TURKEY
the rug guide

Anthony Hazledine

The **HALI** guide to buying carpets,
kilims and textiles in Turkey

TURKEY: THE RUG GUIDE

HALI

Editor
Daniel Shaffer

Associate Editors
Ben Evans, Katie Suckling, Jill Tilden, Lucy Upward

Design
Ysmaën Graïdia

Additional Design & Art Production
Robert Hunter

Production
Liz Dixon

Advertisement Sales
Maro Artimatas

Publisher
Sebastian Ghandchi

Photographs
Anthony Hazledine, Daniel Shaffer, Penny Oakley, Nicholas Purdon,
Ralph Emmerson, Udo Hirsch, Topkapı Sarayi Müsezi, Vehbi Koç Vakfı,
HALI Archive

Acknowledgements
Special thanks to Erkal Aksoy, Mehmet Çetinkaya, Ralph Emmerson,
Abdullah Gündoğdu, Kathy Hamilton Gündoğdu, Gülisdan Hussain,
Deniz Huysal & Ajans Medya, Vedat Karadağ, Lari Meyer, Şeref Özen,
Sarah Parks, and Amanda Phillips, without whose contributions this
publication would not have been possible.

Colour Origination
PH Media, Roche, Cornwall

Printing & Binding
Headley Brothers Ltd., Ashford, Kent

Hali Publications Ltd., a member of Centaur Holdings plc
St Giles House, 50 Poland Street, London W1F 7AX, United Kingdom
Telephone +44 (0)20 7970 4600
Editorial Fax +44 (0)20 7578 7222
Advertisement Fax +44 (0)20 7578 7221
E-mail hali@centaur.co.uk   Website www.hali.com

Turkey/Istanbul Editorial Correspondent
Şeref Özen, Cocoon International Trading Co.,
Arasta Bazaar no.93, 34400 Sultanahmet, Istanbul, Turkey
Telephone +90 (0)212 638 6450   Mobile +90 (0)533 760 6792

TURKEY: THE RUG GUIDE

MEHMET ÇETİNKAYA GALLERY

ISTANBUL'S LIVING GUID
January 2005, year 5 no. 48 / 3.000.000 TL./3 Y
($2/£1.2

TimeOut
İstanbul
in English

Listings of
restaurants,
nightclubs,
cafés and
more...

The hottest bars, most h
parties, jam-packed ven
tips to get by in the city's

make sure to pick this up at the airport or any newsstand in Istanbul !

J. xx
x

OUT on the TOWN

ART : Aesthetics reigns as Istanbul's first modern art museum opens in style
FOOD & DRINK : Traditional fare to warm your heart and shake off those winter blue
CHECK OUT : Dig into the best record stores for everything from Strauss to house

HALI's Rug Guide to Turkey

It is eight years since the publication of *Istanbul: The HALI Rug Guide*. When, in response to demand, it became clear that a revision was due, the idea formed that we might extend our travels beyond 'the city' to include most of the country.

Easier said than done. Any hope that we could produce a comprehensive guide when dealing with a country the size of Turkey and its thousands upon thousands of rug dealers and carpet shops would clearly be foolish. Rather the *Guide* takes the form of a series of suggestions or signposts pointing in a general direction, with arrival at a final destination up to the reader. Each of the three main regional chapters takes the shape of a journey with one place leading logically to the next, with observations on architecture, history, the perfect kebab, in fact anything that caught my eye, because this is my journey and yours will be different.

The content of this guide may lack the erudition expected of an academic author, but I hope it makes up for that with the enthusiasm of an amateur but experienced 'old Turkey hand', and the thoroughness of its research. I have visited every rug shop mentioned in the guide, from the Grand Bazaar to Lake Van, and at least one çay has been drunk in most of them.

There are no instructions here on how to buy a rug, how to bargain, what to look out for, how much to pay, how to avoid the virus of new 'old' rugs, and so on. These are things to learn for yourself, because you are on your own journey, not mine. One thing is certain, however: if you visit every shop in Turkey and never buy a rug, don't worry, because the treasure you will return home with will be priceless. Your memories of travelling in this diverse and spectacularly beautiful country, and your encounters with its delightful people, will be rewarding enough.

If I have a modest hope for this *Guide* it is that before long you dispense with it altogether. The journey really begins when you throw away the map and realise, as Herman Melville did when he wrote in *Moby Dick* that, "...it was not on any map, real places never are."

Iyi yolucuklar
Anthony Hazledine

TURKISH RUGS
ANCIENT AND MODERN

For those attracted by the romance and mystery of the oriental carpet weaver's art, Turkey is indeed the promised land. The Turks (originally nomadic migrants and conquerors from the steppe lands of the East), the Armenians and the Kurds, as well as their indigenous predecessors in Anatolia, have been carpet weavers for centuries, even millennia, and Turkey has been a major commercial exporter of hand-knotted wool pile carpets to the West since the Renaissance period or before.

A generation or two ago, the types of antique Turkish carpets singled out for attention in a publication such as this would have been rather different to those that we see today. Then, typical export production, including the 'classical' period Ottoman carpets represented in Renaissance paintings by old masters such as Lotto, Holbein, Ghirlandaio and Bellini, and also in 17th century Netherlandish paintings, would have been considered the acme of Turkish carpet weaving. Spectacular examples of these 'classical' genres are to be seen in Istanbul's Turkish and Islamic Art Museum.

These types, which are mainly the products of western Anatolian urban weaving centres such as Uşak, as well as later products, particularly prayer rugs, from workshops in and around towns such as Gördes, Kula and Ladik, are well-represented in major public and private collections of historic carpets around the world. The technically accomplished late 19th and 20th century fine silk workshop rugs from workshops in Hereke and Kum Kapı (Istanbul Armenian), with their elaborate Persianate designs, would also have been highly regarded. But that is no longer necessarily the case.

Over the past few decades connoisseurs have learned that the artistic soul of the Turkish carpet tradition lies in the colourful antique tribal and village weavings made in nomad tents and peasant homes in villages throughout Asia Minor, from Bergama and Milas in the west to Sivas and Van in the east, and especially in the hugely productive Cappadocian hinterland of the central Anatolian city of Konya.

The best of these rugs and kilims, whether the directional prayer rugs of Milas, Mujur, Aksaray and Karaman, the medallion designs of Bergama, Dazkırı and Karapinar, the long, coarsely-woven, runner format 'yellow-ground' pieces from Konya (or Avanos), the finely-woven prayer kilims of Kars and Erzurum, or the rustic bedding rugs, covers and ornamented storage sacks made all over Anatolia by the Yörük (Turkish, Turkmen or Kurdish nomads and villagers), to mention but a handful of the myriad types and styles, are distinguished by the superb use of natural dyes, wonderful lustrous wool, and an instinctive understanding of a pan-Turkic design vocabulary.

An even more archaic indigenous tradition, with designs that are arguably traceable back to Neolithic wall-paintings, can be found in the boldly graphic flatwoven tribal kilims of Anatolia, especially those from the Cappadocian heartland, as well as the austere red-and blue weavings of the Yüncü nomads of Balıkesir in the northwest.

While still available on the market, older examples of Turkish rugs and kilims are often in poor condition and fragmentary. Many that do survive owe their existence to the practice of pious donation to mosques and tombs (vakf), and the strict legality of their sale and export is sometimes questionable (where a rug might be considered a 'national cultural heritage' item, an export permit, obtainable from the authorities at the Museum of Turkish and Islamic Art, might be required).

But not all, or even most, of the old and antique rugs and textiles traded in the Istanbul and other Turkish provincial bazaars are Turkish. The great entrepôt is the gateway to the West for heirloom carpets and textiles from the recently independent Turkish-speaking nations in Transcaucasia and Central Asia. Thus one finds glossy-piled Kazaks and Karabaghs, crisply woven Shirvans and Kubas, Azeri flatwoven covers, Shahsavan sumakh bags and Kurdish rugs from northwest Persia, Turkmen tribal rugs, tent and animal trappings, shaggy Uzbek and Kirghiz rugs from Central Asia, and a broad range of exotic and superbly colourful antique silk textiles, costumes and domestic embroideries from the Caucasus and all the lands along the length of the ancient Silk Roads to China.

Of course there are also vast quantities of modern Turkish rugs and carpets on the market. For a century and more from the mid-1900s, Turkish carpet weaving declined disastrously in quality, mainly due to the widespread use of synthetic commercial dyes in combination with harsh chemical washes to tone down their hard flat colours. Much contemporary production is still poorly made, but since the late 1970s there has been a revival of traditional dyes, designs and methods, especially in parts of western Anatolia and the Konya area. Among the best examples of this modern production of both pile rugs and kilims one can now find the 'antiques of the future'.

Daniel Shaffer, Editor, HALI

Fine Rugs & Textiles

19th century Khamseh rug

We proudly present one of the largest collections of antique & new, rugs & kilims

Ceramics & Tiles

As well as Iznik Tiles from IZNIK FOUNDATION,
antique & new ceramics from the most famous
Turkish Masters

*The Byzantium Cistern from the 5th Century
at the basement of Nakkaş.*

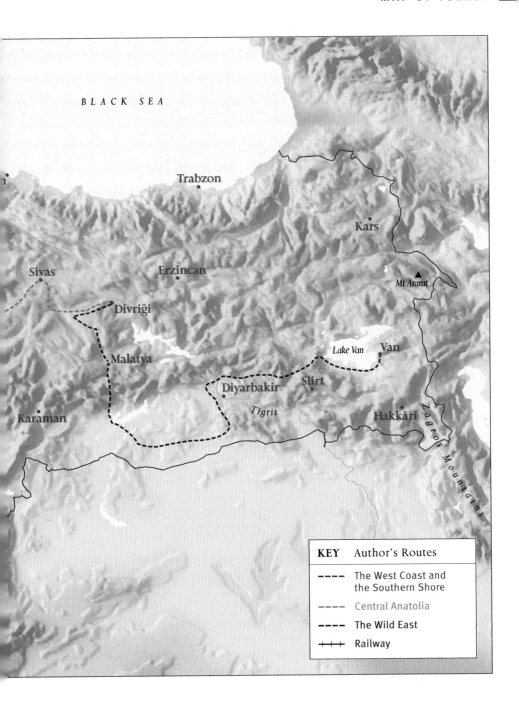

BLACK SEA

Trabzon

Kars

Sivas

Erzincan

Mt Ararat

Divriği

Malatya

Lake Van   Van

Diyarbakir   Siirt

Tigris

Karaman

Hakkâri

Zagros Mountains

KEY	Author's Routes
----	The West Coast and the Southern Shore
----	Central Anatolia
----	The Wild East
+++	Railway

ORIENT BASAR

Mehmet Sağgün

Tuzcular Mahallesi, Paşa Camii Sokak No. 26.
Kaleiçi, Antalya
Tel   +90 242 243 1761
Fax   +90 242 242 0012
Email   orientbasar@antnet.net.tr
Web   www.orientbasar.com

Large selection Antique and Decorative Anatolian, Persian, Caucasus and Turkmen Carpets and Kilims.

Retail and wholesale

All types of restoration and special cleaning services.

bozdağ
antique rugs and textiles specialist

Bozdağ
Established 1972
antique rugs and textiles specialist
finest restoration and cleaning

ARTLINE
PALACE CARPETS   SINCE 1968

We are specialists in custom-made oversize carpets. The best natural materials and dyes are turned into heirloom-quality carpets in the hands of our skilled weavers. Any design is possible, including your own. Up to 300 m² in size, fit for a palace.

Orhan GÜZELMERİÇ
Tavukhane Sokak No: 23
Sultanahmet, Istanbul

Tel: +90 212 638 47 43
Fax: +90 212 638 47 45
Mobile: +90 532 314 15 30
www.artlinecarpets.com

Bodrum Contact
Tel: +90 252 368 91 10

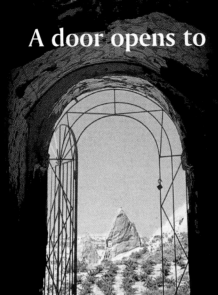

TURKISH MUSEUMS

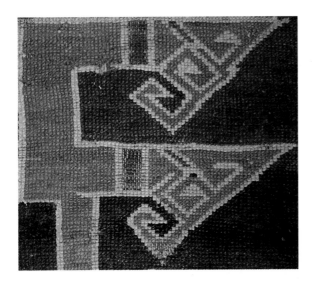

Visitors to Istanbul are soon aware that they are in a carpet-making (and carpet-selling) country.

CARPETS IN ISTANBUL

By John Mills

Most people think they know what they like but in fact few really know what to look for in carpets, how to distinguish the good from the bad, and how to make an informed judgement about what to buy. Yet Istanbul's museums possess splendid collections of early Turkish carpets which are wonderful to look at and enable budding amateurs to educate their taste: the products of tribal, village and court weavers between the 13th and the 19th centuries with their gamut of designs – mainly boldly geometrical in the first two, sometimes small-patterned and floral in the last – and their brilliant colours.

For this is one of the first lessons to be learnt: these were not made by or for people with timid or retiring tastes, wanting pastel shades subservient to decorators' ideas of 'colour schemes' and 'fitting in'. When made by villagers or nomads the carpets were often decoration and furnishing in one. Dyeing wool to obtain pure, strong colours and combining these strikingly yet harmoniously on the loom was the challenge, and this was a matter of pride and skill at a time when the achievement of man-made colour was not so easy and commonplace as now.

1

discovered in 1905 in the Alaeddin Mosque in Konya and were published shortly afterwards. Because of their large size, unique colouring, and designs which differ from other early Turkish rugs, they were at once assigned to the period of the Turkish Seljuk Empire and thought probably to have been made for the mosque when it was built in the 13th century. This belief has remained a cornerstone of carpet scholarship, supported by comparisons with other Seljuk art and only occasionally questioned, but it must be admitted that so far truly definitive evidence is lacking. These fairly coarsely woven pieces have small, repetitive field designs and usually bold, wide borders of stylised 'Kufic' lettering, quite carelessly drawn in places. All are a bit tattered now, though nicely mounted, and some are fragmentary, but they impress by their strange *ton-sur-ton* field colours (for instance light on dark blue, red on red) and the dogged persistence with which

2

First in importance for carpets, as well as the other arts, is the Turkish and Islamic Arts Museum (Türk ve Islam Eserleri Müzesi or TIEM), situated very centrally on the Hippodrome, facing the obelisk and the Sultanahmet ('Blue') Mosque. It is a pleasant place to visit, with a raised courtyard where coffee or tea may be taken. The galleries, on a higher floor, are formed initially by a corridor (7) with cabinet rooms off it, where smaller items are shown, followed by large high rooms where the biggest carpets can be accommodated. Among these are the earliest and most important Turkish carpets to have survived: the so-called Seljuk or Konya carpets (2).

These famous carpets were first

the small designs were extended to make large carpets, something one suspects was not natural for the weavers.

Following on from these early examples, the history and chronology of Turkish carpets is quite vague for more than two centuries. Several pieces of various designs are believed to belong in this period, but evidence is lacking to date them securely. By the mid-15th century, however, many rug designs started to appear in European – especially Italian – paintings and this provides a secure basis for dating. About a hundred years ago several rug designs were named after painters who depicted them, giving us types such the 'Lotto' and the large- (5) and small-pattern (6) 'Holbeins'. The museum has an unexcelled collection of these types, particularly large-pattern Holbein rugs. These show large octagons within rectangles, separated by dividing bands and with additional borders. These individual elements can have many different designs in different colours so the overall design is rarely duplicated.

Another group of somewhat later carpets is formed by those associated with the large weaving area centred on the west Anatolian town of Uşak (7), which continued commercial production well into the 20th century. The best known of these are the medallion Uşaks, often of very large size, which were much exported to Europe. More interestingly, Uşak produced large multiple-niche prayer rugs called safs. These were not exported but used in the mosques, and the TIEM has a range of pieces which vary in their details. Most of these came from the Selimye Mosque in Edirne and are thought to date from the time of its construction in the late 16th century.

The 'named' carpets are obviously the ones which found favour in Western Europe, probably being shipped from ports of western Anatolia, but many other types, from inaccessible places in the centre and east, may only occasionally have been exported. They remained little known and studied until recent years, but the TIEM has many wonderful examples of which only a few are generally exhibited. Many of these come from the collections of the Vakıflar (Pious Foundations), having been removed at different times from mosques and tombs for safekeeping. Awareness of these rugs through their display and partial publication has brought a realisation that the range of designs and types was far greater than formerly imagined, and attaching dates and places of origin to them is still very much a

3

1. East Anatolian carpet, 16th-17th century, Vakıflar Museum, collected from the Ulu Mosque, Divriği 2. Seljuk carpet, central Anatolia (?), 13th century, Türk ve Islam Eserleri Museum (TIEM), collected from the Alaeddin Keykubad Mosque, Konya 3. Konya prayer rug, 17th century, TIEM 4. Central Anatolian kilim saf (detail), before 1800, Vakıflar Kilim Museum

5

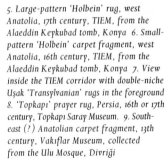

6

5. Large-pattern 'Holbein' rug, west Anatolia, 17th century, TIEM, from the Alaeddin Keykubad tomb, Konya 6. Small-pattern 'Holbein' carpet fragment, west Anatolia, 16th century, TIEM, from the Alaeddin Keykubad tomb, Konya 7. View inside the TIEM corridor with double-niche Uşak 'Transylvanian' rugs in the foreground 8. 'Topkapı' prayer rug, Persia, 16th or 17th century, Topkapı Saray Museum. 9. South-east (?) Anatolian carpet fragment, 13th century, Vakıflar Museum, collected from the Ulu Mosque, Divriği

matter of guesswork (and controversy). Although often badly damaged through long use on mosque floors, their evocative designs, lustrous wool and luminous colours are still a joy.

The TIEM's holdings are not confined to Turkish carpets. There are a few important early Persian carpets, together with pieces from the Caucasus region and Ottoman Egypt. It is also worth visiting the ethnographic section, below at courtyard level, where a range of 19th century rugs and other artefacts may be seen. There are displays of kilims and looms and nomad tents filled with rugs, pile- and flatwoven storage bags, and long decorative bands. Other displays show rooms furnished as in the late Ottoman period, with a curious blend of Victorian furniture and Caucasian, Persian and Turkmen rugs. There is also a very informative display about the use of natural dyestuffs in carpet-making in Anatolia.

Not far away is the small Vakıflar Carpet Museum, set up in 1979 specifically for showing more of the valuable old carpets removed from mosques, including a large group from the Ulu Mosque in Divriği, in east-central Anatolia, which only came to light in the 1970s (1, 9). The small museum building, to the left of the main entrance to the Sultanahmet Mosque, up a shallow flight of steps, was formerly the Sultan's Suite, an annexe to the mosque used as an antechamber by the sultans before and after prayers. Now it, like the TIEM, is a Mecca for an ever-increasing number of Western carpet lovers and collectors who come to Istanbul to see, 'in the flesh', pieces that they may already know from a splendid book published in 1988.

The early carpets from Divriği gain extra interest and importance from their known provenance (many of the other pieces were collected without any documentation) which is at least suggestive, if not definitive, when considering where they might have been made. Many are in fact very different in design and technique from the more familiar pieces from western Anatolia, and an east Anatolian and sometimes Syrian origin is believed for some of them (9). Besides these, in the Vakıflar Museum there are also some Uşak rugs as well as good examples of Caucasian 'Dragon' carpets and a large 16th century Persian 'Vase' carpet.

Display and conservation conditions within the Vakıflar Museum are a cause for concern. The building is not well suited to its task and there is no doubt that the rugs have suffered through damp and neglect. The same, or worse, is true of the early Anatolian kilims (4) in the Vakıflar Kilim Museum on the lower floor, which has not been accessible to the public for some years. A few years ago there was talk of moving the collection to a more suitable building close to the mosque at Fatih, but there is no sign of the project coming to fruition.

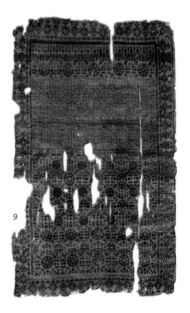

9

It might well be expected that the Topkapı Saray Museum would have a carpet collection among its many other treasures. In fact it does, though a rather odd and unrepresentative one. Unfortunately none of the items are currently displayed apart from one or two late, dull pieces furnishing some of the kiosks.

8

The best part of the collection consists of a group of no fewer than 37 prayer rugs (8) whose origin, whether in 16th/17th century Persia or 19th century Turkey was long the subject of dispute. It has now been established with virtual certainty that those in Persian designs are indeed Safavid Persian, and came as gifts from the Shah of Persia to the Turkish Sultan, thus adding greatly to their importance and interest. Perhaps some at least will one day be put on show.

Some way out of Istanbul proper, up the Bosphorus at Sarıyer, lies the Sadberk Hanım Museum, once a private collection of the decorative arts but now open to the public. This is best visited for its own sake, and for the archaeological displays in a separate wing, but it does have a few 19th century Turkish rugs of types well known in Western collections, but not otherwise to be seen in Istanbul, including some Milas prayer rugs, three rugs from the Kula region, and an unusual small carpet of uncertain origin with a cloudband medallion design.

ISTANBUL'S OTHER MUSEUMS

John Carswell

Istanbul is nothing less than a total museum in itself, and all of its individual museums are an extension of this fact. Basically they can be divided into three categories, dealing in turn with the Graeco-Roman foundations of the city, the Byzantine interlude, and the final phase after the Ottomans captured the city in 1453. It should also be emphasised that when Ataturk created his new Republic in 1924 and moved the capital to Ankara, Istanbul never relinquished its importance as the cultural centre of Turkey, a position which it retains to this day.

When all the foreign embassies moved to Ankara and the diplomats left in Istanbul were reduced in status to consuls, the grand buildings remained and they themselves became quasi-museums. The British Embassy is a case in point. Designed in 1845 as a Florentine palace in magnificent grounds overlooking the Golden Horn, it was the work of Sir Charles Barry, whose architectural career began with a neo-Gothic church in Brighton and finished with the Houses of Parliament. He was nothing if not versatile and his Renaissance essay in Istanbul is a good example.

There are museums in Istanbul which reflect all phases of the city's history, such as the great church of Aya Sofya (3), dedicated by the Emperor Justinian in 537 AD. In 1453 it was converted into a mosque by Mehmet the Conqueror, and in 1935 finally became a museum. Despite its secularisation the structure resonates with its spiritual history, be it the glittering Byzantine mosaics in the dome or the gigantic gilded calligraphic roundels proclaiming the names of Allah and the Prophet Mohammed. Many of the architectural components, such as the eight massive porphyry columns, were reused from earlier buildings.

This is also the case with the enchanting little 14th century Church of St Saviour in Chora, which was transformed into a mosque, the Kariye Camii, in the 16th century. Its decoration was plastered over only to be revealed in the 1940s when the later accretions were removed. The mosaics and frescoes have been splendidly restored, as have the buildings in the immediate vicinity, close to the city walls.

1

Many of Istanbul's museums once had a quite different function, and none more so than Topkapı (Cannon Gate) Saray, the great palace of the Ottoman Sultans. Built in 1459 on a hill overlooking the Bosphorus, Asia and the Golden Horn by Mehmet II as a tangible symbol of his authority, not only was it the palace of the Sultans, it was the administrative centre of the Ottoman Empire, which spread from Persia to the Balkans and throughout Arabia and North Africa. It now houses an extraordinary collection of royal paraphernalia, spread throughout the pavilions of the palace.

It is difficult to know where to start, but before embarking on a tour there is an excellent model inside the entrance gate of the whole complex. There is certainly more than any visitor can absorb in a day, and choices have to be made. There are four successive courtyards in an elegant setting of carefully manicured gardens. The further you penetrate, the closer you get to the inner sanctum of the Sultan himself. The first court was for visitors to dismount, and citizens to pay their taxes. It also housed workshops, storerooms, an atelier for the court artists, a hospital, a bakery and various other ancillary services. The second court was for the conduct of administrative affairs, with the Chancery on the left, beside the entrance to the Harem. The royal kitchens are to the right, designed by Sinan, with a whole procession of tall chimneys rising above the roof. These normally house a selection of one of the greatest collections of Chinese ceramics in the world. These include blue and white porcelain and celadon from the Mongol period onwards. There are more

1. Iznik ceramic mosque lamp, 16th century, Topkapı Saray 2. The Court of Gayumars (detail), miniature from a Shahnama, Tabriz, ca. 1370, Topkapı Saray 3. Interior of Aya Sofya, from Byzantine cathedral to museum

2

3

than 12,000 pieces ranging over five centuries. Only a fraction is on display, but there are many unique pieces, which the cognoscenti come to see from all over the world. Recently, after refurbishment following earthquake damage, the Topkapı kitchens were used for a special temporary exhibition of felts, ancient (11) and modern.

Straight ahead is the entrance to the third court, with

4

4. Late Neolithic anthropomorphic vessel from Hacılar, Sadberk Hanım Museum 5. Ottoman silk velvet cushion cover, 17th century, Sadberk Hanım Museum 6. The Rahmi Koç Industrial Museum 7. Iznik tile panel, 16th century, Topkapı Saray

a pavilion where the Sultan would receive special visitors, foreign ambassadors and local officials alike. For provincial administrators putting a foot wrong at audience meant swift removal from the royal presence and strangulation with a silken cord, in a little room conveniently sited to the left of the gateway.

Entering the third courtyard, on the left is a single storey building set askew from the rest of the complex. Once the royal mosque, and orientated towards Mecca, today it houses the manuscript library, only open to the most serious of scholars. On the right is a series of rooms housing a stunning array of royal kaftans (9) and Turkish silks, the epitome of the Ottoman style. Adjacent is the Treasury, with its mind-boggling collection of gold, silver and jades, many encrusted with diamonds, rubies and emeralds, and thrones inlaid with ivory and mother-of-pearl. Here is the famous Topkapı enamelled dagger, a gift originally destined for a Qajar Shah but never delivered. There are also acres of clocks and watches, coffee-cups, and hanging ornaments, paintings and calligraphy. In the far left corner of the courtyard close to the entrance to the fourth court is a chamber full of Holy Relics, mirroring the Sultan's traditional role as Caliph, responsible for the Holy sites of Mecca and Medina.

The fourth court, with its reflecting marble pool and golden kiosk overlooking the Golden Horn, is the most intimate of all. This was the private domain of the Sultan, with its separate entrance to the Harem. In the 16th century, in order to maintain an impressive silence, communication was by deaf mutes, exchanging orders by sign language. In the evenings the tulip-beds were lit by tortoises slowly moving among the flowers with candles on their backs. This area also contains the Sunnet Odasi (Circumcision Chamber), where the royal princes attained manhood. Some of the

5

finest tile panels ever painted are set in its façade. Besides these, all of Topkapı Saray is decorated with Iznik tile panels of every conceivable design (7). Further decoration is provided by *sebils* or wall-fountains, and not to be missed are the painted interiors, particularly in the private apartments of the Harem.

Retreating from Topkapı Saray, a gateway in the first court leads down to the Archaeological Museum. This was purpose-built in the 19th century by Turkey's first Director of Antiquities,

the artist and archaeologist Hamdi Bey. It houses a magnificent collection of antiquities from all over the Ottoman Empire, such as cuneiform seals from Assyria, and incredible marble sarco-phagae such as the so-called 'Alexander Sarcophagus' dug up at Sidon a century ago. Across the courtyard is the Cinili Kiosk, Mehmet the Conqueror's palace at the end of the 15th century. In Timurid style, it has spectac-

ular tile mosaics around the entrance, and now houses a key collection of early Iznik ceramics, both pottery (1) and tiles.

Staggering away from the riches of Topkapi Saray, the next sensible step might be some refreshment. It is close at hand, a better bet than the always crowded facilities in the palace itself. Just past Aya Sofya, on the left before you reach the Blue Mosque, is the Yeşil Ev (Green House), a charmingly restored 19th century wooden house with a shady garden where you can eat and drink to the sound of a tinkling fountain.

After this stop, you now have the energy to tackle the Museum of Turkish and Islamic Art (Türk ve Islam Eserleri Müsezi), housed in what was Ibrahim Paşa's 16th century palace overlooking the Hippodrome. Ibrahim was Sultan Süleyman's closest friend, but something went wrong, and he also succumbed to the silken cord. The museum houses an unparalleled collection of arts and crafts, calligraphy, metalwork, ceramics and the like. It is a must for readers of this HALI Guide, for it has a unique collection of early carpets, including Seljuk fragments, which complement the Vakıflar Collection not far away across the road. A few years ago the TIEM put on an extraordinary exhibition of artefacts brought for safekeeping to Istanbul from all over the Ottoman Empire before the First World War. An

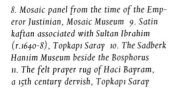

8. Mosaic panel from the time of the Emperor Justinian, Mosaic Museum 9. Satin kaftan associated with Sultan Ibrahim (r.1640-8), Topkapı Saray 10. The Sadberk Hanım Museum beside the Bosphorus 11. The felt prayer rug of Haci Bayram, a 15th century dervish, Topkapı Saray

excellent catalogue by the former Director, Nazan Ölçer, is for sale in the museum shop.

Further downhill and across the Golden Horn is a wonderfully eccentric institution, the Rahmi Koç Industrial Museum (6). It is really a sort of overgrown toy-shop, with everything that every schoolboy ever dreamed of owning – ships, steam-rollers, airplanes, capstans and

engines of every kind, all brightly polished and painted. This is a one-man enterprise and the final touches are a London red telephone box (it works) and a complete French bistro of about 1850 dismantled and shipped from Paris along with two French cooks. It is a charming place for a Franco-Turkish *repas*, if you can stand the noise, due to its popularity with the chattering Turks. I couldn't understand what the collection of old hats in the toilets was about, until I learned that this is another of Rahmi's passions. The latest and most spectacular addition to the museum is a veteran submarine, purchased from the Turkish Navy.

Out of town and quite a way up the Bosphorus is the Sadberk Hanım Museum (8) at Büyükdere, run for many years by Rahmi Koç's sister, the late Sevgi Gönul, for the Koç Foundation. Though a private establishment, it is far and away the most professionally managed museum in Turkey. Housed in a pale yellow wooden *yali*, built around the end of the 19th century, it is divided into two sections; the first devoted to ancient Anatolia (8), Greece, Rome, and the Byzantine period, and providing an excellent short course on the history of Turkey before the arrival of the Ottomans. The second half is unique, and deals with Turkish everyday life, with first-rate col-

HALI
www.hali.com   CARPET, TEXTILE AND ISLAMIC ART

PERSONAL SUBSCRIPTION ORDER FORM

Why subscribe? The benefits to you...
- Save up to to 34% on the HALI cover price ● **FREE** unlimited access to the Auction Price Guide (APG) Online
- HALI e-Gallery – **FREE** access to HALI's dedicated online international shopping marketplace ● **FREE** tickets to the annual HALI Fair in London worth £20 and the concurrent Summer Olympia Fine Art and Antiques Fair
- **FREE** delivery of your own copy of HALI to your home or work address

Yes! Please start my subscription to HALI. I would like to receive the following gift as I am subscribing for 2/3 years:

2 Years ☐

OR

3 Years ☐

☐ **FREE World Time Alarm Calculator** (code 505)   OR

☐ **FREE Mouse mat** (code 515)

(please tick where appropriate)

	UK	Europe	USA & Canada †	Rest of World †
1 Year (6 Issues)	☐ **£90**	☐ **£101**	☐ **£101/US$190***	☐ **£116/US$222***
2 Years (12 Issues)	☐ **£150**	☐ **£168**	☐ **£168/US$319***	☐ **£196/US$372***
3 Years (18 Issues)	☐ **£210**	☐ **£236**	☐ **£236/US$447***	☐ **£272/US$516***

†Airmail rates available on request; *Credit cards will be charged in £ sterling at the current exchange rate

Title (Mr/Ms/Mrs/Miss) _____ First name _____

Surname _____ Profession _____

Address _____

City _____ Post/Zip Code _____ Country _____

Telephone _____ Fax _____

Email _____

PAYMENT OPTIONS

1. ☐ I enclose my cheque (£ or US$) payable to **Hali Publications Limited** for _____

2. ☐ Please debit my credit card in £ or US$ (Diners Club £ only) for _____

☐ Mastercard   ☐ Amex   ☐ Diners Club   ☐ Visa   ☐ Switch

Cardholder Name _____

Card Number ☐☐☐☐☐☐☐☐☐☐☐☐☐☐☐☐ (Switch only) ☐☐☐

Expiry date ☐☐ / ☐☐   Valid from (Switch only) ☐☐ / ☐☐   Issue No. ☐☐

Today's date ☐☐ / ☐☐ / ☐☐   Signature _____

Please supply cardholder's details/billing address if different from above: _____

OUR NO RISK GUARANTEE
If you decide HALI is not for you, simply write to us within the first 30 days of your subscription and claim your money back in full – GUARANTEED!

Publisher

3. ☐ Please invoice me/my company.
Please attach cardholders details/billing address if different from above.

Thank you for subscribing. Please return to: HALI Subscriptions Department, Tower House, Lathkill Street, Market Harborough, Leicestershire LE16 9EF, United Kingdom or fax to: F: +44 (0)1858 468 969   T: +44 (0)1858 438 818   W: www.hali.com

Please allow 28 days after receipt of payment for delivery of your free gift. We would like to keep you informed of Centaur's products and services, including information about HALI via post, by email and/or telephone. Please write to the Circulation Director at Centaur Publications, 50 Poland Street, London W1F 7AX if you specifically do not want to receive this information or email us at: circulationdirector@centaur.co.uk. We will not pass your email address outside of the Centaur group for marketing purposes. We may from time to time make your name, address and/or telephone details available to carefully screened companies who may be of interest to you. However, if you specifically do not wish your details to be passed to third parties please tick here ☐

3131

lections of Iznik, Kütahya and Çannakale pottery, Chinese porcelain, *tombak* (gilt copper), metalware, Qur'ans and calligraphy, and marvellous Turkish textiles (8), embroidery and costumes.

Most fun of all is a reconstruction of a circumcision bed decorated with embroidered towels for a grinning boy. To give it verisimilitude, there is a photo alongside showing Rahmi Koç in a similar situation, sitting up in bed over fifty years ago. He's not grinning! The museum also has an attractive shop and a range of its own publications including catalogues and an impressive museum *Journal*.

It should be mentioned that many of the scholarly activities, exhibitions and publications in Turkey today are sponsored by the private sector, such as the major banks, many of which have their own exhibition galleries. When in Istanbul, it is well worth while checking out what is currently on view.

What else? There are museums in the city devoted to Ataturk, the Air Force, Istanbul porcelain, Beyköz glass, dervishes, Justinian's mosaics, calligraphy, military and naval affairs, painting and sculpture, Ottoman tents, and cartoons and humour. And of course there are the palaces, which successive Sultans built when they got bored with Topkapı Saray.

Of these the most famous pile is the Dolmabaçe Palace, on a vast scale in the best/worst of 19th century taste, built in 1853 by Sultan Abdul Mecit. As the historian Hilary Sumner-Boyd summed it up: "he brought with him one tradition, of extravagance, which might have well been abandoned, and abandoned another, that of impeccable good taste, which had better been preserved". I remember talking to an Ottoman princess who grew up there and asking her what she remembered of it "My dear, it was terribly cold. We had to wear fur coats just to get from one room to another". But Ataturk liked it, and the Spartan bedroom where he died in 1938 overlooking the Bosphorus is still on view.

Just up the hill above Beşiktaş is the Yıldız Palace, smaller in scale and lighter in touch, also 19th century and built by Abdul Hamid II. It has a charming private theatre and small museum in the old apartments. The European inspired garden is laid out with a lake, kiosks and grottoes. It looks like a reincarnation of a primitive painting, complete with white swans.

After all these promenades, if there isn't a café or restaurant on the premises, there is certainly one close at hand. Turkish food and drink is better than museum quality – you can really get your teeth into it. **C**

11

MUSEUMS BEYOND ISTANBUL

John Carswell

In spite of the intellectual and artistic importance of Istanbul, it is only the tip of the iceberg. Even.for ruggies there is another place called – well, Turkey. Although over twelve million Turks now live in the expanded city of Istanbul (it was less than a million when I first got there in 1951) there are other places which should also be added to the cultural road-map.

First of all, Ankara. The political capital of Turkey has a symbiotic relationship with Istanbul, rather like Washington has to New York. Obviously, unless you are a political animal, Ankara is not where the action is. But it is by no means dull, and although many sybaritic Ankarites have week-end hide-aways in Istanbul (I remember meeting the Turkish Minister of Culture surreptitiously slipping away with wife, daughter and dog on the Friday night train to Istanbul) it has much to offer, mostly of a slightly offbeat nature. Historically, there is the Citadel, and

1

various associated classical columns, baths and temples. The mosques are of minor consequence, the exception being an inescapable modern colossus which dominates the skyline.

Near the Citadel is the Museum of Anatolian Civilizations, housed in an old Ottoman caravanserai, which contains the Neolithic sculpture and other artefacts from Çatal Höyük (4) as well as important archaeological finds from all over Turkey. The recently renovated Ethnographic Museum has interesting medieval Islamic material including carved wooden mihrabs and minbars. Of primary interest is the Ataturk Mausoleum, of impressive, almost Fascist, design. It is quite intimidating, but you cheer up when you come to the section with photos of the great man and his motor-car. I last visited it with Lord Gowrie, former British Minister for the Arts, who muttered

2

"Goodness, how Margaret [Thatcher – his boss] would have liked this!" There is also a Natural History Museum, Painting and Sculpture Museum, Railway Museum, Meteorological Museum, Childrens' Museum, and a War Museum. And there is VEKAM, depicting the history of Ankara, and the life of rags-to-riches businessman Vehbi Koç (father of Rahmi, Sevgi and Suna). Ankara is interesting in another way, for a whole generation of expat German architects helped create the new capital in the 1930s. The railway station and the opera house are particularly well worth a visit. You can fly to Ankara any time, but the night train is much more fun. It is extremely comfortable and they serve lots of *rakı* in the restaurant car.

Moving swiftly south, the next stop should be Antalya. Apart from its attractions as a seaside resort, it is the jump-spot for classical sites such as Termessos (steep climb, worth it), Perge and Aspendos. In Side, there is a small museum with some of the most ravishing Graeco-Roman sculpture in the world.

In Antalya itself – a major medieval port – the city walls, fortress and harbour are all fascinating. The new Antalya Museum has a representative display of local antiquities. More sympathetic is the Suna-Inan Kırac Kaleici Museum. Created by Suna Koç and her husband, it is their contribution to the city, with an outstanding collection of Turkish ceramics. Both Suna and her sister Sevgi did much to revitalise the old city by purchasing and restoring old wooden houses.

Moving west to Bodrum, you will discover that if you are Turkish, in the summer it is absolutely THE place to be. It seems as if whole ministries move down there from Ankara, and it is rumoured that if you want to do anything in government circles in the year to come, this is when and where you fix it. Along with Marmaris, the whole of the Bodrum Peninsula is now super-popular, the Brighton Beach of Turkey.

I have mixed emotions, as I first knew it in 1956 when there was only a track into the village and there were less than two hundred inhabitants. Ah well, it's still ravishing, if you can overlook the acres of naked flesh and the politicos. Nearby is Halicarnassus, with its Roman theatre and famous mausoleum.

But the site museum is now in London, for an Englishman called Newton excavated it in the early 19th century and shipped it off to the British Museum.

The only proper museum in Bodrum is on the Citadel, once the castle of the Knights of St John. It contains the finds from various underwater excavations in the area, the first of which was a Byzantine wreck off a nearby islet called Yassi Ada, and involved a British lady diver, an American and a Turk. These three literally invented the science of underwater archaeology at Bodrum that summer of 1956, and the

1. Central Anatolian prayer rug, 18th/19th century, Aksaray Museum. 2. Seljuk star tile, 13th century, Konya Museum 3. Phrygian ceremonial vessel (rhyton), 7th century BC, Anatolian Civilisations Museum, Ankara

3

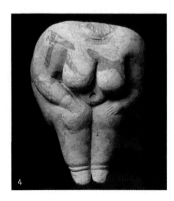

4. Neolithic goddess figurine from Çatal Höyük, 6th millennium BC, Anatolian Civilizations Museum 5. Ankara's Mahmut Paşa Bedestannow the Anatolian Civilizations Museum 6. The Ethnographic Museum in Antalya's Yivli Minare Mosque 7. Doşmealti rug, 19th century, Antalya Museum

7

results of their labours are all there. The most important wreck on view is that of an 8th century ship with an enormous quantity of Islamic glass, which has furnished a close chronology for Islamic glass in the Mediterranean.

It might seem arbitrary to pick out only three towns in Turkey to discuss its cultural attractions. But in their different ways they are representative, and every town and classical site has its own museum, however modest it may be. For starters, Konya, Kayseri, Bursa, Edirne, Iznik, Trabzon, Adana, Diyarbakir, Sivas, and Amasya are worth checking out.

The various Turkish Ministries of Culture, Information and Tourism can all be helpful, but more immediately practical are the first-class *Guides* to Istanbul, Ankara, Antalya and Bodrum produced by Lale Apa and her editor Vildan Yahni. They are a splendid and detailed introduction to these towns, home grown and accurate, well designed and printed, and regularly updated. **C**

ISTANBUL MUSEUMS

Aya Sofya Sultanahmet Meydani   T: 0212 522 9241 / 522 1750

Archaeological Museum Osman Hamdi Bey Yokusu, Gülhane   T: 0212 520 7741

Dolmabaçe Palace Ciragan Caddesi, Beşiktaş   T: 0212 236 9000

Manuscripts & Calligraphy Museum Beyazit Meydani   T: 0212 537 5851

Mosaic Museum Arasta Çarşisi, Sultanahmet   T: 0212 518 1205

Rahmi M. Koç Industrial Museum Hasköy Cad. No: 27, Hasköy   T: 0212 297 66 39/40

Sadberk Hanım Museum Piyasa Caddesi 27-29, Büyükdere   T: 0212 242 0365

Topkapı Saray Museum Sarayiçi, Sultanahmet   T: 0212 512 0480/84 / 522 4422

Turkish & Islamic Arts Museum Ibrahim Paşa Sarayi, At Meydanı, Sultanahmet
T: 0212 518 1805/06

Turkish Tile, Wood and Metalwork Museum Saraçhana Sok 1, Fatih   T: 0212 525 1294

Vakıflar Carpet & Kilim Museums Sultanahmet Camii Avlusu   T: 0212 518 1330

Yıldız Palace Yıldız, Beşiktaş   T: 0212 258 3080

MUSEUMS ELSEWHERE

Anatolian Civilizations Museum Kadife Sokak, Hisar, Ankara   T: 0312 324 3160

Ankara Ethnographic Museum Talat Paşa Bulvari, Opera, Ankara   T: 0312 311 9556

Antalya Ethnographic Museum Yivli Minare Mosque, Antalya

Antalya Museum Konyaalti Caddesi, Antalya   Tel: 0242 243 1604

Ataturk Mausoleum Akdeniz Caddesi Anittepe, Ankara   T: 0312 231 7975

Bodrum Museum of Underwater Archaeology Bodrum Castle   T: 0252 316 2516

Bursa Turkish & Islamic Art Museum Yeşildirek, Bursa   T: 0224 277 679

Diyarbakir Archaeological & Ethnographic Museum Ziya Gökalp Bulvari, Diyarbakir
T: 0412 221 2753

Edirne Turkish & Islamic Art Museum Selimye Mosque, Edirne

Izmir Archaeological Museum Kültür Park, Izmir   T: 0232 483 0611

Konya Ethnographic Mueum Larende Caddesi, Konya   T: 0332 351 8598

Konya Museum Mevlana Mah, Konya   T: 0332 351 1215

Koyunoğlu Museum Konya   T: 0332 351 1857

Mevlana Museum Konya   T: 0332 351 1215

Seljuk Museum Inceminareli Medrese, Konya

Suna-Inan Kırac Kaleiçi Museum Barbaros Mahallesi, Kocatepe Sokak 25,
Kaleiçi, Antalya   T: 0242 243 4274

Turkish Cermaics Museum Karatay Medrese, Konya

Van Museum Şerefiye Mah Haci Osman Sok. 9, Van   T: 0432 216 1139

NEW RUGS IN TURKEY

The history of carpet-making in Turkey is replete with equal measures of fact and fiction, and charts the influence of numerous and diverse foreign elements.

Most of the journey undertaken in this guide focuses readers' attention on places with names that resonate with significance to the ear of rug enthusiasts: Konya, Bergama, Aksaray, Uşak, Kayseri and so on. Although many such towns actually produced rugs, more typically these are convenient labels for rugs collected from village weavers for sale in the nearest large market town. Of course dealers in local bazaars often have more detailed knowledge of the villages where particular rug types are made, but in the West these names are used generically for the rugs of diverse designs from their hinterland. However it is in these countless villages throughout Anatolia that we find the true expression of the Turkish weaving tradition.

Its survival into the 21st century has to a great extent been secured through the pioneering vision and energy of a Ger-

man scientist, Dr Harald Böhmer, whose DOBAG Project, under the auspices of Istanbul's Marmara University, instigated a renaissance in village weaving using traditional methods, designs and, above all, natural dyes, both in Turkey, and beyond its shores.

When he arrived in Turkey in 1960, Dr Böhmer fell in love with the country and its old rugs. He spent much time in the bazaars of Istanbul and elsewhere in Anatolia discovering all manner of beautiful objects (as we hope readers of

Armed with recipes, knowledge and, most importantly, funding from both Turkish and foreign sources, in 1983 village co-operative production of natural-dyed rugs was begun in Ayvacik and Süleymanköy in western Anatolia under the name DOBAG – an acronym of the Turkish words for Natural Dye Research and Development Project. The launch of these rugs marked an important shift in the market: it proved that new rugs could be made that echoed the quality and embodied the character of antique rugs, thereby creating a new low volume market in high quality, relatively pricey, modern rugs.

DOBAG's influence worldwide cannot be underestimated, since its pioneering spirit spawned a renaissance in traditional weaving, preventing the industry from losing its grounding in

1. 'Deco' design rug, Ketenci, Istanbul
2. Sardis 'Mamluk' design carpet (detail), Woven Legends 3. Modern kilim produced for Bereket, Istanbul

this Guide will too). In particular his eye was drawn to the brilliant saturated colours of antique Konya rugs, which he found much more pleasing than the mass of modern rugs on sale. The latter were the products of a commercial industry that, through the 19th and 20th centuries had seen the widespread introduction of machine-spun yarns, synthetic dyes and chemical washes. The homogenisation and standardisation of the industrial process had divorced the act of weaving from its centuries'-old cultural context. This loss of quality sparked Böhmer's scientific curiosity, and he learnt from dealers that the difference in colours between old and new rugs was largely based on the use of handspun yarn and *kökboya* (root dyes).

the traditional societies of the carpet producing countries.

However, it took another Western Turcophile to move this renaissance on a realistic market footing: applying the lessons learned from the small-scale experimental production of naturally-dyed handwoven rugs to the large scale production of high quality room-sized carpets. This was George Jevremovic of Woven Legends who, in 1984, with his wife Neslıhan, began to make market orientated goods with a

variant of the DOBAG formula. His carpets were aimed at high-end retail stores throughout the world. He established production in different parts of Turkey, using designs typical of highly desirable antique decorative carpets from northwest Persia and elsewhere, unlike DOBAG, whose rugs employ designs traditional to the region in which they are made.

Apart from the commercial influence, Woven Legends also had an important creative influence on the Turkish weaving industry. Jevremovic allowed weavers to add their own details in the rugs (the extent of their input was based on the type or line of carpets that they were making). Indeed one of the company's lines, 'Folklife', depends on this principle, since it encourages the weavers to make whatever designs they want. From small beginnings the company now employs approximately 15,000 people worldwide, mostly in Turkey.

These two ventures set quality and artistic thresholds for newly made rugs, and their legacy is apparent in many of the shops that you will visit throughout the country. Turkey is now a place where one has come to expect to find good quality handmade rugs and kilims made in villages to traditional dye recipes. The villages of Anatolia are replete with looms and weavers, and it is rare not to see at least one person in a village walking or talking while spinning wool on a drop spindle. The revitalisation of local economies has been almost as remarkable as the continued innovation of the Turkish industry.

The torch has been taken up by large and small companies alike and it is more common than not for a bazaar dealer to

have his own small production. Many experienced repairers of old rugs and kilims have applied their knowledge and skill to make new rugs, and the results are seen in carpet shops throughout Turkey.

Side by side with this 'renaissance', the Turkish carpet industry continues to produce formulaic, sun- or chemically-bleached pale rugs that take up most space in the large chain stores and the tourist carpet shops. These are not really of interest to us here in terms of either aesthetic merit or material value, since they are manufactured in industrial quantities, and endless bales are shipped abroad by the largest and most powerful Turkish carpet companies. For the sake of the Guide, this part of the carpet business represents industry, while the hand-woven, natural-dyed rugs and kilims made using handspun wool, represent the art and craft side of the divide.

As a postscript, we should mention the production of exceptionally finely knotted rugs from the Hereke workshops. Established in 1843 to supply the royal palaces, today fine Hereke silk rugs are sold in expensive shops on major city thoroughfares. While not to everyone's taste, they are a technical tour de force.

While technique, rarity and colours are important points of reference for a rug seller, the best guide for buying a rug is trusting one's own eye and taste. C

EATING OUT IN ISTANBUL

Andrew Finkel

One of the most pleasurable aspects of touring Istanbul is that much of the really important sightseeing can be done with a knife and fork. Turkish food is reckoned to be one of the world's great cuisines. In fact, it is a river fed by many tributaries, each with its own constantly evolving ambience, rituals and specialities. Navigating even a few of them is both gastronomically and culturally rewarding.

In Istanbul, traditional high culinary culture comes in the form of the Bosphorus meal. This is a highly stylised and by local standards pricey ritual performed at a table commanding a view of this famous waterway. First come the *meze* or cold hors d'oeuvres, then the hot hors d'oeuvres and finally a piece of fresh fish. Look a bit more closely and you see the real point of the ceremony – the bottle of *rakı*, the anise flavoured drink that lubricates conversation and great friendships. The trend in some restaurants is to indulge in quite sophisticated *meze*, and many diners now prefer wine. However, a real *rakı sofrası* (or *rakı* meal) has certain key components – a bit of sweet melon, a bit of salty white cheese, and the contrast of a vegetable like aubergine cooked with olive oil served cold.

Fish, once plentiful, is not a luxury in Istanbul but many still mark the arrival of autumn with the appearance on the menu of a small blue fish *(lüfer)* or bonito *(palamut* in Turkish), a cousin of the tuna. Turbot (usually sliced and fried) appears later in the season. Sea bass and grey mullet are now farmed, but fresh 'wild' anchovies are still plentiful and inexpensive and cooked any number of ways.

In gastronomic terms the Bosphorus on the European side begins at Örtaköy, although this has turned into a neighbourhood of noisy revellers. KIYI in Tarabya is an Istanbul tradition along with FAÇYO in Sariyer or DENIZ LOKANTASI in Kireçburnu as well as the simpler but well-regarded ALI BABA. The Asian side is equally well served. ISMET BABA in Kuzguncuk is equally reasonably priced and serves a neighbourhood clientele. The food at ANGEL, just outside Uskudar, is carefully prepared and there is an inventive array of hot *meze*. KORDON in Çengelköy is elegant and simple and the fashionable, while KORFEZ in Kanlica ferries guests from the European side in its own power boat.

Many of Istanbul's smarter set have deserted the Bosphorus traditions for the meat and two finely chiselled veg of international cuisine. There have been radical improvements in both

The Bosphorus meal in fact has its origins in the humble *meyhane*, or frowsty drinking dens of which the city has many fine examples. The restaurants of the Flower Passage off Beyoğlu used to be famous for beer on tap and fried mussels. The area has since been renovated and to many minds sanitised. Much of the fun has now moved to the back streets. BONCUK on Nevizade Sokak keeps the traditions alive. SAKI around the corner has its fans and REFIK and YAKUP 2 are also popular dives. At ASIR, a short distance away near the police station on Kalyoncu (galley slave) Street, the tray of *meze* still sports *topik* − an Armenian speciality of chick-

1. Guests eating a pudding, detail of an early 18th century miniature painting from the Surname-i Vehbi, *Topkapi Saray*
2. Fresh fish for sale in Istanbul

standard and variety since the days when continental food meant sticking the odd mushroom on a piece of grilled chicken. A new generation of chefs who hail not just from Turkey but Florence or Cape Town have contributed to what is called the 'new Mediterranean cuisine'. The presence of similar ingredients − good olive oil, fresh basil and now fresh porcini mushrooms − and the Turks' own tradition of pizza-style wood-fired bread ovens has helped fuel a love affair with Italian food. Expense accounts rush to the new financial district around Levent to places like ŞANS or the five-star hotels along the Taksim-Maçka axis, or THE FOUR SEASONS in the eponymous hotel in Sultanahmet. CLUB 29 in Ulus combines Turkish and international cuisines and sports a spectacular Bosphorus view. VOGUE in Beşiktaş too has tremendous views and a menu that looks towards the Pacific Rim. LOFT in Harbiye is international with a Turkish tinge.

pea paste enveloping a rich onion and tahini centre.

Many tourists are directed to the restaurant district around Kum Kapı where the high and low traditions of the Bosphorus and the *meyhane* combine. However, just walking around requires running a gauntlet of waiters touting their own restaurants. Unless you are addicted to crowds, the atmosphere is just not pleasant. KARIŞMA SEN ('Mind Your Own Business') right on the coast is a *meyhane* that still attracts a local clientele. Popular with rug shoppers in the Arasta Bazaar, BALIKÇI SEBAHATTIN, halfway to the shore downhill from

3. Assorted chili peppers 4. Fruit seller, detail of a 16th century miniature from the Surname-i Humayun, Topkapı Saray 5. Grilled lüfer (bluefish), a seasonal classic 6. Ripe tomatoes 7. İçli köfte

Sultanahmet, is a *pris fixe* fish restaurant of higher quality than the normal Kum Kapı fare.

One curious phenomenon in Istanbul is the spread of the fast-food emporium. This has been parodied by a new Turkish chain called SIMIT SARAYI which serves the Turkish equivalent of a New York bagel. Normal Turkish food is a hundred times better and not particularly slow. Look out for the the restaurants or *lokanta* that dish out the food people cook in their own homes, served from large trays of simmering

vegetables or meaty stews. You can see everything before you order and it takes no longer to be served a piece of braised lamb in a rich broth than it does a Big Mac. It is hard to get a better lunch (no dinner) in Istanbul than at HACI SALIH'S, an unprepossessing hole in the wall in the Anadol Pasaj off Beyoğlu where a loyal clientele sit in almost reverential silence savouring the food. ÇIYA on the Asian side of the Bosphorus, near the fish market in Kadi-köy, is a rising star. What started as kebab house has now sprouted two sister restaurants a few doors down. One specialises in an exotic array of regional dishes featuring unusual herbs, vegetables or salad leaves you would be hard pushed to find anywhere else in Turkey. This includes a

garlicky sort of leek or a root vegetable with the texture and taste resembling an artichoke heart, a spicy sort of lemonade made from sumac, or for dessert candied whole walnuts spiced with cloves.

There are also several decent *lokanta* around or in the Grand Bazaar. The HAVUZLU caters to a tourist clientele and has a wide variety of food. SEVIM is a more down to earth *lokanta* just as likely to attract a professor from nearby Istanbul University. Harder to find but worth the effort is CAN RESTAU-RANT (Sorgucluhan 19-24, Kapalı-çarsı). Halfway along the main avenue in the bazaar with all the gold shops is an archway leaning to the Esnaf Dernegi (the trades-man's association). From here you take a staircase on the left to a small tiled room with an arched ceiling and excellent dishes like *ekşi köfte* (meat balls in a lemon soured creamy broth) or *ciger sarma* – the nearest you get to a Turkish haggis.

KANAAT, opposite the Süleymaniye Mosque, is incredibly simple but a good place to sample the national dish of cooked haricot beans in a tomato sauce. No better place to meditate on the transience of monumental imperial religious architecture faced with the eternity embodied in a well-cooked bean. The more famous KANAAT – not a chain but a distant relation – is in Uskudar, where there is an extraordinarily broad array of hot and cold dishes and really good desserts.

The main difficulty with purely Turkish restaurants is that they are places where you eat and run rather than places to go out for a leisurely meal. And very often there is no alcohol. There are of course many exceptions – places where you go happily for a business lunch or celebratory dinner out. HACI BABA, close to Taksim, is good, mildly overpriced, but has the advantage of an a outside terrace that is cool in summer. Baked lamb with a savoury rice, iç pilav, along with hunkar begendi (grilled aubergine thickened with a béchamel sauce) is not a light repast but awfully good. BORSA, inside the Cemal Resit Rey conference centre near the Hilton serves traditional Turkish food in Barcelona style chic.

If you are visiting Kariye Cami (St Saviour in Choria) the nearby hotel of the same name has a good dining room called ASITANE whose lengthy menu represents a great deal of culinary research into the history of Ottoman cuisine. Included are several dishes which graced the circumcision feast which Süleyman the Magnificent gave in honour of his sons Beyazid and Cihangir. The young princes were probably standing somewhere howling in the corner, but the guests tucked into almond soup as well as lamb or fowl baked slowly with honey and dried fruit.

KONYALI'S – a famous chain – has a branch in the Topkapı Palace for sightseers. The restaurant, if not too crowded, is far better than the cafeteria. PANDELI is one of the oldest Istanbul institutions. It is over-dependent on groups of tourists, but still clings on to greatness inside a wonderful set of domed turquoise and off-white tiled rooms above the entrance to the Spice Market. Sea bass en papillote is a classic Istanbul dish, and there are good grills and sweets. Lunch-only TUĞRA, the Turkish restaurant in the Ciragan Palace (Kempinski) Hotel prides itself on modern improvisation of historical Turkish dishes. There is no sudden rush of spice here. The flavours are all subtle including veal braised in a mastic sauce or a classic cornflour pudding flavoured with rose water.

BEYTI GÜLER is the Horatio Alger of grilled meat, graduating from a modest eaterie to a grand establishment frequented by visiting statesmen and starlets. He is the only living Turk and only one of two in history to have had a type of kebab named after him – an eyelet of lamb, şiş beyti. The meat is simply cooked in the Balkan style which means mildly seasoned.

The other eponymous kebab is Iskender (or Alexander), named not after the ancient Greek conqueror but a local businessman in Bursa who embellished Turkish doner kebab with tomato and freshly melted butter and then served it with yoghurt on a bed of bread cubes to mop up the sauce. It is a common dish and popular demand has forced many

8

8. Fasulye Piyazi or bean salad 9. Stuffed aubergine, also known as Imam Bayildi 10. Sütlaç or baked rice pudding, the queen of Turkish desserts (All food pictures after Timeless Tastes. Turkish Culinary Culture, *Istanbul 1996)*

lokantas to serve a wheel of doner kebab to their lunchtime trade. Outside Turkey, doner tends to be cut too thick and then allowed to sit around until it goes limp. Here, the meat is grilled to a crisp on the outside and freshly cut. A doner sandwich has all the pleasure and no doubt health-giving properties of a really good bacon sandwich. Many restaurants now sport wheels of chicken doner, served in a thin bread wrap or *dürüm* or, on the opposite end of the cholesterol scale wheels of the spicy Turkish sausage meat called *sucuk*.

9

Whereas *şiş* kebab may be the mainstay of the tourist menu, grilled meats are slightly alien to Istanbul. The best kebab restaurants are run by people from the southeast of the country. The meat should be fresh, simply marinated over-night, not too big in size and where mince is involved, chopped by hand rather than a grinder. Some of the first arrivals to Istanbul, like DEVELİ in Samatya (with branches elsewhere), remain the best.

10

HAMDI'S near the Spice Bazaar in Eminönü is another venerable old timer that serves an impressive array of *meze* as well as wonderful things like pistachio kebabs. There also *çiğ köfte* − raw spicy meat mixed with cracked wheat and eaten in a lettuce wrapper. HANEDAN in Beşiktaş serves similar food in better decorated surroundings.

There are now many posh kebab restaurants that cater to the Istanbul elite, including KÖŞEBASI in

Levent (where Chelsea Clinton ate on her trip here with papa). There are fancier places than NEZIH but probably no better place to sample meat minced by hand and mixed with pistachio nuts or salads with walnuts and soured pomegranate molasses. The most common dessert in kebab restaurants is *künefe*, warmed crisp shredded wheat filled with a special cheese with a sugary sauce. Even better is *katmer* − a buttery hot crepe made from baklava pastry filled with sweetened pistachio.

Fruit is a common desert. A particular treat in season are jellied quinces, which turn a bright red. Funnily enough few restaurants actually serve Turkish sweets. To eat them at their best you have to go to special shops which serve only very simple savoury dishes (boiled chicken and rice or eggs). SARAY − branches in Beyoğlu or Teşvikiye − is authentic; and the SÜT-IS chain isn't bad. Many pastry shops also serve milky puddings. The English torture their children with rice pudding. Here it is baked into a custard, sometimes flavoured with mastic, but always delicious. C

WHERE TO STAY IN ISTANBUL
John Scott

Istanbul is where you stay, even if you don't plan to skulk all day in your hotel room. The city's best-loved short-story writer, Haldun Taner, chose never to own a house, moving on from one rented property to another. It makes equal sense to have a two-base or even three-base holiday, three days in old Stamboul, followed by three days in old European Beyoğlu, topped off with a few days on the Bosphorus or the Princes Islands.

THE OLD CITY

THE FOUR SEASONS is the most luxurious base to explore the Old City. Service makes up for the drawbacks (no swimming pool, sea view, no serious Turkish food). Built as a prison in Turkey's national revival style with turquoise blue tiles from Kütahya, it has been transformed into 55 luxurious rooms and suites, some overlooking Aya Sofya and the Sultanahmet (Blue) Mosque.

Next to Istanbul's best grand hotel is the best small hotel, THE EMPRESS ZOE, started in 1994 by a young San Franciscan, Ann Nevans. The rooms are small but never claustrophobic. Each is different in shape, and the beds, divans and cupboards are in the ergonomic fitted style of old Ottoman houses. Kilim fragments are used as wall-hangings, suzanis are draped over the beds. Many rooms have ingenious mini-*hamams*, complete with marble bench and *kurna* (basin). Breakfast is in the garden, finished off with delicious little home-made *börek*.

The Turing Club's YEŞIL EV (Green House), next to the Roxelana Baths, was Istanbul's first 'restoration' hotel. Though rooms can be spacious, they are in mock country house style and need attention. Ensuite *hamam* bathrooms have been installed in the principal rooms. A reliable fallback with loyal following and leafy garden. The rooms are smaller but more sensibly decorated at AYASOFYA PANSYONLARI, Yeşil Ev's sister establishment – a completely reconstructed street of timber-clad houses under the Tokpapı walls.

Modern travellers in search of news of the East use the

KYBELE HOTEL, unmissable in striking turquoise green, on the street leading from Aya Sofya to the Covered Bazaar. Here, by the light of myriad mosque lamps, journalists, photographers, spies and NGO types exchange tales of (genuine) danger beyond Turkey's borders. The rooms are full of antiques and the mosque lamps securely fitted with few breakages reported in the 1999 earthquake.

Sultanahmet's most comfortable luxury hotel after the Four Seasons is the ERESIN. Besides comfort, the hotel has a feature in common with many small hotels around the Hippodrome, a terrace bar with astonishing views – in this case over the Sea of Marmara on one side and the foundations of the Hippodrome on the other.

Also to die for (not literally, one hopes) is the view from the HOTEL PAMPHYLIA next to the Kybele. Ignore the tobacco-stained red carpet, alarming lift and collapsing bathroom fittings. The view takes in Aya Sofya, Topkapı and Gülhane Park.

Most of the more comfortable small hotels around the Hippodrome rely on good rooftop terraces: The street beside the Ibrahim Paşa Sarayı (the Turkish and Islamic Art Museum) leads first to the friendly TURKOMAN, then to the IBRAHIM PAŞA HOTEL – more closed in, but more attitude, combining ethnic chic terracotta pots and kilims with clever contemporary lighting. Just around the corner is the plusher timber-clad ARCADIA HOTEL. Opposite Sultanahmet's trendy Rumeli Café, the NOMADE is the coolest of the bunch – white-painted wooden floors, patchwork kilim hangings, odd little felt hats on the stairwell.

Still searching? Handy fallbacks are the ARMADA down by the sea walls and, for longer visits, the KUFLEVI, a privately owned house restored by an Englishwoman, Mary Hall, and managed by the Armada. Each floor is a spacious prettily done-up self-catering flat.

THE GOLDEN HORN
Fish have made it back to the Golden Horn without going belly up, so why not hotels? The old quarters of Fener, Balat and Ayvansaray are being tidied up without yet becoming remotely gentrified. Take a copy of Freely's *Strolling Through Istanbul* and park yourself at either the KARIYE HOTEL, a reconstructed wooden house next to the Kariye Cami out on the land walls, or down on the Golden Horn at the DAPHNIS. The Kariye has a peaceful garden restaurant that looks up through the trees at the Kariye, the Daphnis consists of a row of three attached town houses ingeniously knocked together by the owner-architect Defne Yanger who has rediscovered the original frescos. Mainly favoured by visitors to the Greek Orthodox Patriarchate which is almost next door.

THE NEW CITY
FIVE STAR IN TAKSIM

Ordinary luxury hotels are where Istanbul hoteliers have shone in the last decade and the competition is such that prices are miraculously low, especially during the summer. Shop around for the best deals.

The HILTON ISTANBUL was Hilton's first in Europe. Set back from the Bosphorus, the view from the balconies is stunning, a mixture of real city and gorgeous Bosphorus. Ask for a corner room. Lovely gardens, great pool.

SWISSOTEL THE BOSPHORUS feels more like an airport departure lounge when you step into it, and the rooms do not have balconies, but the views over the rooftops of the Dolmabaçe Palace are stunning. The HYATT REGENCY feels like a super-luxurious small hotel and the rooms are sophisticated.

With its excellent new management, the CEYLAN INTER-CONTINENTAL, previously the Sheraton, is quickly becoming the hotel of choice. THE CONRAD is just below Sultan Abdül-hamid's Yıldız Palace and again boasts astonishing views of the Topkapı, the Sea of Marmara and the entrance to the Bosphorus, as well as excellent service.

All roads lead to Taksim Square, and the MARMARA overlooks the hub of Taksim traffic. A brilliant Italian manager, Franco Minozzi, turned a rather minor highrise downtown affair into one of Istanbul's most glamorous hotels in the 1990s. It has since become a little run down but long association with the Istanbul Festival still ensures a healthy quota of divas, conductors, jazz musicians and film directors.

OTHER HOTELS IN AND AROUND BEYOĞLU

Two remarkable old gents preserve the dignity of the old Italianate quarter of Beyoğlu, the PERA PALAS, built for Wagon-Lits in the 1880s and run in an uncompromisingly old fashioned manner, and the BÜYÜK LONDRA, Istanbul's last Levantine establishment, founded in 1892 as the Grand Hotel de Londres, where guests idle the time away playing old 78s in the lobby.

The only hotel on Istiklal Caddesi (the former Grand' Rue de Pera) now pedestrianised, is THE RICHMOND, where the newly refurbished rooms are thoroughly comfortable. The restaurant has a fabulous view over the Topkapı Palace point and the entrance to the Bosphorus.

A handy hotel next to the Galata Tower is the ANEMON GALATA. The rooms with the best views over the Golden Horn are on the third and fourth floors. Once again the staff are extremely welcoming, and the rooftop restaurant has more jaw-dropping views over the Golden Horn and the Bosphorus.

Cihangir, Beyoğlu's uglier, brasher neighbour, has metamorphosed into the new epicentre of Istanbul's café society. It is also a cat's throw from Istanbul's most popular antiques quarter, Çukurcuma. The VILLA ZURICH, typically, is above one smart new café, Laila, and beneath one of the city's best fish restaurants, Doğa Balık (on the seventh floor). The furnishings have worn from plush to adequate in two years. The bathrooms are a little gloomy, but it is very central and affordable.

2

WATERY PALACES

In a city where the ultimate delight is to wake to the flickering reflections of the Bosphorus playing on the ceiling, it remains a mystery why there is such a scarcity of waterside hotels. But things are changing.

On the grand hotel front, there is the ÇIRAĞAN PALACE. Next door to the palace built by Sultan Abdülmecid in the 1860s, the rooms in its long featureless concrete block are large and very large, and the magnificent Bosphorus-side

Galata Tower mark the entrance to the Golden Horn. Upstream, shrouded in umbrella pines, is the ox-red SADULLAH PASHA YALI. The bathrooms are generously Edwardian, and next door in Beylerbeyi there is a proper functioning *hamam*.

A mile upstream, the SUMAHAN ON THE WATER in Çengelköy is soon to join the Bosphorus Pasha and make the Anatolian shore the place to stay in Istanbul. A private launch will whisk you to a brand new boutique hotel, built right on the Bosphorus at its most scenic point by architects Mark and Nedret Butler. The Sumahan is

1. Previous page: Aya Sofya 2. One of the entrances to Istanbul's Kapalıçarşı or Covered Bazaar 3. The dome of the Blue Mosque with the Golden Horn in the background 4. The old walls of Byzantium

swimming pool is heated all year round. But ultimately the Çırağan is just too large for its own good, with staff who lack the wish to please of Istanbul's other luxury chains.

Also on the European shore of the Bosphorus, the BEBEK HOTEL has been transformed from shabby seaside guesthouse to one of Istanbul's smartest, most expensive small hotels. The new look is masculine executive veneer, the view is sensational and the bar downstairs is one of Istanbul's historic watering holes.

The BOSPHORUS PALACE, over on the Anatolian shore, is the only *yalı* (Ottoman-style wooden house) to have been converted into a hotel. An earlier 1890s house on the site was burnt down in 1981 and this is a very reasonable copy in timberclad concrete. Downstream, framed by the Bosphorus Bridge, the domes and minarets of the Süleymaniye and the

scheduled to open in April 2005.

Finally, over the sea and far away to Büyükada, the largest of the four main inhabited Princes Islands. The HOTEL SPLENDID is just that, a twin-domed, splendidly genteel hotel, a short phaeton ride from the quay (there are no cars on the island). The rooms, with inbuilt shower cabins, are modest and the seagulls raucous, but this is another world.

'APART' HOTELS

There is lots to be said for Istanbul's wonderful new 'apart' hotels. The DIVAN HOTEL is a bit pedestrian, but TAXIM SUITES, which the hotel manages across the street (overlooking Taksim Square), is a beautifully proportioned, intelligently run collection of Scandinavian-style apartments, all bleached pine and white covers. Shopping orders are taken each day and kitchenettes include microwave ovens.

The brand new HOUSEZ on Akaretler has much smaller suites, but they are immaculately designed, many with plasma screens, and incredibly good value. Laundry and internet access are free.

In Beyoğlu, along from the Pera Palas, ANSEN 130 is a brand new entry, with twelve designer rooms in an elegant 1900s palazzo at the Tünel end of Meflrutiyet Caddesi. Cool, minimalist, solidly luxurious in a no expenses spared way and at a fair price. One of Istanbul's most respected resident chefs, Mike Norman, is in charge of the elegant dining room downstairs. Finally, ISTANBUL HOLIDAY APARTMENTS is offering an excellent selection of apartments around the Galata Tower. Some have spectacular views, others are with little garden patios.

For information on small hotels, the annually updated *Little Hotel Book*, by Sevan and Mujde Niflanyan (Boyut Yayınları) is recommended. Extra travel information is online at their Small Hotels of Turkey website, www.nisanyan.com. C

5. All roads in the old city lead to the Grand Bazaar

SULTANAHMET

The Four Seasons Istanbul Tevkifhane Sokak 1, Sultanahmet T: 0212 638 8200 W: www.fourseasons.com

Hotel Empress Zoe Akbıyık Caddesi, Adliye Sok. 10, Sultanahmet T: 0212 518 2504 / 518 4360 W: www.emzoe.com

Yeşil Ev Kabasakal Caddesi 5, Sultanahmet T: 0212 517 6785 W: www.istanbulyesilev.com

Ayasofya Pansyonları Soğukçeşme Sokak, Sultanahmet T: 0212 513 3660 W: www.ayasofyapensions.com

Kybele Hotel Yerebatan Caddesi 35, Sultanahmet T: 0212 511 7766 / 5117767 W: www.kybelehotel.com

Hotel Pamphylia Yerebatan Caddesdi 47, Sultanahmet T: 0212 512 0133 W: www.hotelpamphylia.com

Hotel Turkoman Asmalı Çeşme Sokak 2, Adliye Yanı, Sultanahmet T: 0212 516 2956 / 518 3667 F: 0212 516 2957

Hotel Arcadia Dr Imran Öktem Caddesi 1, Sultanahmet
T: 0212 516 9696 F: 0212 516 6118

Ibrahim Paşa Oteli Terzihane Sokak 5, Adliye Yanı, Sultanahmet
T: 0212 518 0394 F: 0212 518 4457

Hotel Nomade Divanyolu Caddesi, Ticarethane Sokak 15, Sultanahmet
T: 0212 513 8172 W: www.hotelnomade.com

THE GOLDEN HORN

Kariye Hotel Kariye Camii Sok 18, Edirnekapı
T: 0212 534 8414 W: www.kariyeotel.com

Daphnis Hotel Sadrazam Ali Paşa Caddesi 26, Fener
T: 0212 531 4858 / 531 4811 W: www.hoteldaphnis.com

TAKSIM

Hilton Istanbul Cumhuriyet Caddesi, Harbiye. T: 0212 315 6000
W: www.istanbul.hilton.com

Hyatt Regency Taşkışla Caddesi 1, Taksim T: 0212 368 1234 W: www.hyatt.com

Swissotel The Bosphorus Bayıldım Cad. 2, Maçka T: 0212 326 1100 W: www.swissotel.com

Conrad Istanbul Yıldız Cad. Beşiktaş T: 0212 227 3000 W: www.conradhotels.com

The Marmara Istanbul Taksim T: 0212 251 4696 W: www.themarmaraistanbul.com

AROUND BEYOĞLU

Pera Palas Meşrutiyet Caddesi 98-100, Tepebaşı, Beyoğlu
T: 0212 251 4560 W: www.perapalas.com.

Büyük Londra Oteli Meşrutiyet Caddesi 117, Tepebaşı, Beyoğlu T: 0212 245 0607

The Marmara Pera Hotel T: 0212 251 4646 W:www.themarmarapera.com

Richmond Hotel Istiklal Caddesi 445, Tünel, Beyoğlu T: 0212 252 5460
W: www.richmondhotels.com.tr

Anemon Hotel Bereketzade Mh., Büyükhendek Caddesi 11, Kuledibi
T: 0212 293 2343 W: www.anemonhotels.com

Villa Zurich Hotel Akarsu Yokuşu Caddesi 44-46, Cihangir T: 0212 293 0604
W: www.hotelvillazurich.com

WATERY PALACES

Çırağan Palace Kempinski Istanbul, Beşiktaş T: 212 326 4646
W: www.ciraganpalace.com

Bebek Hotel Cevdet Paşa Cad. Bebek T: 0212 358 2000 W: www.bebekhotel.com.tr

Bosphorus Palace Yalıboyu Caddesi 64, Beylerbeyi T: 0216 422 0003
W: www.bosphoruspalace.com

Splendid Hotel Büyükada T: 0216 382 6950

'APART' HOTELS

Divan Taxim Suites Cumhuriyet Cad. 49, Taksim T: 0212 254 7777
W: www.taximsuites.com

Housez Süleyman Seba Cad. 60, Beşiktaş T: 0212 259 0114
W: www.housez-istanbul.com

Ansen 130 Meşrutiyet Cad. 130, Tepebaşi T: 0212 245 8808 W: www.ansenuite.com

Istanbul Holiday Apartments W: www.istanbulholidayapartments.com

The Kybele Hotel is ideally located in the centre of the old city of Istanbul. The Blue Mosque, Hagia Sophia, Topkapı Palace, Covered Bazaar and the harbour are all within walking distance.

The Kybele Hotel is a small, family-run establishment. The sixteen rooms, lobby, garden and the library are decorated with authentic antiques. The hotel rooms are comfortable, with modern marbled bathrooms, air-conditioned and with minibars.

We also have an interesting selection of carpets, kilims & textiles in our Yoruk Collection

Yerebatan Caddesi, 35 Sultanahmet 34110, İstanbul, Turkey
Tel: (90.212) 511 77 66 / 511 77 67   Fax: (90.212) 513 43 93
E-mail: info@kybelehotel   Website: www.kybelehotel.com

THE GUIDE

Anthony Hazledine

THE TWO CAPITALS
ISTANBUL & ANKARA

The legend of the founding of the city that became Istanbul is so well known that one hardly dares tell it again, but because it is such a good story, I will.

In the 6th century BC Byzas, a Greek from Megara, set out to found a colony on the shores of the Bosphorus. Before leaving Greece he consulted the oracle at Delphi, taking away the memorable advice that he should "build his city opposite the blind". The city of the blind was Chalcedon, modern Kadiköy, founded a little earlier on the Asian shore by other Greeks from Megara – who must indeed have been blind not to see the strategic advantages of the peninsula facing them (above).

Byzas founded his city and it prospered, levying tolls on the Black Sea grain trade and utilising its pivotal position as a trading centre between Europe and Asia. The city was called Byzantium and a thousand years later this name would be given to one of the most splendid of the great world empires. In the following centuries the city fell under the sway of Medes,

Persians, Athenians, Spartans and Boeotians. Having survived a siege by Phillip II of Macedon the city celebrated its deliverance by issuing coins dedicated to the goddess Hecate, to whom they credited their survival. The emblems of Hecate are the crescent moon and star, symbols that adorn the flag that flies above the city today.

By 73 AD the city is recorded as part of the province of Bythnia, and it remained a prosperous provincial trading city until it was besieged by the Emperor Constantine in

the Western Roman Empire. In total contrast the Empire of the East, with a new capital, a new language and a new religion, was embarking on an epoch of vitality and splendour. Constantinople would become the most magnificent city in the world with its hippodrome, churches, palaces, aqueducts, cisterns and fortifications – monuments that even in their fragmented state still command astonishment and admiration. What traveller of a romantic disposition can forget his first sight of the majestic battered city walls and his entrance into the imperial city?

The Byzantine Empire has in the past had a rather bad press. Gibbon called it "a tedious and uniform tale of weakness and misery" and in the 19th century Lecky was even less stinting in his condemnation, calling it "the most thoroughly base and despicable form that civilisation has yet assumed". This idiotic view had become something of an accepted orthodoxy until challenged by 20th century historians such as Robert Byron, David Talbot-Rice and Steven Runciman.

323 AD, in pursuit of the usurper Licinius who had taken refuge there.

After its destruction and capture Constantine conceived the idea of rebuilding the city and transferring the imperial capital from Rome to Byzantium. From here he would be closer to the centre of the eastwards expanding empire and thus better able to control its economic and military policies. Additionally, with its established Christian population, Byzantium would be more sympathetic to his newly found faith.

On 11 May 330, the city was inaugurated as New Rome, but this was soon changed to Constantinople – 'the city of Constantine.' On the death of Theodosius I in 395 the empire was divided into two parts, the Western Empire with its capital at Rome and the Eastern Empire with its capital in Constantinople, each with its own emperor. In 410 AD Rome was sacked by the Barbarians, and so came to pass the decline and fall of

While the rehabilitation of Byzantium does not need my meagre contribution, it is perhaps apposite to say something about the influence of its art on the West. With its fusion of classical and Eastern elements the legacy of Byzantium can be seen most visibly in the style of architecture known as Romanesque. The art of beautiful books came from the empire

and the magnificent Lindisfarne Gospels are modelled on Byzantine originals. In sculpture there are Byzantine affinities to be found, for example, in the York Madonna, and its presence is strongly felt in the work of the great early painters of Italy. It is argued that the 12th century second Byzantine Renaissance inspired the 14th century Italian Renaissance.

The aspect of the arts that is most relevant to us is of course weaving. For most people with even the sketchiest knowledge of Byzantium the opulence and splendour of the emperor and his court are well known. The luxurious textiles and fabrics with which the court and wealthy citizens clothed themselves were accorded the highest esteem. The most coveted and costly of these were the silks which had to be imported by camel caravan from China, at the time the only place where sericulture was known. The great trans-Asian highways down which these caravans travelled became known as the Silk Road and in later chapters we will also travel these ancient roads.

Legend has it that in 552 AD two monks in the oasis of Khotan in western China sold the secret of the cultivation of the silkworm to the emissaries of the Emperor Justinian who brought it back to Constantinople. In the 6th century the private silk industry was still dependent on state controlled imported raw silk, but by the 10th century silk was being produced in the hinterland of Anatolia and imported raw silk was commercially available. By this time the imperial workshops were operating at Zuexippos, to the northeast of the Hippodrome (2), equipped with very sophisticated looms

judging by the evidence of surviving textile fragments.

The dyeing of murex purple, obtained from a type of shellfish, was an imperial monopoly with illicit manufacture punishable by death. Other colours were obtained from indigo, madder, kermes, brazil wood and weld. Unfortunately few if any of the magnificent products of these workshops survive in Turkey. Most known examples are to be seen in the cathedral treasuries of Europe, having made the journey either as gifts from the Byzantine emperors to foreign royalty and dignitaries, or as precious wrappings for religious relics destined for foreign churches.

When it comes to carpets, examples from all over the empire and beyond would have been available to the wealthy citizen in the city's flourishing bazaars, but

1. Iznik tilework in the Rustem Paşa Mosque 2. The Hippodrome, with the obelisk at its heart 3. 'Janissary' in the Topkapı 4. Byzantine goldwork mosaic in Aya Sofya 5. Carved reliefs on the base of the obelisk in the Hippodrome

6

7

6. Embroidered turban cover, 17th century 7. Ottoman campaign throne inlaid with mother-of pearl, 16th century, Topkapı Saray 8. Aya Sofya, first a church, then a mosque, now a museum 9. Ottoman silk kaftan associated with Sultan Selim the Grim (1512-20), Topkapı Saray

found on carpets are also found on the mosaic floors, but who is copying whom? This puzzle is being worked on by the same team of scholars who are working on the riddle of the sphinx.

The Byzantine Empire had begun with Constantine I and would come to an end with Constantine XI, when on 29 May 1453 the Emperor died defending the walls of Constantinople against the besieging Ottoman Turks. When the double eagle

there is little or no evidence for the production of carpets in Byzantine Constantinople. Local preference seems to have tended more towards mosaic decoration for the floor, and here the distinctive Constantinopolitan School produced work of the highest order. The only surviving remnants of the Great Palace are some of its mosaic floors dating from the 6th/7th century, showing the fine quality and naturalistic style associated with Constantinople. Of course many of the designs and patterns

8

of Byzantium was hauled down and the crescent and star took its place, Constantinople became the only city in history to be a capital of both a Christian and a Muslim empire. After allowing his troops three days to loot and pillage, Sultan Mehmet II set about consolidating an empire that would last until the early 20th century. The Ottomans appreciated and needed the skills of their subject peoples, in particular the Greeks and the Armenians. Later they would offer sanctuary to the displaced Jews of Europe, among them the Sephardic Jews persecuted by the Inquisition in Spain.

The Ottoman court shared with the Byzantines a love of luxurious textiles and the workshops were soon producing silks and velvets for the new regime. New centres of production developed and the city of Bursa, or Brussa as it was then, became particularly famous for its velvets and silks woven in a variety of techniques. Unlike Byzantine work, many examples of Ottoman textiles, both court-made and domestic, have survived and good examples can be seen in both the Topkapı Palace (9) and in the Sadberk Hanım Museum in Büyükdere.

Unable to afford luxurious manufactured velvets, women from the towns, villages and islands of the Ottoman Empire copied their designs onto pillows, cushions, towels and scarves in colourful embroideries that are today keenly sought by collectors (6).

If there is scant evidence of carpet weaving in Constantinople in the early years of the empire, it is clear that work-shops were set up in Hereke, Uşak and Kayseri which remain important weaving centres today. The most important and famous carpets produced in Constantinople during the Ottoman period came towards the end of the empire in the 19th century. Workshops were set up in the Armenian district of Kum Kapı − 'the sand gate' − today a popular tourist area full of over-rated and over-priced fish restaurants. The Armenian weavers produced very finely knotted rugs, often with a silk pile, distinguished by a technique of weaving gold and silver threads into the upper

level warps that created an embossed effect in the pile. They used Persianate designs, the most common being the 'head and shoulders' design prayer rugs. Several of the master weavers signed their work, making us familiar with names such as Zareh Penyamian, Tossounian and Apelian. At the beginning of the 20th century the industry was faltering and by the beginning of the Second World War it was in decline.

Like Rome, the capital it superseded, Constantinople was built upon seven hills. The first hill is the heart of the ancient city and it was here that Byzas and the early Greeks built their acropolis. Later it was where the Byzantines built their palaces and the mighty church of Aya Sofya, and from here the Sublime Porte ruled the vast empire while the sultan amused himself in the nearby Topkapı Palace. It is on the southern slopes of this ancient and evocative hill, among the monuments and ruins of past empires, that we shall begin our tour of the carpet bazaars of modern Istanbul. C

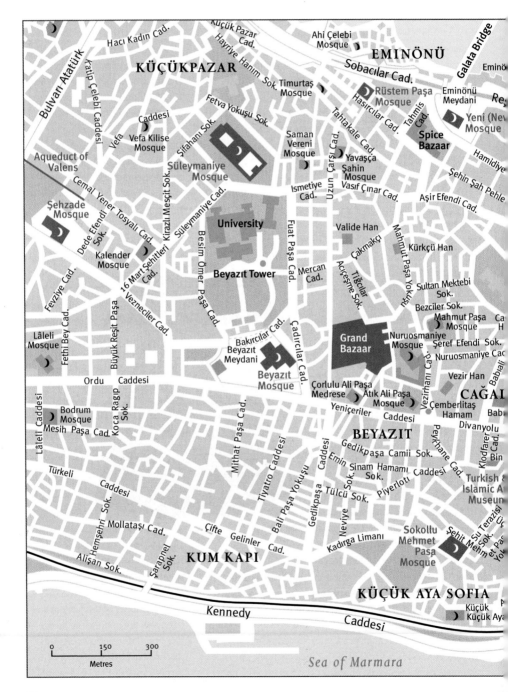

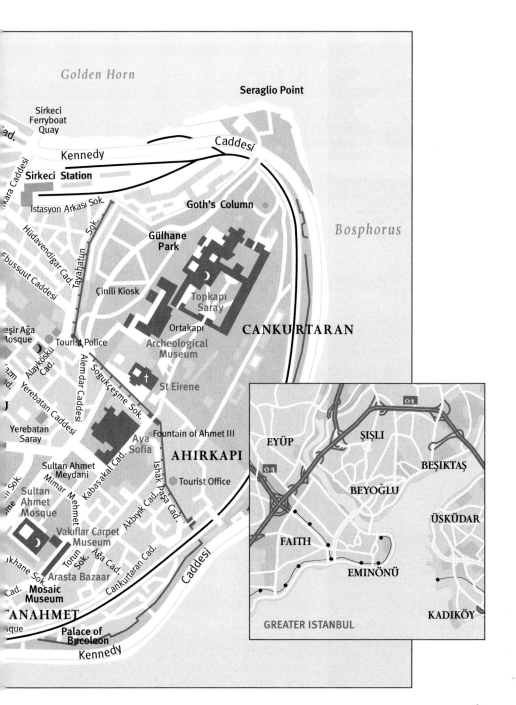

Golden Horn

Seraglio Point

Sirkeci
Ferryboat
Quay

ad.

Kennedy

Caddesi

Sirkeci Station

Mara Caddesi

Istasyon Arkası Sok.

Goth's Column

Bosphorus

Hüdavendigar Cad.

Tayahatun Sok.

Ebussuut Caddesi

Gülhane
Park

Çinili Kiosk

Topkapı
Saray

eşir Ağa
Mosque

Tourist Police

Alayköskü Cad.

Alemdar Caddesi

Soğukçeşme Sok.

Ortakapı

CANKURTARAN

Archeological
Museum

azm
ad.

Yerebatan Caddesi

St Eirene

Yerebatan
Saray

Aya
Sofia

Fountain of Ahmet III

AHIRKAPI

EYÜP

ŞİŞLİ

Sultan Ahmet
Meydani

Mimar Mehmet

Kabasakal Cad.

İshak Paşa Cad.

Tourist Office

BEŞİKTAŞ

Sok.

me

Sultan
Ahmet
Mosque

Akbıyık Cad.

BEYOĞLU

ÜSKÜDAR

Vakıflar Carpet
Museum

Torun Sok.

Ağa Cad.

Cankurtaran Cad.

Caddesi

FAITH

khane Sok.

Arasta Bazaar

EMİNÖNÜ

Cad. Mosaic
Museum

ANAHMET

sque

Palace of
Bucoleon

Kennedy

GREATER ISTANBUL

KADIKÖY

ARASTA BAZAAR & SULTANAHMET

If you are standing in the northern courtyard of the Sultan-ahmet (Blue) Mosque with Aya Sofya to your left and the mosque to your right, then straight ahead of you and up a ramp is the Vakıflar Carpet Museum. This will most likely be closed, which is probably a mercy, as it will save you the pain of seeing important early Turkish village carpets (12) badly treated and poorly displayed. Walk through the large gateway underneath the museum; notice the huge chains that were intended to force anyone on horseback to dismount, and down a flight of steps. Here is an open square bordered by some tourist shops, proceed to the far corner and descend another flight of steps and the Arasta Bazaar is the pedestrianised street to the right (3).

This alley of low vaulted shops was built at the same time as the mosque. The rents went towards the mosque's upkeep as they still do today. The area gradually fell into disrepair and became a home to gypsies who stabled their horses in the broken shops. In 1974 the area was restored and today its 200-metre length is home to 83 shops, the majority of them selling carpets and textiles.

Entering Arasta the second shop on the right is just called HALI and is owned by Adnan Metin. He is a large friendly soul who has been around Arasta for many years. Previously a partner in the Er-Ne-Met business, he now trades on his own, holding a medium-sized stock of mainly old rugs.

Further down on the right-hand side is GALERI CENGIZ owned by two partners, both called Cengiz (Korkmaz and Kara). They have a very large stock which includes many good antique and old pieces and they also have another shop just outside the Arasta Bazaar in Mimar Mehmet Ağa Caddesi. They also claim to have the largest repair shop in Istanbul, and in recent years have been making a name for themselves at international carpet fairs.

Further along on the same side is ARASTA HALI. The owner, Yakup Kaya, is originally from Van in the east, and has been in this shop since 1989. Also with a developing international profile, he has an interesting selection of decorative textiles,

Heading further down the street and on the other side at no.93 is COCOON, owned by Şeref Özen (6) and Mustafa Gökhan Demir. Cocoon has been open since 1995 and has rapidly established a reputation as a prime source for good collectable weavings. Şeref, previously an English teacher, has a particular love of Turkmen rugs and Central Asian embroideries and usually has good examples of both in his large and interesting stock. He has travelled widely in Central Asia, and is well known in Europe and America, where he is a frequent exhibitor at carpet and textile fairs. Like several of the dealers in Arasta who have larger show-

1. *The Blue or Sultanahmet Mosque, with the Bosphorous and the Asian shore behind*

embroideries and chapans (Uzbek silk robes) which includes some collectable antique pieces as well as some older rugs, bags and new production tülüs.

Directly opposite is MAISON DU TAPIS D'ORIENT, opened in 1986 by Mehmet Çetinkaya (5). Born near Elazığ in eastern Turkey, Mehmet studied at art school in Belgium and has brought an artist's sensibility to the appreciation of Asian textiles. This small shop has become one of the best places to find important collectable weavings and textiles in Turkey. Recently he opened a large and beautiful new 'textile art' gallery just around the corner, but more about that later. Today the original shop in Arasta is in the capable hands of his son Said and his long-time assistant Sabri, and you will find an interesting stock of small collectable and decorative textiles including very good new suzanis from Uzbekistan.

rooms in the surrounding streets, Cocoon have a multi-storey gallery in Kucuk Ayasofya Caddesi.

Further down on the same side at no.107 is EYMEN HALICILIK owned by long-time and well-known dealer Ömer Eymen (2). Originally from Malatya (like an astonishing number of Istanbul rug dealers), Ömer was for many years based in Cağaloğlu next to the famous *hamam* (Turkish bath) until he moved three years ago to the Arasta Bazaar. He also has a larger shop just outside the bazaar and keeps an interesting stock of antique rugs that often contains good Kurdish pieces as well as textiles and kilims.

The Sultanahmet Mosque (1) and the Arasta Bazaar (3) are both built upon the ruins of the Great Imperial Palace, almost nothing of which survives above ground today.

But below ground level is a different matter, and beneath our feet at this end of the Arasta are several of the mosaic floors of the Great Palace. A worn stone lion marks the entrance to the Mosaic Museum where these utterly beautiful floors, which probably date from the 6th century AD, can be seen. The museum is open from 9am-5pm every day except Tuesday.

On the corner of the street on the same side as the museum is ER-NE HALI, owned by Murat Metin and his two sons, who also own the five adjoining shops. This business used to

be part of the long established Er-Ne-Met partnership, now dissolved, that traded for many years from this address. They have a huge stock which includes old Persian and Caucasian pieces as well as new production from Hereke and Kayseri.

Leaving the Arasta Bazaar and turning right past the shops belonging to Er-Ne, cross the road to find a three-storey building which will almost certainly have a stunning textile on display in the window and a discreet sign saying MEHMET ÇETINKAYA GALLERY. This is the recently opened textile art gallery (8, 17) belonging to Mehmet Çetinkaya who, as mentioned above, has traded for a number of years as Maison du Tapis d'Orient in the Arasta Bazaar. He has built a worldwide reputation as a purveyor of exquisite textiles, carpets and kilims, many of which now grace major collections. Mehmet was one of the first dealers to understand and promote esoteric Kaitag embroideries from Daghestan and has had a long

affinity with the graphic qualities of antique Anatolian kilims. To visit this spacious well-lit gallery with its superb embroideries, suzanis, kilims, costume and carpets is a sensual treat, and one that is not restricted to the eyes alone since the air is delicately scented by cedar wood shelves and cupboards.

Çetinkaya is part of an interesting development that is seeing a number of leading dealers from the Arasta Bazaar and elsewhere opening shops and galleries in the street that runs downhill from the southern end of the bazaar. Follow it and you will come to the mosque known as the Küçük Ayasofya Cami. This is in fact a 6th century Byzantine church, possibly older than Aya Sofya itself of which it is a scaled down model – hence the name (kuçük means small).

The street leading from Arasta down to the church is wittily named Küçük Ayasofya Caddesi (Small Aya Sofya Street) and at no.1 next to the ruined *hamam* is ER-NE-MET owned by three partners from the original business of that name. They have a large stock of mainly old and antique goods, and if you go up to the second floor you will find a good stock of large and oversize decorative carpets. There is also a large repair shop and a rather nice walled garden out the back.

A couple of shops further along you come to EYMEN HALI-CILIK owned by Ömer Eymen – seen earlier in his Arasta shop. A little further down on the same side (all the shops of interest

2. Ömer Eymen sporting an Aleppo silk tunic 3. The Arasta Bazaar in the shadow of the Blue Mosque 4. Mouthwatering morsels in the Eminönü Spice Bazaar 5. Textile art dealer Mehmet Çetinkaya 6. Cocoon's Şeref Özen in the Arasta Bazaar

are within a short distance of each other and on the left-hand side) is the second shop belonging to Cocoon. Here in a spacious three-floor building they are able to display much more of their large stock of decorative and collectable textiles from Turkey and Central Asia.

A couple of shops further down is the fairly recently opened GALLERY GÖKHAN owned by Hasan Saz, who has been a carpet dealer for many

7. *Pierre Loti in his finery* 8. *The upper floor of Mehmet Çetinkaya's gallery* 9. *One of Sultanahmet's countless cats at home on a rug* 10. *Dealers Ali Turkkan and Burak Aydoğan* 11. *Modern Turkish ceramics on sale in in the Arasta Bazaar*

years and previously had a business in Austria. He keeps an interesting stock of antique rugs, kilims and fragments, and now also has his own production of new Turkish carpets.

A little further down and just before the corner at no.25, you will find MUHTEŞEM TRAVEL on the 4th floor. This business, with its tantalising subtitle 'Cultural and Scenic Adventures', is owned by Vedat Karadağ. Originally from Ankara, Vedat started his career as a carpet dealer in Adana, but has now moved to Istanbul where he will organise whatever cultural or scenic adventure you desire, from visiting Anatolian carpet weaving villages to walking the paths of the high Taurus in search of Alexander's lost legions. Rumour has it that other serious dealers are planning to open galleries in Küçük Ayasofya Caddesi, so this could soon become an even more interesting area for rug hunting.

Retrace your steps back towards Arasta and turn left up Tavukhane Sokak (Chicken House Lane) passing Çetinkaya's gallery on the left and carry on uphill until you reach the southern end of the Atmeydanı. This is of course the Byzantine hippodrome, the shape of which is clearly visible even in its modern manifestation as a large traffic island. Head across it slightly to the right, passing between the southern

obelisk and the twisted stump of metal. This unprepossessing stump is perhaps the most interesting of the monuments that survive along the 'spina' of the hippodrome, having been brought from the temple of Delphi by Constantine the Great. It had been erected at Delphi by the Greeks to celebrate their victory over the Persians at Plataea in 479 BC and takes the form of three twisted serpents, their heads now sadly missing having been lopped off by Turkish and Frankish vandals.

order in any design, using natural dyes, in a number of villages in Aegean and central Turkey.

Leaving Rainbow continue up the hill and look across the road at the corner of Dostluk Yurdu Sokak to find another first floor shop called OBA HALI. This is owned by two brothers, Ali and Daimi Akkuş, who have an interesting stock of old and antique pieces and specialise in Caucasian pieces bought at source.

A few metres further down Dostluk Yurdu Sokak take the first right into Piyerloti Caddesi and look for no.19 on the right-hand side opposite the large municipal building. The street is named after the 19th century French novelist and travel writer Pierre Loti (1850-1923), who was captivated by all things Oriental and exotic (7). He particularly liked 'Stamboul, where

Having crossed the Hippodrome, walk up Terzihane Sokak – the street bordering the southern end of the Ibrahim Paşa Palace which houses the Museum of Turkish and Islamic Art (TIEM) – and on the left you will see the Turkoman Hotel, a popular base for foreign rug dealers. It is owned by well-known carpet entrepreneur Celaleddin Vardarsuyu (whose wholesale and new rugs store BEREKET is just around the corner in Peykhane Caddesi). Continue up Terzihane Caddesi and turn right at the T-junction into Klodfarer Caddesi. A short distance along on the right-hand side you will see a sign saying RAINBOW COLLECTION GÖKKUSAGI HALI KILIM. The shop, located on the first floor, is owned by Bedri Yokuş – also from Malatya – and his partner Ali Bozyak. They keep a stock of old and antique carpets, some kilims, bags and trappings, and also have a large production of new carpets which are woven to

12

13

12. *Anatolian village rug (detail), before 1800, in the Vakıflkar Carpet Museum* 13. *Richly decorated Turkmen woman's hat* 14. *Colourful spice and sponges in the bazaar* 15. *SU.DE's Suat Çapas shows a Jaf Kurd rug in his Binbirdirek gallery*

he was able to camp around dressed in Eastern attire, and spent a lot of time here, pursuing his exotic tastes in a more liberal environment than that in France at the time. He seems to have endeared himself to the 'Stamboulis as a number of locations around the city commemorate his sojourn.

BURAK AYDOĞAN GALLERY, at no.19, was opened in 2003 by Burak Aydoğan (10), who previously traded in the Grand Bazaar. Burak, whose father was a dealer from Erzurum in eastern Anatolia, is one of the youngest and most active dealers in town. In his new shop, with its hidden courtyard of palm trees, he has a select stock of interesting antique pieces, many of which find their way into private collections.

Almost next door is a hotel and carpet shop owned by the three BOZDAĞ brothers, Kemal, Ömer and Muhammet. The shop extends over three floors and has a large and comprehensive stock ranging from decorative carpets to small collectables. Coming from humble origins in central Anatolia, the Bozdağs have built up a carpet business that is an Istanbul institution, visited by international collectors and dealers both large and small. With his engaging manner and ready smile, Muhammet will guide you through their old and antique rugs, carpets, kilims and bags. They are also involved in the large-scale manufacture of new carpets and have extensive repair and restoration facilities near Aksaray in central Anatolia. Their new hotel, still under construction and as yet unnamed, will be ideally suited for the exhausted ruggie, who will be able to lie in bed enjoying a splendid view of the Sea of Marmara whilst ordering a rug from room service.

Retrace your steps to Klodfarer Caddesi and you will soon reach a large open square known as Binbirdirek Sarnıcı or the cistern of a thousand and one columns. Beneath this square (enter from the street below) is a beautiful early Byzantine cistern, its vaulted roof supported on several hundred pillars with carved capitals. A traveller in the early

19th century records the then empty cistern as being in use as a silk manufactory run by Greeks and Jews. It has recently been 'restored' and, in an act of contemporary vandalism, turned into a restaurant and shopping mall, while above ground in the square itself is a structure built to house the ventilation system which is of such ugliness it should bring eternal shame to the authorities that allowed it.

Turn right into the square and a couple of shops along is SU.DE owned by Suat Çapas (15) . Suat has been here for some eight years and is a real rug enthusiast with an excellent and interesting stock of collectable pieces. He particularly likes the minimalist look of Anatolian kilims, but his stock also includes textiles, carpets, bags and fragments. He has some good Kurdish pieces about which he is very knowledgeable.

Practically next door and up on the first floor is ASLAN HALICILIK, one of the district's large wholesale businesses. Specialising in antique Caucasian rugs, Ruştu Aslan conducted business in the Grand Bazaar for many years. Recently he moved here to larger premises where he keeps a large stock of antique rugs and large decorative carpets.

On the other side of the square, up on the second floor at no.6, is KARAVAN ART owned by Muzaffer Kaplan. Muzaffer is the middle brother of a well-known carpet dealing family from Konya, where his younger brother runs the famous shop

Karavan and his elder brother is involved in manufacturing new carpets. In his spacious gallery with marvellous views over the Blue Mosque and across the Sea of Marmara, he keeps a varied stock that includes everything from his brother's new production to

antique and collectable pieces. At present he is starting a new venture selling old decorative terracotta urns and pots for the garden and is beginning production of fountains, basins, vases and similar objects hand carved from travertine.

Facing the square on Klodfarer Caddesi is the Halı Hotel, much frequented by foreign dealers and once again owned by a carpet dealer, Lütfü Bayhan, who keeps a selection of his new production carpets in the hotel.

16

Next door and down a few steps is DINAR HALI owned by Kadir Alan. He offers a restoration service and also keeps a few old rugs. There are a number of other small carpet shops dotted around the square that give the place a jolly atmosphere.

Carry on up Klodfarer Caddesi to reach the main road with the tramlines and cross over Divan-yolu, 'the road to the divan'. The divan was where petitions were brought before the Sultan, but the road is much older than the Otto-man period and more interesting. Originally built by the Roman Emperor Septimus Severus, this road became the main thorough-fare of the new city laid out by

Constantine. Known as the 'Mese' or middle road, it started from a structure known as the Milion situated in front of Aya Sofya and from where all dis-tances in the empire were measured. It followed the course of today's Divan-yolu as far as the modern junction of Aksaray and then divided into two branches, one continuing to the city walls on the Marmara side, the other on the Golden Horn side. It was a grand porticoed avenue down which all the great religious and royal proces-sions took place and all the commerce of the empire flowed. Under the portico's arches the merchants' stalls were grouped in trades with the perfumers nearest the Palace so that their wares could scent the air for the emperor and empress. The fur merchants had their booths in what is known today as Çemberlitaş but we can only wonder where the carpet dealers were and what splendours we would have found there.

A market of carpet dealers can still be found very close to the ancient Mese by continuing a short distance up Babiali Caddesi and looking for a building on the right-hand side

16. Necdet (Mike) Akbaprak of Yörük Collection in his trademark embroidered cap, with visitors to his tassel-festooned gallery 17. Central Asian textiles on display in the Mehmet Çetinkaya Gallery 18. A Turkmen silk embroidered woman's coat 19. A Tajik bridal veil

17

that is usually draped with carpets and kilims. This five-floor building, housing approximately fifty dealers and repairers, is mainly a trade and wholesale centre and a place where a number of dealers with small shops in the bazaar have larger depots. Quite a few of the dealers – who incidentally are nearly all from Malatya – have old and antique pieces, so this is usually an interesting place in which to poke around.

DENIZ CARPETS at no 20, owned by the affable and friendly Hasan Kaya and his saz-playing son Deniz, has a mixed stock of old carpets and kilims from Central Asia and the Caucasus. They have just started a new production of high quality embroideries from the Caucasus in the style of Kaitag and Ottoman needlework. At no.19, another family business, FATIH HALI, is managed by Ali Güreli and his brother and father, who specialise in old and semi-old Anatolian and Caucasian carpets. Down in the basement is BARAN CARPETS AND KELIMS whose owner Nedim Turan has been in the business for over twenty years and specialises in old and semi-old kilims. Opposite Nedim is MERT HALI owned by Erdoğan Özgün, who has a stock of old and antique rugs and kilims as well as some large decorative carpets.

Leaving the Babiali building turn left and then left again down Çatal Çeşme Sokak, then when you reach Yerebatan Caddesi turn right and look out for the Kybele Hotel on the left-hand side. This charming and atmospheric hotel, decorated in a sumptuous late Ottoman style, is the home to YÖRÜK COLLEC- TION, probably the most exotic carpet shop in town. Entering through the hotel you will find Necdet Akbayrak (16), in his trade- mark embroidered cap, holding court in a low room festooned with tasselled hangings, antiques and lamps, while piles of carpets and kilims line the walls in an exotic gloom.

19

18

The place has a wonderful orientalist atmosphere that would have driven Pierre Loti into parox- ysms of delight, and is the perfect place to indulge one's own exotic carpet fantasies. Not only has 'Mike', as he is known, created a fantastic looking shop, but he also has some very good collectable rugs and fragments. He specialises in particular in pieces from cen- tral and eastern Anatolia, and on several occasions I have seen very good antique Anatolian Kurdish rugs there.

As another glass of steaming çay silently appears, this seems to be the perfect place to conclude a hard day spent pounding the ancient streets of Sultanahmet in search of old rugs.

Arasta Hali	*Yakup Kaya* Arasta Carşisi No. 79, 34400 Sultanahmet, Istanbul T: 0212 516 0517 F: 0212 518 5744 M: 0532 217 0104 E: arastahali@yahoo.com
Aslan Halicilik	*Rüştü Aslan* Binbirdirek Mahallesi, Binbirdirek Meydanı Sokak No. 7 Kat: 1 Iletişim Han, Sultanahmet, Istanbul T: 0212 517 9692/93 F: 0212 517 9699 M: 0532 213 1122 E: aslanhali@superonline.com
Aslanlar Halı	*Mevlüt Köse* Tacirler Sk. No.22 Kapalıçarşı, Eminönü, Istanbul T: 0212 526 4362 F: 0212 514 0172
Baran Carpets & Kilims	*Nedim Turan* Baba-ali Caddesi. Babı ali-Ali Çarşısı No. 18/8, Cağaloğlu, Istanbul T: 0212 519 6105 M: 0532 745 8896
Burak Aydoğan Gallery	*Burak Aydoğan* No.93 Sultanahmet, 34400 Istanbul T: 0212 638 6450 F: 0212 518 0338 E: cocoon@superonline.com
Cocoon	*Şeref Özen* No.93 Arasta Bazaar, Sultanahmet, 34400 Istanbul T: 0212 638 6450 F: 0212 518 0338 E: cocoon@superonline.com
Deniz Carpets	*Hasan Kaya* Baba-Ali Caddesi. Baba-Ali Çarşısı No. 18/20, Cağaloğlu, Istanbul T: 0212 527 9871 F: 0212 511 9385 E: yusuf_deniz1@yahoo.com
Dinar Halı	*Kadir Alan* Divanyolu Klodfarer Caddesi, Nüzhet Bey Han No.18/B, 34400 Sultanahmet, Istanbul T: 0212 638 0905
ER-NE Hali	*Murat Metin* ER-NE Hali Carpet & Kilim Arasta Bazaar No. 117, Sultanahmet, Istanbul T: 0212 638 4302 E: er-ne@er-ne.com
	Celal Metin Arasta Bazaar No:117, Sultanahmet, Istanbul T: 0212 638 4302 E: info@er-ne.com
Eymen	*Ömer Eymen* Eymen Halicilik, rasta Bazaar No:117, Sultanahmet, Istanbul T: 0212 638 4302 E: info@er-ne.com
Fatih Halı	*Ali Güreli* Caddesi. Babıali Çarşısı 18/19, Cağoluğlu, Istanbul T: 0212 511 2769 F: 0212 526 8423
Galeri Cengiz	*Cengiz Korkmaz* Galeri Cengiz Carpet and Kilim, Mimar Mehmet Ağa Cad No. 21, 34400 Sultanahmet, Istanbul T: 0212 516 4534 M: 0532 312 7762 E: galeri-cenzig@galeri-cenzig.com.tr
	Atilla Korkmaz, Arasta Bazaar No.157, Sultanahmet, 34400, Istanbul T: 0212 518 8882 F: 0212 518 0694 E: galeri-cengiz@galeri-cengiz.com.tr
Demir Galeri	*Mustafa Gökhan* Demir Galeri Tribalchase, Küçük Ayasofya Caddesi, Sultanahmet, 34400 Eminönü, Istanbul T: 0212 638 6271 F: 0212 638 6270 M: 0532 251 5316 E: tribalchase@tribalchase.com
Gallery Gökhan	*Hasan Saz* Gallery Gökhan Carpets Kilims and Textiles, Küçük Ayasofya Caddesi No.17, Sultanahmet, Istanbul T: 0212 458 7466 F: 0212 458 7467 M: 0532 230 9363 E: carpet@gallerygoekhan.com
Gökkuşagi Halı	*Ali Bozyak* Gökkuşagi Halı Kilim (Rainbow), Binbirdirek Mahallesi Klodfarer Caddesi, Kültür Apt. No.27/6, Sultanahmet, Istanbul T: 0212 517 3633 F: 0212 517 3604 E: rainbowkilim@turk.net
Halı Kilim	*Adnan Metin* Bazaar No. 117, Sultanahmet, Istanbul T: 0212 516 7858 E: hali_istanbul@hotmail.com
Kaktus Art	*Nazan Bahcivan* İshakpaşa Mah.Keleci Sokak No.7, 34400 Sultanahmet, Istanbul T: 0212 638 4480 F: 0212 638 3964

Karavan Art	*Muzaffer Kaplan* Klodfarer Caddesi Dr Şevkibey Sokak, Ortaklar Han 6/2 Sultanahmet, Istanbul T: 0212 638 5211 F: 0212 638 5212 M: 0542 424 1689 E: karavanart@superonline.com
Karavan Halı	*Ali Söylemez* Kervansaray Karşısı Belediye altı No.4, Sultanahmet, Aksaray T: 0382 242 3064 F: 0382 242 3065 E: söylemez@mail.koc.net
Mehmet Çetinkaya Gallery	*Mehmet Çetinkaya* Küçük Ayasofya, Caddesi Tavukhane Sokak No. 7, Sultanahmet, 34400 Istanbul T: 0212 517 6808 F: 0212 638 1553 E: mcetinkaya2002@yahoo.com
Mert Halı	*Erdoğan Özgün* Baba-Ali Caddesi. Babıali Çarşısı No. 18/3, Cağaloğlu, Istanbul T: 0212 528 8559 F: 0212 528 8560
Muhteşem Travel	*Vedat Karadağ* Muhteşem Travel Cultural and Scenic Adventures Mahallesi. K. Ayasofya Caddesi No.25/4, 34400 Sultanahmet, Eminönü, Istanbul T: 0212 458 5750 F: 0212 458 5753 E: info@walkturkey.com
Oba Hali	*Ali-Daimi Akkuş* Binbirdirek Mahallesi Piyerloti Caddesi Dostluk Yurda Sokak Yeşil Apartmentı No. 1, Istanbul T: 0212 518 1677 F: 0212 518 1687 E: obahali@superonline.com
Su-De	*Suat Çapaş* 1001 Direk Mey İletşim Han 7/2, Sultanahmet, Istanbul T/F: 0212 516 5488 M: 0533 238 8916 E: capas@escornet.com

81

1. *Caucasian Sille-Soumak*
   Late 19th century
2. *Caucasian Seichur rug*
   Late 19th century
3. *Anatolian Sarkoy kilim*
   Early 20th century
4. *Anatolian Milas rug*
   Second quarter 19th century
5. *Caucasian Kuba rug*
   Late 19th century
6. *Anatolian Dosemealti rug*
   Early 20th century
7. *Anatolian Sivas silk rug*
   Mid 19th century
8. *Anatolian Karakecel rug*
   Late 18th century

Established in 1952, ER-NE is an exclusive carpet company that prides itself in being one of the oldest in the history of this hand-crafted art form.

Today, the third generation of the Metin family tradition with experience, knowledge and professionalism allied with a global mind set.

Three Metin sons, Nihat, Murat and Cem run the domestic retail & wholesale business from the flagship location that consists of 5 prime front shops in a romantic lane at the entrance to the exclusive Arasta Bazaar in İstanbul, Turkey.

As specialists, ER-NE prides itself on its collection of rare and one-of-a-kind rugs whether Caucasian, Persian, Turkish or Turkomen. ER-NE's exclusive inventory includes an extensive collection of antique hand-woven carpets, kilims and soumaks.

ER-NE wishes you a pleasurable introduction into its realm of carpets providing a hint of the opulence and awe, and the wealth of colour and inspiration you will encounter in our gallery collection. Enjoy!

Regards,
ER-NE Family

ER-NE
CARPETS & KILIMS

**RUG STORE
SINCE 1952
WHOLESALE & RETAIL**

Arasta Bazaar No. 117
Sultanahmet
İstanbul
Turkey
Tel: +90 212 638 4302
+90 212 517 9413
Fax: +90 212 458 5204
Web: www.er-ne.com
Email: info@er-ne.com

Bekir Küden

GOLDEN HORN CARPETS

– Only fine East Anatolian wool from Nemrud Mountain and natural
colours from vegetable dyes are used in our New Line Mahals, Zieglers
and other designs – Bespoke orders of both size and design are welcome
High quality restoration of carpets and kilims

Binbirdirek Mahallesi, Dizdariye Çesmesi Sokak No. 3
Sultanahmet 34400, Istanbul, Turkey
Tel: +90 212 516 05 58/518 30 43 • Fax: +90 212 518 79 90
E-mail: goldenhorn1985@hotmail.com

karavan art

Antique and Decorative
Carpets and Kilims
Established 1978

Beshir Turkmen carpet, mid 19th century

Muzaffer Kaplan
Klodfarer Caddesi
Dr Sevkibey Sokak
Ortaklar Han 6/2
Sultanahmet, İstanbul, Turkey

Tel: +90 (212) 638 52 11
Tel / Fax: +90 (212) 638 52 12
M: +90 (332) 0542 424 16 89
E-mail: karavanart@superonline.com
Web: karavanart.com

KETENCİ HALICILIK

Peykhane Caddesi Üçler Sokak No. 46/1
SULTANAHMET - ISTANBUL - TURKEY
Tel: +90 (212) 518 36 42
Fax: +90 (212) 518 36 48
E-mail: ketencihalicilik@superonline.com

GALLERY GÖKHAN

HASAN SAZ

FINE ANTIQUE CARPETS, KILIMS AND TEXTILES

Küçük Aya Sofya Cad. No.17, Sultanahmet, İstanbul
Tel: +90 212 458 7466   Fax: +90 212 458 7467   Mobile: +90 532 230 9363
E-mail: info@gallerygoekhan.com   www.gallerygoekhan.com

ARASTA CARPET

Turkish carpets and kilims

Uzbek Brocaded Coat
Late 19th century
130 x 105cm

Head Office
Mimar Mehmet Ağa Caddesi 36/1
34400, Sultanahmet, İstanbul
T: +90 212 517 89 43
F: +90 212 518 57 44

Branch Office
Arasta Bazaar 79
34400, Sultanahmet, İstanbul
T: +90 212 516 05 17
E: arasta79@ttnet.net.tr
W: www.arastacarpet.com

ALTUNTAŞ

OLD ANATOLIAN
DECORATIVE KILIMS

MAIN SHOWROOM
Klodfarer Cad. Fırat Apt. No. 16/2
Sultanahmet
İSTANBUL, TURKEY
Tel: +90 212 516 20 11
Fax: +90 212 518 83 92

SHOWROOM
Klodfarer Cad. Kültür Apt. No. 27/5
Sultanahmet
İSTANBUL, TURKEY
Tel: +90 212 517 09 58
Fax: +90 212 638 69 39

Email: altuntaskilim@ihlas.net.tr
www.altuntaskilim.com

BEREKET

Peykhane Caddesi Üçler Sokak No 8
Sultanahmet, Istanbul 34400, Turkey
Tel: (0212) 517 46 77 • Fax: (0212) 638 41 45
e-mail: berekethali@superonline.com

SEMERKAND
Osman & Ulaş

Yağlıkçılar Cad. Astarcı Han No: 25
Kapalıçarşı, İstanbul
Tel: +90 212 526 22 69
Mobile: +90 532 251 8277 / +90 535 289 6443

Welcome!
We wish to be your guide to the
enchanting world of carpets & ceramics...
Every carpet is a collection of messages,
beliefs and images. We wish you a joyful
introduction to this world of carpets by
providing a hint of the beauty and richness
you will encounter in our Galeri 44 Mozaik

⊖ GALERİ 44 MOZAİK

metin
Carpet & Kilim
Bulent Metin

**ANATOLIAN CARPETS AND
KILIMS WITH SPECIAL PRICES**

Binbirdirek Mah. Klodfarer Cad.
Coskun Ap. No: 27/3
Çemberlitaş İSTANBUL
Tel: 00 90 212 517 00 17
Fax: 00 90 212 517 00 16
E-mail: metinhalikilim@hotmail.com

URARTU
Carpets & Kilims

İSTANBUL SHOWROOM
UTANGAÇ SK. NO: 10 - 12
SULTANAHMET 34400 İSTANBUL / TURKEY
TEL: +90 (212) 638 07 95 - 638 07 96
FAX: +90 (212) 638 07 41
E-mail: info@urartu.com.tr

VAN HALI KÖYÜ
(CARPET AND KILIM WEAVING VILLAGE)
VAN EDREMİT YOLU 9 KM. 65200 VAN / TURKEY
TEL: +90 (432) 217 97 65 (3 LINES)
FAX: +90 (432) 217 97 69
E-mail: urartuvan@urartu.com.tr

www.urartu.com.tr

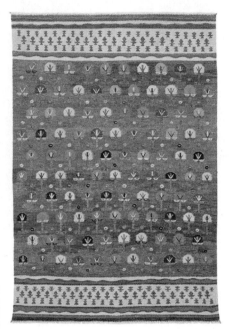

We also have wooden
architectural handicrafts

KAKTÜS ART

KAKTÜS ART
ANTIQUE RUGS AND TEXILE
HAND PICKED FROM CENTRAL ASIA AND ANATOLIA
FOR THE DISCRIMINATING CONNOISSEUR
By Appointment Only

Close to the Arasta Bazaar

İshakpaşa Mah. Kaleci Sokak. No 7/1
34400 Eminönü – İstanbul
Tel: +90 212 638 4480
Fax: +90 212 638 3964
Mobile: +90 532 602 5378
E-mail: kaktusart@superonline.com

ARASTA HALICILIK

Contact: Yakup Kaya Arasta Halicilik, Turkish carpets and kilims
Head office: Mimar Mehmet Ağa Caddesi 36/1, Sultanahmet 34400, Istanbul T: +90 212 517 8943 F: +90 212 518 5744
Branch office: Arasta Bazaar No. 79, Sultanahmet 34400, Istanbul T: +90 212 516 0517
E: arasta79@ttnet.net.tr W: www.arastacarpet.com

Arasta Carpet was established in 1985 selling carpets and kilims from almost every region of Turkey. At the beginning they operated from a small and pretty carpet shop in the Arasta Bazaar located near the Blue Mosque in Sultanahmet, Istanbul. Their mission is to supply the best quality handmade carpets and kilims to their customers at competitive prices combined with perfect service.

COCOON

Contact: Seref Özen Antique Oriental Carpets and Textiles (Central Asian textiles and Corbounan tribal rugs)
Arasta Bazaar No. 93, Sultanahmet 34400, Istanbul T: +90 212 518 0338 F: +90 212 518 0694
E: cocoon@superonline.com W: www.cocoontr.com

Located in the historic Arasta Bazaar in the shadow of the Blue Mosque, Cocoon specialises in rugs, flatweaves and textiles from Central Asia as well as Persia and Anatolia. The names of Seref Özen, who is considered to be one of the foremost authorities on Central Asian textiles in the world, and of Cocoon, have become synonymous with quality service among collectors around the world.

ER-NE RUG STORE

Contact: Nihat, Murat and Cem Metin ER-NE Rug Store, Antique handwoven carpets, kilims and soumaks
Arasta Bazaar No. 117, Sultanahmet 34400, Istanbul T: +90 212 638 4302 F: +90 212 518 0694
E: info@er-ne.com W: www.er-ne.com

Established in 1952, ER-NE is an exclusive carpet company which prides itself in being one of the oldest in the history of this hand-crafted art form. Today, it is the third generation which carries on the Metin family tradition through experience, knowledge and professionalism with a global mind set. As specialists, ER-NE prides itself for its collection of rare and one-of-a-kind rugs whether Caucasian, Persian, Turkish or Turkomen, ER-NE's exclusive inventory includes an extensive collection of antique handwoven carpets, kilims and soumaks.

GALERI CENGIZ

Contact: Cengiz Kara & Cengiz Kormaz Galeri Cengiz Antique Oriental Carpets and Textiles, Mimarmehmet Ağa Cad. 21,
Sultanahmet 34400, Istanbul T: +90 212 516 4534 F: +90 212 518 0694 W: www.galeri-cengiz.com

Galeri Cengiz Rug Co. has the largest and most comprehensive collection of antique collectable oriental rugs in Istanbul. You will discover Anatolian, Caucasian, Turkmen rugs and flatweaves. In addition you will find handmade new carpets including oversize wool and fine silk pieces. Recycled old yarn is utilised in restoration work.

MEHMET CETINKAYA GALLERY

Contact: Mehmet Çetinkaya Küçük Ayasofya Caddesi, Tavukhane Sokak no. 7, Sultanahmet 34400, Istanbul
Branch: Arista Bazaar 151, Sultanahmet 34400, Istanbul T: +90 212 517 6808/458 6186 F: +90 212 638 1553
E: info@cetinkayagallery.com or mcetinkaya2002@yahoo.com W: www.cetinkayagallery.com

Mehmet Çetinkaya Gallery has been the source of the most important textiles, carpets and kilims to emerge from central Asia, Anatolia and the Caucasus. He is the principal developer of the market for rare embroidered Kaitag textiles that have come to Istanbul from Daghestan. Mehmet's Central Asian textile stock includes beautiful ikat chapans, ikat panels, lakai embroideries, suzanis and cross-stitch embroideries.

GOKKUSAGI ~ RAINBOW COLLECTION

Contact: Bedri Yokus Klodfarer Caddesi, Kültür Apt. 27/6, Sultanahmet 34400, Istanbul
T: +90 212 517 3633 F: +90 212 517 3604 E: rainbowkilim@turk.net W: www.rainbowkilim.com

We have a large collection of fine, new, naturally dyed, hand spun wool kilims and carpets in both modern and traditional designs which are immediately available. We can produce our range of kilims and carpets in any size.

ENVIRONS OF
THE GRAND BAZAAR

Start where Klodfarer Caddesi crossed Divanyolu on the previous walk through Sultanahmet, but instead of crossing over, turn left and walk up the ancient Meşe now known as Yeniceriler Caddesi. Pass by the square known as Çemberlitaş, distinguished by the battered column (known as the 'burnt column') held together by iron bands. It is in fact the fire-damaged remains of the Column of Constantine, erected by the Emperor in 330 AD to commemorate the refounding of the city – the only monument from the period still standing. Continue up Yeniceriler Caddesi passing on the right the mosque of Gazi Atik Ali Paşa, one of the oldest in the city having been built only 43 years after the conquest.

A little further on, past the attractive kiosk on the corner, you will see an arched doorway with a sign above it that proclaims Çorlulu Ali Paşa Medresesi and here you should enter. The scene before you is delightful, with the right-hand side of the vine-covered courtyard given over to a *çayhane* full of *narghile*-smoking and *çay*-drinking patrons, while on the left a row of small rug shops display their wares in a riot of colour. Comfortable carpet covered divans in front of the shops provide an excellent place to repose while smoking a pipe and inspecting the wares on offer. Pierre Loti, the high priest of high camp Orientalism, describes the scene in his novel *Les*

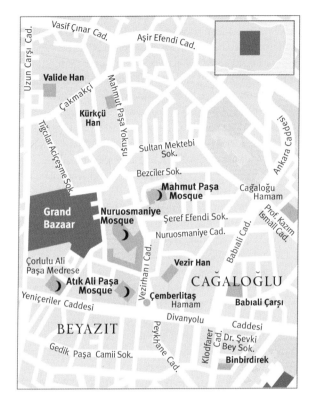

second of the courtyards that make up the Çorlulu Ali Paşa complex. In the first courtyard life revolves around the busy *çayhane* where waiters scurry around with large silver trays full of tulip glasses of scalding tea, while pipe attendants mill around with tins of burning coals to refresh the pipes. But in this courtyard the atmosphere is very different. There is a similar row of small shops on the left but here in place of the *çayhane* is an attractive canopied sa*dirvan* at which the faithful perform their ablutions before attending the mosque built by Ali Paşa, Grand Vizier to Ahmet II, which stands at the end of the garden. A number of the dealers here are hajjis (those

1. The Sardivan in Çorlulu Ali Paşa, where the faithful perform their ablutions
2. A corner of the Ali Paşa courtyard

Désenchantées (1906, trans. Marina Berry) "When he arrived at the square, all the little cafes had lit their modest lamps... and everywhere, on benches, on stools, turbaned dreamers smoked, talking little and in low voices, hundreds of hookahs made a curious whispering sound – water bubbling in the flask as the smoker takes a long deep breath".

Five of the small shops here belong to Şaban Özçelik, who calls his business ANADOLU DOKUMA EVI. Şaban has been in Ali Paşa for 17 years and has a comprehensive range of old and new pieces aimed mainly at the tourist market. The shop at the end is OZ TRUVA, owned by Faruk Gülpekmez who has the distinction of being the oldest business in Ali Paşa. His stock is similar to Şaban's with some new pieces and some decorative kilims.

Upon leaving the courtyard turn right on Yeniceriler Caddesi and after a few steps pass through another archway into the

3. *Sultanahmet Halıcılık, owned by the Kökoğlu brothers* 4. *Adem Dölek of Derya repairing a silk rug* 5. *Abdullah Gündoğdu in the Çorlulu Ali Paşa passage.*

GÜNDÖGDU TICARET, home to one of the Istanbul carpet trade's most prized institutions. Abdullah Gündoğdu (5), who was born in Istanbul and knows every corner of the old city, is one of its best known and liked dealers; a Sufi in spirit, a storyteller in the Hoca Nasruddin tradition, and a rug dealer by profession – a splendid combination. If he is not in his shop he might be pruning the roses next to the *sardivan* and if not then his able repairman Vedat will make you a *çay* while you wait. It will not be long before the amiable fellow arrives, sits down, drinks a glass of tea, and after seeming to lose himself in abstraction will suddenly say "Did I ever tell you about the man who built this mosque, the Grand Vizier Ali Paşa of Çorlulu, and how Sultan Ahmet II had him beheaded in Mytilene? They sent his head back to Stamboul preserved in a bucket of honey and then..."

Next door is SULTANAHMET HALICILIK owned by the Kökoğlu brothers (3), long-time residents of Ali Paşa. They have a varied selection of older and antique pieces and also run a fairly large repair operation. Further along is MEHMET DÖLEK, a respected figure who has been in the carpet trade for over fifty years, the first thirty of which were spent in the Grand Bazaar. Originally a master repairman he keeps a varied stock of old carpets and kilims. At no.13 you will find Şerif Turan, a repairer for twenty years who keeps a stock of mainly old carpets in his shop TURAN HALICILIK. The last shop in Ali Paşa, facing the entrance to the mosque, is ŞENKAYA HALI & KILIM. Adil Şenkaya is another migrant from the Grand Bazaar where he was employed by a well-known dealer before setting up here on his own a couple of years ago. He keeps a stock of old pieces which include rugs, kilims and bags.

who have made the pilgrimage to Mecca) and a slow gentle atmosphere pervades the place, broken by the flapping wings of doves and the soft shuffle of slippers after the prayer has been called.

Several of the businesses here are repair shops and of these DERYA, the first on the right as you enter, is particularly interesting. Owned by Adem Dölek, a repairer for 35 years who specialises in silk carpets, it is one of only two or three left in Istanbul who are able to carry out this highly skilled work (4).

On the left-hand side at no.5 is

Our last stop in the environs of the Grand Bazaar is in Nurosmaniye Caddesi which can be reached by turning left when we leave Ali Paşa and walking back down Yeniceriler Caddesi as far as the burnt column. Turn left here down Vezirhanı Caddesi until you see a pedestrianised street on the right and a large mosque over to your left. The mosque, which stands at one of the main entrances to the bazaar, is built in the Ottoman baroque style and named after the Sultan Osman III, Nur-u-Osman or the 'Light

of Osman'. Turning right from Vezirhanı Caddesi into Nurosmaniye Caddesi, the contrast with the timeless sleepy charm of Ali Paşa could not be more marked. The wide avenue is lined on both sides with large glitzy glass-fronted carpet emporia retailing new and decorative carpets to Japanese tourists. Brilliantined young men in sharp suits are ever vigilant in case one's gaze should inadvertently wander in the direction of the boutique that employs them. This is not fertile ground for those hunting interesting old rugs at sensible prices, but it is mildly entertaining to see this aspect of the floor-coverings trade and I suspect this is where the emperors and the sultans would have bought their carpets, as indeed does Elton John.

There is one place here that does sell antique rugs and it is to be found a short distance along on the right-hand side on the second floor at no.85. KAZAK KILIMS is owned by long time dealer Atilla Topraktepe. Although his business is mainly trade and wholesale, he is always happy to see collectors and serious private customers. He has a large stock of antique carpets of all denominations with usually a good range of Caucasian pieces plus a good selection of large old decorative carpets.

You will find no more antique rugs in Nurosmaniye, but if your interest is in new carpets then cross the to HALI SARAYI. This is one of the older businesses in the street and is run by the three Sefer brothers, fourth generation dealers. They produce carpets in classical designs, some of which have natural dyes and handspun wool, and they have also started using the insect-dye cochineal that has not been used in Turkey for a long time.

Finally, if ultra-fine new silk rugs are your idea of fun. then pay a visit to the shop of long time specialist AVAK SIRINOĞLU at no.63. $\mathbb{C}$

Derya Halı	*Adem Dölek* Derya Halı ve Kilim, Tamiratı Alım Satımı, Çorlulu Ali Paşa Medresesi 36/17, Yeniçerililer Caddesi, Beyazıt, Istanbul T: 0212 512 4929 M: 0535 742 6122
Gündoğdu	*Abdullah Gündoğdu* Çorlulu Ali Paşa Medresesi, Çarşikapı Yeniçeriler Caddesi 36-5, Istanbul T: 0212 513 1510 F: 0212 526 0052 E: a_gundogdu@hotmail.com
Kazak	*Atilla Topraktepe* Kazak Kilims & Carpets, Nuruosmaniye Caddesi Kapalıçarşı, Cağaloğlu, Beyazıt, Istanbul T: 0212 526 1570 F: 0212 512 2533 E: kazakhalikilim@turk.net
Öz Truva	*Faruk Gülpekmez* Öz Truva, Yeniçeriler Caddesi 36/27, Çarşikapı Çorlulu Ali Paşa Medresesi, Istanbul T: 0212 513 4061 F: 0212 513 4061 M: 0532 273 4039
Saray Halı	*Sina Gilani* Kisikli Caddesi 41 Altunizade 81180, Üskudar, Istanbul T: 0216 474 0340 F: 0216 474 0490 E: saray@saraycarpet.com
Sultanahmet	*Kökoğlu brothers* Sultanahmet Carpet & Kilim, Çorlulu Ali Paşa Medresesi 36/6-7, Yeniçeriler Caddesi, Carşıkapı, Beyazıt, Istanbul T: 0212 512 2363 F: 0212 526 0038 M: 0532 261 8189 E. sultanahmethali@ixir.com
Turan Halıcılık	*Şerif Turan* Yeniçeriler Caddesi, Çorlulu Ali Paşa Medresesi 36/13, Beyazit, Istanbul T: 0212 528 2425 F: 0212 585 7333 M: 0536 545 9288
Şenkaya	*Adil Şenkaya* Şenkaya Halı & Kilim, Yeni Çeriler Caddesi Çorlulu Ali Paşa Medresesi 36/14, Beyazıt, Istanbul T: 0212 528 2363
Şirinoğlu	*Avak Şirinoğlu* 63.2 Nuruosmaniye Caddesi, Cağaloğlu, Istanbul T: 0212 519 1635

BURAK AYDOĞAN

ANTIQUE
RUGS & TEXTILES

HIGH QUALITY
HANDWOVEN
ECO
PRODUCTS

GÜNDOĞDU TİCARET

Abdullah Gündoğdu

HALI Magazine Istanbul Agent

Çorlulu Ali Paşa Medresesi
Çarşikapi, Yeniçeriler Cad. 36/5 Beyazit - Istanbul
Tel : 212 513 1510   Fax: 212 526 0052   Email: a_gundogdu@hotmail.com

ASLAN ▼ HALICILIK
CARPET AND KILIM EXPORT

Established 1979

Talish Rug, Caucasus. 2.90 x 1.37m

Binbirdirek Mahallesi Binbirdirek Meydanı Sokak No. 7, Iletisim Han, Sultanahmet, Istanbul, Turkey
Tel: +90 (212) 517 96 92-93 • Fax: +90 (212) 517 96 99 • Email: aslanhali@superonline.com

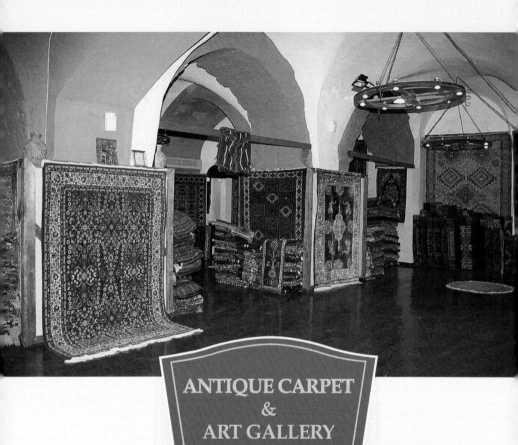

ANTIQUE CARPET & ART GALLERY

Merkez
Molla Fenari Mah
Gazi Sinanpaşa Sokak no. 1
Cağaloğlu, Eminönü, İstanbul
Tel: +90 212 519 55 10/11
Fax: +90 212 528 64 33
E-mail: antiquecarpet@ttnet.net.tr

The Grand Bazaar

Istanbul's Grand Bazaar or *Kapalıcarşı* (covered bazaar) is probably the most famous bazaar in the world. It is certainly one of the largest and is really a small town complete with mosques, fountains, banks, post offices, restaurants, tea houses, money changers and even a bureau for lost tourists, although I wonder how you are supposed to find it if you are lost. And it is certainly possible to get lost among its 64 streets, 4,000 shops and 17 *hans*, not to mention the hundreds of thousands of people who visit it every day. Mehmet the Conqueror started the original building shortly after gaining control of the city in 1453, but it has been rebuilt and enlarged many times over the centuries to reach the size and complexity we see today.

The original bazaar had four gates. Today there are 18 and of these I recommend entering at the Nurosmaniye gate, near the mosque of the same name that we encountered on an earlier walk. The wide main thoroughfare through the bazaar, Kalpakcılar Başi Caddesi, stretches away in a solid mass of humanity, lined on either side by glittering gold and jewellery shops (3).

Enter this river of people and after about two hundred metres look on the left-hand side for a sign over an arched doorway that says Esnaflari Derneği and enter the Sorguçlu Han, one of the oldest in the bazaar. Occupying several of the *han's* original domed rooms is MOTIF GALLERY owned by Ali Türkkan. Ali has a series of smart galleries where he keeps a large stock of old and new decorative rugs and a good selection of large room size carpets. This shop in its small *han* is well away from the main area of carpet activity and to make our way there it is necessary to plunge back into the teeming throng of Kalpakcılar Başi Caddesi.

Now is a good time to get lost. Precise directions at this point would not only be painfully pedantic but would deprive the first time visitor of the great pleasure of becoming hopelessly lost in the Grand Bazaar and wandering aimlessly without a sense of time or place. No sense of time because it is always midday beneath the bright lights, and no sense of place because the extremely irregular and illogical layout offers few comforting landmarks. If you feel a sense of rising panic or

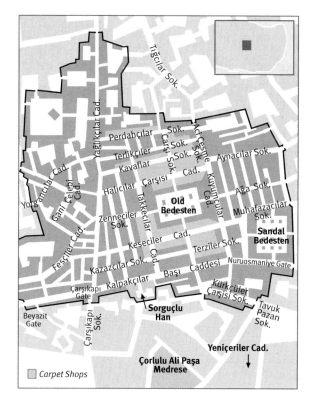

the very well-known dealer Erol Kazancı (6). Erol started work in the bazaar in his uncle's rug shop nearly forty years ago and has built up a successful international business. His clientele includes expats and diplomats as well as dealers and collectors. His large stock includes everything from inexpensive new rugs to highly valuable collectors' pieces and there are few languages in which he will be unable to sell you a rug. He travels widely in the hunt for rugs and over the years many good Caucasian and Anatolian pieces have passed through his hands.

A little further along on the other side is ODABAŞI HALICILIK owned by Ismet Odabaşi, another long time dealer. Ismet has been

1. The shoeshine man points the way to the Grand Bazaar

the hundreds of cups of çay begin to make their presence felt, then remember that all ascending streets lead to the outside.

After spending a pleasant hour or day wandering the bazaar then make for Halıcılar Caddesi, the 'street of the carpet dealers', near the Old Bedestan which is the centre of the bazaar and the original market built by Mehmet the Conqueror. Three shops here at nos.89, 90 and 93 bear the name ADNAN & HASAN and belong to long-time and well-respected dealer Hasan Semerci. He has a good-sized stock of new and semi-antique decorative carpets and also has his own production of Uşak carpets. His straightforward approach, with a minimum of bargaining, has made him popular with the foreign community and he can number UN Secretary-General Kofi Annan among his customers.

Further along on the same side is GALLERY ŞIRVAN owned by

in the bazaar for nearly thirty years and has a stock of mainly semi-old carpets and kilims.

Running at right angles to Halıcılar Caddesi is Takkeciler Caddesi – 'the street of the hat makers' – home to the oldest carpet business in the bazaar, ŞENGOR, which now has three shops, nos. 65, 83 and 98. Originally founded in 1913, today it is in the capable hands of Ahmet Şengör, the fourth generation of the family to run the business. The stock is mainly new Anatolian carpets but it is possible to find the odd antique piece among the stacks. Further along on the same side is another

2. Sea shells decorating an Anatolian animal trapping 3. Inside the Grand Bazaar 4. Hasan Deregözü in his shop inside the bazaar 5. Anatolian kilims for sale 6. Erol Kazanci of Galeri Şirvan

very long established business, AHMET HAZIM. Originally from Kayseri, this is another fourth generation carpet family who have been in this shop since 1940. It is owned today by Ahmet Hazım Evrengil, the business has a good-sized stock of mainly old pieces with a wide selection of kilims. They also have a shop in the Ritz-Carlton Hotel with a selection of large decorative carpets.

Just around the corner in Zennecilar Sokak is KURTOĞLU owned by Mehmet Kurtoğlu. Mehmet has been a dealer in old rugs for many years but has recently taken his business in a new direction. He has begun two new productions based on his own original designs: one of rugs and kilims using natural dyes, the other of striking patchwork kilims.

Retrace your steps back up Takkeciler passing Ahmet Hazım and Şengor on your left and enter the street on the right called Kavaflar Sokak, just past Halıcılar Caddesi. On the right-hand side is another long established shop called MEHMET ERDOĞAN that has a large selection of old rugs and good stock of large decorative carpets in their depot. Directly opposite is SAIT BAYHAN, another long time bazaari who runs the business with his son Mehmet. For over forty years Sait has traded in antique carpets and kilims, but like so many other dealers he is also involved in the production of new carpets. His new rugs, made with natural dyes and handspun wool, can also be seen in the Halı Hotel which is run by his brother Lütfü.

Continue down Kavaflar Sokak and take the first left into Sahaflar Bedestan Kapı Sokak and on the right-hand side you will see HAND-MADE TEXTILE ARTS, a small shop owned by Celal Acikgöz. Celal has had a business in the bazaar for thirty years and specialises in textiles, embroideries, coats and hats from Central Asia along with a few Turkmen rugs and bags. Recently he has started producing a range of clothing of his own design, incorporating fragments of antique textiles. Almost opposite

is another well-established business called THE BROTHERS, run by Zeki Opçin and Murat Ayhan. For many years they have specialised in good antique decorative and collectable kilims, but they often have good Caucasian rugs in their stock as well.

The next small street that crosses Sahaflar Bedestan Kapı Sokak is

7. Textile specialist Mühlis Günbatti
8. Wooden boxes from Central Asia
9. Winter in the Cebeci Han 10. A mini-
Bukharan bazaar 11. Time for a shave.

Terlikciler Sokak and if you turn left a few shops along at no.50 is DEREGÖZÜ owned by two brothers from Malatya, Hasan (4) and Hamza Deregözü. They have a large stock of old and semi-old rugs, kilims, textiles, bags and large decorative carpets. Most of their stock is to be found in their depot, which is in the alley to the side of the Babiali building, and the ever-cheerful brothers will be more than happy to take you there.

Turn right when you leave Deregözü, cross Sahaflar Sokak and you will find a clutch of tiny shops owned by Afghans and Uzbeks who are selling all manner of objects from Central Asia. Here it is possible to find jewellery, textiles, suzani embroideries, knives, costume, hats and more. Some of the stuff is new, some old, and some new but pretending to be old, but all in all this is a colourful and interesting mini Bukharan bazaar (10). The çay on offer in these little shops is usually Afghan-style green tea, which can be a welcome respite from the usual stewed black Turkish çay.

Continue down Sahaflar to the end and then turn left up Perdahcılar Caddesi, looking out for the shop of MÜHLIS GÜNBATTI on the right-hand side (7). Mühlis has been in the bazaar for almost fifty years, since he started work as a cleaner at the age of eight. Today he has one of the finest collections of antique textiles in the bazaar, encompassing everything from Ottoman embroideries to Central Asian suzanis.

Walking back down Perdahcılar there is an interesting little alley on the left opposite Sahaflar called Tacirler Sokak. The tiny shops here are known as dolaps, a Greek/Turkish word that means cupboard. These are not strictly retail or tourist shops but spaces used by small trade dealers working in an ambience far removed from that of the large flashy galleries. Do not expect to bump into Elton John along here.

Most of these small shops are worth looking into and a number of their owners have larger depots elsewhere. The first shop on the right, AKIS HALI, is owned by Himmet Yumuşak and his brother Fezvim, who have a small but quickly changing stock of mainly old rugs. Further along on the same side is AKIF HALI. Owner Mehmet Yollu has a stock of old pieces which usually includes some antique Caucasian rugs. He also has another shop in the bazaar which is to be found in the attractive old İç Cebeci Han. On the other side of the alley is another cheerful soul and long-time dealer, Murat

Sümer, who owns SÜMER NOMADIC RUGS. Murat is mainly a wholesale dealer specialising in old and new decorative carpets. Opposite him is Lütfü Timurtaş, another Malatya denizen, who owns TIMURTAŞ and specialises in old and new kilims, mainly from Yugoslavia.

Return to Perdahcılar, turn left, and continue to the end where you will find Zincirli Han. This beautiful former caravanserai is nearly five hundred years old and is the home of the well-known dealer ŞIŞKO OSMAN. This business is an institution after more than thirty years in the bazaar and Şişko himself is a fourth generation dealer. The business is also

11

10

unusual in that it specialises solely in Anatolian weavings, both old and new, of which they have an enormous stock. Şişko is a grand old gentleman who is preparing his nephew Bilgin Aksoy to take over the business for the fifth generation of the family – surely something of a record.

Another interesting old *han* is to be found by returning up Perdahcılar until it meets Yaglikcilar Caddesi and there turning right. A short distance along Yaglikcilar – a colourful street of textile shops – look on the left-hand side for the entrance to the Cebeci Han (9). This old and picturesque *han* is home to a number of small shops; most specialise in Central Asian textiles but there are also carpets to be found here. On the right-hand side, under the arch as you enter, is ISMAIL DEREGÖZÜ who has an interesting stock of textiles. Next door is TURISTIK ESYA whose proprietor Abdullah also has a good selection of Central Asian ikats, suzanis and embroideries.

On the right-hand corner as you enter the *han* is AKIF HALI owned by Mehmet Yollu (seen earlier in his *dolap* in Tacirler Sokak). Here in a larger space with lots of natural light we can see more of his stock of mainly antique Caucasian rugs. The *han* is given over to small shops dealing mainly in old metalwork and textiles and has an upper level that should also be explored.

If you pass through the gateway at the end of Tacirler Sokak you enter a world far removed from the glitzy galleries and cappuccino cafes that are beginning to proliferate inside the bazaar. Out here are narrow noisy alleys and decrepit old *hans* full of coppersmiths and cobblers in tiny workshops where the air is thick with charcoal smoke and *şiş kebab*. To sit and drink tea in a *çayhane* full of porters and workmen, to a backdrop of shouts and cries from the teeming streets, is for a moment to recapture a flavour of the old Ottoman capital and the greatest of oriental bazaars. ◖

Adnan & Hasan	*Hasan Semerci* Adnan & Hasan Anatolian Carpets & Kilims, Kapalıçarşı Halicilar Caddesi 89-90-92, Beyazit, Istanbul T: 0212 527 9887 F: 0212 513 9359 E: info@adnanandhasan.com
Akıf Halı	*Mehmet Kuruşan* Yağlıkçılar Caddesi, İç Cebeci Hanesi No. 4, Kapalıçarşı, Beyazit, Istanbul T: 0212 519 3450 F: 0212 527 9765 M: 0532 421 2758 E: akifhali@superonline.com
Akis Halı	*Himmet Yumuşak* ve kardeşi, Tacirler Sokak No.27, Kapalıçarşı, Istanbul T: 0212 519 4274 M: 0533 631 1637
Aksoy Halıcılık	*Hasan Aksoy* Tacirler Sokak No: 20, Kapalıarşı, Istanbul T: 0212 511 3389
Deregözü	*Hasan & Hamza* Deregözü Carpets Kilims & Textiles, Çatalçeşme Sk. No: 4/7 Cağaloğlu, Istanbul T/F: 0212 513 1372 E: deregozo@yahoo.com
İsmail Deregözü	*İsmail Deregözü* Yağlıkçılar Caddesi Cebeci Hanesi Girişi No.1, Kapalıçarşı, Istanbul T: 0212 511 8336
Dokuma Evi	*Şaban Özçelik* Dokuma Evi Oriental Carpets, Çorlulu Ali Paşa, Ali Paşa Medresesi No. 36/5, Çarşıkapı, Istanbul T: 0212 519 2341 F: 0212 520 9896
Galeri Sirvan	*Erol Kazanci* Halıcılar Caddesi 50/52/54 Kapalıçarşı, Istanbul T: 0212 522 4986 F: 0212 522 4987 M: 0532 321 0652 E: erolkazanci@superonline.com
Hazım	*Ahmet Hazım* Grand Bazaar, Tekkeciler Sk. No.61-63, Eminönü, Beyazıt, Istanbul T: 0212 527 9886 F: 0212 520 1589 E: ahmethazim@turk.net
Hakıs Halı	Tacirler Sokak No. 27, Kapılıçarşı, Istanbul T: 0212 519 4274 M: 0533 631 1637
Halicilik İnsaat Turizm	*Mehmet Bayhan* Kavaflar Sk. No.33-35, Kapalıçarşı Eminönü, Istanbul T: 0212 526 6295
Hand Made Textile Arts	*H. Celal Açıkgöz* Sahaflar, Bedestan Kapı Sokak No:15, Kapalıçarşı, Istanbul T: 0212 512 2941 F: 0212 425 0525 M: 0532 425 0525
Kurtoğlu	*Mehmet Kurtoğlu* Halı ve Kilim Kapiliçarşi Zenneciler Sokak 24/26, Istanbul T: 0212 519 4003 F: 0212 526 6885 M: 0536 269 29 39 E: kurtoglurugs@yahoo.com
Mehmet Erdoğan	*Mehmet Erdoğan* Kavaflar Sok. No.34, Kapalıçarşı, Istanbul T: 0212 527 9818 F: 0212 255 7674
Motif Gallery	*Ali Türkkan* Grand Bazaar, Kalpakçılar Caddesi 133, Istanbul T: 0212 519 4007 F: 0212 519 4006 E: motifhali@hotmail.com
Motif Halı	*Motif Halı Tekstil* Hüsrevgerede Caddesi 102/A, Teşvikiye, Istanbul T: 0212 327 8095 F: 0212 327 8096 E: motifhali@hotmail.com
Mühlis Günbattı	*Mühlis Günbattı* Perdahçılar Caddesi No: 48, Kapalıçarsı, Istanbul T: 0212 511 6562 F: 0212 527 0987
Odabası	*İsmet Odabaşı* Halıcılar Caddesi No. 41, Kapalıçarşı, Istanbul T: 0212 519 0432 F: 0212 519 0432 M: 0532 312 5391
Old Bazaar	*Sami Müdüoğlu* Old Bazaar Carpets Kilims & Furniture, Can a Sokak 21/B, Saman Pazarı T: 0312 311 4432
Murat Demirkıyık	*Murat Demirkıyık* Pala Halıcılık, Perdahçılar Caddesi, Tacirler Sok. No. 1, Kapalıçarşı, Istanbul T: 0535 723 4919

Sait Bayhan	*Sait Bayhan* Kavaflar Sokak No. 33/35, Kapalıçarşı, Istanbul T: 0212 526 6295 F: 0212 516 2172
Sengör	*Ahmet Şengör* Takkecilar sok. No. 65/83/98, Kapalıçarşı, Istanbul T: 0212 527 2192 F: 0212 522 4115
Şişko Osman	*Şişko Osman* Kapalıçarşı Zincirli Han 15, Istanbul T: 0212 528 3548 F: 0212 526 7287 E: siskoosman@siskoosman.com
Sumer Nomadic Rugs	*Murat Sümer* Kapalıçarşı Tacirler Sokak No. 16, Istanbul T: 0212 526 6085
The Brothers	*Zeki Opçin* The Brothers Textile Arts, Sahaflar Bedestan Kapısı No.12, Kapalıçarşı, Istanbul T: 0212 520 7687 F: 0212 512 6730 E: bma56@superonline.com
Timurtaş Carpets	*Lütfü Timurtaş* Timurtaş Carpets & Kilims Wholesale, Tacirler Sokak No. 11/9, Kapalıçarşı, Istanbul T: 0212 519 3547 F: 0532 262 3564
Turistik Eşya	*Abdullah Tayfunlar* Kapılıçarşı Yağlıkçılar Caddesi, Cebeci Han No. 2, Beyazit, Istanbul T: 0212 528 3412 M: 0532 651 9903 E: teyfun@ttnet.tr

West Anatolian village rug, early 19th century. In its distinctive palette
and use of characteristic minor motifs, this unusual rug, woven in two
narrow pieces and joined, may perhaps be attributed to the village of
Kelez, near Ödemiş (see, e.g. W. Brüggemann & H. Böhmer, Rugs of
the Peasants and Nomads of Anatolia, Munich 1983, pl.80).

MUHLIS GÜNBATTI

Since 1955

OLD OTTOMAN & CENTRAL ASIAN TEXTILES
FINE ANATOLIAN CARPETS AND KILIMS

Marie Claire archives

Perdahçılar Caddesi No. 48 Kapalıçarsı, Istanbul, Turkey
Tel: +90 (212) 511 65 62 Fax: +90 (212) 527 09 87
E-mail: muhlis@muhlisgunbatti.net Web: www.muhlisgunbatti.net

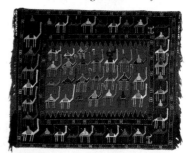

ESKI

Contact: Irfan Karatas   Eski Objets d'Art & Antiques, Cevahir Bebesteni 152-153 (9-10) Kapalıçarşi, Beyazıt, Istanbul
T/F: +90 212 512 5238   M: +90 535 857 5632   E: eskiciirfan@superonline.com   W: www.eskistan.com

For over thirty years we have had the pleasure of welcoming visitors from around the world to our shops in the Grand Bazaar. We have a wide range of antique and semi-antique *objets d'art* from across the Middle East. We look forward to meeting you and, hopefully, showing you something irresistible during your next visit to Istanbul.

GALLERY SHIRVAN

Contact: Erol Kazanci   Gallery Shirvan Antique Oriental Carpets and Textiles, Halicilar Street 50/52/54, Grand Bazaar, Beyazit, Istanbul, Turkey   T: +90 212 522 4986   F: +90 212 522 4987   E: erolkazancii@superonline.com

Gallery Shirvan in Istanbul's Kapalıcarsi (Grand Bazaar) has undoubtedly some of the finest antique Oriental carpets, textiles and kilims anywhere in Turkey. Proprietor Erol Kazanci is particularly knowledgeable in his field and has lectured on antique rugs at various international events and exhibited in many international fairs. Always willing to lend a helping hand in the tough decisions involved in carpet-buying, Erol has an uncanny knack for knowing exactly what it is that will please you and how he can assist you.

L'ORIENT HANDICRAFT

Contact: Murat Bilir   Kapalıçarşi Içbedesten 22/23 Istanbul 34126   T: +90 212 520 7046   F: +90 212 520 7046
E: murat-bilir@usa.net   W: www.muratbilir.com

Portable cultural objects from Imperial Russia. From antique *samovars* to copper water-pitchers, plates, trays, incense-burners and medicine bowls all worn by years of use. Recommended by The New York Times, Frommer's Guide, Delta's Sky magazine and Turkish Airlines' Sky Life magazine.

MOTIF GALLERY

Contact: Ali Türkkan   Grand Bazaar, Kalpakçılar Caddesi. 133, 34440 Istanbul   T: +90 212 519 4007   F: +90 212 519 4009
E: motifhali@hotmail.com   W: www.motifgallery.com

With fifteen years experience in trading textiles and carpets, we are one of the best sources of unusual sizes and we have a large selection of quality stock, including minimalist wool and linen tapestries. Worldwide home delivery, professional cleaning and restoration.

MUHLIS GÜNBATTI

Contact: Muhlis Günbatti   Perdahçılar Caddesi 48, Kapalıçarsı, Istanbul
T: +90 212 511 6562   F: +90 212 527 0987   E: muhlis@muhlisgunbatti.net   W: www.muhlisgunbatti.net

Since 1955, we have maintained an excellent and unique collection of new but mostly old carpets and kilims, antique textiles and embroideries. We have worked continuously to establish long standing relationships of trust, providing the best service with our merchandise in this, the world's largest bazaar.

THE BROTHERS TEXTILE ARTS

Contact: B. Murat Ayhan   Sahaflar Bedesten Kapısı Sokak 12, Kapalıçarşi, Istanbul
T: +90 212 520 7687   F: +90 212 512 6730   E: bma56@superonline.com

Established in 1976, we have an excellent selection of Anatolian, Caucasian and Turkmen carpets and kilims. We also sell tribal grain sacks, yastics, saddlebags and accessories.

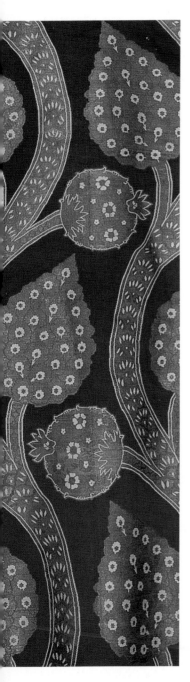

PERA AND BEYOND

The imperial city of Constantinople, later the Ottoman capital, did not extend beyond today's old city, which occupies the peninsula that stretches from the Topkapı Palace to the land walls and is bounded by the Golden Horn, the Bosphorus and the Sea of Marmara. Forbidden to settle in the city itself, foreign merchants, traders and diplomats founded settlements across the Golden Horn, on the slopes that rise up from the seashore to present-day Taksim.

The Genoese were rewarded for their help in dispelling the Latin usurpers of the fourth crusade with preferential trading agreements and permission to found their own semi-autonomous walled town known as Galata. Today it is recalled in the Galata Tower (1) and the name of the bridge that connects Galata to 'the City'. The Galatians repaid the Byzantines several hundred years later by declaring their neutrality during the Turkish siege and refusing to aid the defence of the city. To illustrate that it was nothing personal and just business, on the day of the fall of Constantinople the Sultan signed a *firman* (decree) re-confirming the trading rights of Galata. To the Greeks of Constantinople, Galata and the other towns and villages across the Golden Horn were simply known as *Pera* or 'beyond'.

1

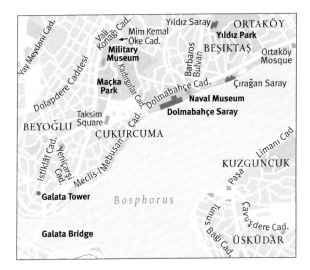

Today this part of Istanbul is the bustling business and diplomatic heart of the city and contains a number of smart and expensive residential areas. This is not rich territory for the hunter-gatherer on the trail of old carpets, but there are one or two places that might be visited if the delights of Gucci and Hermes begin to pall.

The most interesting area is Çukurcuma, a network of steeply inclined alleys that surround the mosque of that name below Taksim Square, bounded by Yeniçarşı and Defterdar and just south of the Galatasaray Lisesi. The area is rapidly becoming gentrified as large smart galleries selling expensive antique furniture replace the small, fascinating junk shops and second-hand dealers who have traditionally traded here. Despite the fact that many of the better antiques were probably bought in London and the small dealers are disappearing, it is still possible to find the odd interesting textile or embroidery lurking in the back of a shop and of course it is great fun looking. TOMBAK, just off Çukurcuma Caddesi, owned by Ahmet Kosedağ (5), is the oldest and most famous shop here and is piled to the ceiling with indispensable junk.

No.4 Faik Paşa is an 18th century house that has been completely renovated and here you will find A LA TURCA, owned by the well-known Erkal Aksoy (2). On three floors of the old house, in addition to a fascinating array of elegantly displayed

decorative antiques and pottery, Erkal has a large stock of carpets and kilims, all of them old or semi-old and aimed at the smart houses and apartments of the neighbouring districts. As well as the decorative kilims for which he is well known he now has a good stock of large old Uşak carpets.

A number of carpet dealers from the old city have opened galleries here, including BURAK AYDOĞAN who also owns a gallery in Sultanahmet. Here in a modern ambience he shows high quality contemporary decorative weavings alongside good antique carpets and textiles.

The well-to-do ladies of Ottoman days spent much time and effort producing beautiful textiles

1. View across the Golden Horn from Sultanahmet of Pera and the Galata Tower 2. Erkal Aksoy of A la Turca

and embroideries for domestic use and for inclusion in the bride's dowry. A good place to look for some of these text-iles and also for lace is at the shop of LEYLA SEYHANLI, who has traded for a number of years at no.10 Altı Patlar Sokak.

A couple of miles away past Maçka Park is the expensive residential district of Nişantaşı which, with its identikit designer boutiques and modern shopping malls, could be in any capital city anywhere in the world. But if you raise your eyes above shop level there are in fact some beautiful belle époque period houses with elegant balconies and interesting architectural details.

On Mim Kemal Öke Caddesi, at no.9, is FCI ŞENGOR, a branch of the family that has the Grand Bazaar's oldest carpet business. Here they deal in new decorative carpets for the domestic market. On the same street at no.5 is GÜNEŞ ÖZTARKÇI, one of Istanbul's very few women carpet dealers, who also deals in new decorative carpets and silk Herekes.

A young and active dealer in the Grand Bazaar, Ali Türk-kan has also recently opened a second MOTIF GALLERY here in Nişantaşı. In this location he sells his own production new kilims with contemporary designs, as well as new carpets that can be woven to customers' specific requirements.

Örtaköy has an attractive pedestrianised district on the shores of the Bosphorus, nestling almost underneath the first

3. Engin Demirkol of Hazal Kelim ve Halı 4. Worry beads for sale in the bazaar 5. Ahmet Kosedağ of Tombak, Çukurcuma's most interesting shop 6. Embroidered Uzbek carpet (detail) 7. The back streets in winter

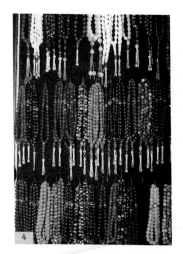

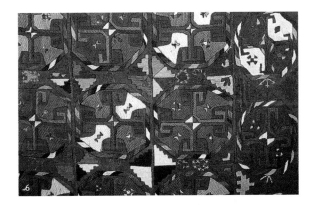

Bosphorus Bridge. Many of the old houses have been renovated and now function as fashionable cafes, restaurants and shops.

On the same street as the ornate baroque mosque, which is rather a good one if you like that sort of thing, is HAZAL KELIM VE HALI. This shop is owned by Engin Demirkol (3), a native of Trabzon and another of the very few women carpet dealers in Istanbul. Engin originally opened her shop in the Arasta Bazaar then, as her business flourished, she moved out to the more relaxed and villagey atmosphere of Örtaköy where she caters to the needs of local and foreign residents. She has a good stock of old and semi-old decorative kilims along with a few carpets, all spread over several floors of her Ottoman house. **C**

A La Turca	*Erkal Aksoy* A la Turca House, Faik Paşa Yokusu 4, Çukurcuma, Beyoğlu, Istanbul T: 0212 245 2933 F: 0212 245 2933
Burak Aydoğan Gallery	*Burak Aydoğan* Decocom, Çukurcuma Street 42/2, Çukurcuma, Beyoğlu, Istanbul T: 0212 245 8792 E: info@decocom.com W: www.decocom.com
FCI Şengör	*Ahmet Şengor* Mim Kemal Öke Caddesi 9, Nişantaşı, Istanbul T: 0212 225 4640 F: 0212 247 9170
Günes Öztarkçi	*Günes Öztarkçi* Mim Kemal Öke Caddesi 5, Nişantaşı, Istanbul T: 0212 225 1954 F: 0212 225 1940
Hazal Kelim ve Halı	*Engin Demirkol* Mecidiyeköprüsü Sokak 27, Örtaköy, Istanbul T: 0212 227 4071 F: 0212 261 3672 E: hazalkilim@superonline.com
Leyla Seyhanli	*Leyla Seyhanli* Altı Patlar Sokak 10, Örtaköy, Istanbul T: 0212 293 7410 F: 0212 261 3672
Motif Halı Tekstil	*Ali Türkkan* Hüsrevgerede Caddesi 102/A, Teşvikiye, Istanbul T: 0212 327 8095 F: 0212 327 8096

HILMI'S CARPETS AND KILIMS

Contact: Hilmi Demirci Osmanlı Caddesi 33/13, Balgat, Ankara 06520 T/F: +90 312 286 5804 M: +90 312 284 6317
E: hilmidemirci@ttnet.net.tr

Contemporary and tribal carpet and kilims. Large selection with reasonable prices. Serving all embassies for almost 15 years. Professional washing and cleaning service.

SEFER

Contact: Kerim Sefer Kerim Sefer Hali ve Kilim, El Sanarlari Tic Gözcü Solak 7, Atpazarı, Ankara 06240
T: +90 312 311 9525/363 F: +90 312 311 9303 E: kerimsefer@hotmail.com

Large selection of old and decorative carpets and kilims from Anatolia. Third generation business with expertise in restoration and cleaning.

19th century Şivas rug, East Anatolia. 152 x 95cm (5'0" x 3'1")

MECİDİYE KÖPRÜSÜ SOKAK NO. 9, ORTAKÖY, İSTANBUL, TURKEY
PHONE: +90 212 227 4071   FAX: +90 212 261 3672
E-MAIL: hazalkilim@superonline.com

ANKARA

When the Turkish Republic emerged from the ruins of the Ottoman Empire, its new leader Mustapha Kemal Atatürk decided that a new capital city was needed: somewhere far from the old Byzantine and Ottoman capital, untainted by the past. He chose a small insignificant town in the middle of featureless rolling steppe land which was known only for its production of a fine soft goat hair with which it shared its name, Angora. In fact it had ancient origins. Originally a Hittite settlement known as Ankuwash, like so many Anatolian towns it would later come under the control of numerous conquering empires – in this case the Phrygians, Lydians, Galatians and Romans. Occupying an important place astride trade routes, it grew under Roman rule to become a large city of 200,000 people. Under Byzantine rule the city began to decline and after its capture by the Seljuks and then the Ottomans it faded out of history and into dusty insignificance.

Promoted overnight to capital, Ankara's remoteness, as well as its unfriendly climate with searing hot summers and freezing winters, made it a very unattractive place for foreign powers to site their embassies or for entrepreneurs to open businesses. The government managed to get things moving by offering free land grants and since then Ankara has grown by the day, attracting more and more economic migrants. As the sea of concrete continues to expand, the extremes of climate are exacerbated by horrific levels of air pollution caused by motor vehicles and the burning of fossil fuels. The introduction of natural gas for home heating should go some way to allieviating the problem, having already proved an effective measure in Istanbul.

As you might imagine, this is not a place rich in purveyors of interesting old carpets, but there is one place that is a glimmer in the gloom, or should I say smog. Arising like an island from an ocean of grey concrete is the hill known as Hisar which was the acropolis of the ancient settlement. The top of the hill is girdled by marvellous Byzantine walls that encircle a neighbourhood of decrepit Ottoman houses, narrow alleys, barking dogs and stinking drains, a perfect antidote to the faceless modern city. It's a miracle the place has survived,

1

of well-known dealers. The friendly and eccentric Fahrettin is really a trade dealer who buys and sells quickly, but he does have a small stock of interesting semi-old and antique pieces which on my last visit included a very good antique Obruk cicim (2).

Having poked around the shops in this area and investigated the early mosque just downhill from Deniz Halı, retrace your steps to the main gate of the Hisar and continue past it, going downhill a little way until on the right-hand side you see a large shop called KERIM SEFER. The building itself is interesting: it is over two hundred years old and is said to have been one of the first Ottoman banks.

1. Central Anatolian village rug, ca. 1800 or before, Gallery Afrodit, Ankara
2. Fahrettin Deniz with a flatwoven cicim

but now there are signs of creeping gentrification as some of the old houses are being done up as restaurants and shops.

To the right of the main gate into the Hisar (3) and hugging the walls are numerous stalls selling spices, dried goods and vegetables. Follow this attractive street and you will soon come upon many small shops selling antiques and carpets (5). This area is known as the Atpazari or horse market, and although the horses appear to have gone there are allegedly 35 rug dealers in these decomposing buildings and shanty shacks. The standard of goods on offer is fairly dire but hope springs eternal and a pleasant hour can be spent here.

There is certainly one shop we should pause at. On the right-hand side going downhill, it is called DENIZ HALICILIK. The shop is owned by Fahrettin Deniz, who has been here for nearly forty years and has been the mentor to a number

2

3. The Atpazari with the main gate to the Hisar 4. Kerim Jefer in his large shop 5. The Atpazari with its rug shops 6. The decrepitly romantic Cengel Han 7. Gallery Afrodit's Mustafa Bulguroğlu

Although much restored the second floor retains its ornate wooden ceiling. A fourth generation carpet dealer, Kerim (4) started work repairing carpets when he was seven years old. Today he continues the business started in Ankara by his grandfather who came from Niğde in 1945. He has a large stock of mainly new carpets on the ground floor but upstairs he keeps a small stock of interesting antique kilims. These are all Anatolian and mostly of local manufacture and Kerim has a good knowledge of the local weaving. This is typical of Ankara where the rug scene, such as it is, seems to focus on local Anatolian weavings, something I find quite refreshing after the Caucasian and Turkmen overload of Istanbul.

Before leaving the Atpazari there is one more shop that must under no circumstances be missed. Just opposite the main gate to the Hisar and slightly downhill is the decrepitly romantic Çengel Han (6), built in 1522, which houses in its arched entrance the best kebab shop in Ankara/Turkey/the world. Allegedly two hundred years old, the tiny kiosk produces kebabs made from lamb reared in the highest pastures and using only the finest cuts. The memory of the doner kebab is so vivid as to produce an almost Proustian moment and there is no doubt that had the great man been a resident of the Atpazari the world of literature would have been enriched by *A la recherche des kebabs perdus*.

The last stop in Ankara is across town in the modern residential suburb of Gaziosman Paşa, a long way from the Atpazari. GALLERY AFRODIT is owned by Mustafa Bulguroğlu (7), an Ankarite who turned from physics to rugs, opening his

present gallery five years ago. Mustafa is probably the best known dealer in Ankara due to his regular participation in various fairs in Europe and America. Despite the rather low-key presentation, downstairs Mustafa has a pretty good selection of antique rugs which includes some fragments of Turkish village carpets along with Turkmen and Caucasian pieces.

In addition to the world famous Anatolian Civilizations Museum, Ankara also boasts an excellent, recently renovated Ethnographic Museum, perched above the city on grounds that include the Painting and Sculpture Museum. The collection includes objects from all parts of Anatolia, and beyond, from the Seljuk, Ottoman and Republican periods. It has an excellent collection of Seljuk wooden architectural elements, most notably a *mihrab* from the 14th century Taşkin Paşa Mosque in Ürgüp. There are also exhibits dedicated to writing implements and calligraphy, metalwork, pottery and porcelain, and religious objects. Some 18 small carpets, mostly from 19th century western Anatolia, are displayed arranged on sliding screens. Many of

these are prayer rugs, including one with a pictorial *mezarlık* (tombstone) design, another in the Istanbul-Bursa court tradition, and examples from the key regions of Gördes, Mucur, Ladik, and Kayseri. Equally interesting, and well explained in wall labels, are displays of traditional Anatolian costume, with examples from Erzurum in the east, Ankara, and the Aegean.

Having explored the Turkish capital's museums, there is little else to detain the rug traveller in Ankara, and if another visit to the Çengel Han can be resisted it is time to leave. **C**

Deniz Halıcılık *Deniz Fahrettin* Can Sokak No.29, Atpazarı, Ankara
T: 0312 324 3622 F: 0532 275 2492 E: denizcarpetshop@hotmail.com

Kerim Sefer *Kerim Sefer* Gözcü Sokak No. 7, Adapazarı, Ankara
T: 0312 213 3604 F: 0312 311 9303 E: kerimsefer@hotmail.com

Gallery Afrodit *Mustafa Bulguroğlu* Koza Sokak 134/A, Gaziosmanpaşa, Ankara
T: 0312 436 2129 F: 0312 447 5948 M: 0532 236 4685 E: afrodit@ada.net.tr

THE WEST COAST &
THE SOUTHERN SHORE

This is a chapter of two halves and for the seeker of interesting rugs one half will be more to his liking than the other.

The cities of the west coast of Anatolia have trading roots that reach back into antiquity. Many have carpet and textile connections that are probably as ancient. Places like Izmir (Smyrna), which flourished as a result of its location at the end of the Silk Road and Bergama, a major marketplace for the incredibly productive looms of Asia Minor, still resonate with history. In contrast the towns of the southern shore are often modern conceits, small sleepy villages that have mushroomed in recent years into large tourist compounds. Ironically, there are probably more rug shops along the southern shore than anywhere else in Turkey, and probably nowhere else has fewer that you would wish to visit. The majority are stocked with goods on sale or return from large wholesalers and are operated by people with little or no real carpet knowledge who may well be running a kebab shop next year. Prices can be insanely high and quality dismally low, but the sales pitch will never be less than enthralling. There are of course exceptions to every rule and here they are all the more welcome.

THE WEST COAST

The best way to reach Bursa from Istanbul is by ferry across the Sea of Marmara. Apart from the pleasures of a short sea cruise which saves several hours of heavy driving, the main benefit will have been to avoid going anywhere near Izmit.

Situated at the head of the Gulf of Izmit on the main road east from Istanbul, the port town is an industrial centre of nightmarish proportions. Smoke and fumes belch from unregulated chemical factories and mingle with the pollution from ancient iron and steel works which together envelop the town in a choking yellow cloud. Huge gas flares from the many oil refineries add the finishing touch to this Apocalyptic scene. Even when driving through on the motorway it is necessary to close the windows and switch off the ventilation. During the day headlights are sometimes needed. How human beings are able to exist in this poisonous filth is a mystery, and to make matters worse many homes were badly damaged in the recent earthquake, forcing people to live outdoors in tents.

BURSA

'Bursa the Green' is also a rapidly growing industrial city which has filthy air in the winter although nothing on the scale of Izmit. Situated on the lower slopes of Mount Uludağ and unable to expand upwards, the modern city has spread over the surrounding plain to accommodate the thousands of rural migrants attracted by jobs in the car factories. The first city was founded here in the 2nd century BC by Prusias I, King of Bythnia, who modestly named it Proussa. Attracted by its extensive thermal springs, the Romans built magnificent bathhouses and turned the city into a provincial capital. Under Byzantine rule it acquired major importance as a textile-producing centre, famed for the production of silk. Sericulture began during the rule of Justinian whose emissary, a monk, had smuggled silkworms and the secrets of their rearing from Chinese Turkestan in

the 6th century. Attacked by Arabs and Turkmen in the 8th and 9th centuries, the city declined. It was fought over by Greeks and Seljuks until the Byzantines re-established their rule, following their expulsion from Constantinople during the fourth crusade. In 1326, after a ten-year siege, the city finally fell to the Osmanlı Turks led by Orhan, son of Osman after whom the Ottoman dynasty was named. These wandering Turks succeeded in establishing a permanent base in Bursa and from here went on to eliminate the remaining Turkmen Emirates in the east of Anatolia and lay siege to the crumbling Byzantine Empire in the west.

This was the beginning of the Ottoman Empire and Orhan set

1. Previous page: Ottoman Stonework in Bursa 2. Milas rug, west Anatolia, 19th century 3. Tile panel, Muradiye Cami, Bursa 4. The Silk Bedesten in Bursa

2

3

about rebuilding the city as its capital. He revitalised the textile industry and in particular silk weaving, paving the way for the production of the most spectacular velvets and woven silks in later centuries as Ottoman power reached its zenith. Although Bursa lost its status as a capital to Edirne, strategically better placed for the final assault on Constantinople, it never lost its affectionate place in the hearts of the Ottomans. Six sultans chose to be buried here and the city was endowed with important mosques and tombs. It also never lost its place as a major producer of exquisite textiles, and even today a few scraps of its illustrious textile history survive.

5. Turkish textiles in Karagöz, Bursa
6. Mini-mosque in the Koza Han
7. Dr Mehdi Kamruz of Minyatur, Bursa
8. Tomb in the Yeşil Turbe, Bursa

The most interesting and atmospheric remnant of Bursa's silk industry is the Koza Han, located near the Ulu Cami and the covered bazaar. Built in the 15th century by Beyazit II this is a typical han: an inner courtyard is surrounded on all sides by approximately a hundred arcaded shops on two floors. The dealers in raw cocoons would be on the ground floor and the merchants selling finished goods on the floor above. Every year in June the courtyard floor becomes a white carpet of cocoons spread out for sale. These days Turkish sericulture is probably in terminal decline and most cocoons are imported from the Central Asian republics, Japan and China. Since a change in the law in 1990 which allowed the importation of raw silk from China, silk production in Bursa has also suffered badly, although some is still carried out, most notably in Bilecik and Sögüt. Today the shops in the Koza Han sell mainly mass produced clothing and scarves, but it is a bustling place with an attractive tiny octagonal mosque in the centre (6) and many teahouses. Close by is the Eski Ipek Hanı or the Old Silk Han, but do not expect to find much *ipek* here as it is given over to shops selling polyester wedding dresses.

A much more interesting place is the nearby Eski Aynalı Çarşi or the Old Mirror Market, and although the mirror makers have gone there is a fascinating little clutch of antique shops. Just inside on the left is SPECIALIST ANTIQUE SHOP owned by Tankut Sözeri who has an interesting stock of small antiques including examples of local embroidered towels or *çevre*. The real find in this shop is Tankut himself, a retired bank manager, active author, part time philosopher and columnist on the local paper.

On the other side of the alley is KARAGÖZ (5) owned by Şinasi and Uğur Çelikkol. The business has two distinct sides. First they are specialists in *karagöz*, the traditional shadow puppet theatre, and they offer a fascinating stock of camel skin puppets as well as mounting regular theatrical performances. Their other specialisation is local costume and the domestic embroideries (10) for which Bursa is well known. They have a comprehensive array of old headscarves with colourful and elaborate edges in a lace technique known as *iğne oyası* as well as *çevre*, beaded wedding caps and silks.

Next door you will find MINYATUR, another interesting shop – or rather shops, as there is also a sister shop on the other side of the alley. This business, which has been here for more than twenty years, is owned by the charming and elegant Dr Mehdi Kamruz (7), who is something of an expert on the local embroideries. In his smart establishment he has an excellent stock of textiles and embroideries, most of them old or antique, including a large selection of *çevre* which he is able to attribute to different towns. He also has old purses, hats, caps and waistcoats and last time I was there he produced from a drawer a wonderful fragment of 17th century Ottoman brocade, most likely from Bursa. This shop should not be missed by anyone interested in Turkish domestic textiles.

9. The Yeşil Turbe (Green Tomb), Bursa
10.Bursa's famous domestic embroideries
11. Tabriz-style tile medallion, Yeşil Turbe, Bursa

To find the few rug shops that Bursa has to offer one must visit the area known as Yeşil which is home to the famous 'Green Mosque' and 'Green Tomb' (8, 9). Tucked away behind the *turbe*, which is interesting for its Persian style decoration

carried out by craftsmen from Tabriz (11, 13), are a few small antique shops that have the odd rug or two. Pickers bring things here early in the morning so you have to get up pretty early to beat the local dealers.

EKINCI TICARET ANTIK, owned by

12. A shop in Bergama 13. Persianate tile portal, Yeşil Turbe, Bursa 14. Rug shops in the old town of Bergama

Zafer Ekinci, a native of Urfa, offers a fairly large stock of antiques as well as a few kilims and carpets (16). A couple of shops further on is Rafet Bircan's SELJUK ANTIK, which also has the odd rug if you get there early enough. A small carpet repair shop, BULENT USTA might be worth a look; they had an antique Kurdish divan cover and a decent kilim on my last visit.

The main rug shop in this area is KARAMURAT TURIZM. It can be found just across the road from the repair shop, occupying an attractive Ottoman house. The inside of the house has plenty of original woodwork and the stock, mainly semi-old with a few antique pieces, is spread over three floors. There are quite a few other small antique shops that cater to the large numbers of tourists who come to visit the tomb and the mosque and most of these shops have a few rugs and textiles. Bursa though is not really a fertile hunting ground for interesting rugs. It has never been closely associated with carpet weaving or trading – certainly not something that could be said about the next place we shall visit.

BERGAMA

Bergama is usually approached by the busy road from the coast but if you are travelling from Bursa go via Balıkeşir and drive through the quiet hills and sleepy unvisited villages of what was ancient Mysia and into Aeolia. However you approach Bergama the outskirts are sprawling, dull and dusty, but do not despair because the old town is picturesque and there are least half a dozen carpet shops worth a visit.

The old town sits at the foot of the ancient acropolis and at the heart of a major weaving district (14). The first settlement on the magnificent acropolis seems to date from the 8th century BC, but it is under the successors of Alexander the Great that the city, then named Pergamon, became a powerful and famous centre of Hellenistic culture (15). Attalos III founded the famous library, which at its zenith possessed 200,000 volumes and rivalled that of Alexandria. It posed such a threat that the jealous Ptolemy forbade the export of papyrus which forced the scribes of Pergamon to revive the use of animal skins as a medium for the copying of books. As a result of this the Pergamenes have bequeathed us both the word parchment and the codex or book of numbered pages

and flatweaves (25). Bergama is rather like Bukhara or Shiraz, in the sense that none of these cities has its own weaving tradition but each has been the marketplace through which weavings from the locale have been traded. The scale of the trade has meant that each of these places has given its name to the rugs that passed through its bazaars. The produce of nearly one hundred villages was traded through Bergama and it is noteworthy that nearly all the carpets that appear in the paintings of Renaissance artists such as Lotto, Memling, Ghirlandaio, Holbein and others are 'Bergama' rugs. The attribution of rugs to specific towns or villages is tentative but names in common

15. The ancient acropolis of Pergamon
16. Zafer Ekinci's antique shop, close to the Yeşil Turbe, Bursa

with which we are familiar. Previously, written documents had taken the form of long scrolls. Since parchment was too heavy and bulky for this format, the practice of binding together individually written folios came into use. The great library was looted by Marc Antony who gave it to Cleopatra as a gift, and it remained more or less intact in Egypt until the 7th century AD. I cannot better the description of its fate than that given by Professor George Bean, *"Then the Caliph Omar, or his significantly named lieutenant, Amir ibn el-Ass, reasoning that if a book was inconsistent with the Koran it was impious, and if consistent, unnecessary, ordered the entire library to be destroyed"*.

There are many settled Türkmen, Yüncü and other so-called Yörük (nomad) peoples in this part of western Turkey who have very strong weaving traditions. Together with Turkish villagers, they have produced great quantities of beautiful rugs

use such as Kozak, Ezine and Yunt-
dağ seem to have some validity.

These days very few antique
rugs from the locale are to be
found in Bergama. What can still
be found, although in rapidly dec-
reasing numbers, are interesting

domestic weavings from Yörük and Türkmen villages. Perhaps the most attractive of these are the grain sacks or *ala
çuval* woven in alternating bands of flatweave and various
types of brocaded weave (19). The old ones often have beautiful strong colours, predominately blue, white and red, and
excellent weaving in good wool. Other things to be looked
out for include woven bands, bags, costume and textiles. Rug
hunting in Bergama is a very pleasant pastime. All the shops
worth visiting are practically next door to each other, and
there is still a chance of finding interesting rugs that are
actually from the area rather than brought in from Istanbul.

*17. Ismail Birol of Bergama 18. Hazım
Özpehlivan's Bergama Halı, hung with
bands and tassels 19. Bergama ala çuvals
20. Muzaffar Narman's unusual nomad
blanket with 'evil eye' symbols 21. Feral
Emir of Damping Carpets in Bergama, a
rare woman dealer in provincial Turkey*

Bergama district is also a massive producer of new carpets
and most dealers' stock reflects this, as well as containing
the usual 'imports', but seek and ye shall find.

The rug shops of Bergama are to be found on Kınık Caddesi on the opposite side of the road to the massive ancient
brick building known as the Kizil Avlu. Starting at the end
nearest to the centre of town the first shop to visit is the
oddly named DAMPING CARPET run by Feral Emir (21) one of
the very few provincial women dealers. Her father, who was
originally from Konya, opened a shop in Bergama over forty
years ago and now father, son and daughter each have their
own businesses. Her stock is mainly semi-old carpets and
kilims along with some of her own new production. Interestingly the shop appears to be built above a vaulted Byzantine cellar which is entered through a trapdoor in the street,

while nearby the ancient Selinus River still flows beneath the road in its Roman tunnel.

At no.29 is TAHSIN BAYANSAL, a respected dealer of thirty years' standing whose stock is mainly metalwork and assorted antiques. He also has a few local weavings which included a good çuval on my last visit.

Muzaffer Narman's OTTOMAN ANTIQUES at no.31 is another general antique shop with a stock of old weavings. Muzaffer has a stack of what he claims to be a hundred çuvals, some of which are old and attractive. He also has local embroideries which included a very unusual child's blanket made by local Kaşıkcı nomads from Atinova and embroidered with strange roundels designed to avert the evil eye (20).

You come next to BIROL HALI, another business that has been in Bergama for nearly forty years. Extending across several adjacent shops, it is owned by Faik Birol, although the day to day running is in the more than capable hands of his son Ismail (17), who greeted me, when I recently visited the shop after a gap of fifteen years, with a cheery "Oh, I thought you were dead." They have three rooms full of semi-old rugs, kilims and cicims, as well as a production of individually designed rugs and felts that are marketed in Italy.

Further along, at no. 59, is BERGAMA HALI. Owner Hazim Özpehlivan was born in the town and opened for business over thirty years ago. His attractive double-vaulted shop, hung with bands and tassels (18), offers general antiques and semi-old kilims alongside local embroidered dresses and coats, and an extensive collection of local çevre.

Carry on a short distance and you will come to ARSLAN CARPET, owned by Sait Arslan, a well-known dealer who for many years has supplied the big boys of Izmir and Istanbul. He has a reasonably large stock of semi-old Bergama area bags, cuvals, rugs and kilims, but ask to look upstairs where he keeps a small stock of older pieces. The last shop on the way out to the acropolis is owned by two brothers and long time Bergama dealers SADETTIN & HULUSI KUŞAK. They have a fairly eclectic stock of semi-old kilims, carpets, local embroideries, costume and assorted textiles. There are one or two other small shops that can be visited by walking back towards the centre of town which is still a bustling market place for the produce of the district.

IZMIR

From Bergama the road hugs the coast south through what was ancient Aeolis to reach modern Izmir, known as Smyrna until the 1920s. Allegedly founded by the Amazons and named after their queen, this is a city with a long and eventful history.

The first traces of settlement date to around 3000 BC and show the people to have been Lelegians and Carians, the original inhabitants of Anatolia. By 1500 BC the Hittites were on the scene and by

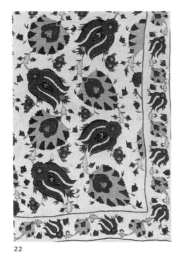

22

23

24

the 1st century BC the Ionian Greeks had settled the city and given their name, Ionia, to the surrounding country.

If we learn anything from history it is that nothing lasts, and in the 6th century the Lydians led by Alyettes destroyed the city and soon the Persians were in control. By the 5th century BC Smyrna was reckoned to be the most beautiful city in Ionia and even today is known as Güzel Izmir.

In the 4th century BC Alexander the Great defeated the Persians and ordered the building of a new city on Mount Pagos, the site of the citadel known today as Kadifekale. From the 1st century BC it was a prosperous Roman city and later an important centre for early Christianity and one of the seven churches of the *Book of Revelations*. In the following centuries it was fought over by Arabs, Byzantines, Seljuks, Crusaders and Genoese until the 15th century, at which point the Mongols arrived and put an end to the squabbling by destroying the place. In 1422 Sultan Murat II conquered what was left and the city became a part of the Ottoman Empire.

The Ottomans granted trading rights to foreigners and the city grew in mercantile importance, thanks to its wonderful natural harbour and strategic location at the end of the spice and silk routes from Persia and China. In the 17th century the Ottomans allowed the export of cotton which further expanded its commercial importance, and in the 18th and 19th centuries merchants from England, France, Holland and Italy, alongside the indigenous Greeks, Jews and Armenians, established large trading companies.

By the early 20th century Smyrna was a sophisticated and cosmopolitan city engaged in the export of various goods including carpets from the looms of Asia Minor. Major weaving towns such as Ushak, Bergama, Kula, Gördes, Aydin and Milas, all relatively close by, produced huge numbers of carpets for fashionable drawing rooms all over Europe and America.

This all came to an end in 1922 when the young Greek state attempted, with Allied encouragement, to annex territory from the disintegrating Ottoman Empire. They were defeated by the forces of Kemal Atatürk, who then occupied and burned down most of the city. The Allies on the whole refused to help the civilians and many perished.

Today Izmir is an enormous modern industrial city of apart-

25

pleasant way to spend an hour. If you are interested in kilims there is one shop here that should certainly be visited. This is found on the first floor and is called KERVAN. The shop is owned by Metin Kıldır and his son Serkan (24), natives of Izmir where Metin has been a dealer for thirty years, the last fifteen in this *han*. They specialise in antique and old kilims of which they have a good stock and also have full repair facilities.

Izmir's best source for antique rugs is not in the bazaar at all but in a rather uninteresting suburban street a couple of kilometres away

22. Ottoman embroidery (detail), western Anatolia, 17th century 23. Busy eateries in a shady Izmir han 24. Izmir kilim specialist Serkan Kıldır of Kervan 25. Bergama 'Holbein design rug, 19th century 26. Ottoman 'court' kilim (detail), possibly Uşak, 18th century

ment blocks and choking traffic, preserving little of its ancient history and practically nothing of its venerable carpet-trading heritage. One or two glimpses of the city manage however to retain some flavour of bygone days. Try taking a stroll and a drink at one of the cafes on the palm-lined harbour front, or plunging yourself into the bazaar area not far from Konak. This is not a covered bazaar as in Istanbul, but a warren of alleys shaded with vines and tarpaulins. Although quite atmospheric it reveals a surprising lack of serious carpet activity; what there is consists of fairly run of the mill tourist stuff.

Most of the carpet shops are to be found in the nearby Kızlarağası Han, which is a good place to visit around lunch time, situated as it is next to an attractive shady *han* given over to jolly and busy eateries (23). Just inside the *han* is a shop owned by AYAN GÜREŞ, a very friendly man who came to Izmir from Bingol over thirty years ago. He has a small stock of mainly new pieces but there were a couple of older bags and trappings hanging around the shop. Dotted about in the *han* are a number of antique shops that might on occasion yield something interesting. In any event poking around here is a

26

in the Alsancak district. SOLMAZLAR HALICILIK is owned by Hüseyin Solmaz, another dealer who moved to Izmir from the east over thirty years ago. He has been a prime source of many very good rugs that have surfaced in Izmir over the years and has supplied major Turkish dealers elsewhere. Unfortunately all this is only a memory these days. No matter where you go the supply of antique rugs has dried to a trickle and most dealers have moved into new rugs. Even so this is the most likely place in town to find collectable antique rugs, kilims and fragments.

27. Ataturk, father of the nation, portrayed in Bodrum 28. The Knights of St John citadel overshadows the port at Bodrum 29. The Southern Shore 30. Ercan Açikel of Galeri Anatolia in Bodrum 31. Sayın Burku of Orhan's Place, Bodrum

THE SOUTHERN SHORE

To travel south from Izmir means a journey through ancient Ionia. Famed for its wonderful climate and natural beauty, it is littered with the ruins of its ancient past and there is still a chance of finding yourself the only visitor climbing over the tumbled stones of a classical city asleep in the sun. The beauty of the landscape is captured for instance on the road from Yatağan to Milas as it passes over pine-covered mountains, lined by rickety wooden stalls selling amber honey. The shock of delight at first sight of the stunningly beautiful coast (29) soon turns to horror as you realise the extent of its destruction. Concrete holiday villas like rabbit hutches sit rank on rank behind wire fences that give each compound the air of a POW camp. The delicate hillsides are gouged out for huge hotel complexes, often in bizarre designs belonging to the Saddam school of architecture. The coast is ruined forever, as we cannot even look forward to the day when they will become crumbling ruins. It is hard to believe that future generations will stroll the twisted steel, broken glass and smashed concrete ruins of these monstrosities as we do the remains of Priene and Xanthos.

BODRUM

Past Milas, still a significant centre for weaving though producing nothing to compare with the pretty rugs of previous generations (2), and through sprawling development is Bodrum. This was ancient Halicarnassus, famous as the birthplace of Herodotus – a fact with little resonance for

today's lager-fuelled visitors. The harbour is dominated by
the small castle built by the Knights of St John (28), and in
the nearby bazaar area by Ercan Açikel's GALERI ANATOLIA.
Ercan, originally from Cappadocia, has been a dealer for
many years and is well known inside and outside Turkey
(30). His stock is spread over two floors with the older more
interesting stuff upstairs.

About a quarter of the way along the harbour front, in an
attractive location with palm trees and *gulets* moored outside, is
ORHAN'S PLACE, owned by Orhan Güzelmeriç and Sayın Burku
(31). Their fair-sized stock includes antique rugs and some good
kilims. They also have their own new carpet production; Sayın
showed me pictures of one of the largest carpets ever woven,
a monster at 19 by 9 metres destined for a Kuwaiti palace.

GOCEK, KALKAN, KAŞ
In antiquity the country east of Bodrum was known as Lycia.
Today it is more prosaically known as the Turquoise Coast.
The rugged shoreline and mountainous interior may once have
afforded the ancient Lycians protection from their enemies,
but it is no match for the relentless march of concrete.

One place that has so far resisted over-development is the
small port of Gocek at the western end of the Gulf of Fethiye.
Surrounded by pine-covered hills, it is popular with the yachting
set, Turkish politicians and foreigners with discreet villas in the
hills behind. With prices expensive
enough to reassure its wealthy
visitors it is affectionately known
as 'Gocheckyourwallet'.

One of the first shops you will
see is BAZAAR ANATOLIA, owned by a
third generation rug dealer, Levent
Şengul. He has mainly new and
semi-old carpets, bags and kilims in
the shop, but older pieces kept at
home can be seen on request.

The town's main rug shop, YUR-DAN CARPET, is in the middle of the harbour front with a beautiful view of the bay. Owned by Ibrahim Yurdan and managed by Yusuf Güler, it has a stock of new and semi-old rugs and kilims. They also have large decorative carpets and a few antique pieces that are produced on request.

Among several other small antique shops in town is one run by Levent Şengul's wife Margo, who sells cushions, textiles and costume.

Further east is Kalkan, once a sleepy Greek village surrounded by olive groves but now in the full throes of total destruction, a.k.a. 'tourist development'. Kalkan is

33

32. Hayri Yaymacı of Orientalia, Kalkan 33. The cliffs behind Kaş 34. Antalya beneath the Taurus Mountains 35. Roman remains in Antalya 36. Mehmet Sağgun with Vedat Karadağ 37. Orient Basar, Antalya

32

popular with the British, who are buying holiday homes as fast as they come off the production line – although the attractions of a mosquito-infested building site, searingly hot in summer and devoid of beaches elude me. Mercifully there is the ever cheerful Hayri Yaymacı (32) and his shop ORIENTALIA. He came here in 1996 from Konya, where he trained first under Ahmet Kavatoğlu and later at Karavan. He has a stock of new and semi-old stuff, as well as a few nice old kilims secreted downstairs. The pleasure here though is Hayri's enthusiasm, undiminished after twenty years in the business.

Not far away is TURKMEN KILIMS & CARPETS owned by the Swiss/Turkish partnership of Henriette Muheim-Dumlupınar and her husband Aykut. They have traded here for over ten years and specialise in semi-old kilims, with a few antique pieces.

Further east along the rugged coast is Kaş, nestling in a beautiful bay backed by high cliffs speckled with Lycian tombs cut into the rock (33). Recent development has seen the small Greek port transformed out of all recognition, but parts of the old village still retain some atmosphere. There is the usual rash of tourist-oriented carpet shops but several are worth a look.

In prime spot on the harbour front is MAGIC ORIENT owned by Mustafa Soylu, born in Beyşehir, who moved to Kaş over twenty years ago. Previously an exhibitor at international fairs he now concentrates on his spacious two-floor shop where he has a large stock, with new and semi-old pieces downstairs and old and antique items, including some respectable kilims.

Close by is KILIM, owned by the Erten brothers from Konya, Ahmet and Lutri. One of several shops owned by the family, they have the usual new and semi-old stock, but particularly like kilims and have several good antique pieces out the back.

Near to the PTT is the shop of Ünal Çelik, another migrant from Konya who definitely wins the best name award with KAŞ & CARRY. Ünal has been in Kaş for nearly twenty years, has a large stock of mainly new carpet sand a selection of older and antique pieces, including, at the time of my last visit, some extra-weft brocaded pieces from Siirt and a small fragment of a classical large-medallion Uşak carpet.

ANTALYA

In any good story the best has been kept to the end. On the border of ancient Lycia and Pamphylia is the huge sprawl of Turkey's fastest growing city (34). On the face of it, Antalya with its expensive marina and mass tourism does not seem the obvious place to find a serious antique carpet shop. The old town though has retained something of a picturesque feel with its crumbling Roman remains (35) interspersed with Ottoman houses in the narrow lanes. Make no mistake though, this is serious tourist country and there are something like fifty carpet shops in town. After you have visited the other 49 make

your way to Paşa Camii Sokak and look for ORIENT BASAR owned by Mehmet Sağgun (36), who not long ago was the subject of an article in *The New Yorker* which portrayed him as a cross between Mahatma Ghandi and Mevlana Rumi and made him a great star with visiting American ruggies, or at least those that believe what they read.

Fortunately Mehmet is far too sensible to believe his own publicity and instead concentrates on what he is extremely good at, which is finding interesting antique rugs. He was born in the Taurus mountain village of Bucak to Türkmen nomad parents who had settled there just after World War II. In 1982 he opened his shop and,

as well as finding time to become a top tennis player, established a reputation as a well respected, well liked and idiosyncratic dealer. He might not even sell you a rug if he doesn't like you, which after the soul-corroding pressure of most shops is a welcome relief.

There is an old Lycian proverb that roughly translates as "Not to have bought a turkey from Mehmet is a far better thing than to have bought a rug elsewhere". As for what you might find in his shop I really couldn't say, you will just have to go and trust your *kismet*. **C**

38. Ancient Lycia, now known as the Turquoise Coast

Arslan Carpet	*Mustafa Arslan* Kınık Cad. No. 75, Bergama T: 0232 632 4661 F: 0232 632 9145 M: 0542 4269181
Ayhan Güreş Carpets & Kilims	*Ayhan Güreş* Old & New, 871 Sokak No. 19, P 82 Kizlarağası Hanı T: 0232 484 1497 M: 0532 235 9132
Bayansal	*Tahsin* Bayansal Ottoman Antiques, Kınık Cad No. 29, Bergama T: 0232 633 2569
Bazaar Anatolia	*Levent Şengül* 48310 Göçek, Fethiye T: 0252 645 1768 F: 0252 645 2479 E: anatolya@ixir.com T: 0252 645 2043 F: 0252 645 2479 E: bazaaranatolia@mail.com
Bergama Halı	*Kazım Özpehlivan* Kinik Caddesi No. 59, Bergama T: 0232 631 6065 M: 0039 338 950 0626
Birol Hali	*Esmil Birol* Kınık Cad. No. 39, 41 & 43, Bergama T: 0232 633 3239 F: 0232 633 1975
Bülent	*Bülent Temel* Halıcı Bülent Usta, Yeşil Caddesi Sancı Sokak No.17, Bursa T: 0224 327 3880 F: 0542 553 9845

Damping Carpet	*Feral Emir* Kınık Cad. No. 27, 35700, Bergama T: 0232 632 6434 E: feralemir@yahoo.com
Ekinci Ticaret	*Zafer Ekinci* Yeşil Emir Caddesi No.3, Bursa T: 0224 328 4785 M: 0532 331 6385
Galeri Anatolia	*Ercan Açıkel* Galeri Anatolia Oriental Carpets and Kilims, Kale Cad No: 1-3, Bodrum T: 0252 316 2468 F: 0252 316 5797
Halı ve Kilim	*Sadettin & Hulusi Kuşak* Kurtuluş Mahallesi Kınık Caddesi No.67, Bergama, Izmir T: 0232 633 1311 F: 0532 293 5786
Kaş & Carry	*Ünal Çelik* Kaş & Carry Quality Handmade Carpets & Kilims, Bahçe Sokak No.3/B Kaş T: 0242 836 1662 F: 0242 836 2389 E: kascarry@hotmail.com
Karagöz	*Şinasi Çelikkol* Kapalı çarsı Eski Aynalı Çarşı No: 12, Bursa T: 0224 210 8727 F: 0224 220 5350 E: karagoztr@superonline.com
Karamurat	*Taner Sağıroğlu* Yeşil Sancı Sokak. No. 3, Bursa T: 0224 327 4905 T: 0224327 5955 M: 0532 317 6225 E: tsagiroglu@turk.net
Kervan	*Metin Kildir* Kervan 871 Sokak No. 19/112, Kizlarağası Hanı T: 0232 425 4919
Magic Orient	*Mustafa Soylu* Hükümet Caddesi 15, Kaş, Antalya T: 0242 836 3150 F: 0242 836 1620 E: morient@superonline.com
Minyatür	*Eski Aynalı* Minyatür Art & Antiques, Çarşı No: 10-11, Kapalı Çarşı, Bursa T: 0224 220 5264 F: 0224 221 5809
Orhan's Place	*Orhan Güzelmeriç, Neyzen Tevfik, Sayın Burku* Orhan's Place Carpets & Kilims Leather, Neyzen Tevfik Cad. No: 40/B, Bodrum T: 0252 316 4571 F: 0252 358 6586 E: info@orhansplace.com E: sayin@orhanplace.com
Orient Bazaar	*Mehmet Sağgün* Tuzcular Mahallesi, Paşa Camii Sokak No: 26, P.K. 271 Kaleiçi, Antalya T: 0242 243 1761 F: 0242 242 0012 E: orientbasar@antnet.net.tr
Yaymacı Orientalia	*M. Hayri* Yalı Boyu Mah. Hasan Altan Caddesi No. 10, Kalkan T: 0242 844 3515 F: 0242 844 3985 E: orientalia@superonline.com
Ottoman Carpets	*Muzaffer Narman* Kınık Cad. No. 31, 35700, Bergama T: 0232 632 0234 E: ottomanarts@yahoo.com
Antik Dekoratif	*Rafet Bircan* Selçuk Antik Dekoratif & Hediyelik Eşya, Yeşil Emir Caddesi No.9/A, Bursa T: 0224 328 0495
Solmazlar Halı	*Hüseyin Solmaz* 1378 Sokak No. 20/B, Kısmet Oteli Yanı, Alsancak, Izmir T: 0232 422 3188 F: 0232 421 9817 M: 0532 232 6224
Specialist Antique Shop	*Tankut Sözeri* Eski Aynalı, Çarşı No. 6, Bursa T: 0224 222 9232 M: 0542 243 0448
Turkmen	*Henriette Muheim-Dumlupınar* Turkman Kilims & Carpets, Yalı Boyu Mahallesi P.K. 53, Kalkan, Antalya T: 0242 844 2097 F: 0532 495 4045 E: henriettemudu@hotmail
Yurdan Carpet	*Yusuf Güler* Cumhuriyet Mah. Turgut Özal No: 15, Göcek, Fethiye T: 0252 645 2295 F: 0252 645 2296 E: yusuf@yurdan.com

Dagestan Kilim

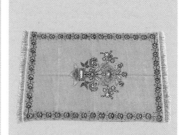

Modern Kilim

Super Fine Kilim

Cradle Soumak

kilim

COMPANY LIMITED

Birlik Mah. 8. Cad 5/12, 06610
Çankaya - Ankara - Turkey
Tel: +90 312 496 09 11(12-13)
Fax: +90 312 496 09 14
Web site: www.kilimcompany.com
e-mail: kilimcol@superonline.com

Saddlebag

Silk kilim - Aydın (Çine)

Sivrihisar Kilim

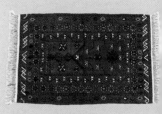

Silk kilim - Konya

SINCE 1985
PRODUCER, EXPORTER, WHOLESALER

You can trust us, because we trust ourselves

THE LARGEST PRODUCTION OF BEST QUALITY KILIMS IN TURKEY
OUR NEW PRODUCTION INCLUDES OVER 1000 KILIM DESIGNS

Konya Kilim, 19th century. 2.12 x 1.36 cm

KAŞ & CARRY
Tribal Rugs & Kilims

❖ Old and New Kilims and Carpets

❖ Custom Made Carpets with Vegetable Dyes and Hand-Spun Wool

❖ Repairs

Ünal Çelik
Bahçe sok. 3/A,
Kaş 07580 Turkey

Tel: +90 0242 8361662
Fax: +90 0242 8362389
Web: www.kascarry.com
E-mail: kascarry@hotmail.com

ORIENTALIA
Motif Turizm Halıcılık ve
El Sanatları San. Tic. Ltd. Şti.

Orientalia was established in 1996 in Kalkan. We specialize in antique and semi-antique tribal pieces from Anatolia and Caucasus as well as contemporary ones. Every piece is carefully chosen by Hayri, who has more than 20 years' experience in carpeting, with consideration of quality and artistic spirit. You will always find some interesting pieces in this unspoilt coastal village, an ideal setting for a holiday.

Contact: Hayri Yaymacı, Yalı Boyu Mah.,
Hasan Altan Cad. No 10
07960 Kalkan / Antalya, Turkey
Tel: +90 242 844 35 15 – Fax: +90 242 844 39 85
Email: orientalia@superonline.com

ORIENT BASAR

Mehmet Sağgün Tuzcular Mahallesi, Paşa Camii Sk. No.26, Kaleiçi, Antalya
Tel +90 242 243 1761   Fax +90 242 242 0012
Email orientbasar@antnet.net.tr
Website www.orientbasar.com

The only source in Mediterranean Turkey for antique and decorative carpets and kilims. Large selection of tribal pieces. Fast and high quality restorations.

Retail/wholesale All types of restoration and special cleaning services.

155

CENTRAL ANATOLIA

The Land of the Seljuks

Anatolia is a state of mind. Not a country or a county but a word that sprawls across the centre of a map of Turkey

Ill-defined and without physical or political boundaries, Anatolia is a Greek word which simply means east. To the sophisticated urbanised Greeks of the Aegean city states it meant a wild and uncouth place beyond civilisation. From the east, from "*anatoli*", came people whose language sounded like *bar-bar* so they called them "barbarians". First came the hordes of Persia and Central Asia, later the Seljuks, and finally the nemesis for the Byzantine Greeks in the shape of the Ottomans. Even today in the big cities of western Turkey there is a tinge of excitement, a frisson when you say you are "going to Anatolia".

The great upland plateau of central Anatolia is a land that has been touched by every empire of the Middle East, from the earliest at the Neolithic site of Çatal Höyük, to the late Ottoman Empire of the early 20th century. This traffic of peoples and cultures has left, among other things, a wonderfully rich weaving tradition, and it is not too fanciful to imagine that weaving itself began in this area. Excavations at Çatal Höyük near Konya revealed what is believed to be the oldest urban settlement in the world, dated to about 7000 BC. Perhaps the most fascinating discovery was the wall paintings that appeared to show motifs which are still being woven into kilims from the area to this day, a continuity of design stretching over several thousand years.

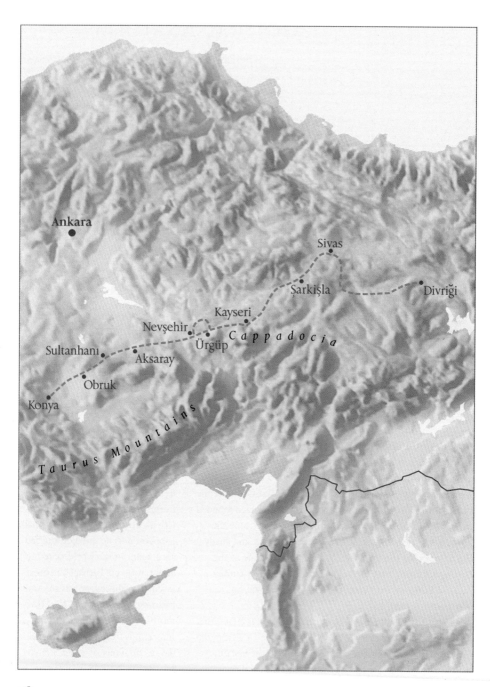

A journey through central Anatolia is a journey through the very heart of Turkish carpet weaving, with every town, village and hamlet giving its name to some wonderful group of rugs. At the very centre of this is Konya, famous for its beautiful kilims, prayer rugs and golden yellow runners. Drive an hour or so from Konya and it is possible to visit Ladık, Obruk, Karaman, Karapınar, Aksaray, Sille and other towns that have produced some of the most sought-after antique village weavings. The people are a mixture of Turks, Kurds, Turkmen and Yörük. They are, as they have been for millennia, pastoralists grazing flocks of fat-tailed sheep on the huge empty plains. Their highly-prized long-staple wool is sold all over Turkey. With its ancient tradition, its important role in the renaissance of rug and kilim production, and its monuments and museums, Konya is a good place to start an Anatolian journey.

In fact any journey to Anatolia should start in Istanbul's Haydarpaşa railway station. Facing the old city across the Bosphorus, it perches on the very edge of Asia. Late Ottoman baroque in style, it has a somewhat stately air about it, looking a little like a mosque or a *medrese*. If you are catching the sleeper to Konya, arrive in time to have dinner in the station restaurant, a wonderfully old fashioned place, its high ornate ceilings hung with hideous chandeliers, potted plants, lace curtains and walls panelled in blue and green Kütahya tiles. There is always a noisy knot of travellers eating *mezes* and getting wrecked on *rakı*. Through the atmospheric blue smog of cigarette smoke it is perhaps just possible to glimpse Graham Greene scribbling in a notebook in the corner. And after the ancient Meram Ekspressi clanks away through dreary suburbs, you fall asleep only to be woken again and again through the night as the train lurches to a halt in increasingly exotic and empty stations.

At some point you stop in dark and deserted Afyon and know you are in Anatolia. When dawn breaks over the endless brown plain the light is different, clear and resonant like the colours in an old Konya kilim, and an eagle hovers next to the track. The plane takes an hour from Istanbul whereas the Meram takes over twelve, but whether this is your first trip to Konya, or your fiftieth, this is the way to arrive.

2. (previous page) The Tomb of Mevlana
in Konya 3. Dervish acolyte at prayer in
the tomb 4. The interior of the tomb of
Mevlana, richly draped with cloth of gold

where we may reflect on the universality of Mevlana's teachings and bow our heads before his enormous tomb, draped
in cloth of gold (4). Although officially a museum, this is in
reality a centre of spiritual pilgrimage (3), attested to by the
crowds of barefoot pilgrims deep in prayer and often weeping.
The Will of Allah triumphing over the dictates of Ankara:
Mevlana would, I imagine, approve.

In the adjoining room, the original *semahane*, or place where
the whirling dance or *sema* was performed, there is a collection of items used in the daily life of the dervishes. These include a number of non-local prayer rugs, but of more interest is
a fragment of a rare Ottoman kilim. Of course in a sense any
kilim made before 1923 (the date of the founding of the Turkish
Republic) is Ottoman, but this fragment belongs to a rare group
of large kilims, often with floral designs, made in workshops
under court patronage and quite distinct from village production. Closer inspection of this fragment, or the prayer rugs, is
not possible because of the reflections caused by the glazed
frames covering them. Oddly enough, there do not appear to
be any prayer rugs specifically connected with the whirling
dervishes of Konya. This is a puzzle given the history of weaving in the area, and is in contrast to the wandering dervishes
of Persia, where the accoutrements of their peripatetic life
have been depicted on a group of 19th century Saruk prayer rugs.

KONYA

Modern Konya is a rapidly growing
city with sprawling industrial and
residential suburbs, but almost
everything of rug interest is to be
found in a small area clustered
around the Mevlana Museum, the
spiritual heart of the city. As famous as the city might be for its
weavings, it is the Tomb of Mevlana
(2), the founder of the mystical
Sufi order of Whirling Dervishes,
that draws most visitors. It seems
appropriate therefore that this
should also be our first stop,

5

Rum, and the roads we travel, the *caravanserais* we visit, and the cities we stay in have all been eloquently shaped by the Seljuk years.

In the 7th century AD the Seljuks are recorded as one of the 24 Ghuz tribes, nomadic Turks living on the borders of Afghanistan. But by the 11th century they ruled vast areas of Central Asia, Persia and Iraq. In 1071, Alp Arslan inflicted a crushing defeat on the Byzantines at the battle of Manzikert in northeastern Turkey, which led Süleyman, in 1078, to declare himself the first Sultan of the Seljuks of Rum, as the eastern provinces of the Byzantine Empire were known. The Seljuks were engaged in almost continuous warfare within an intricate web of shifting allegiances and enmities, far too complicated to be unravelled by a simple rug dealer. They were not

Leaving the tomb complex and its surrounding gardens, we are facing Mevlana Caddesi, later becoming Alaeddin Caddesi which, running in an almost straight line to the Alaeddin Tepesi, is the city's main street. If the Mevlana complex is the spiritual centre of Konya, then the Alaeddin Tepesi is its ancient heart. The Tepesi is a large tree-covered mound encircled by the whirling traffic of the modern city. On this acropolis each successive empire has built its capital upon the ruins of the previous, and over the 9,000 years of its history this has amounted to quite a hill.

This is perhaps the time to visit the Alaeddin Mosque (5), which sits on top of the Tepesi and is Konya's greatest Seljuk monument. It is time also to acquaint ourselves with the Seljuks, because any rug journey through central Anatolia is also a journey through the heart of the Seljuk Empire of

5. Seljuk carved portal on the Alaeddin Mosque, Konya 6. Detail of one of the Seljuk period carpets found in Beyşehir

6

however purveyors of wholesale devastation – that was a speciality of the Mongols. In fact they were highly enlightened providers of social services, endowing medical and theological colleges, hospitals, mental homes, orphanages and poor houses, establishing a welfare state far in advance of that established by Aneurin Bevan in Britain in the early 1950s.

Seljuk art retains certain tastes from its nomadic roots, combined with influences from Persia, China and Byzantium, that together form a homogeneous, vigorous and individualistic style. They created

7. *Konya region prayer rug fragment in the Konya Carpet Museum* 8. *Seljuk period carpet fragment from the Konya region, found in the Mosque at Beyşehir, now in the Konya Carpet Museum* 9. *Medallion detail of a 17th century Konya rug with dragons* 10. *Hüseyin Kaplan of Karavan*

7

masterpieces of architecture and civil engineering alongside works of art in metal, pottery, calligraphy and not least carpets. Which brings us back to the Alaeddin Mosque, for it was there that a group of the most famous and beautiful carpets in the world were discovered in 1905. Most of these carpets and fragments are

8

now on display, along with several related finds from the Eşrefoğlu Mosque in the nearby town of Beyşehir, in the Türk ve Islam Eserleri Müzesi (Turkish and Islamic Art Museum or TIEM) in Istanbul, attributed to the Seljuks and dated to the 13th century.

But who actually made these marvellous carpets? Marco Polo in his *Travels* states that "the Greeks and Armenians in the three major towns of Ikonio [Konya], Kesaria [Kayseri] and Sebastia [Sivas] made the most beautiful and finest rugs in the world", although carpet weaving would of course also have been familiar to the nomadic Turks. But the sophistication of Seljuk woven silk textiles, as well as the enormous size of some of the carpets, point to workshop production almost certainly under court patronage. It is fascinating and instructive to look closely at the designs on the astonishing carved stonework of the surviving Seljuk buildings because nearly all the motifs, including the vine leaf scroll, tulips, arabesques, 'Greek key' variants and infinite repeats of interlocking geometric stars are also found on Anatolian carpets and kilims woven from Seljuk times to this day.

Refreshed spiritually from a visit to the Tomb of Mevlana, and temporally with a *çay* in the shady *çayhane* on the Tepesi, perhaps now is the time to explore the Konya Carpet Museum.

Situated in the basement of the Ethnographic Museum on Sahip Ata Caddesi, this small but very serious collection of carpets should not be missed. First and foremost it has several Seljuk period fragments from Beyşehir (6), including a very unusual multiple medallion fragment. This piece contains the most exquisite purple dyeing I have ever seen, and if anything should be the regal colour of emperors, this is it. There are several other small Seljuk fragments (8) one possibly from Konya, as it relates to

9

fragments in the TIEM with its wide Kufic border. The similarity of this border to the calligraphic blue tilework in the Gök Medrese in Sivas (42) is fascinating. There are also several pieces that have been removed from the *semahane* at the Mevlana complex, including a white-ground Selendi 'bird' carpet and a beautiful 17th century Konya rug (9) with dragons in the medallions. Another rare carpet with an attribution to 15th century Konya has a red field filled with winged animals/birds of a type similar to those on certain 19th century northwest Persian sumakh bags. Along with several other very early and beautiful fragments (14) there is an excellent collection of 18th and 19th century prayer rugs (7) and yastıks (pillow faces) from local villages. This very superficial precis is in contrast to the wonderful depth of the col-

lection and is intended as the merest of hors d'oeuvres.

Of course the museum has spoilt you for anything you are likely to find in the carpet shops of Konya, but Seljuk fragments aside there are the occasional good 19th century Anatolian village and tribal weavings to be found, and what pleasure there is in the search. A good place to start is back at the Mevlana complex looking towards the Tepesi, because a hundred or so metres up Mevlana Caddesi on the right-hand side is Konya's foremost and most famous rug shop.

KARAVAN (10, 13), despite its name, is not an old *caravanserai* but an old *hamam* (Turkish bath) with the original domed rooms that formed separate bathing areas for men and women now being the principal rooms of the shop. Karavan was started in 1982 by Asim Kaplan, one of the founders of the famous Young Partners, a shop that became an institution for an earlier generation of dealers and collectors. Karavan today is run by the delightful Hüseyin, youngest of the three Kaplan brothers (10), who presides over the most interesting shop in town with charm and patience. Their stock is enormous – everything from collectable antique carpets and kilims to startling new *tülü*, traditional Anatolian weavings with a long silky pile used by shepherds for clothing and bedding (11). Karavan also have their own production of good quality kilims, sumakhs and cicims to complement their large stock of semi-old kilims gathered by Hüseyin on his forays throughout Anatolia. Hüseyin also likes Ottoman textiles, so it's always worth poking around in the darker recesses of the shop and if you are lucky he will bring out his excellent collection of *çevre* (embroidered ceremonial towels).

11

11. Anatolian tülü or long-piled shepherd's rug (detail) 12. Mehmet Uçar of Ipek Yolu (Silk Road) in Konya 13. Hüseyin Kaplan and his team inside Karavan 14. Çintamani design carpet fragment in the Konya Carpet Museum

12

If you walk through Karavan's exotically decorated rooms you will find a small door that opens into the repair shop of MEHMET AKAR. Although working closely with Karavan, Mehmet runs his own business, a family affair that includes his son and brother-in-law.

Retracing our steps to the Mevlana complex, in the street that borders it to the north we find the latest incarnation of Young Partners or GENÇ ORTACLAR. It is now run by Mustafa and Kazım Büyükerkek, sons of one the original founders, who opened this shop in 2000. They have a stock, like many other Konya dealers, of their own production new kilims, but down in the basement there are also several piles of old pieces with some interesting antique Anatolian, Caucasian, and Kurdish kilims and saddlebags. They also have a depot of large decorative carpets in the alley behind Karavan.

Literally just around the corner from Genç Ortaklar is LOTTO CARPETS & KILIMS, run by the brothers Mehmet and Galip Doğan. They do not have any antique pieces and specialise in their own production of new kilims. Returning again to Mevlana Caddesi, after a few metres take the first right-hand turn before you reach Karavan into Naci Fikret Sokak, and facing you at no.1 is IPEK YOLU, whose owner Mehmet Uçar (12) is an internationally well-known dealer, an interesting man who runs probably the only non-smoking rug shop in Turkey. He was born in the Taurus Mountains into a nomadic family belonging to the Sari Keçili or 'yellow goat' tribe, and became one of the early converts to natural dyeing, even learning some recipes from his grandmother who wove *zili* (flatwoven covers). He has a big production of new kilims and some carpets, with up to one hundred looms in the Taurus and around Konya. In his shop, alongside the new weavings, he keeps some semi-old and antique pieces.

Back on Mevlana Caddesi and a little way past Karavan is a small shop called OTTIMO, run by the Canbaz brothers, Yılmaz and Bülent. They have a stock of semi-old carpets and kilims, doing most of their business with Italy, a result no doubt of Yılmaz's fluent Italian.

Next door is another small shop, GALERIE SELJUK, owned by

Mustafa Temiz, who has been there for thirty years. He also has a stock of semi-old things and decent enough touristy bags and kilims and, bizarrely, he is also fluent in Italian and spends a lot of time in Italy.

Almost directly opposite, on the other side of the road, look up at first floor level and in the jumble of advertising boards pick out one saying AHMET'S PLACE. Confusingly the entrance is through an unconnected ground floor shop, but persevere because up the stairs awaits another institution. Konya seems to be full of them. The business was founded in 1970 by the late Ahmet Kavutoğlu (18), who served as mentor and teacher to the young Turks who would go on to found Young Partners. Many of the great Konya fragments and kilims that today grace major international collections originated here. It is unlikely that you will find such pieces these days, but ask his sons Ahmet and Mustafa Yalcin Kavutoğlu to take you down to their basement and who knows what *kismet* has in store.

Back again on Mevlana Caddesi, the first small street on the left is Bostançelebi Sokak and a short way down at 10/a is NADIR CARPETS & KILIMS owned by Nadir Gezgin (19). Another long-time Konya dealer, he has been in the business for thirty years, and although he does not speak English, do not be put off, as his friendly manner will prevail. He has a small mixed stock of new kilims and some older pieces and

14

13

it is certainly worth having a dig around. On my last visit I spotted an interesting *heybe* (double don-key bag), clearly of Sivas origin, with a date and inscription in Armenian script.

Next door to Nadir is MIHRI LIMITED run by brothers Ali and Emin Özdemir, sons of a carpet dealer father. The stock is mainly their own new production kilims but there is the odd old piece to be found. Investigate the shop on the other side of the alley which also belongs to them.

15

16

Just around the next corner at no.4 is OSMANLI HALI-KILIM owned by Zeyid Yaman. Really the name is a misnomer as this is an antique shop with a few old rugs, but Zeyid, who has been in the shop for twenty years, has a good eye for interesting things. His stock of antique marble troughs, mortars, pottery, oil lamps, amber, Çanakkale jugs, paintings and old wood printing blocks might be just what you need after all those new kilims. If your taste is for Ottoman baroque furniture, then a visit to the first floor showroom will not fail to delight.

To reach the wonderfully named DERVISH BROTHERS CENTER it is necessary to walk back down Mevlana Caddesi towards the tomb and turn right at the roundabout, then keep going for several hundred metres and look for the shop opposite a large hotel. Although the shop no longer has any connection with its sadly missed charismatic and eccentric founder, it still promotes its dervish origins and claims connections with international Sufi groups. Üzeyir Özyurt, the owner, has a large atmospheric shop well stocked with old and semi-old kilims, a few antique pieces and a range of his own production of angora wool kilims.

From here it is a short walk following the signs in an easterly direction to the Koyunoğlu Museum. This private museum has a first floor ethnography section displaying embroideries, carpets and kilims. Although some of the exhibits are awful and the dating is annoying, with several pieces given 18th century dates despite being a kaleidoscope of chemical colour run, the display is an instructive collection of local types. There is a good Obruk cicim and a very nice Mut kilim on show along with a couple of 18th century Konya rug fragments. Like many provincial Turkish museums this place does not receive many visitors. Therefore one often has the pleasure of having the museum to oneself, but the downside is that there is usually a reluctance to turn on the lights. Carrying a torch on museum visits is not as ridiculous as it sounds.

The last place we visit in Konya is the most extraordinary of all and it's not even a rug shop. YAFES SINOP, who claims descent from the Seljuks (and why not?) is a second generation spice merchant (16) whose father dabbled in a little natural dyeing for a hobby. When the *kökboya* revolution began, Yafes was drafted in by Young Partners to find the secret of dyeing purple, a process others had re-discovered but wouldn't reveal. With his knowledge of herbs and spices Yafes eventually found the secret and from then on started experimenting with other colours. Today along with his spice business he has a small production of naturally dyed kilims.

The real joy though is a visit to Yafes' extraordinary *han*, which is situated in the back streets near the market (ask for directions at Karavan). The entrance is down a short flight of steps into a sunken courtyard surrounded on three sides by low rooms. The open area in the centre is a most astonishing

15. *Central Anatolian kilim (detail)*
16. *Yafes Sinop, the old magician of Konya* 17. *An eagle waits among the hidden treasuresin Yafes Sinop's han in Konya* 18. *The late Ahmet Kavutoğlu, mentor to a generation of yopumger Konya carpet dealers* 19. *Nadir Gezgin*

jungle of dye vats, piles of wood, old pots, broken furniture, strings of weird dried roots, sacks of onion skins, powdered madder, skeins of dyed wool, crates of live partridges and thin cats slinking in and out. Mummified birds including a pelican hang from the eaves and on my last visit as I peered into the gloom of a dark corner overhung with cicims I froze to find I was staring into the eyes of a live brown eagle (17).

In the buildings surrounding the courtyard is a warren of small interconnecting rooms intoxicating with the scent of spices and stacked with bales and spilling sacks of dried flowers, roots and herbs. Shelves from floor to ceiling contain jars of every spice and simple in the sorcerer's treasury, and as old ladies flit in and out buying pinches of magic dispensed in twists of paper, the enigmatic old Seljuk magician serves the most delicious spiced tea I have ever tasted.

for its kilims and prayer rugs, many with a characteristic stepped mihrab (niche) design. Another half an hour and the road reaches Sultanhani, which is a good place to stop.

Sultanhani is a clean, pleasant, sleepy little town and has two main claims to fame. Its most obvious is the spectacular Seljuk *caravanserai* (22) built in 1229. This impressive building is a reminder of the importance of these ancient roads. Built approximately 18 miles apart, or the distance a camel caravan can travel in a day, the *caravanserai* offered within its massive walls safety and comfort for the traveller. They provided warehouses in which to unload the merchandise, stabling and food for the animals as well as food, lodging and a *hamam* for the men. Royal foundations like the one here have superbly decorated entrance portals, the stonework lavishly carved, leading into a courtyard with a small square mosque in the centre.

Sultanhani's other less well-known claim to fame is that it is the carpet repairing capital of Turkey. A number of the big city dealers have their own workshops (21) and many a foreign carpet sent to Turkey for repair will end up here. There used to be nearly a hundred workshops in town but now there are perhaps half that number. Although these are not open to the public, it should be possible to obtain an invitation.

There are a couple of little rug shops dotted around town catering to the visitors to the *caravanserai* and out on the road

SULTANHANI, AKSARAY, NEVŞEHIR

After shaking off Konya's dreary industrial sprawl, the road east to Cappadocia becomes a straight black line swimming in the heat haze. The Anatolian Plateau is a dusty brown featureless plain as flat as the sea and ringed by mountains that never seem to get any closer. The road passes anonymous villages shimmering in the distance and large flocks of sheep are reminders that this is carpet country. An hour from Konya is Obruk, famous

to Aksaray, KARAVANHAM HALI AND KILIM owned by Ali Söylemez has a few reasonable old kilims among its stock.

Back on the Silk Road and it is a short drive from Sultanhani to Aksaray, another town famous for its carpets and in particular its beautiful old kilims. Today there is little evidence of former weaving glory to be found in this market town where probably nothing much has happened since Sultan Ruknuddin was murdered here in 1264. Although there are no carpet shops to see there are a couple of buildings well worth a visit. Just across the bridge spanning the Melendiz River is the 'leaning minaret of Aksaray' (24), an early brick built tower with the greatest 'lean' in Turkey. The local museum has a small collection of rugs, but disappointingly none are on display. However, it is well worth a visit anyway as it is housed in an interesting Karamanoğlu period *medrese* embellished with excellent stone carvings (23).

Back on the road to Nevşehir the mountains at last appear to be getting closer, while hills and unfolding valleys begin to intersperse the empty plains. The road passes Ağzı Kara Han, another great Seljuk *caravanserai* founded by Sultan Keykubad in the 13th century. Despite being the main town of Cappadocia Nevşehir has little to detain the carpet traveller. A rather cramped and unattractive town surrounding a main road that bisects it from east to west, it has just two shops that might be worth a visit.

Approaching from the Aksaray direction on the left-hand side near the centre is EMNIYET GALERI run by Celal Paylan. This is really a trade shop with a large stock of semi-old kilims, but Celal also has an interesting pile of the big grain sacks known as *ala çuval*. Heading out of town on the Ürgüp road, Nevşehir's other rug shop is to be found on the right. ANATOLIA ANTIQUITE is a family business run by Nail Taşkesen and his son Adnan, who are mainly trade wholesalers of new rugs but have the odd semi-old piece in stock. They also have a second shop further

23

out of town near the Nevşehir Museum on Yeni Kayseri Caddesi.

The museum has an interesting archaeological section downstairs and upstairs a display of ethnographic items including kilims and rugs. These consist mainly of late undistinguished weavings with chemical colours and no labels. There is a notice saying that local dealers have donated most of the pieces: I should think they would have been glad to get rid of them. With the wealth of interesting local weavings and the amount of spare time available to provincial museum employees there is no excuse for this sort of travesty.

20. *The yard-man at Yafes Sinop's Konya han* 21. *A rug repairman in Sultanhani*
22. *The Seljuk caravanserai in Sultanhani*
23. *An ancient stone carving in the courtyard of the Aksaray Museum*
24. *The leaning minaret of Aksaray*

24

UÇHISAR, GÖREME

From Nevşehir it is a short drive into Cappadocia. Enough has been written elsewhere about its unique and bizarre landscape (28) to render any further embellishment here redundant. Perhaps less well known is its interesting weaving culture that has produced both piled rugs and kilims. The old kilims are particularly beautiful with their repertoire of ancient motifs rendered in glorious colours. The palette of those pieces attributed to Cappadocia is slightly more pastel in comparison to those of Konya, where the colours are more saturated, the difference due perhaps to the mineral content of the volcanic waters.

No one as yet feels confident enough to attribute these kilims to specific villages and the generic term Cappadocia must suffice. Not quite the same situation applies to the piled rugs and there are some specific attributions, especially to the town of Avanos. One of the particularly interesting attributions concerns the group of yellow-ground long rugs, often with 'Memling'-gül designs, which are ascribed in the literature to Konya (25). A number of knowledgeable local dealers attribute these rugs to Cappadocia, possibly with good reason. Until the early 20th century the population was a mixture of Greeks and Armenians living alongside the Turks. The Armenians in particular have always been regarded as superlative craftsmen and it seems highly likely that they were skilled dyers and weavers who took their recipes and skills with them when they left. I have seen examples of rugs from Yahyali woven before the exodus, and afterwards when the Turks took over the dyeing and weaving, and the decline is obvious. Certainly the yellow-ground long rugs all appear to be old and do not seem to have been woven after the 19th century.

From Nevşehir the road passes Uçhisar, 'the top fortress', a village built into and around a towering pinnacle of rock (27). With stunning views and stylish hotels carved out of the tufa, it serves as a tranquil base from which to explore the region.

A couple of kilometres down the hill from Uçhisar is Göreme, a village famous for its 'fairy chimneys' (1, 31) and also home to the most impressive rug shop in Cappadocia.

25

26

Ömer Tosun was born just up the road and served an apprenticeship in his uncle's rug shop in Ürgüp before opening his own INDIGO GALLERY. Ömer (30) soon established himself as a serious dealer with a great knowledge of local weavings. Although his business now includes two hotels and a travel agency, he has not forgotten his rug roots, as you will see if you pay a visit to his basement. Here among some interesting old Kurdish, Caucasian, and Turkish rugs he has a small collection of the so-called 'Konya' long yellow rugs that he categorically attributes to Avanos. He also has several other old rugs of local origin including some with Armenian inscriptions and a beautiful pair of runners, possibly from Sille, with a very unusual inscription in Greek,

25. Locally woven antique yellow-ground 'Konya' runner at Kirkit Halı in Avanos 26. Cappadocian woman weaving mats from palm fronds 27. The Cappadocian town of Uçhisar, or 'top fortress' 28. The unique and bizarre Cappadocian landscape 29. Camels wait patiently in Cappadocia

further attesting to the fascinating ethnic mix of earlier years. Upstairs Ömer has a large general stock, including many semi-old rugs and a selection of new kilims from his own production. He is also expanding his repair workshop into a purpose built facility.

There are quite a number of shops in Göreme selling semi-old and new carpets, and apart from the personality of the owner there is little to distinguish them. Opposite Indigo is ROSE CARPET run by Hasan Uludağ, with a general stock of tourist-oriented goods. Göreme, as well as being the smallest of the Cappadocian towns, seems to me the nicest, and a stroll around its hobbity streets will soon reveal its rug shops. Also worth mentioning in Göreme are SULTAN CARPETS run by Mehmet Daşdeler and EXPERT HALI run by Süleyman Kalcı.

AVANOS, ÜRGÜP

About ten kilometres from Göreme is Avanos, which more or less marks the northern edge of Cappadocia. Avanos is a small town in the process of growing into a larger one and is sprouting some charmless blocks of new housing in the process. Don't be put off but head across the river and up into the old town, which is still atmospheric with its traditional houses. Although pottery is the main concern here and the ceramic shops outnumber the rug shops, there are a couple worth visiting.

KIRKIT HALI, run by the Diler brothers, Ahmet and Yasin, is in the centre of town and has been trading for over twenty

31

30

years. The brothers, whose mother and grandmother were weavers, have a large stock of semi-old Turkish and Persian pieces along with their own production kilims woven in Uşak. In the back room they have a collection of antique pieces that may or may not be for sale, including some very nice 'Avanos' long yellow rugs (25). The enterprising Dilers also have a travel agency and a *pansiyon* in a traditional house.

Leaving Kirkit turn left and follow the sign pointing up to the old town and after a short and pleasant ramble you will find HITAŞ. This family-run business was started by Ömer Tokmak (33) in 1975, selling pots and carpets. In 1983 he started producing a few natural-dyed kilims with designs thought up by his sister and now has eighty looms in the Taurus making naturally dyed carpets. The designs are still quirky and charming and Ömer, a delightful man, will show you around his courtyard and storerooms, full of dye plants and dried roots. If the charms of Avanos prove irresistible then Ömer and his wife will rent you a quiet terrace room with a splendid view of the town.

On the road to Ürgüp a short detour can be made to the beautifully restored *caravanserai* at Sari Han. This 13th century building is, as its name suggests, a pale yellow colour and inside there is a cool teahouse and a large inner hall that is used on summer evenings for musical performances.

Ürgüp lacks the charm of Göreme, with a main street full of new buildings and big hotels, but it does boast one of the best rug shops and nicest dealers around. Muammer Sak, who runs AKSA HALICILIK (34), is a native of Konya who moved to Ürgüp in 1980 and has established an enviable reputation as a dealer in fine kilims. His stock is mainly good quality old and semi-old pieces, but he also has some first rate antique Anatolian fragments and complete kilims. He has a good knowledge of local weavings, communicated with charm and modesty. A flick through his photo album reveals an array of well-known dealers and collectors who have found their way to his shop.

There are a number of other rug shops clustered together a short walk up Kayseri Caddesi, but none with the gravity of Aksa. SILK ROAD CARPET run by Yaşar Sucu, an established dealer, has a large stock of new carpets and kilims. Practically next door is LE BAZAAR D'ORIENT run by Murat Güzelgöz, a long established business with a stock of new carpets and kilims. BEST COLLECTION AKSOY CARPET SHOP, run by the Aksoy brothers Ismet and Cemal, established dealers with a good reputation, has a few semi-old pieces among their stock of new kilims.

KAYSERI

Leaving Cappadocia, a short and pleasant drive across a flat fertile landscape dominated by the snow-capped volcano Mount Erciyes brings us to Kayseri, an ancient city and important carpet centre. Known in antiquity as Mazaca, it sits at a cross-

roads of the great trade routes of Anatolia and was a trading city of the Assyrians/Hittites in the 2nd millennium BC. It was a major junction on the 'Royal Road' established by Darius the Great, which ran from Susa, his Persian capital, to Sardis. In the days of Persian domination in Anatolia a camel caravan could cover the 1,677 miles in ninety days.

The Romans renamed the town Caesarea, hence its modern name. Under the Byzantines and later the Seljuks the city grew in importance as a centre of commerce, learning and art and after short periods of occupation by the crusaders, the Mongols, the Karamanoğlu and the Mamluks, it fin-

30. Ömer Tosun of Indigo Gallery, Göreme
31. The 'fairy chimneys' of Göreme
32. Old central Anatolian prayer rug
33. Ömer Tokmak of Hitash in Göreme

ally became part of the Ottoman Empire in 1515.

It is difficult to know how long carpets have been woven in and around Kayseri, but by the end of the 19th century it was famous for its production of finely knotted, cotton wefted, pale coloured rugs and carpets. These were sometimes piled in silk but more often in cotton, which was chemically treated to give it a silk-like sheen. Intriguingly the cotton used in old Kayseri carpets was imported from England and the old name in Turkish is *Mançester* carpets. They were woven by Armenians in Kayseri and by Greeks nearer to Nevşehir and were made in all sizes from small prayer rugs to room size. A popular design was startlingly simi-

34. Muammar Sak's Aksa Halıcılık in Kayseri 35. Old central Anatolian carpet fragment

Turkish parents buying two large Kayseri carpets as part of their daughter's dowry. The final blow has been the cheap imports of carpets from China, Iran and India so the 'Kayseri' you buy today is just as likely to be a 'Peking', 'Tehran' or 'Delhi'. Despite these depredations, Kayseri is still a major weaving centre and in particular produces huge numbers of kilims, while in the town itself there are something approaching three hundred dealers.

Today Kayseri is a thriving commercial centre with the remains of its illustrious history interwoven with the fabric

lar to the medallion and spandrels design found on Safavid carpets and book covers from Tabriz in Persia, and shows Eastern influences seeping westwards.

The Kayseri carpet tradition is in serious decline. The first blow was the emigration of the Armenian and Greek weavers at the beginning of the 20th century and the deterioration of the colours and the quality of the weaving in pieces made after their departure is clearly seen. Another blow has been a decline in the tradition of

of the modern city. Highly unusual Seljuk *kumbets* are dotted around the city along with contemporary mosques and *medreses*. The black-walled citadel, built originally by the Emperor Justinian in the 6th century and rebuilt by the great Seljuk Sultan Keykubad sits at the commercial heart of the city, a stone's throw from its three bazaars. Encircled by narrow streets packed with shoppers and traffic, the bazaars are wonderfully atmospheric, colourful and almost totally tourist free. The *kapalıçarşı* is the main bazaar with over five hundred tiny shops selling everything the heart could desire.

Well, not quite everything because they do not sell carpets, and to find Kayseri's best known dealer it is necessary to leave the *kapalıçarşı* and find Cumhurriet Caddesi, where just around the corner in Tennuri Sokak and facing the 13th century mosque is YÖRÜK HALICILIK owned by Nurullah Özçilsal. This is a family

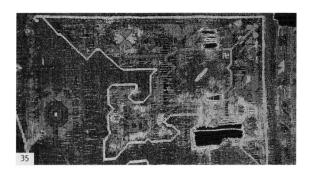
35

business started by Nurullah's father in a tiny shop in the *kapalıçarşı*. Nurullah took over after completing his university studies in English literature, expanded and moved to larger premises. It has come a long way since the days of selling to the backpackers and tourists who used Kayseri as a base before the development of tourism in Cappadocia. Today the business is concentrated on the production of new kilims, which Nurullah does in prodigious quantities and various qualities, some of which can be seen in his basement. In the upstairs shop he has a few older cicims and çuvals.

Next door to Yörük is another long established business, TURAN TURISTIK TESISLER, owned by Turan Mutlu, who has a few semi-old pieces among the predominately new stock. The small streets around here are packed with dealers, probably most of the three hundred are here. Located mainly in a number of commercial buildings there is little to choose between them if you are looking for new carpets and kilims. And don't worry if you can't find them, they will find you. If the sight of piles of brand new carpets stacked to the ceiling in trade warehouses begins to pall, then plunge back into the mêlée of shoppers and ask directions to the Vezir Han.

Although built in the 18th century, this *han* has the ambience of something much older. The outer courtyard is surrounded by tiny shops, most of which function as slaughterhouses. It is often necessary to step around pools of blood and heaps of steaming sheep's entrails to reach the inner courtyard, and one of Turkey's most delightful carpet *hans* (37). This court-yard is surrounded by small shops on two arcaded floors, the ground floor being given over to merchants dealing in sheep-skins, leather, cotton and raw wool, while the first floor is

occupied by rug dealers, repairers, hat makers and *çayhanes*. replace the cars and vans parked in the courtyard with camels and this scene has changed little since Darius last stopped by to drink a cool *ayran*. The rumour is that the Vezir Han is due to be closed and 'restored' because it is unsightly and unhygienic. One can only hope that the local beauracracy will proceed with its usual endear-ing inefficiency.

Climb the stairs and make for NO.112, KAPLAN CARPETING, run by Mahir Kaplan. Not that many people speak English here, but the friendly and helpful Mahir, a retired teacher, is fluent in several languages. His stock is like that of most of the other small dealers, a mixture of old and new carpets and kilims with a sprinkling of bags and trappings. Like most of the dealers in other non-tourist places, these are trade dealers, so don't expect to find the big important pieces that are on sale in retail shops. But what you might find are interesting local bags, trappings and bands, and at very reasonable prices. Another delight of these shops is the lack of pressure and hassle, where a transaction is conducted at a pleasant provincial pace with a man who might be the third generation of his family selling carpets in the same shop.

Next door to Mahir is OTANTIK HALI owned by Mehmet Bugur, a

36

36. *Central Anatolian yatak (long-pile bedding rug) with a Memling-gül design* 37. *A wool merchant's wares at the Vezir Han in Kayseri* 38. *The façade and minarets of the Çifte Minare Medrese in Sivas* 39. *Zekeriya Kartal's Sultan Bazaar, Sivas*

friendly man with a mixed stock of kilims and carpets. OKÇUOĞLU HALI VE KILIM run by Mustafa Okçu at no.62 is mainly a repair shop but he does have a few pieces for sale as well. ERCIYES KILIM IMALATI, owned by Mustafa and Mehmet Kefkir, is mainly concerned with making kilim cushions, but they are also repairers. Another family business concerned with making cushions and bags from kilims is YILMAZ HALI run by Mahmut and Yavuz Yılmaz at no.95. Hacı Davut Yılmaz at no.25 runs KAISER and has the usual stock of mixed pieces with some semi-old kilims, as does Alattin Ilter who owns ILTER HALI at no.97. Around a corner in a sort of inner inner courtyard at no.96 is KARAKOÇ KILIMCILIK owned by Fuat Karakoç. He has a good-sized stock of semi-old

kilims with some interesting looking older pieces lurking in the heaps.

Descend the stairs to ground level and walk through a passageway and you find yourself in a courtyard with a domed ceiling supported by squat heavy columns. This is the 15th century *Bedestan*, another atmospheric little *han* now housing a small clutch of carpet dealers. The main shop here is IDEAL HALI AND KILIM owned by Savaş Imamoğlu, who has a fairly large stock of old and new pieces and will perhaps show you a copy of the obscure American novel by an unknown writer in which he is mentioned.

37

Close to the rather splendid city walls, near Turan Caddesi is the Gürgüpluoğlu, a beautiful Ottoman house restored and opened as an ethnographic museum. It has, amongst other things, a collection of yastıks in cicim and kilim technique, interesting because of the local attributions. It also has a proper old *Mançester* rug and a strange 'Shiraz'-like rug with an intriguing attribution to Ürgüp. There is also a yurt on display, presumably belonging to Turkish Turkmen.

The road to Sivas heads northeast from Kayseri and follows yet another route trodden since antiquity. It passes another of the royal *caravanserais*, the 13th century Sultan Han or Palaz Sultan Han, and continues on through pleasant farmland. The villages hereabouts have a rich weaving heritage and a particularly beautiful group of rugs are attributed to Şarkişla, which we pass a little over halfway.

SIVAS

At 1,275 metres above sea level, Sivas is the highest city on the central Anatolian plateau and is probably Hittite in origin. It first appears in history as the Roman city Sebastea that later became the capital of Armenia Minor. It prospered under the Byzantines until it was captured by the Danişmend Turkmen in the 11th century, and then fell to the Seljuks of Rum in 1172. It flourished under the Seljuks who built mosques, *medreses*, hospitals, and libraries, becoming one of the most important cities in Anatolia. At the junction of the Persian-Baghdad caravan route, Sivas became a centre for the exchange of goods and ideas, but after the usual demolition job by Tamerlane it has sunk into a pleasant provincial torpor, little visited by tourists but boasting some of the most magnificent Seljuk buildings in Turkey.

Probably the most famous of these is the Çifte Minare Medrese, founded in 1271 by the Grand Vizier of the Mongol Ilkhan of Persia. Only the façade and the twin minarets exist today, but they still convey the superb artistry of the master stonecarvers (38). It is a little difficult to stand far enough away to enjoy a view of the whole building, because it stands just a few yards away from the front of the Sifaiye Medrese (40). This is an earlier building, founded in 1217, and functioned as a sort of early psychiatric hospital offering a variety of treatments. Amazingly it was still in use as a hospital until 1916 and today its pleasant courtyard is a *çayhane* surrounded by a number of carpet shops.

Just through the magnificent portal on the left is ÖGUZHAN BAZAAR run by Fikri Ceniklioğlu and his son Oğuzhan. Originally from Divriği, a nearby town that seems to have produced a disproportionate number of carpet dealers, Oğuzhan is the third generation of his family to enter the business. They have a mixed stock of new and old carpets and kilims. Directly opposite is SULTAN BAZAAR (39) owned by Zekeriya Kartal, a native of Sivas. He also has a mixed stock of old and new, with some cushions and bags but upstairs he has some older more interesting pieces. He showed me an interesting cicim yastık from Sivas and some antique kilims.

Inside the courtyard opposite the tomb of Sultan Keykavus is ZUMRUT KILIM, a shop with a small stock of old and new kilims. This *medrese* has a sleepy, faraway feel about it and is a charming spot to drink a *çay* under carpet and kilim festooned

arches. Behind the Sifaiye Medrese on Osman Paşa Caddesi is UYGAR ANTIK run by Mehmet Tetiker and his son, who has the splendid Seljuk name of Alpaslan. Originally from Malatya, this is another three-generation business which has a large stock of mainly new

40. The Çifte Minare Medrese, Sivas
41. Incised Seljuk period relief carvings on the Gök Medrese 42. Seljuk tilework frieze in the Gök Medrese 43.The imposing portal of the Great Mosque in Divriği 44. Seljuk double-headed eagle on the stonework at Divriği

carpets including some new kilims from Şarkişla. There are also a few older pieces here and I was proudly shown an early 20th century rug from nearby Zara that had been woven by Armenians. Half of the shop is given over to general antiques and there are interesting examples of old Armenian metalwork, including a beautifully carved rifle covered in arabesques identical to those seen on the Seljuk buildings.

A short walk away on Cumhuriyet Caddesi is the stunning Gök Medrese, another building founded in 1271. Although officially closed and boarded-up for restoration, a kind word to the watchman might secure admission. Despite its neglected condition this is a magnificent building and its marble portal is carved with tree of life motifs (41) and strange groups of fantastic animals within a leaf shape. Looking at these one might detect a similarity to the *vaq* animals on later carpets and again wonder what role Armenian craftsmen had in all this.

Just inside the portal there are several rather ruinous rooms, but up in the dome are the remains of blue tilework decorated with Kufic type script. The similarity of this decoration (42) to the major borders of the Seljuk carpets found at Konya has already been mentioned, and it is doubly intriguing to find that these tiles were made by a master tile maker, a certain Kaloyan of Konya. It's a short step from Kaloyan to the very common Greek name of Kaloyanni, and not a huge leap to imagine that the builders and designers of these great monuments were Greeks and Armenians. They were after all the products of technically sophisticated and long-settled cultures. The skills of architect and builder are abilities unlikely to be highly developed among nomadic peoples.

DIVRIĞI

Before leaving these Seljuk dominated lands of central Anatolia there is one final pilgrimage to be made, and not a carpet to be seen. Leaving Sivas on the road south to Malatya we are following the old caravan route to Baghdad. After some seventy kilometres the road reaches Kangol, the town that has given its name to the famous Anatolian sheep dog. These beautiful beasts are kept not for their shepherding skills, which are nil, but for their ability to kill a wolf, or anything or anyone that gets anywhere near their flock. From Kangol head due east and wind through bare hills to reach the town of Divriği, home of the most spectacular Seljuk building in existence.

The Great Mosque and Hospital complex at Divriği was built in the 13th century when the city was the capital of the Mengücek Emirate, which had existed under the rule of the Seljuk Sultan Alaeddin Keykubad ı. Inside the building are a number of beautiful and unique architectural features and it was here in the early 1970s that a highly important group of historic carpets was discovered. Discussed elsewhere in this guide, subsequently these were taken by the authorities to Istanbul, where they are now on intermittent display in the Vakıflar Carpet Museum.

ted that this effect harks back to the Seljuks' nomadic origins on the steppes of Central Asia, when decorated weavings were hung against the plain wall of the tent. Perhaps I have been too long in these Seljuk lands but these great portals look to me like memories of the ancient ensi at the yurt's doorway. ☾

Beautiful though it may be, it is not to see the inside but the outside of the building that we have travelled this far. The portal of the hospital, known as 'the Gothic Portal' (43) has an exuberance of floral motifs including tall lily or palm-like plants that are found on no other Seljuk building. These have the decorative feel of ancient Egypt or Palmyra, if not an Art Nouveau carpet by Voysey. The west portal of the mosque, which is interestingly named the 'Textile Portal', contains what is probably the most famous image from the mosque, that of the Seljuk eagle (44) shown in both single and double-headed forms. The north portal of the mosque, known as the 'Baroque Portal' has carving in such high relief and undercut so deeply that it appears unconnected to the stone beneath.

This magnificent building shows brilliantly the contrast of the highly ornamental entrance set against an utterly plain wall, which is the genius of Seljuk architecture. It has been sugges-

Ahmet's Place	*Ahmet & Mustafa Kavutoğlu* Mevlana Caddesi No. 60, Konya T: 0332 351 2055
Aksa Halıcılık	*Muammer Sak* Belediye Sarayı Altı 38, 50400 Ürgüp T: 0384 341 4348 F: 0384 341 4888
Anadolu Kilim	*Mehmet Sepik* Anadolu Kilim The Textile Gallery, Şifaiye Medresesi İçi No.19, Sivas T/F: 0346 224 1762
Anatolia Antiquite	*Nail & Adnan Taşkesen* Esentepe Mahallesi Ürğüp Street No.46, Nevşehir T: 09384 213 1758 F: 09384 213 1758 M: 0532 274 7497 E: adnantaskesen@yahoo.com
Arlekin	2 Organize Sanayisi Yaylacık Çaddesi No.11, Konya T: 0332 239 0744 F: 0332 239 1019
Bazaar Şhirvan	*Orhan Yagcioğlu* Park İstanbul Caddesi Tutluhan Kat:1 No.113, 380040 Kayseri M: 0352 232 1795 E: bazaarsirvan@hotmail.com
Best Collection	*Cemal Askoy* Best Collection Aksoy Carpet Shop, Yahya Efendi Cad. 8, Ürgüp T: 0384 341 4105 F: 0384 341 2610
Dereli Kemal	*Yafe Sinop* Baharatçısı Şifalı Bitkiler ticaret Ltd, Şti Selmiye Caddesi Piri Mehmet Paşa Med. No.3, Konya T: 0332 350 8588 F: 0332 351 1887
Derin Halı	*Mustafa Derin* Derin Halı ve Kilim, Cumhuriyet Mahallesi, Tennuri Sokak, Hüsrefoğlu İşhanı Kat 2/28, Kayseri T: 0352 231 8460 M: 0542 455 8247
Derviş Brothers	*Üzeyir Özyurt* Mevlana Alanı, Otel Balıkçılar, Yanı Mimar Sinan, Sok. No. 6/A, Konya T/F: 0332 351 5467 M: 0532 266 0270 E: derushbrotherscentre@hotmail.com
Emniyet	*Celal Paylan* Emniyet Galeri Eski Halı ve Kilim, Atatürk Bulvarı No.38, 50100 Nevşehir T: 0384 213 5091
Erciyes	*Mustafa-Mehmet Kefkir* Erciyes Kilim İmalatı, Vezirhanı Üst Kat No.25-26, Kayseri T: 0352 222 4556 F: 0352 231 3580 M: 0535 363 4605
Ideal Halı	*Savas Imamoğlu* ideal hali kilim, Camikebir Mahallesi Bedestan İçi No. 3-4 Kayseri T: 0352 222 1131 F: 0532 435 3360 E: savas64@yahoo.com
İlter Halı	*Alattin İlter* Camikebir Mahallesi Vezirhanı, No.97 Kayseri T: 0352 232 4100
Galeri Selçuk	*Mustafa Temiz* Mevlana Caddesi No. 53/D, 42030 Konya T/F: 0332 351 5036 M: 0532 326 4060
Genç Ortaklar	*Mustafa Büyükerkek* Civar Mahallesi Şehit Nazim Bey Caddesi No. 2/A, Karatay, Konya T: 0332 351 0707 F: 0332 351 4979 E: youngpartners@hay.net.tr
Indigo Gallery	*Ömer Tosun* 50180 Göreme T:/F: 0384 271 2351 E: indigo@indigo.com.tr
Ipek Yolu	*Muammer and Mehmet Uçar* Ipek Yolu Silk Road, Mevlána Caddesi Nacifikret Sokak No.1, Konya T: 090 353 2024 F: 090 332 7658 M: 0542 811 0483 E: ipekyolutr@superonline.com
Kaiser	*Hacı Davut Yılmaz* Kaiser Orient-Teppich-Bazaar Export and Wholesale, Camikebir Mahallesi Vezirhanı Üst Kat (Kervan Saray) No.25, Kayseri T: 0352 222 8371 F: 0535 776 9488
Kaplan Carpeting	*Mahir Kaplan* Cami-Kebir Mahallesi Vezirhanı Üst Kat No.112, Kayseri T: 0352 232 7194 F: 0536 215 1297 E: mahirkaplan@hotmail.com
Karakoç	*İbrahim Karakoç* Camikebir Mahallesi Vezirhanı No.66, Kayseri T: 0352 222 1800 F: 0542 772 3312
	Fuat Karakoç Camikebir Mahallesi Vezirhanı No.96, Kayseri T: 0352 222 1800 F: 0352 231 1714

Karavan Inc.	*Hüseyin Kaplan* Mevlana Caddesi No. 63, 42030 Konya T: 0332 351 0425 F: 0332 352 7842 E: karavanhali@superonline.com
	Ali Akar Mevlana Caddesi, Kizilay Pasajı No. 16, 42030 Konya T: 0332 352 0317 M: 0532 771 9072
Kirkit Halı	*Ahmet & Yasin Diler* Avanos T: 0384 511 4542 F: 0384 511 2135 E: kirkit@gediknet.com
Le Bazaar d'Orient	*Murat Güzelgöz* Kayseri Caddesi 32, Ürgüp T: 0384 341 7262 F: 0384 341 8612 M: 0543 574 1309
Lotto	*Galip Doğan* Lotto Carpets & Kilims, Şehit Nazimbey Caddesi Civar Mah. Celal Sk. No. 2/C, 42030, Konya T: 0332 353 2544 F: 0332 350 4909 M: 0542 637 3267 E: lottocarpet@hotmail.com
Mihri Ltd.	*Ali Özdemir* Mevlana Cad. Bostançelebi Sk. No. 9-10, 42020 Konya T: 0332 353 0608 F: 0332 350 2013 M: 0542 361 5187 E: mihriözdemir@hotmail.com
Nadir Halı	*Nadir Gezgin* Nadir Halı Kilim Pazari, Mevlana Caddesi Bostançelebi Sokak No. 10/A, Konya T: 0332 352 0590 F: 0532 621 0637
Oğuzhan Bazaar	*Fikri Ceniklioğlu* Şifaiye Medresesi İçi No. 13, Sivas T: 0346 224 1762 F: 0346 224 1763
Okcuoğlu Halı	*Mustafa Okcu* Camikebir Mahallesi Vezirhan Üst Kat No.62 Kayseri T: 0232 7430
Osmanli Halı	*Zeyid Yaman* Mevlana Cad. Bostan Çelebi Sokak No 4, Konya T: 0332 351 3934 F: 0532 633 1760
Otantik Halı	*Mehmet Buğur* Camikebir Mahallesi Vezirhan Üst Kat No.26, Kayseri T: 0352 232 3630 M: 0542 522 2787
Ottimo	*Yilmaz & Bülent Canbaz* Melvana Caddesi 53/E, 42030 Konya T: 0332 350 9494 F: 0332 353 4226 M: 0532 326 4056
Quality Carpets	*Ahmet Erten* Quality Carpets & Kilims, Mevlana Caddesİ Bostançelebi Sokak No: 19/102, Konya T: 0332 351 72 43 F: 0332 350 7139
Rose Carpet	*Hasan & Hüseyin Uludağ* Göreme 50180, Nevşehir T: 0384 271 2272 F: 0384 271 2551 E: rosecarpet1@hotmail.com
Silk Road Carpet	*Yaşar Sucu* Kayseri Caddesi 30, Ürgüp T: 0384 341 4126 F: 0384 341 4126 E: silkroad_urgup@yahoo.com
Süleyman Kalıcı	*Süleyman Kalıcı* Göreme T: 0384 271 2349 E: expert@turk.net
Sultan Bazaar	*Zekeriya Kartal* Şifaiye Medrese İçi No. 2, Sivas T: 0346 225 2775 M: 0542 251 2942 E: sultanbazaar2000@hotmail.com
Sultan Carpets	*Mehmet Daşdeler* 50180 Göreme T: 0386 271 2030 E: sultanhali@hotmail.com
Taşkent Halı	*Hacı and Mehmet Şahin* Cumhuriyet Mahallesi.Cumhuriyet İşh No.6/D, Kayseri T: 0352 222 4534
Okmak Hitaş	*Ömer Faruk* Cami Sokak 11, 50500, Avanos T: 0384 511 45 87 F: 0384 511 2787
Yılmaz Halı	*Mahmut ve Yavuz Yılmaz* Camikebir Mahallesi Vezirhanı Üst Kat No.95, Kayseri T: 0352 232 7553 E: salı@ttnet.net.tr
Yörük Halıcılık	*Nurullah Özçilsal* Cumhuriyet Mahallesi. Tennuri Sokak No. 28/B, Kayseri T: 0352 222 1455 F: 0352 222 6710 M: 0522 219 5289
Zümrüt Kilim	*Cemalettin Yılmaz* Şifaiye Medresesi No. 16, Sivas T: 0346 225 1983

New Tribal Weavings

Established 1982

brahim Köse

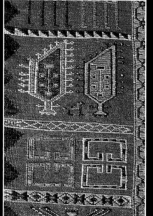

'karavan INC.

Halıcılık ve El Sanatları
Sanayi ve Ticaret A. Ş.

Antique and Decorative Carpets and Kilims
Established 1978

We have a large selection of antique and semi-antique carpets and kilims.
Our production of new carpets and kilims range in design from traditional to
contemporary, using extraordinary wool, mohair and vegetable dyes.
We welcome custom orders and offer top quality restoration and cleaning services.

Contact: *Huseyin Kaplan*   Mevlana Caddesi No. 63, 42030 Konya, Turkey
T: +90 (332) 351 04 25/350 96 96 – F: +90 (332) 352 78 42
E-mail: karavanhali@superonline.com

The finest antique carpet collection in Anatolia

Uşak-1814

indigo gallery

Göreme - TURKEY
www.indigo.com.tr

BAZAAR ahtamara
Retail & Wholesale

ESTABLISHED 1979   SABAHATTIN ABI
Fine Decorative and Old Carpets and Kilims

LARGE INVENTORY I EAST ANATOLIAN, PERSIAN, CAUCASIAN
AND KURDISH CARPETS AND FLATWEAVES

HEAD OFFICE
K. Karabekir Cad.
PTT Sk. No. 5, Van
Tel: +90 (432) 214 32 53
Fax: +90 (432) 216 81 37

SHOWROOM
Kutlugün Sk. No. 25
Sultanahmet, İstanbul
Tel: +90 (212) 458 40 56
Fax: +90 (212) 458 40 57

BRANCH
Arasta Bazaar No. 55
Sultanahmet, İstanbul
Tel: +90 (212) 518 43 94

www.bazaarahtamara.com I Email: info@bazaarahtamara.com

THE WILD EAST

Assuming that the mines and dogs don't get you and you have a bit of a taste for adventure then travelling in eastern Turkey is a delight.

If Anatolia was an ancient illusory concept then eastern and southeastern Turkey have become a modern nightmare. Unlike other areas of Turkey which have a predominantly Turkish population, the east is predominantly Kurdish and this has sometimes led to strife.

The Kurds claim an ancient heritage and a long association with their homeland and regard the Turks as relatively recent occupiers. They have been identified with the Carduchi, described by Xenophon as fearsome warriors who attacked the Greek army from their mountain redoubts with armour piercing arrows. They themselves claim descent from the ancient Medes, which is interesting because these Medes/Kurds developed a religion known as Zoroastrianism, whose priests were called 'magi', and it seems likely that the New Testament's three wise men from the East were in fact Kurds. Even today

there are fifty thousand Kurds in Turkey who belong to the highly secretive Yazidi sect, whose rituals have never been seen by outsiders. They believe among other things that Malak Ta'us cried for seven thousand years and filled seven jars with tears and these were used to extinguish the fires of hell.

Whatever the truth of these claims, it is a fact that for thousands of years the Kurds have lived along the Tigris and Euphrates Rivers and in parts of the Taurus, Zagros, Pontus and Amanus Moun-

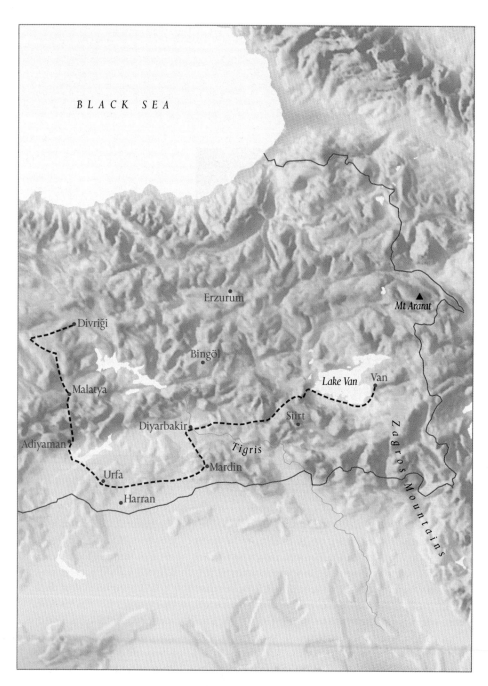

BLACK SEA

Erzurum

Mt Ararat

Divriği

Bingöl

Lake Van

Van

Malatya

Diyarbakir

Siirt

Adiyaman

Tigris

Zagros Mountains

Urfa

Mardin

Harran

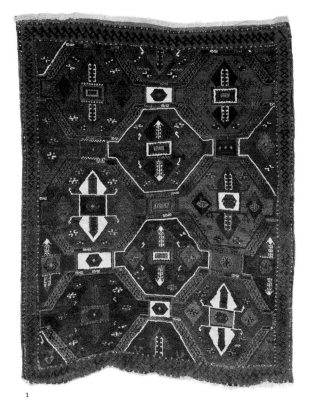

discouraged because if the land-mines don't get you the wolves and the kangols will.

Assuming that the mines and dogs don't get you and you have a bit of a taste for adventure then travelling in eastern Turkey is a delight. The fighting has obviously had a disastrous effect on tourism, but that is now slowly beginning to rebuild itself and the locals will be pleased to see you. Along with empty roads, stunning scenery and delicious food, the East has some interesting little rug shops rarely visited by Westerners. Apart that is from Americans on 'aid' projects.

Although the Kurds share a strong ethnic identity, they have proved difficult to unite politically,

1. *East Anatolian Yörük rug, 19th century*
2. *Gültekin's holed but beautiful antique Kurdish rug in the Malatya bazaar*

1

tains. Modern political boundaries mean that these areas are now in four different countries: Turkey, Iraq, Iran and Syria. Ever since the founding of the republic, Turkey has pursued a policy of denying a separate cultural and ethnic identity to the Kurds. This, along with a general economic neglect of the Kurdish areas, resulted in 1978 in the formation of the PKK, an organisation pledged to fight for a Kurdish homeland. The Turkish state responded with its military might and the result has been a civil conflict in which thousands have died and some two million people have been displaced.

However, with the capture of the PKK leader in 1999, the war has subsided to a few skirmishes in isolated areas. Travel is now possible in almost all the Kurdish areas and the army will soon tell you if they don't want you around. Strolling off to picnic on some remote mountainside is to be thoroughly

divided as they are into eight hundred different tribes. These are organised on lines similar to the Scottish clan system, and a man (or woman) is firstly and fiercely loyal to his own chief and tribe.

One thing they do have in common is a wonderfully rich weaving tradition that encompasses everything from thick shaggy long-piled rugs made in the high mountains to fine and delicate kilims from the plains. Even today many Kurds in the high wild mountains live lives that have changed little over the centuries, pursuing their occupations as shepherds and farmers. The weavings associated with this traditional lifestyle are still to be found, and unusual local and domestic items turn up in the small rug shops. Beautiful woven bands used to secure loads onto animals, saddlebags, animal decorations and items of costume are some of the ethnologically interesting items that can still be unearthed by the diligent seeker.

MALATYA

Malatya is a good place to start a rug foray into the Kurdish lands of east Turkey, particularly if you like apricots, because the Malatya district produces a staggering eighty per cent of the world crop of the dried fruit. They are delicious but be aware that the attractive golden yellow ones with smooth skins are chemically treated to look like that, and it is the wrinkly brown ones

that are the real thing, a lesson learnt in apricots that will be well remembered in rugs.

Malatya is another ancient city at an important junction of the southern Silk Road, and was a garrison town on the eastern frontier of the Roman Empire. The modern city was established in 1838, a few miles from its ancient site. It is a busy commercial place with smart shops on tree-lined avenues that give it a prosperous Western feel, unlike the rest of the Kurdish areas apart from Van. There are upwards of a hundred small dealers in town, but the few that have shops are nearly all conveniently found in one building, the Elmas İş Han in

the central market area on Akpinar Meydani. This is a centre for trade dealers, so not everyone speaks English, but it will not be long before someone appears who is happy to help.

At no.27 is OSMAN TIMURTAŞ and his son Murat, who have a stock of mainly new pieces with a few older things. They also have a pile of beautiful plain handwoven covers or blankets which I had not seen elsewhere and they produced for my perusal a rather splendid old runner which they said came from Malatya. Just along the passageway at no.37 is ŞENCAN owned by Muharrem Şencan, who has a stock of mixed old and new pieces which, on my last visit, included a fine old Mujur/Kirşehir prayer rug. At no.35, Ramazan Karabulut of PALANCIOĞLU keeps a stock of new and old pieces including some nice çuvals from Malatya, while on the ground floor at no.7 is GÜLTEKIN KARDESLER, owned by the Gültekin brothers,

Mehmet and Ahmet. They have a reasonable sized stock which includes a number of interesting older pieces, and on my last visit they had a splendid antique Sauj Bulag Kurdish rug (2), the beauty of which was only marred by its atrocious condition. They also had some interesting examples of costume, including an unusual coat from Zara near Sivas.

A couple of shops along at no.4 is a repair shop owned by Ramazan Yakut, while at no.92 is HAZAR HALI, which is owned by Ahmet Cek and is another shop with a small mainly newish stock mixed with some older pieces that included a rather good Elazığ rug. Next door is KAYHAN HALICILIK owned by Ramazan Kayhan, who has a similar stock to his neighbour but also had a good complete *heybe* (double bag) from Malatya.

There are quite a few other small shops in this *han* that might reward a methodical search, but we are going to leave the Elmas İş Hanı and visit Malatya's most important dealer. Ask for directions or perhaps someone will show you the way to another commercial building not far away called the Pak Kazanç İş Hanı. This *han* is across the Akpinar Meydan and a short walk through the back streets, but before leaving the Meydan and on the other side from the Elmas İş Hanı is a small shop at no.17. This belongs to ISMET ÖZER, who also has a stock that includes some older kilims and bags.

Having found the Pak Kazanç İş Hanı it won't be that difficult to locate ALI DINÇARSLAN because he is the only carpet dealer in the building and he has no fewer than six shops here. A native of Malatya who has been in the business for more than twenty years, Ali is rarely in the shop these days as he spends most of his time attending to his cotton thread business. The everyday running of the shop is in the more than capable hands of his nephew Erhan, who is charming, helpful and speaks perfect English. They have a large stock with many old and antique pieces (3) including some good Anatolian kilims. As a little light relief after working your way through six shops full of rugs, look at his small collection of antique flintlock rifles, most of them with beautiful carved stocks, probably of Armenian workmanship.

4

3. *Ali and Erhan Dinçarslan of Malatya with a 17th/18th century west Anatolian 'Transylvanian' design prayer rug* 4. *East Anatolian Yörük rug, 19th century*

ADIYAMAN, URFA

The road due east from Malatya heads into the mountainous Kurdish heartlands, but following the old Baghdad caravan route we head south towards the hot flat plains of Syria and one of Turkey's most exotic bazaars. The road starts well enough through miles of orchards, particularly beautiful in the autumn

5. *The ancient citadel at Urfa* 6. *Looking down to the Plains of Syria from the citadel* 7. *Long-piled regional weaving attributed to Adiyaman in the Urfa Bazaar* 8. *The Pools of Abraham, Urfa* 9. *Kurdish Yörük prayer rug at Ali Dinçarslan in Malatya*

when the apricots and the poplars are turning yellow in the little valleys and riverbeds. After some fifty kilometres the road enters the mountains, where it twists and turns through ravines and hangs above torrents before finally debouching into the rather nondescript little town of Adiyaman. Although a number of interesting weavings are attributed to Adiyaman (7), these find their way to bazaars in the bigger towns, and there is little here to detain the rug traveller.

From Adiyaman south the country becomes flat and parched, the endless brown plain dotted with ugly patches of cotton. The temperatures here in the summer are ferocious and even in winter the land seems subdued by heat and temperatures are in the mid-twenties. This arid wilderness is being slowly irrigated with water from several massive and very controversial irrigation projects. The damming of rivers and subsequent creation of huge lakes has meant the flooding of numerous villages with the resulting displacement of thousands of people and the inundation of a number of unique archaeological sites. These facts have been well reported around the world but what is less well known is that these enormous bodies of water are changing the local climate.

A couple of hours south of Adiyaman and a few miles from the Syrian border the road finally reaches one of Turkey's most intriguing and exotic cities. With its strong Arabic and Middle Eastern influences Urfa is unlike anywhere else in the country. Occupying a strategic position on the Silk Road from Antioch to Nisibis and controlling the pass from Anatolia to Mesopotamia has meant that the city has been fought over for millennia. It has been occupied by Hurrians, Assyrians, Parthians, Seluicids, Romans, Byzantines, Armenians, Turkmens, Arabs and Crusaders to name but a few. Its origins are lost in time, although some identify it with the Old Testament city of Ur.

Legend also connects the city with the Prophet Abraham and a cave at the foot of the citadel mount, said to be his birth-place, is visited annually by thousands of pilgrims. Near to the cave and surrounded by elegant mosques and medreses are the beautiful Pools of Abraham (8), which teem with sacred carp, the eating of which is said to cause instant blindness. According to the legend the fish come from the time when Nimrud became incensed with Abraham's monotheistic tendencies and hurled the prophet from the top of the citadel into a fire below, but divine intervention turned the flames into water and the sticks of firewood into fish.

Renamed Edessa by Alexander the Great, the city later became a vibrant centre for the development of early Christianity and was a home to many groups and sects such as the Nestorians and Chaldeans. It was the capital of the Kingdom of Armenia when, in 1229, it succumbed to the machinations of Count Baldwin of Boulogne who founded the County of Edessa, the first crusader state in the east. Since then any traces of its Christian and in particular its Armenian past have been systematically removed, although the name Urfa is known to the modern Armenians as an embroidery stitch.

Sanliurfa, 'glorious Urfa', to give it its full name, is a fast-growing rather characterless place, but the old town clustered at the foot of the citadel is an atmospheric warren of old streets thronged with Arabs and Kurds, many in local costume. Built from pale yellow limestone, the mediaeval houses are romantically decrepit and separated by narrow alleys alive with dirty children.

The *kapalıçarşi* or covered bazaar is wonderful, noisy, exotic and real. It spills out from its five hundred year old building into a maze of tiny alleys packed with shoppers and merchants. The air is thick with smoke from the many kebab stands for

9

which Urfa is justifiably famous, although on the menu of apocalyptic meals it would be hard to choose between a fish that will blind you or a kebab that can be lethal, containing as they sometimes do an evil parasite.

Inside the *kapalıçarşi* things can have changed little over the centuries, with all the merchants of a particular trade still clustered in specific areas, their tiny shops often not much bigger than a wardrobe. Lest we should forget that we are in one of the great entrepôts of the Spice Road, Urfa is famous for red pepper and the bazaar is a mosaic of colour from the open sacks in front of the spice shops. Many traditional trades are still found here, including knifemakers, tinsmiths, coppersmiths, engravers, gunsmiths, saddle-makers and even one ancient man making *tambors* from fresh sheepskins.

8

In the cloth bazaar there are tattooed, kohl-eyed Kurdish women laden with gold jewellery who are buying bolts of opulent velvet embroidered with silver thread. With the noise, the smells and its wild and colourful population, this *kapalıçarşi* makes its more famous

shops here selling older pieces and even some of the shops with new rugs might well have something older in the stack.

Entering from the main road, then the first shop of interest is No. 7 close to the entrance. SANSAL TICARET is owned by two brothers, Eşref and Vedat Sansal. Interestingly, they do not sell new weavings at all but mainly old kilims. Although their stock is not ancient, they do have some interesting old weavings from the locale, including çuvals and saddlebags. On my last visit they pulled out a long narrow flatweave decorated with knotted pieces of cotton which they said was Kurdish work from Adiyaman, and struck me as being unusual.

A little further along at no.35 is Urfa's best known and most respected dealer, Müslüm Sarac (13), who owns SARAC TICARET. He has been a carpet dealer for thirty-five years in his tiny shop, having taken over from his father who had been there for fifty, and who had, in his turn, taken over from his father. He has a reasonable sized stock of mainly semi-old pieces, which include some very interesting local weavings. Among these I would number some flatweaves that clearly seemed to my eye to be from Afghanistan, although I was assured by Müslüm that they were in fact local Urfa weavings. The interesting conclusion must be that these kilims were woven by the settled descendants of Turkmen from Central Asia.

Just around the corner in the next han is BAYDAG, owned

cousin in Istanbul seem about as exciting as Habitat.

The carpet bazaar is in the part known as the Sipahi Pazari and can be found either by spending an hour or so drifting around the main bazaar until you stumble across it, or more prosaically by entering from the main road almost opposite the Edessa Hotel.

These days most of the shops are selling new machine-made carpets, a reminder that this is very much a bazaar for local consumption and tastes. There are still a few

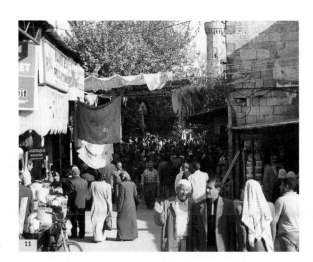

by Abdurraham Baydağ, who also has another shop in the
modern shopping centre just below the Hotel Edessa. His
stock is mainly of new kilims, but again there is the occasional older piece to be found. There are a few other shops in
the environs of the *kapalicarsi* and the Hotel Edessa, but these
are in the main selling new rugs to the pilgrims and tourists.

After the noise and frenzy of the bazaar, the cool green
shade of the tea gardens that surround the Pools of Abraham
is a perfect place to rest and perhaps ponder on a fantastic
Edessan textile legend. King Abgar V, who ruled Edessa in the
first century heard of the teachings and miracles of Jesus and
invited him to Edessa in the hope of a cure for his sickness.
Unable to go, Jesus sent a textile bearing an image of himself
"that had not been painted by hand". Having cured the king,
this textile, which became known as the 'Image of Edessa' or
the 'Holy Mandylion', spent the next nine hundred years in
the city, the object of pious veneration. In 944 the 'Image of
Edessa' was taken to Constantinople, where it remained until
1204 when it disappeared during the ravages of the Fourth
Crusade. In the 1350s there was the 'historical' emergence of
the Turin Shroud, and the rest as they say is history. Well
that's the legend and what better place to contemplate it
than in these tea gardens that cover the site of the great
Cathedral of the Holy Wisdom that once housed the relic.

A little over a kilometre due north of the Pools of Abraham
and the bazaar area is the city museum. This is an interesting
stroll that passes several churches now in use as mosques and
crosses the Karakoyun River close to a beautiful early Byzantine aqueduct. Scattered about in the courtyard of the museum
is an intriguing collection of carved stonework from various
periods and cultures which includes a splendid representation
of the Man with beasts. Upstairs in the museum are photographs showing felt making and silk and cotton weaving and on
display is a beautiful silk spinning wheel, all of which attest
to the importance of textile weaving in the area. Embroidered
çevre, some with metalwork, and an unusual framed embroidery
with a 17th century date, along with examples of costume from
Urfa and the Harran are also on display. Several traditional
carved wooden doors from Urfa are also to be seen including
one particularly beautiful example full of intricate 'carpet'
borders and a Tree of Life.

*10. The bell tower of an old church finds
a new role as a minaret at the Ulu Cami,
Urfa 11. The entrance to the teeming
kapalıçarsı, Urfa 12. Mule in the Urfa
Bazaar 13. Urfa's best known carpet
dealer, Müslüm Sarac*

14. *Toys for the boys, Kurdish style, in Mardin* 15. *Schoolboy in Mardin* 16. *Old padlock on a door in Mardin* 17. *The walls of Diyarbakir, high above the Tigris* 18. *A view into Syria from the old town in Mardin*

MARDIN, DIYARBAKIR

The most interesting way to reach Diyarbakir from Urfa is to take the main highway due east, stopping to visit the town of Mardin on the way. Running parallel with the Syrian border, the road is dead straight across a land that seems to be suffering some Biblical punishment. Temperatures in the summer have been recorded at 63°C and nothing grows except the odd patch of cotton, further debilitating the exhausted soil. The occasional small villages are of the utmost poverty. Single storey rectangular buildings are made from the brown mud of the plain, into which they will one-day dissolve back. The villagers appear to own nothing except a conical pile of dried dung cakes for fuel. This may be Mesopotamia but the Garden of Eden it is not.

The old town of Mardin is very picturesque by contrast with its flat-roofed Arab style houses straggling up the side of a steep hill crowned by a castle. Because it has been very close to the areas of recent fighting it has been little visited by tourists in the past few years. Although there are plenty of police and army around (14) it is a fascinating place to visit with its stunning views into Syria (18) and its colourful Kurdish populace.

From Mardin it is due north to Diyarbakir and the countryside begins to lift and rise, dotted with flocks and herds, fields and trees, a pleasant relief from the punished plains of Syria. After passing army checkpoints the road eventually reaches the valley of the Tigris River and a sprawl of scruffy suburbs gives way to the awesome black walls of Diyarbakir. This is one of the world's most ancient cities, having been founded by the Hurrites in 3000 BC. This was where caravans carrying Cyprus copper crossed the Tigris on their way to trade with the Hurrians at Van. Its history of conquest and occupation would fill a book, so perhaps it is enough to say that it has been occupied by 26 different empires. Its most lasting and stunning monument is its ominous black basalt city wall (17) nearly 5.5 kilometres in circumference. It is said that the only two man-made objects on earth that are visible from space are the Great Wall of China and the walls of Diyarbakir.

The modern city long ago burst from the restraining girdle of its walls to spread over the surrounding plains. This is a very Kurdish city that in recent years has been swamped by many thousands of often penniless refugees displaced by the fighting. Shanty towns have sprung up around the walls and the old city is packed with people. You do not have to venture far from the main thoroughfares to be aware of poverty and to feel a little ill at ease with the gangs of street boys who will soon be in your wake. There is something wild and tense about the place, which has also been a focus of political agitation.

Of course the true rug hunter is not put off by any of this: he is only intrigued and quite rightly because there are a couple of interesting shops here. A very good place to start is literally just inside the walls at the Mardin Gate. The gate itself is well

worth investigating because carved around the portal are cartouches of opposed animals and bands of Kufic type script. These appear to date from the time of the Akkoyonlu Türkmen occupation of the late 15th century.

Just inside the walls is the Deliler Han constructed in the black and white stonework typical of old Diyarbakir. It was built in 1527 to house the guides taking pilgrims to Mecca. In the 1980s it was converted into a hotel and can serve as an atmospheric base from which to explore the city. In the corner of the courtyard of the Buyuk Kervansaray, as the *han* is now known, is the shop of its resident carpet dealer, the affable FADLI SAHIH. Fadli (23), who is from Diyarbakir, has been in the hotel for the last four years and has a fairly large stock which includes some older pieces as well as costume, dresses and scarves, all of local Kurdish origin. Sitting in the shade of

the chinar trees with the splashing fountain as Canan the tame red parrot flies about overhead while looking at rugs in Fadli's corner is certainly one of life's rug moments.

If you can tear yourself away from the Kervansaray's courtyard to enter the mêlée outside then turn right and head toward the centre of town up Gazi Caddesi, affectionately known as the 'street of thieves'. Keep on the same side of the road and after the central crossroads keep going until you come to the 16th century black and white building known as the Hasanpaşa Han (20). This is another delightfully decrepit *han* with old men sitting around the canopied fountain in the centre, and a feeling that not much has changed here over the centuries.

Occupying one whole side is a shop called SUR BAZAAR 21 (21),

which belongs to Diyarbakir's premier dealer, Sait Sanik. Born in Diyarbakir, Sait took over from his father who was a carpet dealer in the bazaar and opened up here in the *han* in 1983. He has a large and interesting stock spread out under the colonnades and three inside rooms, with lots of local weavings, including animal bands and trappings, saddlebags, çuvals and kilims. Sait is generous in imparting his knowledge of the various Kurdish weaves, and here again I saw flatweaves that looked astonishingly like Uzbek or Afghan work (19), but he assured me they came from Beritan and Şavak nomads in the Bingol area. He also had some beautiful naturally-dyed twill covers or blankets made by nomadic Kurds in the Hakkari area and northern Iraq, all in all an education.

The lovely old Hasanpaşa Han is unfortunately destined for res-

toration, and in anticipation of this Sait has opened another shop on the other side of the road to the right of the doorway into the Ulu Cami (Great Mosque). There he has a stock of newer smarter pieces with quite a few carpets and some good Van area kilims. The shop is also worth visiting for the wonderful view from its back windows which look down into the courtyard of the mosque with its beautiful stonework and Corinthian columns.

In front of the Ulu Cami is an underground market that contains two more carpet shops. As well as the usual mixture of old and new pieces, Faizi Allgöz's MESOPATMIA CARPETS, had some interesting and unusual black cicims that were apparently Diyarbakir work. The other shop had no name but appeared to have some older pieces as well as general antiques.

Back above ground and facing the mosque the bazaar area sprawls off to the left, and although not as exotic as Urfa it is lively and interesting. Walk along the alley on the left hand side of the mosque and you will find a number of tiny shops selling harnesses and general farming equipment. Some of these have attractive hand-woven animal bands and blankets among their stock and one venerable old man told me that he had been a merchant there for seventy years.

A little further on and around the corner is a carpet shop called HACI BABA, owned by Muharrem Mimaroğlu, who has the usual general stock of mixed old and new pieces, but also a few unusual looking semi-old kilims, no doubt of local manufacture. A few shops further on is TIGRIS CARPETS, an old

established business owned by Cavit Satici, who has been in this shop for over twenty years. He has a stock of mainly new pieces with a few semi-old rugs and kilims in the stack. Further into the bazaar are various other small booths carrying on what must be rapidly disappearing traditional trades, among them an old man making wooden pack-saddles for mules, which he was covering with pieces of an old kilim.

VAN

Our next stop is as far east as we shall go. A long drive on empty roads passing through the seldom visited towns of Silvan, Bitlis, and Tatvan, around the southern shore of Lake Van and through the mountains, brings us finally to the city of Van. The town is dominated by the so-called Rock of Van, a vertiginous outcrop crowned by a picturesque citadel (30), or rather the remains of several citadels. The building of main interest is the unique mud brick structure (28) that was at the heart of the capital of the Urartian empire.

The Urartians came about as an alliance of small local tribes in the 9th century BC to resist the might of the Assyrians. In 580 BC they in turn were attacked and wiped out by the Medes, after which they faded from history until they were 'rediscovered' in the 19th century by the likes of Henry Layard, the excavator of Nineveh. The relatively few surviving artefacts show them to have been superb craftsmen, particularly in metalwork, which frequently depicts the sacred tree flanked by guardian genii.

After the demise of the Urartians the Armenians emerge as a homogenous people occupying most of the lands of eastern Anatolia. Occupying a strategic buffer zone between opposing cultures, the area around Van has been fought over continuously between the powers of East and West. For a while in the 12th century, there was even an autonomous Kingdom of Armenia. Regarded as traitors by the Turks for backing the Russians, at the end of the First World War they were subjected to the forced deportation that caused countless deaths and contributed the modern Armenian diaspora. But although the people have gone, the vestiges of their culture remain at such beautiful and poignant places as Ani and Akdamar.

19. Sait Sanik with Kurdish flatwoven bags 20. The 16th century Hasanpaşa Han, Diyarbakir 21. Stock spread under the colonnades at Sur Bazaar 21, Diyarbakir 22. Syrian Orthodox priest with two orphans at the world's oldest church, St Mary in Diyarbakir (3rd century) 23. Fadli Sahi

There is also the memory of their great skill as craftsmen, something that was illustrated when the finest silversmith in Van told me that he had learnt his trade from his father, who

in his turn had been apprenticed to an Armenian.

The other great Armenian tradition still being carried on is of course weaving, and there are many historical sources that attest to its antiquity in these parts. Bone instruments used in weaving have been found in nearby Armenia dated to the 2nd millennium BC, and in the 5th century BC Herodotus wrote that "the inhabitants of the Caucasus dyed the wool with a number of plants having dyeing qualities and they used it to make woven fabrics covered with drawings which never lose their brilliant colour". Within living memory Armenian dyers have been famous for their beautiful lasting colours, in

particular 'Armenian red' made from the *kermes* beetle. Arab histories record that in the 8th century AD taxes levied from Armenia included twenty rugs, and the Arab historian Yaqut writes in the 13th century that "the Armenians make huge rugs in the town of Van. The rugs made in Kalikali were called 'khali' after the name of that town".

Modern Van is a peculiar place because, having travelled so far east, there is nothing 'oriental' about it, and unlike other ancient cities in Turkey there is no old town. The old city at the foot of the citadel was destroyed by Ottoman artillery in 1915 after the Armenian populace had barricaded itself inside. The modern city, sited a kilometre or so inland, is laid out on a grid pattern and consists of utterly undistinguished eurostyle concrete buildings and anonymous Western style shops selling designer clothes and mobile phones. The town is

surprisingly wealthy for this part of Turkey and what it lacks in architectural merit it makes up for by the friendliness of its inhabitants and the beauty of its situation, surrounded by high, often snow-capped, mountains and facing the turquoise lake.

Van's carpet shops neatly fall into two categories, huge and small, and lacking any main *kapalıçarşi* they are dotted about around the centre of town. Far and away the largest and most important rug business is URARTU, owned by Tahir Abi (26), which is found very close to the central crossroads. Tahir was born near Hakkari and is from the Gevdan tribe who are known for the excellent kilims they weave. He started out selling sheep to Syria but in 1983 he turned to dealing in rugs and kilims and is today the biggest dealer in eastern Turkey. His shop is large and there are six floors of it, each stacked to the ceiling. A large proportion of his stock, and this applies to all the carpet shops in Van, consists of new sumakhs, kilims and carpets from Iran. Tahir is also a large producer of new kilims, having 250 looms in local villages. They weave what are known in the west as Van kilims but these in fact come from the Hakkari area and the ones being produced by Urartu are of excellent quality. He also has old and antique Kurdish pieces, including some very good kilims and some rugs of Persian Bijar origin.

24. Detail of a 19th century east Anatolian kilim saf (multi-user prayer rug) 25. The finest tailor in Diyarbakir 26. Tahir Abi of Urartu in Van. 27. A family portrait in Van 28. Ruins of the Urartian mud-brick citadel on the 'Rock of Van' 29. Typical scene in the Diyarbakir bazaar

If you can't find quite what you are looking for here then ask to visit the 'carpet village' Tahir has just constructed nine kilometres out of town. Built in caravanserai style, this place is for tour groups and coach parties, and alongside demonstrations of weaving has a further bewildering quantity of stock. Most of the stuff here is new but there was a very nice pile of old animal bands in one of the rooms and for those with the stamina there might be other treasures to be found.

Tahir belongs to a large extended family many of whom

are also in the carpet business. A close relative, Sabahattin Abi, owns the next biggest rug shop in town, BAZAAR AHTAMARA. Located just off Maraş Caddesi, a short distance from Urartu, this is another shop with six floors of rugs. Again a large proportion of the stock is new weavings from Iran, but there are are also older local Kurdish kilims and some carpets to be found.

In a side street off Cumhurriet Caddesi, next to the Asur Hotel, is a small shop called EASTERN ART GALLERY owned by Fevzi Bozbay. Besides the ubiquitous new Iranian goods, a few older Kurdish rugs are to be found there.

Further away on Hastane Caddesi, in front of the Urartu Hotel,

another small shop, CARPET AND KILIM URARTU, has a stock of mainly new pieces, as does GALERIE AVSHAR in the street to the side of the hotel.

The local museum is worth a look and includes some old 'Van' Hakkari weavings, several of which are unusual and attractive. Especially beautiful are some of the Hakkari end finishes where the warps have been woven into a web and then plaited into long tails in much the same manner as the women plait their own hair (in fact some of these warp tails have human hair woven into them). Also exhibited are a number of Urartian implements labelled as textile tools. These include horn needles, loom weights and a shedder and in view of the scarcity of Urartian remains, are clearly very rare.

Around the museum on Cengiz Caddesi is a little cluster of rug shops: there are two on the other side of the road facing the museum and several in an arcade next to it. There are more small rug shops in the grid of alleys bordered by Cumhurriet Caddesi and Karim Karabekir Caddesi, but as these all have similar stock they do not really require separate mention.

This is as far east as we can travel across Anatolia and the end of this journey. In a few miles we come to the Persian border and that is another story. We hope these ramblings have whetted your appetite and the end of this guide is the beginning of your own journey. There is no pretence that this is a detailed or comprehensive guide: in fact perhaps the opposite, because to quote the American painter Georgia O'Keefe "Nothing is less real than realism...Details are confusing. It is only by selection, by elimination, by emphasis that we get at the real meaning of things." **C**

Atasoy	Maraş Caddesi No.8/B, P.K 65200, Van T:0432 216 1234 E: atasoyart@hotmail.com
Baydağ Halı	*Abdurrahman Baydağ* Baydağ Halı & Battaniye ve Kilimcilik Bedesten Çarşısı No.40-42-47, Şanlıurfa T: 0414 215 6469 F: 0532 316 8658
Bazaar Ahtamara	*Sabahattin Abi* Bazaar Ahtamara K. Karabekir Cad. PTT Sokak No. 5, Van T: 0432 214 3253 F: 0432 216 8137
Dinçarslan	*Ali Dinçarslan* Pak-Kazanç İş Hanı No. 48-49-50-51, Malatya T: 0422 323 9378 F: 0422 324 5490
Eastern Art Gallery Oriental	*Fevzi Bozbay* Cumhuriyet Caddesi Turizm Sokak 5, Asur Oteli Altı No.5, Van T: 0432 216 3753 F: 0432 216 9461 M: 0532 453 3077 E: nomad_fevzi@yahoo.com
Eski Halı	*Osman Timurtaş* Eski Halı ve Kilim Ticareti, Akpınar Meydanı Elmas İşhanı No.27, Malatya T: 0422 323 9095
Gültekin Kardesler	*Mehmet Gültekin* Elmas İshanı No. 7, Akpınar, Malatya T: 0422 322 2779 M: 0535 613 0702
Hacı Baba	*H.Muharrem Mimaroğlu* Bakırcılar Çarşısı, Yeni Karşısı No.9/A, Diyarbakır T: 0412 221 0986
Palancıoğlu	*Ramazan Karabulut* Palancıoğlu Halı Kilim Ticaret, Akpınar Meydanı Elmas İşhanı Zemin Kat No.35, Malatya T: 0422 326 1315
Saraç Ticaret	*Müslüm Saraç* Sipahi Pazarı No.35, Şanlıurfa T: 0414 215 7612
Sur Bazaar 21	*Sait Sanık* Gazi Caddesi, Hasanpaşa Hanı No. 10 Diyarbakır T: 0412 221 6209 M: 0542 433 0562
Tigris Carpet	*Cavit Satici* Bakırcılar Çarşısı, Yeni Han Karşısı No. 36 Diyarbakır T: 0412 228 5396 M: 0535 820 6889
Şansal Ticaret	*Eşref & Vedat Şansal* Sipahi Pazarı No.7 Şanlıurfa T: 0414 217 0778 M: 0536 327 6750
Şencan Halı	*Muharrem Şencan* Elmas Is Hanı No. 37, Malatya T: 0422 324 1877
Urartu Carpets	*Tahir Abi* Van Edremit Yolu 9. Km 65200, Van T: 0432 217 9765 F: 0432 217 9769 E: urartuvan@urartu.com.tr

ADVERTISERS INDEX

Born in 1936 in Vienna, Zvi Jagendor family to escape the Nazis. Educated at Oxford, he later emigrated to Jerusalem where he taught English and Theatre Studies at the Hebrew University. His first novel, *Wolfy and the Strudelbakers*, was longlisted for the Booker Prize 2001.

Wolfy and the Strudelbakers

'A most impressive novel full of narrative power and unforgettable description.'   *Jewish Chronicle*

'The delight is in the comic detail, even when the matter is serious.'
                                                        The Times

'For all its gentle humour, what this outstanding mosaic of stories reveals above all is the endless cost to those who are not merely estranged from their homelands, but also from themselves.'
                                        Bryan Cheyette, *TLS*

'... the novel reads like the best kind of personal memoir, full of the little intimacies of family life, and written with a sustained and generous vision of the particular joys and disappointments of finding your way in a foreign land. Jagendorf's prose, appropriately, covets a childlike simplicity and directness of observation. At times you think of *Dubliners*, or Seamus Deane's *Reading in the Dark*...

Jagendorf's novel ... itself feels like a surprise piece of news that deserves a wider audience. It was rightly included among the Naipauls and McEwans on the Booker long list; it would be a small travesty if Wolfy did not inveigle his way at least into the final six.'
                                        Tim Adams, *The Observer*

'Although Wolfy's attempts to reconcile his past with his new homeland form a coherent story, the narrative proceeds like a dream. Everything trembles, alive with joy or pain or the remembrance of both. There are lyrical flashbacks to Kristallnacht in Vienna as Onkel Otto runs for his life through the streets, and then there's the scar that Wolfy's father hides – just something else he brought to England under his shirt. Every character leaps into life with a telling detail or phrase. From the lugubrious Onkel Mendl, the strudelbaker – who speaks one-third Yiddish, one-third German, some English "and some connecting bits he made up" – to the mischief-making adolescent Wolfy, these are personalities of vitality and charm.

Jagendorf handles the material with astonishing finesse, balancing the playfulness with a delicate and sensuous world of touch and smell, evoking a fragile world threatened by sorrows that cannot be forgotten. As the book moves toward its end, it gathers together all its light and darkness, and eases into elegy.'

James Hopkin, *The Guardian*

COMING SOON: THE FLOOD

COMING SOON:
THE FLOOD

a novel

Zvi Jagendorf

HALBAN
LONDON

First published in Great Britain by
Halban Publishers Ltd.
2018

www.halbanpublishers.com

A CIP catalogue record for this book is available
from the British Library.

ISBN 978-1-905559-92-3

Typeset by AB, Cambridgeshire

Printed in Great Britain by
CPI Group (UK) Ltd, Croydon CR0 4YY

For Molly

and in memory of E.M.

You who will emerge from the flood
In which we have gone under
Remember
When you speak of our failings
The dark time too
Which you have escaped.

To Those Born Later by Bertolt Brecht

Broken Dolls

CONSTANZA'S SINGLE EYE stared at her without blinking. Would she ever blink again? Biddy had cracks in her scalp and clumps of her hair were torn out. Poor thing. The flock of dolls lay huddled against each other like captives in a harem in a deep window of what had once been the Abyssinian palace. Their legs were asplay, arms set stiffly in gestures of surprise and helplessness but their faces were still composed and made up with the pink, red and blue of cheap cosmetics. Here and there cheeks were scarred, toes missing and limbs chipped. Ada inspected her girls, victims of another break-in. They needed more attention than she had been able to give them. The big trial coming in a few months was taking up all her time. It was to be filmed but there was no television set-up. So she had got the job of putting together makeshift studios out of formica panels and home improvement materials in the storerooms of an old ice factory soon to become a communications centre. The Big Shit was locked up safe and snug in his cell, watched over day and night. He was protected but her dolls were of no interest to the state and they paid the price. The last burglary was the worst. She had found them thrown across the floor, pissed on. Some had been split open in a search for money, raped and disembowelled by a beast.

The insurance man found it difficult to understand that she had given each doll a name and insisted he write them down. He couldn't spell Sophie. Idiot in a crew cut.

So get a doctor, Ada. Get a doctor.

1

Doctor! Duktur! Yalla Duktur.

The shouts had come from Mamilla after the last shooting incident across the ceasefire line. A sudden crack-crack, a tight drum-roll. Pause. Then the ambulance siren, distant, louder and louder until the wild, wailing beast was practically under her window. Then the quiet again, the town's wounded quiet under the ragged wind.

Duktur, Duktur. Wai wai wai.

Again the cry for help rang in her head like hammer blows on corrugated iron.

But *her* doctor was no army man. Au contraire. He was Kronberg, the philosophy professor turned art dealer, toy doctor and general electric repair man and, sad to say, he was leaving Jerusalem, going back to Würzburg where they were making him an honorary city elder and director of the Witness Archive. Pity he was leaving. He held the bruised heads and unhinged limbs of her girls the right way. Firm fingers but no pressure. He knew where they all came from, Bulgaria, France, Bratislava, Dresden, and looked at them with a mad stare that made her laugh. 'Displaced dollpersons,' he said, 'even rare ones, have accidents. They got here by accident, picked up in a hurry, then discarded by children who discovered the sun and the sea unlike you.'

He was unusually frank with her and over cups of coffee under the wobbling, overloaded bookshelves of his study-hospital-laboratory he asked her why she lived by herself in the gloomy Ethiopian mansion and why she wore only black and chain-smoked Gitanes. 'In hell that is what they smoke, one Gitane, one column of ash stretching into *Ewigkeit.*'

Ada was curious about this spare, grey-eyed German with his high forehead and old-fashioned steel glasses. She had only dreams and photos of her father but she could think of Kronberg as something close, a patron or even a lover, traditional and firm in his old tweed jacket but worldly and in possession of a multitude of secrets. One of these was the nature of his relationship with his younger friend Tomas who sold second-hand books and prints from

2

a barrow and half a shop near the market and painted through the night in a ruin he had made into a studio just above no man's land.

Ada would meet them together at the lunch table d'hôte run by the two formidable ladies from Berlin in their flat behind Jason's Tomb in the best part of town. You got there by skirting the dark, gaping mouth of the Hasmonean burial cave lurking between gardens of quietly rich apartment houses then walking up a gravel path into a line of people waiting for a table in the small, grey and cream painted dining room with its ever-burning strips of fluorescent lighting. Frau Hermine and Frau Gertrude were known as 'Die Tanten' or 'The Dodas' – 'the aunts' – to their clientele but the cosy nicknames didn't dull the gossip about their lives in Weimar bohemia before the war. The severity of their hair styles and the pointed absence of any man in their establishment added spice to their stolid home cooking of pale green and brown dishes heavily dependent on kohlrabi, barley and slabs of tough, government-subsidised meat which attracted the students, bachelors and civil servants for the generous portions needed to combat winter chill in rented rooms. Hermine called Ada 'die kleine Französin' because of her black Parisian sweaters and skirts and her eternal Gitane, and she took a maternal interest in giving her second helpings.

'*Essen Sie mal Fräulein Ada*' she would tell her off if she showed signs of a lack of appetite. '*Vous devez vous forcer à manger.*'

Hermine knew many languages but drew the line at Hebrew, which in her view belonged rightly to clerics and fantasists and could never be imposed on modern, civilised women like herself.

Ada first met Tomas when she was struggling with a wintry day's stew of stringy meat and doughy kohlrabi. Kronberg joined her table and introduced his friend.

'Hello Ada, where's a smile? That's better. It's time you greeted my good friend Tomas. You should have lots in common. Ada is also a painter and understands dolls better than anyone.'

Tomas nodded and smiled at the glass-covered table top.

He was small and finely built with a pale fine face and a mass of black hair just beginning to turn grey in irregular flecks. When he placed his hands on the glass top of the table Ada was astonished to see how rough and scarred the skin was and how prominently the veins pushed against the brown skin. He allowed Kronberg to order the dishes and ate with strict concentration pausing to rest now and again, seemingly unaware of the animated conversation going on between his companions.

Ada had seen them occasionally at the Hermon Café around the corner and at concerts but had never spoken to them together. Perhaps she imagined it, but there seemed to be a 'leave us alone' cordon around them as they sat reading and smoking under the tall pine trees in the café garden.

Now Kronberg was talking, waving hands in protest against the disaster of no man's land and the neurotic consequences of living in the duller half of a provincial town sliced in two but masquerading as a capital city.

'Buried in a dead end with two traffic lights that's where we are. Convince me any life is possible in this cul-de-sac? Life! You are always too close to streets which end in ugly walls and barbed wire. Push through some thorns and bang it's the middle of a minefield. Even if you try to ignore it and spend your days right here in the Bauhaus ghetto with the professors and the civil servants and the pastry shops, the border creeps after you. It's just over there behind the bus stop, too near, too tempting, too frustrating. A man wants to escape, but how? If you could cross over without getting shot, where would you find yourself? On the Hejaz railway Kingdom of Jordan branch? What railway? We're in a fool's cage with a flag over the wire and a nanny from the United Nations to keep the idiots from biting each other. Hopeless.'

He attacked his slice of meat with abandon, going red in the face as he sawed with his knife and chewed. He loved to lecture but coaching the occasional student in Greek or Latin didn't give him enough opportunity.

Ada was not free enough of winter chills to compete with

4

Kronberg's energetic rhetoric but she tried to defend the town as a magnet for those who were looking for the last stop to nowhere.

'OK, it's the end of the line, there isn't anywhere to go from here, but that's what attracts borderline people and hunger artists. Jerusalem is a kind of madhouse but rent is cheap and the treatment is free. Neglect and indifference. So, there is the occasional suicide. Somebody takes a jump off the roof of Terra Sancta College. Somebody else gets naked and wanders down the railway track shouting in German and waving fists at the trees. But basically it gets by. The mad do their mad work and look after each other. The others do whatever God tells them.'

The promise of a secret, fantastical Jerusalem, of lairs in deep, empty shells of Armenian houses, inside grand patios turned into makeshift apartments, behind the decaying facades of Ottoman mansions, barricaded convents and half-empty pilgrims' hostels had beckoned to her when she had come back from Paris with nowhere in particular to go, carrying a stack of canvases with a few black skirts and sweaters and her dolls and books in an otherwise empty trunk. Here, in a neglected town still not recovered from the violation of being chopped in two but displaying its wounds like dirty bandages on a beggar's body, she would find a place. It would be isolated from the demanding, noisy business of the rest of the country and it would be close to the border, the edge where one life came to an end at a STOP DANGER sign, and another life began right opposite as in a mirror, close by but unreachable. Here she would encamp, like a wily mountaineer on a ledge over a precipice, protected by DANGER BORDER from people looking over her shoulder, people she had no wish to know.

She didn't need comfort and the wounded town offered little of that. The resentful isolation and poverty of the religious quarters repelled her, the few commercial streets were like an empty theatre waiting for an audience and in the greener quarters, away from the border line, the neat apartment houses where well-combed ladies gossiped in German and maids beat carpets on balconies reminded her too much of the Carmel in Haifa where she had grown up. Yet

5

close by, a street or two away, the deep gardens of once-prosperous Arab houses summoned her in to spy a life she hesitated to approach. The broken pots of flowers, the weed-choked boxes of herbs, the thirsty trees and the hungry cats were traces of families who had lived there and fled. They awoke in her a troubling sense of being left over from some distant life of her own, of which she retained only blurred, unstable images. She looked at the houses filled up with new families, altered by makeshift additions and partitions, loud with the noise of competing radios and voices summoning children and felt the absence of people she didn't know. Perhaps they were neighbours still but out of sight on the other side of the Old City wall. Perhaps they were watching her through binoculars from the parapets, a little black figure smoking a Gitane hesitating by the gates of Villa Shibli Jamal, unable to decide where she would make her next address –

DANGER BORDER?
STOP NO MAN'S LAND?

Where else was there?

Aunt Perla's symmetrically neat flat on the Carmel above Haifa port told her too clearly who she had been years before in a spartan world of soap, white underwear, white cheese for breakfast and supper and supervised homework followed by classical music and quizzes on the radio. Her aunt's crisp head nurse's uniform with its red Star of David hanging out to dry on the balcony was a banner of dedicated service which made Ada feel sick and hungry for the chocolate, coffee, salami and nicotine brought by Suzi her mother whenever she returned from abroad, turning the flat into an island of luxury and dissolute eating, smoking and drinking for a week or two. Suzi was never in the same place for long. In Bonn with the Reparations Commission, in Paris with the embassy, in Washington on some mysterious mission. Ada was used to seeing her in the in- betweens, glamorous and talkative in well-cut European clothes and smelling of the kind of perfume that stayed in your nose after a kiss. Until it all stopped.

6

Now the monotony of her weekly visit to her mother in the ward, trying to think of things to tell her, hoping she would smile or talk nonsense or laugh was a burden she found hard to bear. Lately she had taken to phoning and listening to the few words and pointless questions that told her Suzi was there. By bus it took four hours, each dragging minute an anticipation of the ordeal to come. So when she finally got back to the dark town late at night she welcomed its lack of traffic lights and its empty streets. The pale, unsteady flicker of an occasional street lamp was all she needed. It lit up her friendly wave to the rusty bullet-holed DANGER BORDER sign in three languages as she skirted Mamilla below the Old City walls and walked up towards Emperor Haile Selassie's Abyssinian mansion, set up to be his royal family's refuge from Mussolini but now a dark beehive of airless corridors, rented rooms and apartments, one of which was her home and the unsafe haven of her dolls.

Tomas looked up from his plate and wiped his lips delicately with the paper napkin.

'Come to my ruin and you've got the dead end smack in front of you. I mean the real end of the road, not Kronberg's abstraction. In the right weather it smells like no other place in town. There's a wind of trouble there. Unmistakeable. Come, I'm not even going to try and sell books this afternoon.'

The line of lunch clients outside had disappeared and a cold, unpleasant and gritty wind was whipping through the quiet street in the empty afternoon. The stone houses round about looked like small fortresses left over after the civilisation they once protected had vanished. Only the occasional tinkling of a piano showed there was life behind the narrow windows and the flower boxes.

Ada walked between the two friends, resisting an urge to link her arms with each and skip down the road singing the Marseillaise. She didn't know them well but weren't they all comrades, survivors of a shipwreck, thrown together by a great storm onto a coast lined by small houses in which mothers and daughters hid among the carpets and hard sofas doing piano practice and polishing the silver, afraid to open their doors because of the cold wind and the monster *DangerBorder* lurking outside?

Tomas's studio was a patched-up ruin of what once had been a simple Arab peasant's house with an animal pen. Thick bare walls of roughly hewn stone must have supported a domed roof where now a flat roof of concrete blocks cut through the building's original grace. It was cold inside. Perched like a mountain goat on the steep side of the valley where the border lay, it confronted the Old City wall and breasted the cold wind whipping up grit and sand from the deep ravine beneath. Beyond the arched window towards the horizon the desert tumbled on indifferently, unfolding itself in more and more shades of grey and pale yellow until it disappeared, swallowed under the mist by the sudden rift valley, the sunken Dead Sea and the wall of mountains in Jordan.

Tomas went to the window pushed it open roughly and squinted.

'Breathe,' he said. 'Tell me what you smell.'

They stood next to him. Kronberg sniffed minimally like a suspicious cat. Ada opened her mouth and took a deep breath, filling her lungs with the cold air. She felt the rawness on her lips and in her throat but couldn't smell a thing. Tomas stared at the open window.

'It's the dryness. So it's not there. Human and donkey shit should be there, wet earth, soaking thorns and goats' stink, barbed wire rusting in the rain and wet air out of caves. That's what you should be getting but it has all gone. If it doesn't rain soon everything here will crumble away. It'll all collapse into one dry hole under no man's land and disappear. Then there'll be nothing between us and them on the other side. We'll be pushed together, nose to nose, lip to lip, belly to belly. Then what will the UN do? Where will they draw the line?'

Ada looked at Tomas to see if he was serious. He seemed to be getting ready to launch himself out and fly across the valley. His open palm was slapping impatiently on the cracked window pane.

Then he jumped onto the deep recess of the tall window and waved
HOO HOO HOO YADLEDOO DALOO. He yodelled incongruously
into the wind, cupping a hand to his mouth, the muscles on his neck
were straining and his eyes popping with the effort.

When the thin answering echo came it was backed up by a
donkey's bray and the groan of a labouring engine, perhaps a bus
struggling up a hill in Silwan, the village on the other side.

Tomas closed the window.

'I'll make some tea,' he said and lit the kerosene cooker and the
small heating stove. The familiar, sickly mineral smell spread
around the room curling like a fog into eyes and mouth and nostrils,
warming the air only to make it unbreathable.

Kronberg arranged himself on a deep window ledge and closed
his eyes.

Against a wall Tomas had propped large, apparently empty
canvases, rolls of paper and columns of books. A couple of graceful
clay water pitchers, one upright the other overturned seemed to be
posing for someone to draw them. Prints of Byzantine mosaics and
colourful advertisements for German cars torn from magazines of
the thirties were stuck irregularly around the room. Elegant women
in tweeds stood by Daimlers and Mercedes watched over by the
Virgin in gold and Christ Pantocrator. The German women looked
polished and bored, the cars polished and perfect. The only painting
hanging on a wall was of a white domed roof swelling like a full
moon in a night sky with a large pot of gaudy flowers broken and
scattered against the edge of the plump curve. An incongruous
bathtub stood precariously on the roof and in it lay a figure of a
woman painted red and green, naked but wearing a straw hat.

Ada had no way of telling if it was Tomas's work but she didn't
ask. A large Javanese puppet hanging from a hook in the ceiling
twisted in the draught. Its face was malevolent with a mauve and
yellow meanness. Its lower parts were hidden by a skirt of elaborate
batik. She noticed a large brown folder on the floor near Tomas's
work table.

'Can I have a look?'

Tomas grunted as he looked for sugar and glasses.

She opened the folder. It was a chronicle of ruin in black and white. Barbed wire climbed over crumbling walls. Broken terraces lay like open drawers in front of hollowed-out houses. Trees were twisted by drought or neglect. Gardens were surrendering to thorns and disorder. Overturned tables lay among food and plates scattered around like fallen leaves. The barbed wire incongruously snaked around everything, high in the trees, pushing out of windows and doors, twisting among grape vines, filling up waterless goldfish pools with knotted metal spikes.

Among all this Ada noticed a striking charcoal sketch of a bearded young man staring full face off the sheet of paper. He was drawn with broad, confident lines. The forehead with thick eyebrows and the heavy eyes with caves of shadow under them dominated the broad nose and drooping mouth. The jaw line stressed by the beard was aggressive and cocky. The mop of hair was thick and black and glistened like silk. Something had been written under the drawing then smudged out.

After the sketch there were drawings of a barge or a clumsy kind of tug with a large fat man asleep on his back under the hull. His belly, swelling up towards the ship seemed like a primitive round anchor and under the fat folds of his stomach his robe was wide open revealing a penis nestling in a cocoon of grey pubic curls. Ada closed the folder.

'You manage to work every day?'

Tomas poured hot water into glasses full of green mint leaves.

'You think selling old books and maps would make a life?'

He sat cross-legged on a straw mat and sipped the tea. He looked at her directly, eyebrows raised a bit as if to say: What about you?

'They are full of sorrow and anger, your drawings, ruins, interrupted lives, that terrible wire. No lies about where we are. You don't beautify it.'

She wanted to ask him about the dome and the scattered flowers and the woman with the hat in the bathtub but Tomas pointed at her impatiently.

'So?'

'Dolls,' she said. 'Dolls and things.'

She looked for help from Kronberg but he was curled up like a big cat in the window sill.

'I paint them in stories, doll people getting into trouble, running away. Getting lost, dreaming. Getting pregnant and having abortions. Women. Nearly all women. If they break they can be stuck back together. If they break too much they can be thrown on a doll heap and their parts can be reused. I tell their stories in bits and pieces.'

'To whom?'

'To the Ethiopian monk who visits me and to Kronberg and a few others.'

She pointed at the charcoal drawing.

There he was, jowlier than in Paris, more self-important, the eyes half closed against the inanities around him.

'Milo…?'

Yes, back from New York.

He looked at her as if to ask her something but didn't and twisted his head in the direction of the Jordanian army post.

'Didn't you hear there's more trouble about his house. The ceasefire line again. The Jordanians say it goes through his kitchen. But we've got a different map, so it's a quarrel. The UN have been snooping around once more.'

Kronberg levered himself off the window seat.

'What did I miss? It's this kerosene fug. It's poison and should be outlawed.' He looked from one to the other and at the open folder.

'Ah there's the wizard himself, the professor of apocalypse. You seem to have got Milo in a rare hopeful mood, Tomas. What did you give him to smoke?'

'He was actually full of talk and plans. He's back, his new woman is on the way and he wants to cook up some sort of theatrical extravaganza for the end of the world or the opening of the trial, something no-one has ever done. He's having a party in a couple of

11

days. Come with me if you like. Who knows, it might turn into a frontier incident and make us feel important. The École Biblique diggers now think his cistern was used in St Jerome's time so the Vatican might get involved in his plumbing.'

Ada had kept her distance from Milo Banet ever since his return to the city. She ignored his phone calls, left his notes unanswered and if she encountered him in the street or in a café, was always in a hurry to get somewhere else. She wasn't unhappy to notice some hesitation in the way he tried to approach her. Let it be, she said to herself. The bastard is partly human. He hasn't managed to sweep me into his dustbin with yesterday's half-smoked cigarettes and last week's bottles.

In their years together in Paris he had also been hesitant at first, unsure of himself, even withdrawn and wary. Though he spoke French fluently and imitated the latest philosophical jargon pretty well, he was vulnerable and on his guard, careful not to be caught out and shamed as a verbose hick from the Levant with a taste for silk shirts and leather jackets.

'You look like a pimp,' she had told him. And he took it as a compliment. What a life he could live, running a stable of women who depended on him and were afraid of him, nibbling sugar from his hand one moment and cowering in the corner the next if he raised his eyebrows in scorn.

Ada could read his fantasies and pretensions the way she guessed the plot line of a crime novel or a B picture and as he gained confidence the plot got thinner. She watched him bathing a German girl in his melancholy charm, working on her fear and fascination as he played the part of a haunted Hebrew prince, restlessly searching for release from the bonds of his past. The next stage was reading *Les Liaisons dangereuses* together or Henry Miller, after which came the predictable denouement. Ada heard the gasps and thuds of their lovemaking in the apartment she and Milo shared and would go out early for the bread, and prepare the ceremonial breakfast, as she did with each new doll. Then they would dip in silence into the wide bowls of bitter coffee. He would prepare his exit by being solicitous in an offhand way and mention the amount of work waiting for him at his desk in the library. The girl was left with Ada as a prize to sketch and paint as long as she lasted. The women were sometimes embarrassed by her presence and disappeared, but often were quite ready to talk and submit to the questioning look and swift brush and charcoal of the third and mysterious member of their unstable triangle.

For Ada these were not only his dolls but hers as well. She made their flesh betray itself and submit to her designs. She drew them savagely and knowingly, for wasn't she a discarded doll herself? She put them in exaggerated postures of seduction and defencelessness but also slipped glints of mockery into their eyes. Often she drew them as mechanical dolls on the edge of being women. They were damaged and could bleed. They sweated and bore marks of love bites or bruises, but they had no will. They wanted nothing and so they were doomed. Ada didn't name them because they were all versions of one commodity, food for a man who never stopped being hungry. In this scene she was Leporello with a brush but she wasn't just keeping score, she was in the play herself. She painted herself as a virgin soldier in khaki uniform, three stripes on her sleeve, unpleasant stains of sweat under her armpits, hair drawn back tight, standing at a bus stop outside a military camp. Unlike the naked dolls of Paris she was ungainly and top-heavy in her ill-fitting uniform with its too tight shirt and barrel of a skirt and she stood, waiting like a shabby armchair on stocky legs. Her shoes were shapeless and dusty and her ankle socks looked as if they were roughly cut out of threadbare diapers. Ada painted herself like this again and again, adding to the ungainly figure touches of grotesque detail and scribbling over the canvas insulting phrases in Hebrew slang, ugly enough to embarrass even herself. These she never showed to Milo or to anyone. They were her private and obsessively distorted memory of how they had met outside the Sarafand Army camp one winter a few long years ago.

He was sitting in a jeep by the side of the road whistling something classical and admiring his profile in the driving mirror.

13

He was waiting for a friend from the barracks, but why not take her? The friend would find a bus to get home.

'Where do you want to go?' he said.

ADA, WHERE DO YOU WANT TO GO?

Voices in her head multiplied the question obstinately, in dreams and in unspoken conversation during the day. Sometimes it came from Aunt Perla, or from a man in a raincoat and a felt hat who spoke hurriedly and indistinctly in what could have been German.

To Milo, at the bus stop, she said, 'Too far for you.'

'Beirut, Damascus, Aleppo?'

'Carmel, near the park.'

'Jump in, sergeant.'

He began performing for her as soon as he switched on the engine. She had rarely been spoken to as a woman before and she was lost. When he showed off his knowledge of languages, of food, of jazz, of Greek beaches it was all for her. She was being shown worlds of adventure. She was being led out of khaki drabness into a great and glamorous light. Why else would he talk like that? Why else would his voice vibrate so when he described swimming at night between rocks named after gods and goddesses? Ada was repelled and hypnotized. The night swimming promised sex just as Aunt Perla's soap, mouthwash and starched uniforms banished the very thought of it. Perla was suspicious of her niece's breasts in their white brassiere because they were traitors, fifth columnists working against a woman's autonomy. Shame on those twin white flags waving surrender to the cunning enemy encamped outside the virginal gates. So when Milo took her forcefully on Perla's hard but broad sofa, breaking her virginity and whispering words of encouragement if not affection she was teetering somewhere between pleasure and disappointment. She had wanted something like this to happen eventually, but here? At Perla's, under the Käthe Kollwitz print of a starving child? In this way? With him? In uniform? And what about the mess?

He left that to her and after a civilized cup of coffee and a quick shower and farewell kiss, he was gone, saying he had to be back at

14

the camp leaving her a telephone number and the remains of a packet of condoms.

Next morning at breakfast Perla said 'I heard you talking in your sleep when I came back from the shift. Did you have a bad dream?'

'Some trouble with the army,' said Ada spreading more white cheese on her slice of wholewheat bread.

'If there's any misbehaviour, report it to the commanding officer,' said Perla, 'I know they take a light view of anything to do with women. But if you nag them enough they'll have to do something about it.'

Perla considered herself an authority on military matters as she had volunteered to serve in the British army as a lorry driver in Egypt during Montgomery's campaign against Rommel. 'Yes,' she would say 'Corporal Perla Maiberg was an expert at digging lorry wheels out of sand. It was girls like us from Palestine that kept the Eighth Army moving. We had a reputation.'

In Tomas's studio it was growing dark. Ada looked out of the window at the valley. Weak points of light were starting to appear in the scattered houses on the other side. The wind was beginning to sigh more loudly and whistle and she searched in vain for a drop or two of rain on the dusty window pane. Tomas and Kronberg were talking quietly, head to head. Ada felt something of an intruder. When she said she was going, Tomas said, 'Come again whenever you feel like it. I'll show you where I put the key so you can get in when I'm not here. You can try working here if you like. I'm not in all the time and the light is good if it doesn't give you a headache.'

When she left the 'ruin' the few battered trees on the path up the hill towards the old railway station were creaking and bending in the wind. It was cold and raw and she felt a longing for home, though she didn't know what that could be. It wasn't the Carmel flat which seemed like a too shiny copy of somewhere else. Supposedly it meant a place where everything began, mother, father, child, safe walls, toys, soft clean linen, bright windows and music somewhere? She felt deprived of such a place and had been looking for it ever since childhood in the illustrations of books and in stories. Or she conjured one up around a pretty tower-shaped clock with a moon face which worked erratically now but had been brought by her mother from her home. In bed she would hear its whirr and ting as promising something comforting which fell into place while rooms and windows and smells of rain swam in and out of her consciousness and she fell asleep.

Perla sometimes spoke of a small apartment with a balcony overlooking a playground where Ada had been taken by her father and mother.

'You sat still on the rocking horse and watched the other children for hours. If Hitler hadn't marched in you'd probably still be there, watching, a woman on a rocking horse. You were a champion at watching others enjoying themselves.'

When Ada got to the Abyssinian palace Eyob Mulugeta, the tall monk from the nearby monastery who served as a kind of concierge, was standing at the main gate waiting for her.

'You had a visitor Madame,' he said.

He called her Madame even though they had become good friends and would sit together in the evenings with cups of strong tea listening in silence to the birds and the slowly fading noise of the street as the shops and garages closed and hawkers of nuts, matches and candles gave up and left the pavement.

'The visitor, he gave this letter for you.'

It was a postcard photo of Marlene Dietrich in American army uniform.

Ada, my darling niece, I'm here for the big trial. I have been summoned to teach your apprentice translators the art of speaking for the devil. Must see you, Rudi

She had first seen Rudi May in Paris when he was on the European leg of his lecture performance, Speaking for the Devil: A Ventriloquist at Nuremberg.

He had announced himself over the phone as 'Rudi, you know, your dear mother's brother,' and saying he had little time between Paris and Amsterdam called her out to meet him at a café opposite St Sulpice.

He picked her out quickly enough and kissed her on both cheeks.

'Look at you, the lady in black. And I expected an Amazon, a Mädchen in uniform, like your army photographs. But you still look like my sister Suzi, pure white skin and big eyes. We must catch up on what you're doing. Tell me, how are my formidable sisters?'

They sat there the whole evening while he heard nothing about his sisters but gave a vivid recital of his own adventures and achievements, beginning with the Nuremberg Trials where he had been one of the translators.

'Didn't your mother tell you about it? I'm sure she did. I sent photographs and long letters. But perhaps you were busy playing at doctor with the boy next door. How is she?'

Ada's mother would hold a glossy photograph in her long white fingers and they would all look at it together. It showed a large room like a meeting hall with men sitting on a dais with flags behind them and others sitting stiffly in rows like in a big classroom full of discipline and there were soldiers in white helmets standing on three sides of the room. Her mother pointed to a small blurred patch of white face at a table. That's Uncle Rudi she said. He's got earphones and he's wearing the American uniform. And those are monsters, she added, pointing to two rows of white faces sitting in the dock in front of a line of standing soldiers.

Rudi didn't stop for an answer about Suzi.

'I did write about it in many American newspapers and gave talks on the radio but you need to tell that story live for it to make a strong impression. That's what I'm doing on my tour. I act the scene out and bring people right into the middle of it all.

'And I've got some good photos, high drama; real courtroom stuff. Ladies and Gentlemen, I present Rudi May in the translator's role! *Taram*!!'

He spread his arms like a conductor marshalling his orchestra.

'I make it personal you see. After all it's my drama as well, even if I was only one of a team. Imagine! There they are across the room, the whole gang of them: Goering, Keitel, Speer, Kaltenbrunner and they have to speak through me. I am their mouthpiece.

'All that thick German. That hateful Nazi jargon. Dreary, thumping sentences and words a foot long. Grim stuff. Hours of it. But it stuck with me. Even today sentences suddenly pop up out of nowhere.'

He cleared his throat and puffed out his chest:

Das Ziel dieses deutschen Vorgehens soll eine in der Zukunft liegende internationale Lösung der Judenfrage sein, die nicht von falschem Mitleid mit der 'vertriebenen religiösen jüdischen Minderheit,' sondern von der gereiften Erkenntnis alle Völker diktiert ist.

'Bla bla und wieder mahl bla. How come those words didn't stick in my throat? That's what people ask me. They can't imagine me just doing the job as if it was normal. And I tell them. No. No problem at all. Rudi's throat is stick-proof, it's like the Suez Canal – anything that floats can sail through.'

He put a finger to his lips.

'Honestly, hand on heart, there was no vomiting by me because of what they said. I was tough and it was a test of wit and endurance.'

He arranged a pack of cigarettes, matches and a coffee spoon on the table to represent his position in the courtroom.

'So there I am, Rudi, facing them on my right and the judges to my left. I'm sitting still but it's like I'm moving between them, like a ping-pong ball. Click for German, clack for English.

'After a while I don't look at the villains at all, it takes my mind off what they are saying. I am no eyes, just ears, Rudi All-Ears. So I hear their sentences pushing their way, through the vocal system, like a column of soldiers, marching up to the front, *links, rechts, links, rechts*. And, ladies and gentlemen, before it is actually spoken, I know what the bastards want to say. Yes, I am ahead of them and I mean to stay there. Click and clack.'

He flicked a table tennis backhand over the cups on the café table.

'For this you need stamina like an athlete in a relay race. You get the baton, you run and have to pass it on in a hurry. No time to think. Run, pass it across again and again until the end and it's all over. Next day we start again. And the pay was good and the bourbon and the smokes from the PX were extra good. There were plenty of parties so we didn't get depressed or worn out. Rudi May a Yank at Nuremberg!'

He stopped for breath. There was a thin film of sweat on his brow.

'So, how are my sisters and how are you faring in Paris?'

He seemed sorry he had got to the end of the Nuremberg relay race. He looked at his watch and then at Ada for approval.

He was remarkably smart in a grey pin-striped suit that looked tailor-made and a military style raincoat. His perfectly regular features and white unblemished skin were those of a film star of the thirties: Ada could see him as Laszlo in *Casablanca*, even though his hair was a bit too curly to be taken seriously on a Resistance hero. His lips were feminine, pliant and plump, lacking only lipstick to seal them as a woman's and his eyes, unlike his speech, were dreamy, grey, sad and slow.

Ada had heard many stories about the clever, charming rapscallion Rudi who fled Vienna by himself or with a Swedish or perhaps Swiss dancer even before anyone realized what was about to happen. Perla would say he knew no rules. He used his charm like a hypnotist to make everybody do his will, especially the girls. He would walk into the house a completely different young man from the one who left only a few hours before. He was wearing the same clothes, the same felt hat and raincoat, the same briefcase under his arm but if he went out a travelling salesman in buttons and straps, he came back a count from an operetta. Where had he been to make that change? No-one in the family knew what to make of him. 'We all knew he was brilliant but at what?'

Ada could hear the hard edge in Perla's voice. She had been left to deal with their parents in their shuttered apartment as the clamour in the streets grew more and more menacing and the need to flee became urgent. She was the older sister and the quick-moving Rudi had gone.

Ada looked at him and saw traces of her mother, the same sad eyes, similar soft and regular features, the same sensual mouth. In spite of the bravado, Rudi's eyes, like her mother's, seemed to be searching for someone who would assure him of his worth and absolve him of bearing false witness and profiteering.

He had not come to see them after the trials, according to Perla, because he felt guilty at abandoning them all but they suspected there were other reasons though no-one spoke about the obviously German girl laughing next to him in one of the Nuremberg photographs who reappeared years later still laughing in a photo of a Thanksgiving gathering at Rudi's house in Oakland.

Trying to fall asleep Ada replayed that Paris meeting in her head but the Rudi she imagined now was a blurred copy of the handsome man in the café. She tried to reconstruct their conversation but her mother's face kept floating in. Ada wanted Rudi to look at her but he didn't and she was left, as sleep took over, with no Rudi and only her mother apologizing for letting the milk boil over again.

RUIN

MILO RANG HER at the ice factory the next day. She was in the middle of organizing a fittingly sober décor for the makeshift studio in which legal experts and historians would debate the day's proceedings of the big trial. Most of her work consisted in beating off the attempts of her bosses, ignorant and dazzled by the unknown medium of television, to make the studio resemble a furniture showroom or the lobby of the King David and she went on doggedly with her plan hoping they wouldn't notice till it was too late.

Milo had an idea to discuss with her. He realized how odd it was they hadn't really spoken to each other since he arrived in town but he didn't labour the matter. He wanted her help. He was cooking up a project, a fantastic project and he needed her to join in. Only she could handle it. Would she come to his place tomorrow? Other people would be there and it would be interesting.

I'll go, thought Ada, and I'll bring Rudi.

When she met Rudi at his hotel she saw a thinner, paler and altogether less flamboyant man than her companion at the St Sulpice café. The good looks were there as were the curly ranks of his shiny brown hair but he looked ill at ease with red eyes, perhaps from lack of sleep, and he wore a crumpled shirt that might have served him as a pyjama.

He embraced her and confessed immediately to being upset.

'I've only been here for 24 hours and I feel completely out of place. I've been in some strange towns but this must be the strangest.

The taxi driver asked me if I'd sell him my jacket and then they serve herring and sour cream for breakfast. It's not natural. The whole place is not natural. It's driving me to drink but the bar is never open. How can you live in a place like this?'

Ada took his hand like a doctor and stroked it to calm the patient down and ease the discomfort.

'You get used to it. In the end you give in.'

'You make it sound like tuberculosis. All I see from my window is a clump of thin trees and a bald lawn. Where is the old part? You know, the real thing.'

'On the other side. It's in Jordan and you can't cross over. Only Christians can do it, Easter and Christmas.'

She guessed Rudi was playing the game of the ignorant tourist protesting because a bedside lamp flickered and the water pressure was weak. Surely he knew the town was divided and the Old City forbidden territory. He's acting the stranger, she thought, preparing to meet his sisters after all these years as if he had never been their little brother. Now he was a new man, a Californian and an international lecturer and expert. She wasn't sure of what he was an expert but it had something to do with language teaching and bringing people of different cultures together and it involved a lot of travelling.

'If you want to see the Old City, you can look at it from Notre-Dame, a convent roof on our side of no man's land. It's quite interesting, and upsetting, like a puzzle you will never solve. We can go and do that later.'

Rudi looked at his watch.

'I mustn't be late for my meeting with the young translators. Where is Terra Sancta College?'

She put him in a taxi and arranged to meet him before going to Milo's for the next evening's event.

Standing alone outside the hotel she realized she couldn't go to the ice factory and deal with the officious bustle and the distracted workers who were supposed to be helping her. Instead she would collect some of her drawing materials and take up Tomas's offer of his ruin as a place to work. When she got to the house it was already afternoon and the steep hillside was lit by the stern glow of the winter sun which made the broken terraces, the olive trees and the house itself stand in strict separation from each other as if ordered to arrange themselves on some tilted military parade ground. Ada fumbled for the key under the stone Tomas had pointed out to her. It was large and heavy, not the kind you could carry around unless you tied it on a chain round your neck or tucked it into a peasant's broad cloth belt. The lock was stiff and she had to work with both hands till the door swung open and the room was hers.

The unfamiliar smell of a stranger's living space hit her immediately. It was spicy and backed up by smoke, kerosene, orange peel and a tinge of sweat. A large mattress she had not noticed before lay on the floor in an alcove. Some clothes were strewn around it and a colourful cloth had been spread over all haphazardly. A bottle of arak peeped out from beneath the tassels.

Ada walked over to the wall and the painting she had noticed the day before. Looking closely she could make out something scribbled under the naked woman in the bathtub: *tear at the heart of the sitz cutout where the cunt hides leave in a hurry betray witness*

She settled into one of the window recesses with her charcoal and drawing block and, impelled by she knew not what, began to draw a children's playground with seesaws and wooden horses and swings and slides but empty of children. Only blurred and shadowy adult figures stood around the playground's fence and one at the gate lifted a hand in a gesture, perhaps of goodbye.

She drew the scene a few times and couldn't bring herself to put children into it. Instead she put clocks, pots, kettles and meat grinders in the yard, on the swings and the wooden horses. On the seesaw she put two broken geranium pots, one on each side.

The light outside had softened and the room, though cold, had a restful, resolved look as if its emptiness was a deliberate and calm rejection of the randomness and clutter outside in the haphazard city with its unfinished pavements and forgotten trenches and naked, whitewashed blast walls blocking the doorways of houses.

23

Ada didn't put any light on and when Tomas came in he found her asleep in the window with her drawings scattered around her like handkerchiefs. He didn't wake her but put the light on in the kitchen corner and lit the kerosene stove to take the chill off. He sat at the kitchen table for a while looking at Ada's small black shape curled up in the window. In repose her face was that of a child, soft and round, shaped by shadows rather than bones. Between the blackness of her hair and the high neck of her sweater the white of her face glowed like a street lamp at night. Only the long tapering curves of her eyebrows spread a bold black repeated pen stroke across her forehead.

Tomas lay down on his mattress and waited for the call to prayer from the other side. He liked to listen with his glass of arak and ice. The rolling ribbon of sound, first thin and single, then fuller and bolder as it was joined by other calls from beyond the walls and across the valley, played a ragged, irregular accompaniment to the tinkling of ice in his glass as the pale cloudy liquid spread the good news into his throat.

Arak Akbar.

When the mosque chorus was in full cry, Ada woke up and swung quickly off the window recess. She saw the light from the kitchen and Tomas with his glass stretched out on his mattress looking at her.

'Have a drink, it helps with the dark.'

He poured her a glass and came over to the window. They watched the last gleam of day surrender as points of light began to signal from houses in the valley and beyond.

Tomas picked up some of the drawings she had dropped on the floor.

'You didn't see this from here,' he said.

'No.'

'There's no playground. The kids run about in trenches and caves. So where's your playground?'

'It's where your roof and bathtub is.'

Tomas laughed.

'That's right here, down there in the valley. I can see the roof at night when there's moonlight but it's gone by dawn. It's an abandoned ghost roof.'

Ada picked up the rest of her drawings.

'The woman in the tub, she doesn't look abandoned.'

'No she isn't. You're right. She's just been left behind but not forgotten.'

Ada collected her things and headed for the door.

'Thanks for letting me come. It's good this place.'

Tomas stood with his back to the window and waved.

'Come any time, even when I'm here. There's room.'

Puppets

THE NEXT TIME she saw Tomas was in the crowd of guests at Milo's party.

She had brought Rudi who was in a far better state. He had met the apprentice translators and found them appreciative and even in awe of the man from Nuremberg.

'You should have seen them perk up when I played them my precious recording. First Goering's voice, annoyed and too loud and then mine, calm and objective; I warned them about the dangers of falling into the drama trap.'

'Never dramatise the defendant,' I told them. 'Don't hate him. Stay cool and calm. Stick in your laboratory and report on the experiment. Leave the drama for your friends in the bar, afterwards. I hope I didn't make it sound boring. I promised them an exercise with long German sentences and a stop watch. That could be fun, something to look forward to.'

He certainly didn't look boring. Rudi the charmer, the international Californian, was dressed for Milo's party in a white suit and a golden yellow shirt with an open collar and a wine-red cravat carefully tucked inside. Once there he put down his present, a bottle of Irish whiskey, with a flourish and clapped his hands boyishly at the yelps of enthusiasm from the jaded drinkers of arak, laboratory-concocted vodka and Cognac Medicinal.

Milo's 'party room' was the grand reception room of a rich Arab's house which apparently was in its turn built on a sheikh's tomb and a Byzantine hermit's cave.

Faded, chipped inscriptions in Arabic and Greek on bits of broken stone stuck haphazardly into the walls were interpreted one way or the other by self-appointed experts and the repeated violations of the grave's holiness had occurred so far back that no-one cared. The room was totally white with a great arched ceiling that invited the world into its tent or shut it out depending on your mood as you looked up and around then rested your eye finally on a curved recess holding two deeply-set windows looking out towards the north and the Old City.

The crowd in the room was noisy, Grapelli and Django were beating up the rhythm as dancers, drinkers and talkers pressed up against each other and conversation became shouting and smoke took over from air. *Sweet Georgia Brown* was getting the crowd to stomp and sing when Ada found herself face to face with Milo by the food table. He was sweating and flushed, giving his dark complexion an explosive livid coating but he was enjoying himself and the deep lines on his face stretched happily into a series of grins and laughs as he greeted his guests, waved and shouted names across the room.

'Enfin, Ada'le, cara bella,' he said, 'where have you been? I've been looking for you?'

'Not so far away.'

'Don't you miss me? Because I've been longing to talk to you for weeks. I'm heavy with a magnificent project and you're the midwife. Without you it can't happen, it's no go. I mean it.'

What's he trying to do, she thought. What's this enthusiasm? Is this the professor of despair?

'Look at this,' he said, taking a glossy card out of his jeans pocket. It was a photograph of the nuclear cloud over Hiroshima.

'And this.' On the reverse was a drawing of a ship with the head and shoulders of a bearded man sticking out of a turret above the deck. In his hand he held a bird. It was Noah.

'What are these, illustrations for a Bible class?'

'No. They're outlines for a show like no-one here has ever seen. It's about the end of the world. It's a warning. We present the Flood

27

as an auto-da-fé for our time. This we will do here in Jerusalem, in the street with the trial inside and the warring hosts outside and screw any bastards who try to stop us. You are the only one I can trust to make it come out right. You've got the knack. You see things right.'

He put his drink down and hugged her. Alcohol and tobacco were there and she felt the warmth of his body through their clothes. She returned his pressure calmly, balancing herself carefully on both feet like a wrestler judging an opponent.

'You know I'm doing the set-up for the television broadcast of the trial.'

'Nonsense. That's not real. It's drudgery. It's politics. Eichmann, that's all stuck in the past. What we'll do is an act of defiance and revolution. It's going to show all the shits and the whole world that we are not blinded by self-pity. We're not pale ghosts. And we can look at the worst without fear. We're alive, maybe not for long, and we have something shocking to say. You may not want to hear it but listen people, it's us. Tell me I'm a bullshitter.'

He looked at her with cunning eyes and a knowing grin.

'I'm not talking nonsense. You must know it. You know me better than anyone.'

Django's rippling cascades were bouncing faster and faster around the arched room, pushing voices higher and louder so that the babble seemed to lift the white tent off its moorings like a balloon filled with noise. On a rickety card table by the window the poet Julius stood in his baggy jeans and khaki shirt. His legs were bandy like an old sailor's, his boots were so misshapen that some large animal might have chewed them up and spewed them out, and he was waving his blue beret, shouting a No Man's Calypso through his beard into the wall of sound:

O THE MANDELBAUM GATE
SHE A MIGHTY FINE GATE
O THE MANDELBAUM GATE
SHE BE CLOSE AT EIGHT

28

O YOU GOTTA BRING A PASS
OR THEY KICK YOU UP THE ASS
AND YOU NEVER GET TO HEAVEN
THROUGH THE MANDELBAUM GATE

Somebody turned down the music and from one end of the room
came the strangled sound of a trumpet. It was pitched high and
rough and at first the tune didn't appear, hidden behind false starts,
spurts of sound and sudden changes. Then it resolved itself into a
free and rousing version of 'Viva Espana' and the whole crowd, even
the drunks, swung into the irresistible half-march, half-dance of the
paso doble.

Milo took Ada into the middle of the dancers and she waved at
Rudi who seemed to be dancing with two girls and had taken off
his jacket. He was flushed and there were sweat stains under his
arms. The neat curly crown of his hair had collapsed and thrown
woolly strands in all directions. The carefully tied cravat at his neck
was gone. As he bounced up and down, both his hands pointed at
the ceiling forcefully as if he was commanding heaven to get the hell
out of his way.

This isn't California Rudi, she thought. He's becoming one of
us, a borderline madman.

Eventually the trumpeter ran out of breath and the mass of
dancers dispersed into small knots of people talking more quietly
in different parts of the room. Tomas came over to Ada and took
her by the hand.

'Come and I'll show you the cistern. There's a full moon and it's
worth seeing.'

He seemed much more composed than anyone in the noisy, tipsy
crowd. His face in the dim light had an ascetic, almost Nordic look,
with his white skin stretched tightly over the sharp angles of his
cheek bones. His blue eyes floated over lips as straight as thin pencils.
He's a kind of Robespierre, she thought. A cold flame. He's outside
all this sweat and noise.

She looked round to see what Milo was doing. He was laughing

29

with Rudi and some others over the plates of olives and the remains of the punch.

She followed Tomas out into the garden. Everything was pale blue or black in the crisp and cold moonlight. The broad stone terrace with its table and chairs seemed like the deck of a ship in a silent sea bounded by the black shapes of tall cypresses and stunted olive trees. Tomas beckoned to her from the head of some stairs hewn into the stone beneath the house. He took a torch out of his pocket and led her down rough, uneven steps into a hole or a cave or even a storage basement of the house. It was dry but smelled of water and slime and the wet coats of animals. Strewn around on the floor and in recesses were clay storage vessels and empty jerry cans. Tomas's torch picked out a white enamel tray. FRÈRES MATOUSSIAN EXHIBITION LE CAIRE was printed across it in bold black letters. It was hardly chipped and seemed to have some connection with a stove or some kitchen utensil which had been taken away or perhaps looted. Tomas's light wandered irregularly round the walls. He seemed to be looking for something. Then it stopped at a shelf in the rock and he took her by the hand to show her. 'Feel this,' he said, guiding her fingers over the rough damp stone. 'Do you feel something? And this?' He took her other hand and moved them both in small circles next to each other on the wall. He had turned the torch off and his hands were guiding hers firmly in the same circling repetitive movement. 'What is it?' she asked, feeling foolish at not being able to come up with an answer from the touch of her hands. He seemed eager she should make something out with her touch in the darkness but she could get no further than the shapeless roughness of the rock under her fingers and the fear of creeping things or of slime that kept her muscles resistant to Tomas's guiding hand.

'They're breasts – a woman's breasts and her belly beneath them – don't you feel it?'

She started to laugh but suppressed it sensing Tomas's seriousness. 'Couldn't it just be the shape of the rock? There are plenty of natural bumps and hollows.'

'Yes, but there are more of them in the same arrangement. I've found a few and I haven't looked everywhere.'

The thought of Tomas's hands feeling the rock methodically, inch by inch, and groping in the dark for bellies and bosoms seemed so absurd that she couldn't restrain her laughter. He had moved further away and was pointing the torch beam at a higher stretch of the rock.

'Milo also laughs at me,' he said. 'But I bet there's something up there. I need a tall ladder but it's almost impossible to get something like that down the stairs. These cisterns or whatever they were once, graves or caves or the way into tunnels, they bother me. I see a house and I imagine what kind of hole it is sitting on and where it leads to. It's quite bad sometimes. I sit at my window and look at the houses opposite on their side and it's like I am seeing the hollow roots of a big tree pushing through the earth in all directions but especially towards me.'

Tomas led her up the stairs and they stopped in the garden. He seemed excited and eager to talk and as he talked his hands moved around him like wings.

'When I was a kid I heard our neighbour, old Berko, talking to my father. He was telling him about tunnels in the earth. And he said that when dead Jews got buried they waited in their graves for the tunnels to open up and when the time comes they would roll through them for thousands of miles till they ended up in Jerusalem. Then they would stand up, the dead would. My father laughed but I remembered.

'I used to draw whole maps of underground tunnels especially when I was living with the Poles. They didn't have any paper so I drew on anything, the walls (I'd get smacked for that), with chalk on the floor, with a knife on the bark of trees, with sticks in the mud. But I never really got to crawl into something deep underground. There was too much mud and wet earth. Anyway I don't remember.

'It was only when I got here that I came across cisterns and tunnels cut in the rock. The first ones I saw at some archaeological site made me feel dizzy with recognition. It was a smell I had never smelled before

31

but I knew it, stone and heat and dry earth. No shit, no dead dogs, nothing wet. They had cleaned it up, even put glass over some scratchings on the wall. But that didn't interest me. It was the hole itself, like an open door and the tunnel that led you deeper but you couldn't crawl into it. They gave me a good feeling, some kind of confidence that I would be safe, that I would be dry, that I wouldn't rot.'

It was cold but Ada hesitated. She didn't want to go back into the crowd and the light. Tomas was quiet now and had drawn his slight body and delicate head into something like a cocoon in the dark, or a statue. She put a hand on his shoulder and he shook himself as if coming out of a reverie.

'If we stay much longer out here they'll have to thaw us out.'

He took her hand and they went back into the room.

Many of the guests had gone and the lights were being turned off. Couples who couldn't drag themselves away were lying on cushions whispering and embracing. Rudi was nowhere in sight. A few people were gathered around Julius, who was singing a Sufi chant in a hoarse whisper and keeping rhythm with a shoe on an empty pail. Kronberg emerged from the dark, walking unsteadily with a fixed, unnatural smile on his face. He looked at Tomas, 'Where have you been hiding. I thought you'd perhaps gone home.' He smiled distantly at Ada. Tomas said nothing. He walked to the door slowly and Kronberg followed him leaving Ada standing in a smear of spilled wine and cigarette butts.

She went over to where Julius was singing and sat on a mattress between a couple of apparently sleeping bodies. Julius was using one of his boots to beat out the rhythm and she noticed that there were more holes in the sole than leather. The grey sock on his foot was in even worse shape. But he looked healthy and warm. His thick black, silky beard tumbled off his pale face onto his chest and his lips moved within the hair like small red fish wriggling in a net. To Ada he looked like a young, well-fed prophet. Julius raised his eyebrows, questioning her without interrupting his chant, 'LI-LLAHI-RABBI-L-ALAMIN, AR-RAHMANI-R-RAHIM…'

32

She sat and swayed, letting the soft hissing and guttural sounds lull her into a passive and receptive state. In Julius's mouth the words took on an odd English colour but the Arabic prevailed and spread comfort with its slow, drumming repetitions – *mercylordworld, mercylordworld, mercy, merciful, mercy...*

'Drat this!' Julius said suddenly. He had stopped the chant and was struggling to put his boot on.

Ada crawled over the mattress to help him.

'Beware lurking scorpions.' He watched her free the laces and guide his foot inside.

'Unnatural kicker. Where have you been Darkness? Why haven't you come to visit? It's weeks now and I have no female audience for my randy philosophers. Don't tell me you've been avoiding me because of the shooting in my back yard. It was all a misunderstanding. Idiocy. They sent two garbage trucks for the annual cleanup and one of them reversed into the barbed wire and knocked over two empty oil drums which rolled down the hill making a terrific noise. Bang Bang Hashemite. Bang Bang Israelite. Sha Shtill Silenzio United Nations.' He put a finger to his lips.

'You know, Julius, it's not the shooting. It's the big trial I'm working for. The television studio I'm setting up.'

Julius looked interested.

'Do you think we could get my philosophers in front of the cameras? One failing they don't have is stage fright. Puppets have to perform. It's a matter of life and death for them. If they don't perform gangrene sets in. Also here.' He pointed at his forehead.

'Where's Tomas?'

'He went home, with Kronberg.'

Julius whistled and pointed in the direction of Tomas's house.

'He'll huff and he'll puff and he'll blow the house down. It's just a push and everything goes.'

'What do you mean,' said Ada.

'He wants Tomas to go with him to Würzburg. There's no no man's land there and he'll have money and a nice set-up. Kronberg knows how to handle the Germans.'

33

'So, if Tomas agrees what's the problem?'

'Right. But who is Tomas?'

'Come, I'll walk you down to the road.'

The room was quite dark and there was no sign of Milo. A sweetish smoky smell hung in the air. It was the kind of hasheesh smuggled in from Lebanon; Milo had ways of getting it whatever the police did.

As they walked out into the night Julius led the way up a rough path to the remnants of the old Turkish military bandstand at the top of the hill. There was no wind and no sound of any kind. They stood on the little, oddly shaped platform with its floor of broken tiles and crumbling balustrade and looked at the slope leading down to the valley. There were no lights in the scattered houses. But Tomas's place was lit up at the entrance and at the windows.

Ada tried not to look but her eye was drawn to two figures by the open door. The smaller one was hunched over and seemed to be covering his face with his hands. The other seemed to be staring impassively or fixedly at his companion. Then abruptly he turned away and started walking down the hill towards the Hebron road.

'You see said Julius, Kronberg knows about Tomas, or knows most of it. But that doesn't stop him being cruel, because he thinks he knows what's best for him.'

'How do you know all this?'

'Well, unlike you, Tomas isn't put off by fireworks. Anyway he comes to me for tea and arak and I read him stuff and we talk. He likes the puppet philosophers too. He's got unusual ideas for them. There's a neat mixture of metaphysics and handyman in him. When I get a threatening letter from the Greeks about my roof repair or the new telephone line I show it to him and he's very good at thinking up delaying tactics, better than lawyers and free.'

'Look, Darkness, why go searching for a taxi at this time of the night. Come and sleep over. I've left the stove on. It's warm and cosy, if you don't mind the stink.'

For Ada Julius was a famous celibate and therefore could be a friend without complications. He would only fall in love, and then

34

briefly, with an impossibly idealized creature. She was sometimes even a woman, often a quite ordinary transient, an exchange student in town for a while or a dreamily earnest Dutch lady seeking enlightenment. But quite often it wasn't a real woman he worshipped hopelessly. Once it was Sappho to whom he wrote love poems and Diotima to whom he composed verse letters. But there was also Monica Vitti, Margot Fonteyn and a stone, the German inscription carved in beautifully elaborate Gothic lettering over the door of a Templer house in the German Colony: MACHE DICH AUF! WERDE LICHT; DENN DEIN LICHT KOMMT.

He had an obsessive love for the inscription, a verse from Isaiah, placed there in 1890 by the devout Christians who built the house when they settled in Ottoman Palestine. A day didn't go by without him visiting it, standing by the steps at the front door and mouthing Luther's German as if it was a spell made to banish all darkness. She had seen him there herself, loitering in the rain, probably hungry, unkempt, a gleam in his eyes, his beret soaked through. He was afraid the tenants would try to remove it or harm it in some way because it was German and hateful to them. He had considered appealing to them to take care of it and volunteer to clean it of soot and bird droppings but his friends had convinced him that it was a bad idea. It would only draw attention to something the family may not even have noticed. As it was they became suspicious of the strange man who kept watch at their door and had the police come to look him over. After a brief talk the officer treated him as a harmless oddity and put him down as yet another one of the collection of salvation seekers who wandered about Jerusalem with prayers in their pockets.

'I'll come,' said Ada. 'Thanks.'

Julius's house was built on ground that had at some stage belonged to the Greek Church. They claimed it was part of the complex of a basilica, traces of which had been dug up and which might have occupied quite a stretch of the hill around the ruined Turkish bandstand. But the winding border line and Jordanian protests made the dig too problematic and Julius was allowed to pay rent to the Greeks on condition he made no changes and didn't dig in his garden. Margarian, the Greeks' lawyer, would pay visits to discuss the rent and make sure Julius was not digging or disturbing the status quo in other ways. He was a small distinguished-looking gentleman, an elder of the small Armenian community and he always wore a suit and a shirt with a tie even in the hottest weather.

'Mr Julius' he would say, 'only in pots. This geranium and this basil, even this tomato whatever you like, put them in pots. Such way there is no digging and everybody is happy. The earth, you know, belongs to Almighty God who gave it to the Greek Church.'

He would point at the sky and at the ground with a two-handed all-inclusive gesture that left no room for argument. Margarian quite liked the idea of having a poet for a tenant and consulted Julius on the rhymed birthday greetings he sent his nieces in Pasadena but made it clear that he could not expect to get ahead in life if all he did was write poetry and edit copy for the newspaper at night. 'Do your parents agree for you to become a poet?' That was his way of saying that Julius's economic future was, to say the least, doubtful and no way would he allow a daughter of his to marry him even if he converted and became an Armenian Christian.

Julius battled with the ill-fitting iron door, gave it a mighty kick and a gust of warm fetid air hit them as they stepped down the stairs that led into the room. Two large puppets hung from the hook at the centre of the domed ceiling. They were long, stick dolls with roughly moulded scornful faces, painted brown, green, pink and red. One head was topped by a conical hat, another by a turban. Swinging slightly next to each other, occasionally meeting nose to nose, bulging eye to staring eye, jaw confronting jaw, they looked like a pair of duellists in some Arabian cursing contest performed before an amused Caliph and his court.

'There's your bed,' said Julius and pointed to a mattress placed in the broad arched recess of the window. 'Not enough blankets but we can leave the heater on.'

He sighed and walked heavily over to his bed, untied his boots, then flopped down fully clothed and began to snore.

Ada sat by the window and watched the puppets. The weak light from the one bare bulb in the kitchen robbed them of any individuality. They loomed there, strung up and idly floating, like large exhausted birds seeking a surface on which to land. She knew them well. She had been with Julius when he had wheedled them out of the difficult, eternally angry Sasson brothers in their impossibly crowded and filthy shop in Jaffa Road. The sign above the entrance in faded blue paint proclaimed: BROT RS SASSON W RLDWI E B ZAAR but it was hardly visible and behind the years of dust, the shop window seemed to display nothing but random piles of wrapping paper, cardboard boxes, old telephone directories, some cracked mirrors and a framed photograph of a bearded old man in a turban.

The brothers (some said they were twins but this was by no means clear), were frail, bony and stooping dark men in their sixties who had opened their shop just after the First World War and filled it with toys, dolls, music boxes, conjuring sets, masks and paper hats and all kinds of bric-a-brac they had bought in the course of a world tour a few years later. No-one knew why they had stocked their shop with such things rather than the more usual kitchen ware or cosmetics or fake antiques. They presumably made some kind of living, which could not have been so hard as neither had married. But by the time she and Julius came to know them, their shop had become a dark mouldy fortress, piled high with unmarked cardboard boxes and parcels wrapped in newspaper, while the two of them kept guard against customers from behind forbiddingly high counters.

Julius had penetrated the shop's defences by falling through the door dragging Ada with him one very wet and windy morning, bringing down on their heads a heap of paper parasols from Shanghai. They were sheltering from the storm and had no idea of what was in there. But when the brothers Sasson, taken by surprise,

37

had satisfied themselves that their door was undamaged they agreed to sell him an umbrella. Much later Julius realized how unusual this was. The Sasson brothers had hardly let any one into the shop for years, let alone selling anything, not even an umbrella. They did not even admit it was a shop and were conducting an interminable law case with the municipality claiming the property should be taxed as a storage space and that nothing had been sold there for twenty years. But the sight of Julius and Ada, wet through, her coat drenched, his beard dripping, a woollen cap pulled over his ears and his army surplus bomber jacket unbuttoned because it could not fit around his two sweaters, failed to arouse the usual antagonism. Instead of snapping at them like nervous dogs and shooing them out into the rain they stared at them in silence and when Julius spoke to them in English, apologized for their rough arrival and promised to pay for anything he had accidentally broken, Ezra Sasson climbed a ladder, rummaged among the boxes on a high shelf and threw down a towel.

'From Manchester,' he said, watching Julius dry his face and pat Ada's hair.

'So am I,' said Julius. 'From Manchester.'

They both stared at him and Ezra, making a lot of noise grunting and pushing boxes from one side to another until he finally found what he was looking for, threw a small item wrapped in faded newspaper at Julius who caught it.

'Also from Manchester.'

Julius unfolded the paper, his eyes smarting from the dust, a red and green and yellow tin music box with a handle appeared, shining and brightly painted with clown faces and suns and moons. He took it in his palm and turned the handle. The tinkle was remarkably loud and filled the crowded shop.

O I do like to be beside the sea side.
I do like to be beside the sea.

Julius sang alongside the tinkle in the falsetto of a lisping girl. The Sasson brothers laughed.

Julius bought the music box and an umbrella then became a regular visitor to Bazaar Sasson, discovering partly by accident and partly by cunning in roundabout conversations that they had a hoard which they were reluctant to show and wouldn't sell; certainly not to idiots who pushed their way into the shop and asked for ping-pong bats or crayons.

Gradually he found out about their Czech masks, Russian dolls, wind-up cars, motorcyclists and tanks from Germany and stick puppets from Java by way of Amsterdam. But he was careful not to show much interest in buying. Just looking, he would tell them. After putting them off their guard he enlisted Ada in an attempt to buy them.

When she entered the gloom of the shop one evening with Julius she saw the two brothers in the light of the one bulb looking like sharp beaked parrots perched behind dirty glass in some desolate zoo. One wore very thick glasses, the other had a flat cap on his head but its peak was missing.

They peered at her, ignoring Julius.

All were still for a while.

Then Ada, on cue, rummaged in her bag and brought out Roxana, her one Turkish doll. She was all spangles and scarves and once had a veil but her left arm was missing, pulled off and trodden on in the last rape and robbery. She placed her gently on the counter in front of the brothers like a patient on a stretcher.

They all looked at the invalid doll in silence.

'Maybe you have a spare arm to fit her,' said Ada.

Without saying anything Sami Sasson bent down and crawled into the space under one of the counters. They saw nothing but heard crackling and tearing noises and Sami saying '*Pas ça, pas ça, merde...*' sneezing as the dust penetrated his nostrils. Then he surfaced with a tin biscuit box, handed it to Ezra who prized open the lid with a teaspoon revealing a miscellany of doll parts, heads, hair, arms, legs, dresses, handbags, jewellery.

'Here. Look,' said Ezra pushing the box at Ada as if accusing her of criminal neglect. Then he seemed to lose all interest in her

39

and resumed a conversation he could have begun with Julius during an earlier visit.

'Amsterdam is too dirty. The dogs make *kaka* all over the *trottoirs*. But there are things from all over the world because the Dutch made an Empire like the British so ships bring stuff all the time.'

'Like what things?'

'Stuff …batik and also gongs and moving dolls and silk and jewels.'

'So did you bring batik?'

'Some.'

'And moving dolls?'

'A few.'

'I've found an arm,' said Ada, 'and I think it fits.'

They watched her trying to ease the arm into the hole under Roxana's shoulder. It almost fit so Kronberg would have to be consulted but the arm was much darker than the rest of Roxana's chubby pink body and too long. So Kronberg would have to operate.

She was going to say: How much? When she remembered Julius's threat, if you mention money directly they'll throw you out. So she put the arm on the counter and put her nose back in the biscuit tin as if she was still searching.

Julius made a move.

'People today don't appreciate those moving dolls. They buy things with batteries but before you can say Bob's your uncle, they stop working.'

Sami laughed, '"Bob's your Uncle but he's done your dad. Ask your mum, ask your mum," – that's the song the British soldiers used to sing in the street outside here by the beer shop.'

Julius detected a moment of nostalgia and seized his chance.

'I think you can make the moving dolls dance to music you play or songs you sing. You have to practise but that's what they can do. Isn't it?'

The brothers looked at each other then Ezra moved the ladder to another corner climbed up and pulled a parcel off a shelf piled high.

Julius unfolded the wrapping paper delicately as if he was removing a shroud. The angry faces of two Javanese puppets stared straight at him from their lair. Their beaks and bulging eyes were those of the Sasson brothers. They were dressed in brightly coloured batik skirts still crisp and uncreased.

Julius stayed calm.

'Someone should write words and songs for them. Then they could dance. That is what they were made for. Lying on a shelf in a parcel is like being dead for them. Like being buried.'

Ada felt the tension and wondered if Julius hadn't gone too far.

'You can do this, write words and songs?' said Sami.

Julius stretched out his arms like wings and in a half voice, soft and breathy, turning his head to right and left, sang out the Sanskrit chant he had learnt from a travelling American beatnik on his way to India to join Allen Ginsberg: *Sambasada Shiva Sambasada Shiva Sambasada Shiva, jay jay Om.*

Ezra looked startled as Julius repeated the chant again and again but he gradually sunk into himself and contemplated the puppets with his hands behind his back. Then he seemed to wake up, scribbled something on a piece of a page torn out of a telephone book and gave it to Sami who returned it impassively.

'We give you them,' said Ezra, 'but not completely. When you finish what you do with them you will bring them back. In good condition.'

The men shook hands, leaving Ada staring at the pile of doll parts and one-armed Roxana on the counter.

In the room the airless heat and Julius's snoring made it impossible for Ada to sleep so she put on her coat and went outside into the clear fresh night. The only sound breaking the stillness was the howling of jackals from the direction of the watershed and the desert. The chill air cleared away all her tiredness and filled her with energy as high as if she had just drunk a strong cup of coffee. To get her blood flowing she started to walk in the direction of the bandstand. When she got there she was surprised to see the lights in Tomas's house still burning. The light they cast into the night was so strong that the house looked like a cruise liner sailing through a dark sea.

The path down from the bandstand was treacherous – full of holes and sudden dips. Loose stones and cement blocks tested her balance at every step. Concentrating on where to put her feet she didn't notice Tomas till she was almost up against him. He was standing in the dark just outside the pool of light created by the open door. He had no coat no shoes or socks either and he was trying to light a cigarette. Tomas showed no surprise but looked at her as if she was some inanimate object, a tree or a wheelbarrow which had come between him and his concentration on striking a match. He finally succeeded and inhaled the smoke with a sigh. She recognized the sweet smell.

'I couldn't sleep,' she said. 'Julius…'

'The big snorer,' he guessed. 'I can practically hear it from down here and when he dreams he sings. You could have stayed here. I'm a quiet sleeper.'

'We saw you and Kronberg earlier, at the door. I thought of coming down but you looked as if you'd had enough.'

'Kronberg is a good friend. I owe him a lot. But sometimes it gets to be too much. Here have a pull on it, it'll help you stay warm.' He offered her the joint. His outstretched hand trembled and his eyes moved restlessly as if he couldn't decide where to look, at her or the darkness surrounding them.

She inhaled, knowing it would do little for her in a situation like this, on a doorstep, in the cold, with jackals calling in the hills and no wine or music.

'Kronberg is going to Würzburg?'

'He goes wherever he wants. Aren't you cold? You are. So come inside and stop shivering.'

He led the way into the brightly lit room. For a while they stood there awkwardly not far from the door then he took her by the hand and led her to the broad window recess. He boiled some water and made tea with mint leaves. They sat there sipping the hot fragrant drink and Ada noticed that the large painting of the dome and the roof and the woman in a bath had been taken down and was now propped up against the wall. It had been worked on. The bathtub was more like a trap and emphasized in thicker strokes imprisoning the woman whose face had been distorted and painted over and was now more a feline mask. The hat previously on her head was now hovering above it like a straw halo. The night sky had tongues of fire in it…She wanted to ask him about it but she didn't know how. He pointed to the painting.

'I found that bathtub in a scrap yard by the railway station. There was lots of stuff there from houses that had been looted, broken furniture, ironwork, tiles, copper boilers anything. The yard was pretty filthy, all that sand and rust but the tub was still white under the dirt, almost new. It had a name, the firm I suppose, PAULAINE. That was my mother's name, Paulina. So I bought it. It was useless because I couldn't fit a bathtub in here. And for a while it stood out there by the door. It didn't stay white for long, not with the pigeons and the dogs around here. But it made me imagine I remembered her. It made me think I remembered her in the bath squeezing a sponge over her back. But I must have made it up.'

'So you painted her.'

'No. I don't remember what she looked like. Maybe the hair and the shape of her face. But if her name is Paulina she must look like a cat, why not?'

He pointed at the painting and laughed. 'Then I realized, it's in the Bible. She's in a tub on a roof. David spies her and sends her husband into the minefields. She's soaking in the tub on a roof near no man's land but downstairs the house is empty because they've all run away. Somebody told them the soldiers were raping their daughters. But they forgot her. Fools, they were looking for bathtubs and copper boilers, not their daughters, not their wives.'

From outside there was a noise of stones being kicked and something metal falling over with a clang. Somebody cursed in a loud voice and then shouted 'Hello, is anybody there?'

Tomas went to the door and found Rudi dishevelled and holding a bleeding hand up in a Roman salute.

'Shit,' he said. 'How long is it going to take them to fix some street lighting? It's like the belly of the whale out there.'

Rudi looked quite wild. His suit was stained with spilled wine and his face had livid scratch marks on cheeks and brow.

He looked at Ada without surprise.

'I put the girls in a taxi and I started up the hill to get back but got off the path in the dark and I didn't see any lights. So I pushed on and I seemed to be going down instead of up then I fell into some kind of hole or trench. I had to pull on putrid thorns and barbed wire to scramble out and I blundered on for a bit till I saw your light. So the party isn't over?'

He smiled at them, returning to his old self.

'What are you drinking? Tea! Clever idea. Let me wash this blood off.'

He went into the bathroom and when he came out he sipped the tea with pleasure and stared at the painting. He seemed a bit drunk still.

'Who's the beauty in the tub?'

'Bathsheba,' said Tomas.

Rudi half looked at the painting and yawned.

'D'you have a blanket?' he asked. 'I think I have to rest a bit or I'll get into more trouble.'

He took the blanket Tomas gave him and went over to a straw mat in a corner wrapped himself around like an old soldier put his jacket under his head turned to the wall and fell asleep.

'Come' said Tomas. 'It'll be too late to go to sleep soon.' He led Ada to his mattress and they both lay down in their clothes. He covered her gently with a blanket and she let the warmth creep around her and lull her. He was near her, she could hear his breathing and smell traces of the hasheesh but he lay still. We are like children, she thought, children run away from home, lost and overtaken by sleep.

FAMILY

RUDI RANG HER and said he was staying longer than he had planned. The translation workshop was going well and Ulli, his wife, was coming to join him. He had wanted Ulli to meet his sisters for ages and now was the time but he needed to go first with Ada, perhaps this weekend, to straighten things out because of the many years they hadn't seen each other and 'All the misunderstandings, you know.'

In the bus he asked her about Suzi directly for the first time.

'I got hints from Perla but nothing direct. She had some kind of breakdown? I figured that out. She can beat it, you know. They keep coming up with better medicines. Do they know about meditation here?'

Ada closed her eyes and Rudi didn't press her.

He would find out soon enough, all the things he had avoided mentioning, the questions he had preferred not to ask in his impersonal but self-congratulatory letters that would turn up like mosquitos in a sweaty night, offensive, troubling, demanding to be dealt with.

Meanwhile the steady rumbling progress of the half-empty bus rocked him till he closed his eyes, sighed and sank back in his seat. His handsome, well-shaven face, dabbed that morning with a delicate fragrance, could have been drawn by a Florentine master. Feathery long eyelashes caressed the milky skin beneath them, lips formed a graceful bow and the nose brought no coarseness into the picture but gave the pleasing lines a manly, tapering signature.

'Why shouldn't he be pleased with himself?' Perla would say.

45

'God knows he's had everything his way since he was in short pants. At school they called him Lucky Rudi. He broke the rules but he was hardly ever caught. So now he's the all-American star, touring the world in his Nuremberg show and making it a story with a happy end. Cultural Exchange and Cooperation! Popcorn and ice cream. Fine if you have a pool in the garden and a car that looks like a wedding cake. What can they know about the real world in California?' She made it sound like an amusement park.

From her bedroom years ago when she was still at school Ada would hear Perla and Suzi reading Rudi's letters out loud to each other, adding little tunes of their own to liven up the dry reportage.

Dear Sisters,
My recent trip to Scandinavia with a Californian young leadership delegation was an unqualified success. *Tra la lalala*
I met many important people in the field of cultural communication and language teaching including Gunilla Unqvest whom you must have heard of and who is very interested in my idea of operating a network of language schools in areas of political and military conflict. *Tam te tam tetamtetam*
After many long but interesting meetings with experts I was able to find time to see the sights including the royal palace, the Viking Information Centre and an ultra-modern fish-smoking plant. *Phooooo*
In a month I travel again. This time to attend a Cultural Exchange Fair in Tokyo where I will address one of the main sessions on: SPELLING FOR PEACE.
I hope you are both well and the princess too.
Birthdays are coming up soon
SO STAY HAPPY
Your brother,
Rudi
PS I checked with the Swedish Red Cross to see if they had any record of Walter but there was nothing.

'Is Papy hiding with Uncle Rudi?'

Young Ada was desperate to find her Papy because Suzi had promised that he would be home some time soon and when he didn't come she didn't like to talk about him too much or answer the girl's persistent questions. They had some small photographs in a brown envelope. Oma and Opa looking startled, straight at the camera as if it was going to jump at them. School journeys. Suzi in a white dress and Papy by her side in a suit. One was of a picnic on a hillside with big trees all around. They said that the baby doing a push up on the blanket was Ada. But Ada wasn't interested in that baby. She looked and looked at Papy trying to make out his smile and burrow into his eyes which were screwed up against the sunlight.

Suzi told her that Papy was very strong and clever and had gone in a train to find a place for them all to be safe till the war was over and then they would be together. But he had got lost and they didn't know where. After the war they asked Rudi to look for him because Rudi was right there in Nuremberg and could get cars from the American army. But nothing.

Ada would lie in bed listening for a car to stop in the quiet street or for a knock on the door. It was always at night when she listened not expecting him to come in daylight, in the bright sunlight and the heat or when she was busy doing homework. How could Papy come in the middle of logarithm tables or the Hasmonean wars or even a game of draughts with Lilah next door? No he would come when it was quiet in the night and only she was waiting and he would bring light with him.

She learned not to talk to Suzi about Papy and found a friend in school whose father had been killed in a war though she was lucky and had a grave to visit once a year with her mother and brothers. Still Ada could tell her about Papy, even making up stories so that she would have a more real father who said and did things and not just a name and a small photograph with creases so that from staring at it you saw nothing.

This weekend Suzi would be home and as they climbed the stairs Ada felt some pity for poor Rudi who was about to face sisters he had not seen for so many years and whom he had kept at bay with letters which read like totally favourable school reports. However he showed no signs of nervousness as he bounced up the stairs and stopped at the door next to the array of little cactus-bearing pots which Ada had made at school.

Perla looked them over, her blue-green eyes startling in her sunburnt face, and put a finger to her lips. 'Suzi's asleep.'

She hugged her brother in an embrace that combined emotion with inspection and kissed him on the mouth before tilting her head to one side, opening her astonishing eyes wide. Her crown of goldish brown hair had been specially brushed for this moment and she stood there fragrant and fresh from the shower in her crisp checkered dress, Peruvian bead chain and freckles marking her bronzed skin, like an athlete past her prime but full of the energy of races run and waves defied. Every morning she put her body to the test in a session of gymnastics on the balcony snapping commands she had picked up in the British army. When she read Greek stories about gods and heroes in school Ada imagined Perla as Atalanta running fast and gracefully in a short dress that barely got to her knees. Men were running after her trying to catch her but she was faster. They lay panting by the wayside as she sped on and on and on.

'Bubi, it's you Bubi I can't believe it's you.'

Rudi must have winced at the sound of his childhood nickname but Ada felt a twinge of jealousy as she linked Bubi to a home with a father and a mother and sisters who called you from the balcony in the evening.

'Bubi come up and have your supper, it's getting late.'

Perla melted away at the sight of him. All her professional strictness, acquired in the army and honed on the doctors and patients of the hospital orthopedics department, surrendered to a genuine, almost girlish happiness at seeing her brother. She patted his arm vigorously as she led them into the bright living room with its astonishing view of the port town and the sea and they sat at the table for the ritual welcome of coffee and cake served on thick, plain china, a poor relation of the delicate blue and orange porcelain of Vienna which was set out for visitors in the room with the heavy sideboard and the three Turkish rugs under which Bubi used to hide his tin boxers and racing cars.

Perla watched her brother drink with hungry, enquiring eyes. Maybe he was a Californian pedlar of magic, spreading a naïve optimism about a better world to be founded on language learning and cultural exchange. Maybe he had been lucky to avoid actual battles like those in the wake of which she had driven her truck often filled with exhausted, roughly bandaged soldiers. She didn't really hold it against him that he had landed the Nuremberg job and turned the mass of hateful and nauseous jargon he heard into a cabaret featuring himself, the heroic, eternally hopeful translator. All that was unimportant. Here was Bubi come back to them, perhaps for good?

'How do you like it here? Isn't it lovely? You should have seen it when we moved in. This street was nowhere, shrubs, stones and mud in the winter, thorns and dust in the summer. The nearest house was a donkey ride away. Now there's a fine cinema across the road and they've promised ceiling fans for the summer. Why don't you stay longer? We'll put you up and find work for you. Isn't it wonderful how we caught that butcher?'

Rudi seemed wrapped up in his cake and coffee, his head bent over the cup and plate as if to shield himself against the shower of questions. He pointed to his mouth full of poppy seed cake and smiled appreciatively.

'This is something you used to make at home, isn't it? It takes me back all the way. Sister Perla's *Mohnkuchen*. What an attraction. My friends couldn't get enough of it. A piece of this bought me two bike rides round the park.'

'Forget the cake, Rudi. Tell us everything. Rudi, tell us about your wife. You hardly mention her in your letters and you called her Cookie, that couldn't be her real name.'

There was a gasp from the door and Suzi appeared barefoot in a thin pyjama top.

'Bubi,' she cried, and flung herself at him, almost knocking over his coffee. She wrapped her arms around his neck and hung on him whispering his name again and again.

'You're wearing perfume.'

'Only aftershave.'

She stood back to look at him acknowledging Ada with a glance and an appreciative roll of her eyes.

'You look so fresh and new, like a present we just opened. Rudi, I'm so glad to see you. We wondered if you'd ever come.'

She sat down next to him and held his hand.

'We thought perhaps your wife didn't want you to because your sisters would eat you up.'

She kissed his hand.

'But look at me. She needn't be afraid. I couldn't harm anybody.'

Suzi looked thin and fragile in her blue nightgown. Her jet black hair had streaks of grey in it and her dark eyes dominated her small pale face giving her the look of a night creature. Her white arms and legs seemed to hang haphazardly from her body as if unsure of what their function was.

Ada went over and kissed her mother's forehead. It was damp and there were smudges of eye make-up here and there. Suzi looked at her and frowned.

'I'm not looking my best today, that bus ride is suffocating and who can keep calm jammed up against a large woman with stuffed bags and a live chicken clucking under her feet?'

She hugged her daughter looking at Rudi as if to display her possession.

'What do you think of her, Bubi? We thought we'd lost her to Paris but she came back, though how she doesn't die of boredom in the dust heap where she lives now, I don't know.'

Ada watched the three of them beginning and interrupting competing conversations, stopping and starting, finishing each other's sentences, laughing at incidents remembered or forgotten,

50

picking German words and phrases out of the past, singing bits of popular dance tunes.

Ich bin die fesche Lola, der Liebling der Saison!
Ich hab ein Pianola zu Haus in mein Salon...

She saw how they avoided any mention of the parents left behind in the doomed Community Home for the Aged. They all seemed younger as if taking a cue from Rudi, even the lines of strain on her mother's face had softened, giving way to the old vivacity in her voice and an undercurrent of laughter. Suzi was particularly amused by Bubi's descriptions of his journey across Europe with his Swiss girlfriend. She made him repeat his imitation of the florid, many-chinned German official finding fault with the photograph on his forged passport because it made him look less 'Arisch' than he really was.

'*Echt arisch mit zutch blau eyes that's me*,' said Rudi who had dyed his hair for that journey.

'But I think he really knew I was fake and let me get away with it. He had something in his eye that wasn't all Nazi. Maybe not. I suppose even in those days I was looking for the best in people.'

'Candide,' said Perla. 'Is that how you found your wife? You didn't write us about it, did you?'

Rudi didn't answer immediately.

'I sent you photos so you'd know but I wasn't going to make excuses. I didn't want to explain. I wasn't sheepish and I didn't feel guilty. I left all that behind years ago. I'll tell you what happened when I left Vienna. I had a photograph of Mama and Papa in my wallet and I let it fly out of the train window. One minute it was in my hand between my fingers. The next it was gone. I let it go. It wasn't an accident and it wasn't deliberate. It blew away. It was a sign you know, the things you're supposed to hold onto at all costs, they're a burden, if you're honest with yourself, like heavy winter coats smelling of mothballs. They weigh you down. I was travelling in an express train away from it all, and fast. I felt strong for a while. The fizz didn't last but I wasn't afraid and that kept me going

51

through London, the Blitz and everything. After the war, when I got the Nuremberg job and found Ulli, she was much younger, not much more than a girl, but she had a toughness I recognized and admired. She had got away. Stuck in that hell she had pulled herself free. The deadly schools and poison almost choked her but she resisted. She hid her Mickey Mouse in the mattress and at night she mouthed the Anarchist songs her father taught her before he disappeared. Ulli was like an orphan scrabbling for a life in the ruins. I suppose I became something of a father, for a while, anyway. Perla, you have to break down barriers between people and resist the poison like Ulli's father did, like his dead comrades. There was resistance in hell and nobility too. We'd be fools to ignore it. We weren't the only victims and we weren't good at resisting.'

¡A las barricadas! a las barricadas! por el triunfo de la Confederacion.

He hummed the song from the Spanish civil war and swung his hands in a mock salute to Perla. He had not fallen on the barricades of Madrid and Barcelona. The true believers were dead in unmarked graves. But Rudi was borrowing their trumpet call to rally his troops in the inevitable battle with his sister.

She stared at him.

His cheeks were flushed and his body, perched on the chair like a bird, seemed ready to tense muscles and take flight at any moment.

Perla rattled her beads.

'Listen to yourself. Other people. Other people. They can take care of themselves. We have to look after our own. We couldn't then, we hadn't a clue. And look what happened. You threw their photo out of the window? You got rid of the mothballs and the baggage and did a high wire act? We left our parents behind and you make that some kind of achievement, a declaration of independence! This is a proof of good health? Don't you have any shame? One hundred spelling seminars in twenty countries can't ever put that right. And can marrying a German girl heal you?'

'Why do you think I need healing, Perla? I became normal that's all. I stopped thinking "them and us". I really did. It's all of us, Perla, not them and us, and till you see that you will only crash into every wall, fall into every ditch and end up a mess of unhealed wounds, angry with everybody except yourself.'

Perla's eyes were like icy blue darts aimed between Rudi's ears.

His voice now calm and resonant betrayed no emotion as if he was lecturing at an international seminar. It was the voice of reason, a reason so obvious that it took an extreme form of blindness not to see it and it made Perla mad. She twisted her beads in one hand as if to make a sling out of them but she spoke in a controlled voice.

'You do need healing. You need healing from fake happiness. You wrap your head in cotton wool soaked in eau de cologne and it smells good doesn't it? You prefer sanitised kitsch to what every normal person sees in front of his nose. It's flattering. It puts you on a pedestal as one of the chosen. A visionary. What vision? You can't even see what violence you did to yourself when you pulled the liberated Rudi out of your head. That Rudi is a fake.'

She could have been a prosecutor bearing down on the accused across the courtroom with indisputable proof of his forgery in her hand.

'We all need healing. You too. All that stuff is unfinished for us. I used to think like you. Just do something brave and bury the past. Join the British army. Grow muscles. Fight the Germans. Keep moving. Don't look back. But it's no use. We're infected by that helplessness and that's the wound that won't heal. We have to admit it and live with it. It will never heal. Not for you. Not for us.'

There was a truce of sorts as both looked at Suzi who was curled up in her armchair, eyes closed.

'Have you ever heard me talk about them, ever?' was Suzi's answer to Ada's questions in the past. Not that Ada asked much about her grandparents. But she did look at the photo of the old couple all bound up and stiff in black, especially Opa who wore his lawyerly collar so high up his neck that it seemed to be squeezing his head off. *Rechtsanwalt Ossias Maiberg* it said on the rubber stamp at the bottom. Suzi murmured in her sleep.

'The pills make her sleepy,' said Perla. 'She just drops away in the middle of whatever's going on...'

They looked at her.

Will they talk about it?

Ada knew they wouldn't. Not in front of her. They could quarrel loud and shamelessly but not that. They would find a time to be alone and whisper it all out, heads close together, conspirators. This was absurd as she knew everything, always had. But Perla insisted on treating her as a minor or a new recruit whose job was to obey orders and ask no questions. Perla knew at heart how ridiculous this was but her fixation with the past meant that Ada had to remain a young girl, kept away by her wise elder aunt from the abyss of the unpalatable truth.

That Suzi had tried to kill herself was the truth. Also that she had thrown up her job in Bonn with the Reparations Commission and arrived home distraught, angry and sick, her good looks veiled by a grey curtain. Ada was summoned back from Paris but her presence made things worse. Domestic quarrels about shower protocol or where knives and spoons were supposed to be became insane tugs of war. Suzi hated the sun and wouldn't go to the beach. Suzi took all flies as insults. She sprayed her room with vile substances against mosquitoes and ants which poisoned the air and spread an oily chemical film on the tiles. In the shower knots of her hair blocked the drain and her ranks of German shampoos, headache pills, mouthwash, hand cream, and eye paint commandeered the shelf space. Then the politics. She accused Perla of chauvinism and lack of interest in the Arab victims of 1948. 'Everywhere they go they need police permits. They need permits to go and pee and it makes no difference to you. You look at everything from under your 8th army cap as if you were still fighting Rommel. He's dead, didn't you know? It's different now. We're not going to be invaded any more.'

With Ada there were quieter moments when they sat in the Bahai gardens, lulled by the evening cool and the gentle curve of the flower beds dropping like flocks of butterflies from the Shrine of the Teacher towards the port and the bay.

Suzi was curious about Paris and Milo.

'You're not in love with him anymore. You think he's some kind of genius, and you're good friends and you share a flat. So you cook for him and iron his shirts? And what does the genius do for you? What sort of friendship is this? You're the woman so you give too much. And does he notice? What are you hanging on to by staying with him?'

Suzi hardly knew Milo and considered him with a kind of amused suspicion when she saw him with her daughter during her brief visits home to Haifa. She had a nickname for him, Napoleone which she shortened to Polly and tolerated his airs because he seemed to be making Ada flourish, turning her from an unformed, burdened girl into a self-sufficient and energetic young woman. She encouraged this, bringing her daughter clothes and books and art materials and encountering Perla's low estimation of the young man with reminders to her sister of certain British officers who found comfort in Corporal Maiberg's arms during the war.

'Yes but that was the war,' Perla would say, lamely.

Talking with Suzi quietly like this in the Bahai gardens Ada was almost persuaded that her mother was recovering and that coming home had done her good. But her speech was oddly irregular. There were gaps and hesitations when she could hear Suzi's breathing as laboured as if she was straining and marshalling all her strength against some physical obstacle.

As a young girl she had never thought of her mother as weak or vulnerable. Suzi was a laugher, even frivolous in comparison with Perla's lack of nonsense. In the summer she wore flowery dresses which she made herself and straw hats with large floppy brims and sometimes a ribbon. When her friends came before going out to a café to dance they sat on the balcony, women like her in bright dresses and men in white shirts with close-cropped hair like soldiers. They would smoke and drink coffee and laugh loud and talk even louder all at once. There were men also who came without the others to take her out. One Ada liked a lot because he played Monopoly with her and didn't mind if she finished with all the money. He worked in the port like her mother and had a jeep and a name like Buldiczenny but even longer and unpronounceable. He was special because he could get Ada onto lovely white ships in the dock and joke with them about sailing away all three to Greece and France. But when he did go away on a ship for a week he didn't take Ada, only Suzi.

Suzi patted Ada's knee.

'You should go back to Paris and your life. Staying here is a waste of time for you. Perla shouln't have got you to come. For what? To keep an eye on me when she's at work? Anyway I'm not staying much longer.'

'Didn't you leave that job?'

'Yes I left, but they'll take me back. I know the work better than anyone.'

'I thought you couldn't stand it any more.'

'I can't. Those men in dark suits at the table with me, what were they doing? They were allocating blood money for power stations and railways and cargo ships and big cars for politicians. It was very polite and businesslike, like lawyers opening a will after the funeral. They never raised their voices. Then at my desk in the next room I had to turn the radio on to make some noise, anything, Doris Day, Brahms, Ella Fitzgerald. 'Pennies from Heaven' – anything to help my mind wander away from the reports of projects and the fantastic sums of Deutschmarks I was typing. But it was no use because outside I had an additional job – to fend off the hungry fish from Tel Aviv desperate for money for their pet developments. It was hell. And we have no shame. I had to stop them undermining each other in front of the Germans. They accused each other of exaggeration and lying, just to get a bigger hand in the Deutschmark purse. Who can sleep after days of that?

'There was so much insomnia and it brought Walter back. One day there he was – Walter. You know what it's like when you're not sleeping. I thought I saw him. In the street or on a tram I found myself looking out for him. Twenty years after he left. A man with his build or a head shaped like his from the back or a walk like his, almost a run, arms swinging … and I looked, I looked too closely

56

for good manners. It got me into trouble. But mostly I was ashamed of myself for losing control.

'It never happened before. Didn't I miss him all those years? Perhaps not enough. You saw I lived pretty normally. I had friends and there were men I liked and spent a lot of time with. We didn't put a candle in the window for Walter even though you missed a Papy. But Papy was like a character in a book, wasn't he? You made him up out of stories, stories I told you or some you told yourself like the one about your doll falling off the window ledge and Papy finding it and putting its legs and arms back in their places.'

'That didn't happen?'

'No, you made it up.'

'But over there in Germany at the office where I worked, only there, he began to butt in. He came and didn't leave. He was sullen and quiet and I could feel he was angry I didn't remember him enough. From behind my shoulder he kept his eye on my work and together we stared at the columns of type and numbers under the heading of the Bundesentschädigungsgesetz. They climbed on and on and spread themselves like ladders naked on the white paper. And my eyes and hands strained to get the paragraphs and columns right. Tipp-Ex was a defeat and the Germans wouldn't stand for it. But I was listening for him and you know what he was telling me. You have to know. He was telling me to get out of there. *Get out Suzi! Quick, get out!*'

She took hold of Ada's hand and pressed hard.

'Isn't that what I tried to do?'

Rudi and Perla had abandoned the battlefield and gone to rest and Ada sat watching her mother sleeping like a baby, breathing quietly through soft pouting lips. Sickness had made Suzi passive and defenceless. Sometimes her voice turned back to childhood and she became a girl again begging for some favour or asking for protection from an undefined threat. When she was like that her eyes went blank and yet Ada couldn't help searching for some sign of cunning behind the mask. Her mother was there, in retreat perhaps, but she was there, hiding and could be found. She was not far. Yet she couldn't come back by herself. She needed a guide.

Perla's salon, though, wasn't a place to entertain weakness. It was a room designed to encourage positive thinking. The light in it was bright with the great sky and the distant sea forming shifting alliances with wind and cloud to sweep the white walls and spare brown furniture with an apparently continuous healthful glow. Even in winter the sun was never completely defeated but sent squibs of intermittently strong light into the room as if to say I'm still here. Perla's table had a full vase of flowers on it most of the time, usually red, rarely beautiful but always crisp and sometimes stiff and pointed like a cluster of spears. Her framed photos were mostly collections of soldiers posing over the bonnets of lorries and jeeps and some prim white circles of nurses on hospital lawns. On one wall etchings of thorns arranged in ascending order marched up invisible steps. They were tame and pretty, robbed of their putrid, barbed threat. Near them a couple of neat desert landscapes made the wilderness look clean, safe and distant. Only the large Käthe Kollwitz print of a hungry child stood out rebelliously over the sofa. Its dark lines of misery and the anguished eyes in the child's upturned face threw a cold European shadow over the Mediterranean brightness. Ada thought the print belonged to a man Perla had loved years ago but she knew nothing more.

She had grown up here but it seemed to her now a strange even alien place. It was the home of Perla's certainties. Its lack of mess and shadow, even its prevailing smell of soap and toast in the morning, seemed wrong and out of date to her. It was like some moral principle learned at school, good in theory but inapplicable and adrift when it came to the confusions and complexities of life in the world. Perla would tend this space till she died, guarding it from change and unaware of its inevitable decline and decay. In her eyes it would always be white, bright and new, the first house on a street which had slowly gathered around it. Like a firm, once-sterile bandage in place for years, it had covered the old wound till only a scar remained, ignored as much as possible, but a reminder, if one touched it in the night, of what would not go away.

Ada had never been so disturbed by what was an ordinary familiar place. Her discomfort made clear to her why she would rather be in her dark, decrepit Ethiopian rooms with their wobbly tiles and their smell of cats and damp where there was no big sky at the window and no reach of water anywhere and the one certainty outside was the closeness of the ceasefire line and its dilapidated markers, the twisted, bullet-struck signs announcing DANGER BORDER in three languages.

Ada left Rudi with his sisters and took the first Saturday evening bus back to Jerusalem. She tried not to listen to the chatter on the radio about the impending trial but closed her eyes and worked at guessing where they were from the grumble groan and whine of the engine and the pace of the bumps and swerves, especially when the slow climb up to the city began.

Eyob Malagueta knocked on her door almost as soon as she got back. She had just put the light on and was inspecting her dolls for any signs of distress.

'A gentleman Tomas was here Madame but he didn't leave a message.'

Eyob seemed to want to come in and talk. He towered over her at the door in his black robes like a cypress in the dark. He seemed ill at ease about something and looked over his shoulder before he came in and closed the door.

She made some tea and they sat by the window as they always did listening to the few sounds of the night. A radio boomed for a minute and was switched off. Cats yowled. The iron gate of the Palace of Exile creaked in the wind.

'How is your family back home?'

He looked at her with concentration as if he were inspecting a fruit tree for signs of blight.

'Not much work and no money for marrying my sisters.'

He made a deprecatory gesture with his hand as if to sweep his family's troubles out of the window and into the dark street. Blood specks swam in the soft white and brown of his eyes. He was unnaturally quiet, sipping his tea with birdlike nips.

'Is something the matter, Eyob?'

'Madame Ada is angry with me?'

'What? No, why should I be angry?'

'You did not speak to me in days.'

'I went to see my family and often when I come home at night you are in your room and the light is out.'

'Yes, I lie there thinking. I do not sleep.'

Ada had only the vaguest idea of the rules of the monks' life. Were they supposed to pray at night? Eyob didn't seem a very ascetic type. And he seemed to spend all his time in the Palace of Exile rather than the monastery round the corner. He had got used to smoking a Gitane with her and occasionally drinking something stronger than mint tea. Cognac Medicinal was probably against the rule but Ada didn't feel guilty about that. It was such a rough drink and hardly pleasurable enough to be a sin. She hoped she wasn't the reason for Eyob's sleeplessness and tried to change the subject.

'You know I am working for a kind of film about a trial here in Jerusalem.'

He looked uninterested and Ada felt she might be insulting him by assuming he knew nothing about television. As for the Big Shit, why should he know anything about him?

'I do not sleep now for many days, even weeks.'

He stopped, waiting for her to help him. Ada gave in: 'Is there some trouble?'

Surely there was no confession in the Ethiopian Church so she hoped she was not leading him in that direction.

'This, this is my trouble.'

He shook his black robe as if he was getting rid of the crumbs lodged in its folds.

'The Church makes me angry for myself. I say Eyob what are you doing here? Will you do nothing till you are old and sick and put on a heap of sacks to die. The Church brought me here from

Ethiopia but I am nowhere and in the night when I hear a car outside I want to jump into the street and throw myself under.'

He was trembling. Ada poured him a glass of cognac and he drank it quickly with the grimace of shock that the unbelievable rawness produced every time.

'If you are so unhappy you can leave, can't you?'

As she said it she knew how stupid it was, as if he could just walk out of the monastic shelter into streets where his height and colour would make everyone stare and the kids shout Kushi Kushi and where would he get clothes to fit?

'I would like to study. I can repair electric and radios also sewing machines.'

He looked hungrily at her stack of canvases and sketch books and the large work table with models of the television studio and some dolls' heads in a basket. Her brushes, pens and pencils and her boxes of buttons and scraps of cloth and cameras and fragments of old tiles strewn around haphazardly on every surface clearly fascinated him.

'You will teach me?'

'What?'

'To draw a face on paper in black and then with colour. I will draw your face and you will draw mine. If I learn this well I will perhaps find work outside. Why do you have him?'

He pointed to an unsteady tailor's dummy Ada kept in a corner.

'It is like a stranger in your room. He never eats or sleeps but he keeps watch.'

'This is a dummy I bought from a tailor but it is not a man or a woman. It is like a big doll without a face or arms. I can make it into whatever I want even an animal like a bear or a big bird.'

Eyob clapped his hands and laughed.

'Madame Ada, I beg you this favour, let me have this dummy. Only for a short time. Let me make something on it. I will learn to do this.'

'Take the dummy any time, Eyob, but treat it gently it's old and unsteady.'

The dummy and the whole conversation seemed to have improved his mood. He drank more cognac and talked quite loudly about the petty quarrels and jealousies in the monks' world. Only one thing made him talk reverently in a quiet voice, his long trunk swaying as he spoke.

'One thing I wish for myself to do if I stay a monk. I would go to Deir el Sultan in the Holy Sepulchre. The Ethiopian holy place needs young monks to fight with the Coptics who want to take it away from them. *G A N A V I M!*' he said loudly.

This surprising Hebrew word – THIEVES! – was a war cry flung across no man's land, over the barbed wire and the wall towards the great church and up onto its roof where Eyob's embattled countrymen wrestled with their rivals over feet and inches of sacred stone, brick and dried mud.

Ada closed her eyes. She was tired after the journey and Eyob's visit had been more demanding than usual. She stood up and put out her hand.

'Good night Eyob, you can take the dummy tomorrow. And we'll talk more about the drawing.'

'Thankyou Madame Ada' and he was gone leaving traces of Medicinal and sweat in the air.

Border Fragrance

Tomas came to see her at the ice factory which was becoming the television and communications centre even though hardly anyone walking along the airless corridors and arguing loudly in the makeshift rooms really knew what that meant. The shabby concrete floors continued to sweat grime while new walls of some synthetic material that shed white powder if you touched it were springing up haphazardly. Somebody had decided that heavy old government desks were necessary and a line of these with the support of battered filing cabinets stood by one of the entrances like welfare petitioners. Hollow shouts mixed with booms and bangs filled the air. The poor acoustics made normal sounds monstrous and quiet conversation impossible. But a team of electricians who looked more in the know than anyone else were confidently rolling wheels of cable in all directions and threading bunches of black red and green wires down stairwells and across ceilings.

There were rumours that a foreign television director had been hired to put an end to the chaos and had been given absolute authority over the whole project. Ada's work area kept moving around and she was surprised that Tomas was able to find her and had no story of blundering through naked carpentry and into camouflaged toilets before reaching his goal.

He stood by her work table and moved one of her studio models around with a perplexed look.

'Don't worry Tomas,' she said. 'Whatever I know about this

63

wonder I get from books. Look here,' she pointed to a stack of books and magazines piled up on the floor. 'There's no-one to ask. Everybody here is a major expert on the Big Shit but nobody knows how we are going to show him to the world in moving pictures on something called television.'

'Kronberg has taken off for Würzburg,' he said.

'He's gone?'

'No. He went to talk to them about the Archive and his budget. He won't do anything till he's sure. Kronberg doesn't trust anybody, not even the Germans. Are you busy or just pretending?'

'I'm my own boss here, a lot of my work I do at home.'

'So let's go to *Die Tanten*. Don't you long for chewy kohlrabi and not quite unfrozen meat?'

'I thought you liked to eat there.'

'I do but somebody has to take my attention off the food and you're the one.'

Ada felt a welcome lightness even gaiety in Tomas's manner. The intense, almost hurtful sharpness she had noticed in the past was absent and he seemed unburdened as they walked through the crowd in the market street past the piles of fruit and vegetables spilling onto pavements and headed for the lunch ladies behind the Hasmonean Tomb. Frau Hermine, her stout body wrapped in a deep blue apron, stared at them with raised eyebrows and a questioning smile.

'Und wo ist der Herr Professor? He is not well?'

Tomas explained and they sat down. The little room was crowded and Ada felt warm and relaxed as conversation in a babel of languages bounced around her head. It seemed like a family gathering, a strange family sure enough but with a marked tolerance of each other's strangeness. Eating by himself at a corner table with a book propped up on the salt cellar was Hugo Flamm who it was said had written three doctorates on military history but submitted none and devoted his life to editing other people's work and looking after his collection of First World War headgear. He could sometimes be spotted on King George Street of an evening wearing a highly polished Prussian cavalry helmet which went well with his big Alsatian dog, his handlebar moustache, stiff bearing and tweed jacket. Yet he was a pacifist and had avoided serving in any army.

Tomas had become silent and was eating with his head down, hunched over his plate as if he was afraid someone would snatch it away. He curled inwards like that sometimes when Kronberg was making one of his speeches and Ada took it either as a form of resistance or a disciple's respect. She brought him out of it with a remark about the kohlrabi. He looked at her, startled. Perhaps she had interrupted a reverie that had taken him elsewhere, far away from this table and his companion.

'I was thinking about Würzburg. Kronberg wants me to go with him.'

'Yes, I heard from Julius. What would you do there?'

'They'd give me a studio and a teaching job too if I want it. Kronberg says they're keen. His family was very well known there. For him it would be coming home.'

'And you?' She felt a surprising rush of anger at Tomas's passivity and jealousy at Kronberg's hold over him.

'I don't know.'

'You'd lose quite a lot by going wouldn't you? You won't know what till you're gone. And you'd be more dependent...on Kronberg even than...'

'Even than I am now.' He finished her sentence and smiled like a mother contemplating a wayward child's naughtiness. 'He pulled me out of deep shit. You don't know how crazy I was. Nobody would go near me. They didn't understand what I said so I quarrelled. You know what I looked like? I looked like a sack of orphanage clothing and I must have smelled like it too. Kronberg saw me in Taamon Café quarrelling with the waitress. He stopped it, you know how people take notice of him, and we started talking or he sat me down and did the talking. I don't think he let up for a whole night.'

Come on Kronberg, shut up, Ada shouted in her head. Shut up for godssake and let someone else talk. Make room for Tomas. Don't take him away.

'So you always get on now?' she asked as neutrally as she could.

'Who gets on all the time? But I don't pull a knife any more and I've learned to keep quiet. I couldn't keep quiet until I met him. I didn't know what it was. He helped me find it.'

'Funny, Kronberg isn't exactly a man for quiet. He's got opinions about everything and doesn't keep them to himself. He lays down the law to anyone who'll listen.'

'You don't like him much, do you?'

'In Paris I'd love him. I can see him legs stretched out, Campari in his glass, entertaining the young with some theory made up in Tübingen in the good old days. But here...we're in hiding. We get bad dreams and dizzy spells, so going on like he does with this brimming confidence of his beats me down. I feel like closing all the doors and sleeping for a week. But I admit he's attractive. There aren't many like him around. He's got *savoir faire*. He is ageless and spare, a bit demonic too if you come to think about it. And where does he get his permanent sun tan from, hell fire?'

Tomas laughed.

'If Hermine overheard you, wait for the gossip. The Demon Professor and the Dark Maiden – a good topic for the Berliner club. But since he isn't here and can't defend himself we shouldn't give in to gossip. That's something he hates though he can't stop doing it himself. We should be going before it starts to rain.'

The weather had changed. The dusty grey and yellow dryness which seemed to have settled on the town for good was giving way to swiftly moving black and white clouds and a new fresh smell of earth that came with the change in the direction of the wind. There were hints of rumbling far away which could have been thunder or explosions in one of the quarries outside the town. Loose shutters began to slap and clatter in the irregular gusts. The lunch room was emptying out as people hurried away to beat what looked like a storm.

'Come to the ruin with me. It's quite spectacular in a storm and then you'll smell the apocalypse like I told you.'

Bent against the wind, they hurried through the empty streets.

Occasional drops of rain hit the ground with an exaggerated splat as if to say *dash dash*. Even the desert in the distance had shed its hopeless monotony and was now a patchwork of light and shade, of black, grey and yellow watched over by ranks of clouds on the move. Now more than ever the town seemed to be balanced precariously on an edge, on some kind of foothold between what people had built and collected and fortified and what was naked and unpeopled and empty.

It was raining quite hard when they got to the hillside where the house was perched. A thin mist was snaking through the valley below and the stones and trees nearby were losing their painful sharpness as a damp cloak enveloped them and drew them into the surrounding blur.

The house inside was washed in a pale grey light, whiter by the windows and darker in the corners and depths of the room. Tomas didn't put on the light and led Ada to the window. He had forgotten to take his coat off and she took hers and his and draped them over a chair. It wasn't cold. It was very still as the growing turbulence outside was muted by the thick walls and let itself be felt only by an occasional undefined tremor. They could have been hiding in a shelter from an air raid or looking out at an underwater world from the dark of a diving machine. Tomas seemed to be staring out of the window at the mist but his eyes were closed. Ada stroked his cheek with her fingers.

'Praying for a miracle?' She said.

'It's you.'

He turned, cupped her face in his hands and kissed her. His face was still damp from the rain and fragrant with the new smell of the wind and the coming storm. He kissed her roughly at first, biting at her lip, then softer till they were at rest head to head. After a while he held her face and looked at her, as if from a distance, his eyes inquiring and troubled.

'What?' she said.

He didn't answer but drew her to the bed they had shared chastely

67

on the night of Milo's party and undressed her like a father, slowly, carefully. Kneeling, he rocked her in his arms and she felt herself grow lighter, like a fruit hanging on its branch. Yet he was the lighter one in their lovemaking, focused and nimble, then slowly losing himself in the folds and paths of her body as she enveloped him.

With his boyish, muscular body stretched out next to her she listened to the spattering of the rain on the windows and the thud of the wind hitting the ill-fitting frames. What if a great gust hit the house, tore out the whole window and sucked them, bed and all, into the valley? No man's land would be their bedroom and the United Nations Truce Supervisors would be called in to inspect them and decide who was violating what. She wasn't ashamed of her imagined nakedness. Let them be ashamed for disturbing us. We are the real peacemakers. We are the stillness inside the storm.

She snuggled close to Tomas's warmth. His stillness was magnetic. She wished she could enter it and let it enfold her like the tunnels that opened up to him in his imagination. They would help each other through, sometimes he would lead sometimes she would slide ahead snakelike through the corridors of rock and the smell of water would lead them on.

Tomas mumbled and opened his eyes. She brushed his forehead with her lips.

'I was thinking we might be sucked out by the wind into no man's land just like this, naked.'

He didn't answer but took her forcefully, hastily into the tunnel of his making, asking her wordlessly to trust his quick body to lead her in and out of darkness and back into the stillness of the room at the heart of the storm.

They lay there for a while, not talking. Then he helped her up and led her to the window. It was trembling less in the weakening gusts and the rain wasn't hurling itself at the glass. Instead it sounded like jugfulls of water spilling against the panes. The first stage of the storm was passing. Tomas brought a blanket from the bed and draped it over her shoulders then he opened the window and a wave of fresh, damp air rolled into the room.

He stood there naked.

'There's the smell. Now while it's fresh and strong.'

He took her by the hand and put her directly in the wave of air. She shivered but it was not cold. She tried to fill her lungs and only managed little intakes of breath. The dampness was strange but not unpleasant as it covered her face and breast like a soft towel.

But where was the apocalypse? She couldn't find it. There was earth and a rancid tinge of weeds, hints of sewage and, above all the dampness that soothed everything.

She didn't want to disappoint Tomas so she took a few deeper breaths and said 'I think I know what you mean. It's border perfume. It's made up of whatever is ours and whatever is theirs and the rain stirs them into each other. But it doesn't last. The rain doesn't last.'

He closed the window. 'It's more complicated than that,' he said, 'but you're getting there. You're on the way.'

Then they went back to bed to listen.

Ship Of Fools

'Ship Of Fools, That's the title for now.'

Milo was outlining to a group of friends and neighbours and possible performers what he would be working on. He had summoned them to the house and given them arak and a joint or two for those in need. The newest arrival was his American woman, Jordan, who had broken off an engagement to be with him and spent a lot of time on the phone trying to calm her parents who imagined her naked and lost in some desert encampment with no doctor or clean sheets for hundreds of miles.

To Ada she seemed more Milo's equal than the string of young birds who hung on him for a month or two then vanished. Jordan was older and seemed to know what she was doing even though she was openly puzzled by the strange society she found herself in. She had a doctorate in anthropology to finish and clearly was not dependent on Milo the way so many of his women were. She had to be glamorous, of course, but her beauty was of a severe kind like her well-cut clothes. Her brown hair was pulled back, giving her face a sculptured shape with prominent cheekbones and full lips and there was an American cleanness about her which was unmistakeable. You could, even without looking closely, see the miracles worked by religious dental care and faithful attention to skin and hair as well as seasonal attendance at the Temple and regular skiing holidays in Colorado.

Milo went on, one hand gently stroking Jordan's neck, 'This play is us. We are on the edge here closer than anyone imagines to the end…of the world…and closer than most people ever get to a dangerous and invisible line, where death waits. But you can't put us into a play. Who would be interested in us? We are odd, an eccentric collection. We don't represent anybody. Not a country or a religion or a tribe. The police would call us weirdos and, some of us, drunks. They think of us as outsiders and misfits. But we know things that others don't know. And we're not afraid.'

Ada recognized the music and the seriousness of the delivery. He was like an Arctic explorer encouraging his companions to go out into the ice storm for one last attempt at the pole.

'So what do we do about it?'

He raised his voice and brought in Chairman Mao: 'We are guerrillas and surprise is our weapon. When everybody everywhere is watching the little Nazi in the dock and feeling good about justice and retribution and munching peanuts, we open our show. Where? Near enough to make a disturbance. For us there are no prosecutors, no witnesses, no judges and especially no prize criminals – only ourselves and our audience, only the mirror we hold up to them. By some fluke we think we are survivors, the Book tells us we are a family of Holy Fools crowded into a ship called an "Ark" and sailing to the end of the world. But we are going to drown too. The Book is a joke – on us. We drown to peals of cosmic laughter.'

There was silence as Milo's music worked its magic.

'But, Milo, we don't drown. Remember? There's a universal drainaway. The waters recede and everything starts all over again,' said Julius.

Although Julius and Milo were close friends, the poet thought Milo's pessimism wilful and overdone, especially when it was performed before an audience. Milo had originally wanted the play to end with the Ark floating aimlessly in the universal flood, the passengers starving, beginning to eat the animals and each other and Noah running out of birds to send in search of dry land. But after many arguments Julius had brought Mr Margarian in to plead the cause of Mount Ararat as a symbol of the (God willing) victorious struggle of the Armenians against so many evil powers.

71

'If you make Noah, the just man, overlook Ararat you will incur the scorn of the believing Jews but worse you will have all the wide-flung Armenian communities of the entire world against you. Ararat is like Sinai for us. It is where the world begins again…in Armenia. So if you erase it in a public performance here in Jerusalem, the name Milo Banet will appear in the catalogue of our persecutors together with Sultan Abdul Hamid the Cruel Turk. Why would you want this, my friend?'

No-one ever won an argument with Mr Margarian so Milo reluctantly gave up his idea of rewriting the Biblical story though he stuck to it for rhetorical purposes.

He took a sip of his arak and looked around at the group. He had dressed for the occasion. His black shirt was new, his coal-black beard was carefully trimmed and Rudi's yellow cravat was blinking like a traffic light from his neck. Jordan's work, thought Ada. She's out to sweep away the small-town scruffiness for ever and make him presentable to the salons of Berkeley. She felt a brief pang of loss in anticipation.

This evening the group was small. Apart from Ada, Tomas, Julius and Rudi there were a few people who lived on the slopes around the old Turkish bandstand, some students from Milo's seminar on Satan and Eros and two specially invited guests, Martin Baldwick, the British Council representative and Père Félix, a renegade Dominican monk and archaeologist who was seen in the habit of his order only at costume parties and spent a lot of time in cafés and cinemas and in the beds of young diggers and women of all types and persuasions.

Rudi had come back from Haifa and his sisters with a lot of energy and enthusiasm for whatever night life the town had to offer. He had become a regular at Fink's bar and would drink and swap jokes in Viennese dialect with the host till late into the night. Whatever foundation employed him in California they must have agreed to extend his stay considerably because he had moved from his hotel to a guest room in the Convent of the Soeurs de Sion and was on the best of terms with the Mother Superior who asked him to give informal classes to the nuns on peacemaking through language teaching. He kept a strict regime of running in all weathers, an hour every morning, which fitted in well with the ascetic ideals of the convent and brought him briefly face to face with neighbours hurrying off to morning prayers before work. After more evenings drinking with Milo, he began to show a real interest in the Ship of Fools project, telling Milo that his experience with cultural bureaucrats all over the world would come in handy for steering the ship towards performance and putting it under an international spotlight. And anyway the universal ideal beyond the pessimism was close to his heart. He considered the Ark an experiment in cultural cooperation in the face of disaster. Indeed it went further because in the Ark cooperation was achieved between humans and other species as well, something that none of his conferences had ever dreamed of discussing.

Ada was warming to Rudi. She noticed more of his energy and enthusiasm for good causes and less of the prima donna. His trainees in the translators' class which now met rarely had done well and were not only coping heroically with barrages of German syntax but were developing, to his approval, the professional distance necessary for work with nauseating material. He had them translate diatribes from *Der Stürmer* and bits of Goebbels' speeches, insisting on secrecy since a leak would have cost him his job. Bad enough that he had to explain to a suspicious customs officer at the mail depot that these documents were for an academic project and not evidence of his diseased and dangerous mind.

Milo was struggling to paint a clear picture of a project he had imagined in brilliant technicolour but with considerable vagueness. His core idea, now that he had to abandon the pessimism of the doomed Ark going nowhere, was the isolation of Noah and the refusal of people everywhere to understand his warnings about the coming catastrophe.

'Nobody wants to listen to Noah. He's an old *nudnik* and he smells bad. Even his wife makes fun of him and she has to be dragged spitting and drunk into the Ark. So while all around us a festival of self-congratulation is going on and everyone is gloating over our prize Nazi, we will show a whole civilization going under because they stupidly think they are safe and normal and that anybody who doesn't think so is mad. That's what we must show. Not just the miracle of survival and God's rainbow and all that, but the end of the world and the colossal drowning of everything, obliterated like Pompeii and Hiroshima in the middle of a normal day. We'll do it just like that – in the middle of a normal day, in the street on a platform on wheels like the local people did in Chester six centuries ago. Right, Martin?'

Baldwick nodded and fidgeted on his cushion. He seemed ill at ease and strapped down in his blue suit and polka dot bow tie. Milo cultivated him because the British Council might be called on to support the first performance in the Holy Land of an English miracle play even if it had been radically rewritten and was going to be acted in a polyglot babble of languages. But Martin was nervous because he was too close to no man's land and didn't want to get mixed up in any incident caused by drunks on this side or bored soldiers on the other. His predecessor had been to one of Milo's parties and had been picked up by a police car after neighbours reported a man singing loudly in a foreign language sitting in the middle of the Hebron road. It took him a while to convince the patrol he had not strayed across the border in the night.

Milo went on.

'It makes things easier for us that the Jews don't take the Ark and Noah story so seriously. It's not as sacred or as emotional as Abraham and Isaac.'

'*Exactement*,' said Père Félix, 'Noah to you is only a goy, and a drunk like all goyim and you didn't draw him, paint him and illustrate him in a thousand ways like the church did. So your man in the street has no idea of what the Ark looks like, a big bathtub maybe, or what Noah looks like, perhaps like Popeye, nor of course that Noah is a theological archetype of Jesus Christ. He is a forerunner of the Saviour.'

'Even when he gets drunk and displays his penis?' said Milo.

74

'Not intentionally, my friend. He is asleep after a drink or many drinks and it is his bad son Ham who takes the parental bird out of its cache. I think some of your rabbis say he buggered him.'

There was quiet for a bit.

'Ham is black isn't he? Isn't he supposed to be the father of all black peoples?' said Jordan. 'That's why he's out of line and shameless according to the Book. OK, so the Hebrews also had white prejudice about Africans and sex. Too bad for them, but how can you ignore it today, honey? You have to show prejudice up for what it is. Or you could change it. Make Shem the bad son. Have the arch-semite expose Papa's penis and all. That should stir things up.'

'What's so important about Noah's penis?' said Rudi who had only the vaguest idea of the Bible story. 'If the play is about a trashy civilization going down the drain and it's only saved by a bunch of fools who volunteer to start the whole thing over again, then the point must be: What civilization do they set in motion? What's the good of it if they are only going to repeat all the crap? I say let the band of fools agree on the principles of a better world at the end. The finale could be a hymn to Universal Cooperation and Peace including animals. I think I could write that.'

Milo looked uncomfortable. The discussion was moving in wrong directions and the last thing he needed was a general debate on a project he was determined to control by himself. He had wanted to impress the British Council man with the daring originality of his idea and show off the artistic talent at hand. But Ada and Tomas had kept quiet, he had made the mistake of introducing Noah's penis and now Rudi was rewriting the end with his own Ode to Joy and Carnival of the Animals.

Jordan felt Milo's frustration and put her hand in his.

'I guess I'm new to this project and I've never seen anything so ancient – not in Europe and not in the States. It's got great potential. But what I know is you can't run for the finish till the basic plan is in place and that's what Milo is up to. Once you've got the words and the lyrics and know what the Ark looks like the whole package is going to change.'

'The Ark looks like a floating tower of Babel,' said Julius. 'It is dizzy with sounds. Animal voices on all levels mingle with human languages and create a cacophonic din, a soundstream which propels the heavy ship onwards. I didn't say forwards did I because there is no direction in the Universal Wet. Every way is forwards and backwards and sideways too. Only upwards and downwards are not to be.'

There was silence for a while. Then Baldwick and most of the others waved goodbye and tiptoed out into the night.

An air of dissatisfaction hung around the room and mingled with the smoke. Milo stood up abruptly, unwound the yellow cravat from his neck and tied it quickly and expertly around Julius's eyes.

'You are the scapegoat Julius. You are the prize talker of shit here. And you're going to pay for it. One bleat and you're finished.'

'NOOOOO GO TO BLOODY HELL' shouted Julius and humming to himself, adopted a Japanese wrestler's pose.

Milo grappled with him from behind and he flailed about with feet and hands making loud animal noises. He was considerably larger than Milo and tried to pull off the cravat but Milo held his hands down till Julius, now red in the face and sweating, began to kick and yell.

'SLIMERATS STOOLPIGEONS FAKERS ARSEHOLES'

Spit dribbled from his lips and his beard fanned out in rhythm with his shouting and head-butting. But these crises of unspecific anger, secretly directed against real and imagined editors, politicians, social climbers and rival poets, didn't last and soon he was a woolly heap on the floor in the midst of some broken glass with Milo sitting on him looking apologetically at Jordan.

'Useless talk brings out the worst in us.' He bent over Julius and patted him on the back and with a mock expression of worry leaned over to see if he was breathing.

Then he called over to Félix, who was lying on a cushion smoking.

'So, *mon Père*, what chance the Holy Church gets wind of this and protests to the government?'

'What could they protest about?'

'Blasphemy. Bestiality. Buggery.'

Félix's answer was to free his lungs of smoke and sigh deeply.

'Why should Holy Church care? A troop of amateurs with an exaggerated sense of their importance drags a cardboard Ark up Ben Yehuda Street in Jerusalem and makes a disturbance outside the court house till they are stopped by the police. So what? You take yourselves too seriously, my friend. Just because you consecrate a little cabal here by the border doesn't turn you into the Albigensian Heresy. Be honest, this place is too boring so you are engaging very hard to create excitements like the soldiers who shoot across the lines to keep awake. The only things not boring here are deep under the ground but you can die of ennui looking for them.'

Félix's cynicism and morbid fascination with religion and the past were among the things he had in common with Milo. He looked like Jean Gabin gone to seed. His grey-haired crew cut was still tough and manly but his face was a turnip pierced by a commanding Gallic nose while his sharp blue eyes ruled over a permanent and startling red flush. It was hard to imagine him in the robes of a monkish order but when he spoke about his past, which was rarely, he hinted at troubled years in a French seminary and some sort of disgraceful suspension. Yet he still had contacts with the Catholic establishment on both sides of the border and was sometimes sent on errands useful to both parties in the unresolved dispute. Because of this a blind eye was turned on his sporadic digs in out-of-the-way sites and his activity in the illegal finds and forgeries market rarely got him into trouble.

Tomas was busy drawing Julius lying on the floor with Rudi's cravat in his hair. On the paper Julius's head stood out detached from the rest of his body like John the Baptist's head on its platter. His eyes looked like black shells holding milky pearls while his hair and beard spread thick black wire in all directions.

Ada didn't want the evening to end in smoke and frustration so she made a suggestion even though she knew it would make trouble for her.

'I can make a pretty good model for the Ark, not full size but quite big. I'll use stuff lying around the Television Centre. Nobody knows what's there and what it's supposed to be used for. If anybody asks I'll say it's a prop for when children's television starts.'

'Fine' said Milo, 'great.' He looked relieved that something so tangible had come out of the evening. He cupped Jordan's face in his hands and kissed her.

'You are wrong, *mon Père*,' he said, stroking Jordan's cheeks. 'We are not as negligible as you think. Maybe it's not because of who we are but we happen to live right on a big sore on the international buttock. It stings all the time and it can't be ignored. So they're going to take notice even if we're not the Comédie-Française and the newspapers will be here anyway for the Big Shit.'

He had regained his confidence.

'I love you,' he half whispered to Jordan. Then loud to Félix, 'don't be jealous, we'll give you a part. Maybe even Noah. Why not? A goy, a drunk, tall and learned in theology. Perfect. Just be yourself, *mon cher*.'

Ada watched Jordan as she leaned against Milo's shoulder with her eyes closed. There was something graceful and calm about her, none of the tension and suppressed hysteria that Milo's cruel charm so often induced in women. She wasn't afraid of failing to impress the lord and master. Not Jordan. Money, thought Ada, money and Berkeley. Twin protector deities hovering over the beautiful and learned American maiden making sure she emerges from every encounter unscarred, perfect, summa cum laude. Ada felt ashamed of her lack of generosity. Why should she secretly wish to see such perfection debased, stained with tears and mud, left to fly back home with a suitcase full of torn underwear and diaries packed with illegible complaint? What good would that do Ada? And Milo? He could straighten up. There were more spectacular conversions in history. She entertained for a moment the absurd picture of Milo, fattened up in checkered Bermuda shorts walking the family dog along a suburban street or parking the family car in one of those garages where you flung aside the door to open Ali Baba's motorcave.

Jordan got up and that was the signal for dispersion.

Tomas was even quieter than usual as they walked down the hill.

'When is Kronberg coming back?' Ada asked.

'There's some court case that has become complicated. His family's property. So he's lonely and wants me to join him.'

'You'd go?'

'Maybe.'

They stood at the door of his ruin.

'Don't go' she said. 'It's worse when I'm lonely.'

He pulled her close to him and they went into the warm dark room. It smelled of kerosene and orange peel. It was their Ark.

A Great Miracle Happened Here

'Ulli is on the way.'

It was Rudi on the phone in a state of some agitation.

'She was supposed to come when she leaves her library job but this is so sudden, so quick. I was on the phone telling her about the Ark and all the goings on at Milo's place and she said: that's it I'm coming. She's always been impulsive but this…Do you think they allow couples to stay at the Convent or will we have to take separate rooms?'

It was hard for Ada to think of Rudi as somebody's husband. Uncle, brother, tennis partner, but husband? He was so self-contained, neat, brushed and agreeable. There was no husbandly rust in his workings, no echo of another voice in the pauses of his conversation. He was his own act, solo, shiny and finely tuned. A shirt of Rudi's stained by a rancid trickle of baby drool was unthinkable. And what about a wife asking him to pick up milk and carrots? It wasn't natural. Yet soon he would be registered as half of a double and Frau Hermine would say, if he came to lunch alone: *Und wo ist die schöne Frau Ulli?*

What could she be like – this German waif pulled out of the Nuremberg ruins and brought to California to be the wife of a man who had turned into a compulsive traveller? What did she know about Rudi? What had he told her about Vienna and the family? Did she know about the photograph he let fly out of the train window? In the snaps he sent his sisters she was always laughing, often with a glass raised in a toast, sometimes with party ribbons in her hair. It was Thanksgiving or New Year, inevitably a festival. She looked young and sturdy with short blonde curls and glasses. Rudi was usually in the background, often in shadow, not quite one of the party. He looked out, beyond the camera, as if he was searching for an opening and needed a pair of binoculars to show him how far he had to go to find it.

Then Ada found herself unexpectedly in the middle of Eyob troubles. The monk had disappeared. He hadn't been seen for a few days but no-one paid particular attention at first. He could have been meditating in a cave or a deserted orchard in Ein Kerem. There was some desultory searching and a party of monks was sent to scour the woods and terraced slopes at the outskirts of the town. They came back with finds of discarded clothing including a clean black Hassid's coat intact with a single condom in one of the pockets, but no trace of Eyob. Then one of the senior monks came to see Ada because they had found a book of sketches and a tailor's dummy in his room and made the connection with Ada's painting. He was an old wizened man, bent over and skeletal but fluent and tactful in his enquiries.

'Maybe Madame has heard something of Eyob? He has been learning to make drawings with Madame? Eyob is very young man and has been very sad for his mother. It was possible he should go back to Ethiopia. Did he say something to Madame?'

Whatever she said might be harmful to Eyob so she stalled.

'He was interested in making drawings and I began to show him and he said he would work sometimes outside and sometimes in his room.'

She wondered if drawing was forbidden to the monks but she heard no censure in the old man's voice.

'And the big doll with no head?'

'It is an old one used by tailors to measure what they make, like suits or dresses. He liked it so I lent it to him.'

'It is not witch doll for magic?'

'No, it is called a tailor's dummy. You can find them in one or two shops on Jaffa Road.'

He didn't look convinced.

'But where is the head?'

'Such dummys do not have heads. They are made that way.'

He looked suspicious.

'So why some pins are stuck in this doll, all over?'

'They must have been left over from when it was in a tailor's shop. They use pins to hold together the clothes they are sewing.'

He clicked and sucked on his false teeth and looked around the room. Noticing the pile of dolls by the window, he burrowed in his robe and pulled out a small pair of glasses. He inspected the dolls and sighed.

'These, Madame,' he pointed at the window, 'such things are for playing by young girls?'

'Yes, but I collect them.'

It wasn't clear whether he understood.

'You are Jewish person?' he asked.

'Yes.'

'You must not pray to dolls. It is written.'

'Of course not. I keep them like in a shop.'

'To sell?'

He seemed to understand something and she jumped at the opportunity.

'Yes, to sell to tourists for dollars.'

He smiled hesitantly and nodded.

Ada was perhaps cleared of the suspicion of witchcraft and idolatry but she was concerned that a link had been established between herself and Eyob's disappearance.

At Fink's bar a few nights later she asked Félix for help. Although he lived in a pleasant flat stuffed with books and potsherds in a good part of town he was a wanderer in spirit and took off on solitary expeditions, sleeping rough. So he was an expert in detail on the lay of the land around the town in the only direction you were free to walk, to the West. The deep terraced valleys, the derelict wells and cisterns next to the bare concrete houses of new immigrants, the occasional spring, the crumbling agricultural storehouses, sheikh's tombs, crusader ruins and relics of the 1948 war, all these were his territory. He walked the steep goat paths, brandy flask in his pocket and though he neither kept a journal nor had a camera he came back full of talk. He called his beat Terra InFelix because it filled him with sadness. 'There's something left hanging out there, something waiting for a sign to bring it to life. Spring only seems to do it. But even Spring can't remedy the *tristesse*. Sad the way one hill folds into another like it's surrendering and even the birdsong, it is too quiet. There aren't enough trees. So much emptiness and beneath the ground so much buried and lost.' Then he might pull out of a pouch a few purple and white stones of a mosaic or the green neck of a small glass flask and stare at them as if he could hypnotise them back into fullness.

Ada bought him a glass of Armagnac.

'My friend the monk has disappeared. You know all the caves and the derelict houses around the town. You could keep an eye open for a tall Ethiopian monk.'

'How do you know he hasn't got rid of his habit?'

'I don't think he'd do that.'

'Don't underestimate a monk's desire for liberty. Look *ma chère*, it's not the right weather but I'll make a short reconnaissance for your man. And why do you concern yourself about him?'

'He spoke to me frankly and I feel responsible in a way.'

Félix rolled his eyes and promised to give it a try.

Winter was settling in. There were a few flurries of snow and days of rain but the wind was now in charge of the town. It encountered walkers from unexpected angles at street corners with cold gusts that stung eyes and nose and blew grit into mouths through closed lips. It changed the direction of rain to horizontal so that flying drops met a face like pellets aimed to hurt. It blew into all the spaces left undefended around doors and windows so that the warmth created by kerosene stoves inside spread in patches only like an unfinished jigsaw puzzle. No room was ever really warm. And people sometimes just took to their beds under heavy down covers brought from Europe by families unconvinced, in Vienna or Breslau, that the real problem in Palästina would be merciless heat rather than cold feet.

In the town's sleepy commercial streets they were brightening up the shops for the coming Festival of Light, Hanukkah. Ribbons, silver paper and red and gold party decorations, put away the year before, appeared again. Strings of party gold and silver coins nestled on the toys, shoes, handbags, and shirts that shopkeepers hoped the season would help them sell. At the heart of each display, like a lighthouse in an aquarium, stood a menorah. Some were of traditional silver or brass but others were compositions of sea shells, jerry-built out of bottle tops and coloured pebbles, even old gun barrels and tin cans clumsily welded together. The seasonal formula in bold letters, often stretching across the window like a garland, completed the picture

A GREAT
MIRACLE HAPPENED HERE

But in certain shops you could detect the ghostly influence of another December Festival, also celebrating a miracle, whose name could be mentioned only in a whisper. Wallets and leather gloves were placed on shiny white crinkly paper simulating snow. Little sprigs of plastic holly hid shyly behind a box of cigarillos or a bottle of fiercely expensive whiskey. For some reason Christmas hints were directed at men only, rich men of the world who had seen Regent Street and the Galeries Lafayette and didn't give a fig for the isolationism of ghetto obscurantists. As for the gentiles, the Christian Arabs, the diplomats and the United Nations personnel, many of them could celebrate Christmas on the other side by way of the Mandelbaum Gate and for those who stayed behind there were one or two shops hidden away in less frequented streets where you could buy pork and ham and pies and Christmas decorations and even order small Christmas trees from Nazareth or Jaffa.

*

Jordan and Milo quarrelled about Hanukka. Jordan was used to a warm family celebration with cousins and friends and presents. The candles on the menorah had always made a deep impression on her. As a girl she counted their progress from one to eight with a suspense and pleasure she never forgot. Later the anthropologist in her linked the emotion to the magical power of counting spells and fire rituals in tribal cultures. But here with her window facing the Temple Mount in the grey cold mist she felt the old tug and started looking for a menorah among Milo's coffee makers, smoking apparatus and chipped Armenian tiles.

Milo was incredulous. 'Why would I have one of those pyromaniac toys? Candles? You know where they can stick their candles. Who gives a shit about the Temple and fake miracles? It's kitsch, pure insufferable kitsch. What's next, latkes and cherry brandy?'

Jordan was hurt. The quarrel showed her how far away from her old life she had come. The familiar scenery of her world had vanished and in its place was this strange marginal and polyglot collection of people who seemed to belong nowhere but on a narrow and dangerous frontier and even made this an article of faith. Were she not so closely involved she might have made a study of them observing their withdrawal from the town where most of them worked, their resistance to its official pieties and their disdain for its displays of flags and patriotism. She understood how drawn they were to the lost half of the city over the wall and how its Moslem and Christian character and its babel of languages – Armenian, Greek, Arabic, English – offered them a fantasy of variety, mystery and worldly freedom from the tribal enclosure. They were in one place and longed to be in another. Not New York or Paris but a place that was, she guessed, absurdly similar to where they already were. It was only the other side of the coin. Milo had shown her the old Mandate piastre coin they used to flip for heads or tails. On one side was a palm tree, on the other the legend PALESTINE. You flipped shouting ETZ (tree) or PALESTINE. But the piastres were gone with the British, and the Tree and Palestine were separate for ever.

Jordan understood the sadness of this but why the grudge against the menorah? Why the anger against this harmless handful of light? She needed someone to share her troubles with.

That evening she walked over to Tomas's ruin and found Ada there alone drawing sketches of the Ark and masks and costumes for Noah, the animals and the family. She sat at the sturdy carpenter's table Tomas used for work under a lamp that gave an unstable, intermittently weak light. Ada's chalk-white skin and coal-black eyes made her face a Japanese mask. Jordan resisted an impulse to smile and say Hi, like one did at home. This kind of unearned, easy, quasi-friendliness was treated with suspicion here. So she made straight for the sheets of sketches.

'How's it going?'

'It's a big mess. When I come up with something that seems OK he says no.'

Some of the Arks were colourful and gay as if they were competing in a regatta or on display in a carnival but others were dour and businesslike, as ponderous as hippos in mud.

'What does Milo want?'

Ada didn't answer.

'Do you think he has a realistic idea of what's going to be?'

'A few hours before the big day he will.'

'What's making him do this?'

Ada looked surprised.

'I hope you haven't asked him.'

'No, I didn't but…he seems very different here from when we lived in the States. He wasn't so prickly over there. Here it's as if he's in a fight all the time. Who's he fighting? Why does he hate Hanukkah?'

Ada laughed.

'You should have seen him staging a Black Mass on Yom Kippur years ago. Hanukkah is peanuts, child's stuff. He was almost lynched for barbecuing a rabbit that Kippur. People on their way to synagogue smelt him out and broke into the garden. They were wearing white but they wanted blood. He had a revolver and he threatened them. So they just cursed him and his children's children and went back to their fast day. You see it's murder to resist here. You have to put your whole mind to it because it's the least natural thing to do and yet you've got to resist to hold onto your self-respect. If you don't think with the herd you mustn't shut up, you have to work hard at showing it.'

'Lighting candles would compromise him?'

Ada laughed.

'It would make him feel like Nanny Fanny in the kindergarten. It would threaten his manhood. Milo would never do it, even for you. Stay away from it.'

Listen to me, thought Ada, the retired Sultana telling the current harem favourite how to handle the capricious commander of the unfaithful. She wouldn't tell Jordan about Christmas Eve years ago and the times she and Milo had, in the pitch dark of a cold December night, climbed the steep winding path up Mount Zion to the Dormition Abbey to watch the Midnight Mass. The church was paces away from the ceasefire line and the Old City wall but the night hid the barbed wire and the sandbags and every year a crowd of students from the University and the Art School filled the outer aisles of the massive, unlovely church to listen to the echoing chants of the service and catch a glimpse of the monks and the bright, coloured robes of the officiants. They stood pressed together ragged and wrapped up against the cold like young barbarians stranded in imperial Rome and waited to be impressed by something they knew nothing about: Christian mystery and pomp, organ thunder, incense and flickering lights. Milo was uncharacteristically silent about all this even though they returned twice. He knew the Latin of the Mass from his studies and Ada watched him closely to see if he would mouth the responses. But he stood stock still throughout the service, his eyes fixed on the massive pillar with St Michael holding a sword in front of them. Milo's dark face was frozen in concentration. Back in the room where they lived he drank half a bottle of Cognac Medicinal to warm up and spent the rest of the night reading. She woke up late to find him gone but he had scrawled on one of her canvases lines of St John of the Cross:

Oh mi Dios Cuando sera
Cuando yo diga de vero
Vivo ya porque no muero.

Later he said he fell asleep drunk and remembered nothing except waking up cold, stinking of alcohol and going outside to pee.

If I wrote that I did it in my sleep but don't paint over it. I'll stare at it till it reminds me of something. She left him sitting in front of the canvas and when she came back at night the verses were painted over and he was lying on their mattress smoking.

Did it remind you of anything?

You can talk to him in Spanish,

Oh mi Dios, Oh mi Dios.

Look what you've done.

Ada felt a sisterly pang for Jordan. The lovely young American was a traveller in a strange country where she couldn't understand the road signs and was likely to misread the gestures of the natives who might be trying to help or were misleading her out of impatience or a lack of compassion. Milo was possibly in love with her but how could he offer her anything but a dangerous and rocky path to stumble along? There was something unyielding and irresponsible about him even today, even with this new woman whose health promised to lead him away from the destructiveness and self-wounding that had marked his life.

She put a comforting hand on Jordan's arm.

'It's a difficult place and this is an odd crowd. We're jealous because you're healthy and we are hypochondriacs. We think we've got all the going diseases and the world won't cure us. People must have said to you: Why did you come here, are you crazy? Haven't you heard that? Well, they mean it. Milo can never do candles because if that's what sane people do, he'd rather be sick.'

Jordan returned Ada's touch for a second and without saying anything walked out. Through the window Ada saw her climbing up the path, bent against the cold wind, arms crossed against her breast. She looked frail and diminished as the surrounding greyness absorbed her, like it absorbed the stunted trees, the crumbling bandstand and the rusty, creaking signs warning DANGER BORDER.

Tomas came back that night with news about Eyob. Père Félix had come to his stand in the market and told him the Ethiopian monk was safe and living in a house in Sataf, a village abandoned by its Arab population in the fighting of 1948. Félix heard about him from the Kurdish men of a nearby immigrant village who found him roaming the terraces near their bare breeze-block houses looking for food. Though they had no common language they took pity on him and gave him cheese and fruit. They said they saw smoke so he must have found a way to warm himself. When Félix climbed the path to the village he found traces of a fire in one of the crumbling houses but no Eyob.

Ada wanted to set out for Sataf immediately but Tomas pointed out that there was no bus and it would be late by the time they got there. The army used it as a training ground so it would be dangerous as well as useless. Tomas had other things on his mind. He had a letter from Kronberg.

They sat down in the window and were silent for a while as the wind rattled the panes. Tomas unwound the thick scarf from his neck, pulled an envelope out of his pocket and began to read.

Why do I feel so at home here? It doesn't make sense or it could seem monstrous and shameful. It's not as if I walk through my past life every day. The city was flattened by an enormous air raid near the end of the war and the historic parts were rebuilt by the work of women (no men around) to look like it was before the war. So it's as if it didn't happen. All neat and clean, an architect's drawing. Yes, I recognize parts well enough but I didn't grow up here. Not in this doctored photograph. Our street and our house have disappeared so why do I feel at home? I last saw father and mother when they came out on the steps of our house to say goodbye. They stood there looking straight ahead, Dr Kronberg and Emilia, upright and stiff, real Germans. They wanted the neighbours to pay attention, I suppose, though that was something real Germans would avoid. I have some strange urge to approach people in the street and say: I was born here, you know. I had to leave but now I'm back, back home. They would run away from the madman. The tribunal inquiry about the property goes on. They are very correct of course and young. They would like it all to be over but their own rules bind them. Meanwhile I address school assemblies in buildings that have no past and in a German that must seem to them an ancient language. Yesterday I stared at the rows of boys in the hall. They looked like eggs in a box and as the headmaster introduced me I blotted them out and thought of you. I pictured you, dear Tomas, at work, bent over the paper spread out on your table. I see your shoulders and hands moving with the lines you spread across the sheet. I look at the back of your neck, tense with concentration and your hair sometimes more brown, sometimes dark. The school hall and its boys are gone but you are there while I watch. Then I got up to speak when I had to, I am used to this sort of thing by now, and said what was expected of me: some accusation, in the right direction, some anger but also regret and hope that, if the past was faced, the wounds would heal. As I prepare for such addresses I think of how our city remains wounded by its war, handicapped by amputated streets and neglect, an orphaned city. I am not surprised how little I miss it. I don't carry Madame Zion in my heart, only you.

When will you come?'

Tomas's voice softened to a murmur but his face when Ada took his hand was impassive.

'He's sure I'm going to join him.'

'What did you promise?'

'It's not what I promised, it's what he decided. Since we've known each other he has made our decisions. It was the way it had to be.'

'He doesn't own you.'

Tomas was silent.

'He fought me for my life when I was destroying it. I needed to have everybody against me. I stank of anger I didn't talk, I just quarrelled. With Kronberg I failed. I couldn't turn him into an enemy. I used to hit him and bite and I drew blood. They were mostly nightmares but not always. I tore up books. I smashed up his study and I succeeded in making him angry. So we fought. It usually ended with him wrestling me to the ground. It wasn't so hard. He was stronger then and I was puny. He called them lovers' quarrels.'

Tomas cupped her face in his hands.

'You must have known or guessed. Who can keep secrets here? But what people say is a joke, a caricature. People don't know. No-one knows but two.'

'And me?'

'You know me now. You didn't know me then.'

He looked pale and thin framed in the window, the tip of his nose still red from the cold outside. A frown of concentration tightened the skin around his eyes which now stared at the big canvas on the wall as if he was trying to throw beams of light at the painted scene.

'When your parents are suddenly not there you first think they're coming back any moment. You wait up at night for them. Then there's room for nothing but anger because they've abandoned you, stuck you with strangers in a dirty hovel full of smoke. Then the smoke chases everything out of your head except you want to run away and breathe. Then you get used to it and cough and draw with chalk on the floor and forget. Kronberg pushed me to remember even if I almost strangled him for it and he made me think I couldn't live without him.'

Tomas looked at her as if daring her to avert her gaze. She didn't. He stood in front of her and stroked her face. His hands were still cold.

'Believe me, you would have run like a frightened rabbit from me. You wouldn't have been able to stand me. Pity from a distance, maybe. You must have read about people like me in the paper but to deal with me, talk, sleep with me in one bed? Never. It was like a gangrene on me and nothing could scrape it off. Women noticed it from a mile away. *Look there goes that strange Pole. You know what happened to them!*'

Tomas was speaking mockingly, aggressively, his voice rising to a high pitch and his hands a vice pressing against her cheekbones. Ada felt the mounting tension in his body and didn't know how to restrain it. He kept on talking but it was more noise than words. She couldn't wrestle him to the ground like Kronberg. She couldn't stifle him or shout over his voice. So she pressed her head against him and hung there, her arms around his hips like a lifebelt. When his voice grew calmer she pressed her whole body to his and breathed in the smell of his clothes, the gritty wind in them, the fragrance of orange peel, the acrid kerosene, the paint, soap powder of the latest wash and the mustiness of wool stored in a suitcase through the long summer. This is the flavour of no man's land, she thought, it's not the end of the world. It's our world, where we live.

An early bus took them next morning to a crossroads just outside the city, past the cemetery and the two quarries, both still silent before the day's business of pestering the rock began. Then they walked along a trail which followed the bed of a valley. On both sides steep slopes exposed lines of terraces like ribs on a naked torso.

The recent rain had put some gleam into the pale grey stones and the ground was soft and muddy. Soon they started to climb steeply up the slope and at first a few trees and then signs of cultivation, irrigation channels and plots of soil began to give a domesticated character to the abrupt hillside. Then shells of stone houses with gaping holes for doors and windows appeared, scattered on both sides of the path holding onto the slope precariously as if resisting the slippery slide to the bottom of the valley. The climb was strenuous and they stopped to rest on the remains of a stone wall.

The rain had given fragrance to the air but it was countered by a stale breath that seemed to be coming from the empty shells of houses. *Yoo Hoo.* Tomas gave his high pitched no-man's-land shout. *Yoo Hoo Eyob Eyob Yoo Hoo.* In the morning silence the echo was dramatic, swooping back, pure and unchanged, from the opposite flank of the valley far away. But no answer from Eyob. They climbed further into what must have been the heart of the village. A muddy pool of water surrounded by a sturdy, undamaged wall was fed by a trickle flowing out of an opening in the rock above. The water made a crisp metallic tlip tlip sound as it fell into the pool. With a nimble jump Tomas climbed over the rock above the pool and disappeared. Ada sat still transfixed by the sound of the water magnified by the hollow shell of the wall surrounding the pool. She closed her eyes and tried to ignore the flies trying to burrow into her ears and nostrils. Then she heard Tomas's voice seemingly from within the rock. 'Hey!'

'Hallo,' she answered, too lazy to get up. There was silence for a while, then Tomas's head appeared in the opening of the rock above the pool. 'Come up – it's worth it.'

She climbed over stones that may once have been steps with difficulty and found herself at the entrance to the tunnel that led water from its source to the pool below. Tomas was crouching inside, his hands flat against the limestone wall.

'Look how smooth. It's like the flank of a big soft cow, forget the stone. Feel it, it's alive.'

Tomas was excited. He patted the rock as he spoke.

'The village has been deserted for years but there's no dirt or shit in here. It's like it's been swept and the walls polished every day or at night by the people who lived here, come back just to clean it.'

Ada crouched down near him. Although she was smaller than Tomas she felt large and clumsy here as if she was disturbing some natural equilibrium of rock, water and air. She was sitting in what had been the lifeline of a living body and now it was sterile, a channel of water with no purpose.

'Who cares if it's clean. It's all wrong,' she said.

'What?'

'This empty village. This water going nowhere. The broken walls. The quiet.'

She felt the chill of DANGER BORDER sneaking into the tunnel, even though it was miles away from the ceasefire line and the barbed wire.

She and Tomas were intruders. They had crossed over a non-existent line and crawled into the heart of a left behind land where water kept trickling from its spring like fingernails growing on a corpse. If they stayed till dark surely searchlights from somewhere would stab at the terraces and the stone walls looking for them, trying to scoop them out of their hiding place.

She shivered so visibly that Tomas pressed her close.

'I'm cold and hungry, let's get out.'

They crawled back into the light and she called for Eyob again. Her shout startled some birds but there was no answer. They pushed their way through clumps of thorns into the gaping mouth of one house after another. Strewn here and there in all the emptiness there was debris, rusting shapes of metal unconnected to any recognizable object, fragments of pottery crushed into the earth, discarded tins of army rations, even a roll of toilet paper and in one shell of a house the sooty marks of a recent fire and some orange peel. Eyob's trace.

They gave up to return to the city and go to work.

SHPITZ

THE OLD ICE factory was now called EXPERIMENTAL TELEVISION CENTRE. Gradually more of its grey, bleak heart was turning into offices, some inhabited by people sitting behind old desks talking into new phones. Somewhere hidden away behind makeshift wooden walls a studio or a control room was still taking shape. Although it wasn't talked about, the underlying fear of the officials in charge was that the famous foreign correspondents, the BBC people, the American networks and all the rest, would find the locals incompetent, ignorant and unprepared. Old Soviet jokes about Radio Yerevan in Armenia weren't much comfort to them as they saw themselves turning into a similar example of provincial clownishness. However a saviour had been found. Lewis Meredith was a Welsh theatre director who was married to the daughter of a heavyweight in the London Jewish community who had whispered into the ear of the ambassador who had called it a recommendation from the highest quarters in the media world. Not that Lewis was a known quantity. He wasn't. He had directed plays here and there and had some not so well documented connections with television drama in Cardiff and Manchester. But Lewis Meredith agreed to come immediately so the largest office with a window, two phones, more or less stable walls and an armchair was put together and dusted off to receive the new Director, immediately nicknamed Shpitz.

Ada was called in to meet him a few days after he started work.

She was surprised to find the office had an anteroom with a secretary, some shiny leaves in pots and, on the wall, a framed aerial photograph of Massada, pink in the setting sun, looking like an arrangement of biscuits on a tray. The door to the inner office was open and a man beckoned to her to come in. It was Meredith standing by his desk with one foot on a chair and one hand worrying his black goatee. Ada noticed an elegant suede shoe and a red sock between it and the trouser cuff. He put out a hand, keeping his shoe on the chair.

'Very glad to meet you. Lewis is my name. They tell me you were at the Beaux Arts in Paris and everyone calls you Ada. So Ada, did you know Renée Farkash? She might have been there in your day, a really talented stage designer, wonderful flair and sense of colour. Made the buggers get on their feet and cheer when the curtain went up. Perhaps you've heard of our production of *Volpone*. No? Quite notorious. We had a large woman playing the lead. Dressed her in scarlet furs. Became quite famous afterwards as a television cook. Yes…so Ada, well…you are in charge of design and serious stuff like that. Truly, I'm looking forward to working with you. I may be the director, formally and all that but you'll find out I'm a team fellow. I really believe in co—llab—or—ation.' He separated the syllables as if they were a musical flourish and marked the end of the word with a click of his tongue.

He was thin with a bony, pointed face (hence Shpitz) and deep-set blue eyes. His hair was thick and deep black and lay across his head and broad forehead like the coat of a sleek animal. The whiteness of his skin was phenomenal.

Ada noticed a bottle of Medicinal and a chipped Turkish coffee cup on one of the shelves in between a couple of fat folders and thought: *Shpitz, you are a quick study*.

She invited him to a Hanukkah party.

Jordan had seemed so upset by the absence of seasonal candles that Ada arranged a gathering in her Ethiopian rooms so they could get round Milo who was out of town for a few days and mark the festival. Perla, in Jerusalem for a nurses' meeting, would be there and Julius, Rudi, Félix, Tomas and whoever had heard there was a chance of getting some foreign drink. She bought doughnuts and various sticky pastries and made a potent hot punch with the help of some lab alcohol from the Medical School. The menorah (borrowed from a neighbour that morning) was put on the window recess and, ignoring the fire hazard, she arranged her dolls in ranks behind it like the Vienna Philharmonic Chorus in drag.

Taking stock of the room before the guests came she was struck by how permanent it looked and yet it had the feel of a stage set arranged and lit for an audience. Her paintings, some stacked, some standing against the walls, a model of Noah's Ark on its shelf, her books, sewing machine and even the bright mess of cloth fragments, sketches and bric-a-brac on her work table filled it with a personality she assumed must be hers. Not in Suzi and Perla's place, nor in the other rooms and apartments of her life had she felt such sympathy between herself and four walls. The fading Abyssinian Palace of Exile with its rickety stairs and dark corridors had become a place that suited her melancholy and her love of old stones and walls that seemed to stay upright by some law unknown to the architects who built rectangular housing projects in a hurry on bare hillsides. Here she felt like a lizard in the sun, protected by something like another layer of skin from the clamour of the town in one direction and the desolation of no man's land in the other.

The party became noisy very quickly. The candles on the menorah once Jordan had lit them soon melted and were forgotten as the loops and curves of Sidney Bechet's clarinet brought out the jitterbugers among whom, Père Félix taller than everyone else, flushed and broad shouldered, hovered over the bobbing heads like a buoy in a sea swell. He was dancing with a surprised Perla, prompting her into dizzy twists and turns as he swayed around her singing in his mellow baritone:

Quand la vie
Par moment me trahit
Tu restes mon bonheur.

Ada enjoyed watching Perla forget her professional crispness as she was drawn out by Père Félix's charm. She had come probably expecting the usual coffee and cake chatter and had been ambushed by the strong punch and the jazz and the unusual Frenchman who knew the Egyptian desert and sang like Charles Trenet.

Rudi, on the other hand, was ill at ease, chain smoking and hovering by the window on the edge of the room looking anxiously about him as if he expected a police raid. Ulli's arrival was imminent and he had spent days planning for every contingency, hunting for American coffee, shampoo, soap and thick towels. His friend, Schwester Clara, the Mother Superior, had shown much ingenuity in turning his bare room into a cosy nest for a couple. She had moved in a sofa and rugs from her own apartment and spread embroidered coverlets over every flat space. On the bed was the most delicate of all the community's treasures, a band of purple silk bearing the motto AMOR VINCIT OMNIA embroidered in gold thread. It had been saved from a pillaged sister convent in Lebanon.

Rudi was troubled about Ulli and the coincidence of her arrival with Christmas. In California they had never bothered with festivals except for an occasional Passover Seder and a regular Thanksgiving and Ulli had only painful memories of her Nuremberg childhood, so there was no reason Christmas should come up. But his short stay in Jerusalem had changed Rudi. He had lost his indifference to religion. The eery quiet that crept through the city on Friday evenings when the streets emptied, the traffic stopped and the smells of cooking for the Sabbath meal drove the stray cats crazy, put him in a restless searching mood. He would walk alone through dead streets as the light faded, listening to the clatter of loose shop signs in the wind and the forlorn trill of an ignored burglar alarm. Somewhere up some stairs above the uncleared garbage or through an alleyway there were prayer rooms. He would see men dressed in black with children trotting behind them hurrying, always hurrying to the evening prayer. He imagined the rooms to be like poky workshops or bare rooms of political clubs where a weekly negotiation went on between the men and a hidden figure of authority who dealt out famine and wealth, life and death. Rudi himself had never been in such a place though he had been inside a large synagogue with an organ in Vienna. What fascinated him was this suction which drew fathers and children through streets and into alleyways and up stairs every Friday evening. On the other side, Félix had told him, something similar happened. The narrow streets that led down to the El Aqsa Mosque became rivers of men heading for prayer. Rudi imagined them all together, hundreds and hundreds, downing foreheads on the cold stone of the mosque floor like sheep grazing and he felt the isolation of a lone swimmer adrift in a sea ruled by mysterious, dangerous currents. Christmas became in his mind one of these with Ulli sucked down into its overwhelming centre.

The party was quietening down when Lewis arrived. Framed in the doorway to survey the room and wearing a shaggy black and white sheepskin coat he looked like the Knave in a pack of cards. Soon, a glass of punch in one hand and one of Ada's Gitanes in the other, he was describing his production of *The Merchant of Venice* in Cardiff which had been picketed by the Association of Jewish Ex-Servicemen.

'Good people, all of them but completely off the wall. They were too wooden-headed to realize that Shylock was the hero, dammit. The only honest man in the whole of Venice. He was also taller than all the others. You see I wanted an athletic, manly Hebrew. No sloping shoulders and flat feet. More a weight lifter than a bookworm. The actor was Welsh and he had a lovely basso voice.

'*When Jacob grazed his uncle Laban's sheep*.

'He bloody well sang it like a hymn in chapel. The buggers in the gallery liked him too. That show did more for the Jews than Benjamin Disraeli and Groucho Marx any time, take my word for it.'

The pointed black beard under his chin punctuated his speech like a jumping exclamation mark.

Bechet had been turned off and the room was warm and

humming with conversation when Ada noticed Jordan standing by the work table leafing through a folder of sketches and drawings. She looked over her shoulder.

'Strange things your dolls get up to. They're really women on the way to something else, like caught in the act of running away. Some of them look totally real, this one. Fascinating.'

She picked out a drawing in coloured chalk of a Malian beauty with a nun's headdress and a silver cross on her graceful breast. Milo had liked to play nuns and priests with her.

'Did you know her?'

Ada didn't answer immediately. On the tip of her tongue was the whole frenzied Parisian episode with Oumou, and Milo's infatuation to the point of proposing marriage.

'Why the nun's get-up? She couldn't really have been a nun. Some kind of fancy dress?'

'Yes, she was a dancer and she liked theatrical stuff. She was always in and out of one costume or another.'

More out than in, thought Ada, seeing underwear strewn around the flat and Milo in tears refusing to eat for days when Oumou once disappeared. Then, when devious messages by telegram began to arrive from Nice and Marseilles his grief turned to anger and he bought a knife with which to kill her.

'Was she a friend of Milo?'

How innocent this American beauty is, thought Ada. *Doesn't she suspect the naked nun of anything? Don't they teach French erotic classics at Berkeley?*

'Yes, she was one of his girlfriends in Paris.'

'A special one?'

'They were all special while they lasted.'

She regretted saying that but the truth was quicker than her tact and there was some anger in her against Jordan for opening all this up. Surely it was all confessed and forgiven between her and Milo. Or was it?

Jordan persisted.

'And you, how did you fit into all this?'

She wasn't looking at her as she asked, her eyes were fixed on Oumou and her fingers traced the curve of her neck.

Ada needed to get out of this conversation. Julius joined them.

'If you want to know anything about those women, don't ask Ada. She just painted them, never asked questions.'

He pointed to Oumou, 'Behold the Queen of Sheba. Her perfumes were so strong that Solomon lost his erection and fainted. Seriously, Ada, there are some good stories here and you're not telling. Why?'

Lewis was looking over Jordan's shoulder.

'And this is what you do when you're not working for us? Very handsome indeed. They don't seem like local flowers or haven't I been looking in the right direction?'

Ada had enough.

'I don't know why we're looking at these. It's all old stuff. Most of it I should have thrown away. They're nothing I'm proud of.'

She scooped up the sheets and put away the folder. She shouldn't have left it on the table with the room full of people. But it was there because she couldn't help interrogating her past with Milo. The women in the folder were an intimate history she had made a weak effort to forget. It was a history of a hidden wound surfacing in the faces and bodies of the women and in the doll mechanisms that competed with their lively flesh. She could not bring herself to look at the cruel paintings of herself as a soldier. They were like confessions of a crime. No force in the world could make her read again the base, sordid language she had scrawled over that scene. But the ghost of it hung over her like a bad memory of a violation inflicted by herself on herself.

Jordan was sulking in a corner with a glass of punch when Milo walked in. He was red-faced in his black sweater and leather jacket and was carrying a small Christmas tree in front of him like a bouquet.

'Where's Père Félix? This is for you, you old bastard. Now you've got to decorate it à l'anglaise or I'll give it to the British library.'

He looked around the room, blew a kiss at Perla and went over to Jordan. He was elated.

'We got some money out of the British Council. They think Noah's Ark here is a great idea. One of their directors in London is a fan of the mystery plays and did Satan for the York festival. Why are you looking upset, sweet, didn't you light the candles? Did it make you homesick?' He was trying, in his way, to soften his sarcasm with concern.

He took her in his arms and stroked her back but she responded only half-heartedly. Still holding her he looked over her shoulder at Ada, 'There was a police car in the street by the monastery gate. A bunch of cops as well. Could be something to do with your friend.'

The party was splitting up into small groups. Perla was singing Vera Lynn songs, her arm linked with Félix's. She was a little drunk and melancholy and did the sad voice of the troops' sweetheart with eyes full of tears: *We'll meet again don't know where don't know when.*

Ada was worried about Eyob. 'He must have got into trouble.' She whispered to Tomas and they left the room and hurried round the corner to Ethiopia Street where the Church and the Monastery stood behind a high wall and an iron gate painted sky blue. The courtyard was strangely bright in the intermittent moonlight. Tall cypresses stood on guard and the irregular chalky paving stones glowed despite the dark. No light at all came from any of the windows of the ramshackle houses hugging the round white church. They didn't know where to go so they chose a door at random and knocked. No-one answered. Tomas tried his yodel. Yoohoo Yoohoo hoo. Still nothing.

Ada searched for the Amharic phrases Eyob had taught her when they made a bet she couldn't get them right.

First she banged hard. Then, '*Yikerta.*'

And again, '*Yikerta dehna neh.*'

That ought to be something like, 'Excuse me, hello.'

There was a movement on the other side and a figure covered in black with a weak torch in its hand opened the door.

'*Selam*,' said Ada. 'English?'

It seemed to be a man.

'English, yes. Please?'

'We are looking for Eyob.'

Silence.

'Eyob. Is he here?'

More silence, then he pointed the torch at one of the other doors in the row and fluttered long bony fingers in a gesture of dismissal. He turned abruptly and closed the door.

Tomas banged hard and long on the door, which was at last opened by a young monk holding an orange. The room behind him was brightly lit though no light filtered out through the small window.

Ada felt more confident.

'Eyob? We are friends. Is he here?'

The monk motioned them to come in.

The room was empty of furniture except for chairs arranged in a square along the walls under gold and red religious paintings. The monks in the chairs looked identical to Ada, wizened old men in black. It seemed like some sort of tribunal or committee. Then she recognized the elder who had come to see her about Eyob and addressed herself to him.

'We apologise for coming so late. But we heard news that maybe Eyob has been found and we came to see.'

There was silence.

'Who is the young man?'

'He is my friend. He accompanied me in the night.'

The elder took off his glasses and then replaced them. The line of black robed men remained perfectly still.

'Eyob is held with the police. He is found but he is closed up in Moskobiyye.'

The police station and lock-up were in the Russian Compound where pilgrims had once been housed in fortress-like buildings alongside the big Orthodox church.

'Maybe we can help,' said Ada.

But there was no answer.

103

'Sorry, good night,' and they were out of the door.

'That jail is a stinking hole,' said Tomas who had been there a few times. 'The Ethiopians will get him out soon enough. The police don't like to mess with churches. It gets too complicated.'

When they got back to the room it was almost empty and stale with smoke and the smell of spilt alcohol. Jordan was still there on the sofa, seemingly asleep. Perla was stroking her hair.

'He outdid himself tonight, the Grand Turk. Look at her. She's shell-shocked.'

Félix appeared from the bed alcove and took Ada aside.

'Milo was beastly in the extreme. For no reason. So she asked him about that Africaine in Paris. Not tactful maybe but he acted as if she stuck the finger in his eye. He called her Betty Boop and Nancy and more. She wasn't listening to the signals so she kept on asking and he put his hands on her shoulders and looked her right in the eyes and said: "She was the best godalmighty fuck in the world."'

'OK, not polite, but he said it in a voice of great reverence and regret like he was mourning the fall of a civilization. Pity for Jordan.'

They all stood over the sleeping Jordan like relatives by a hospital bed. Ada had seen this all before, the distraught victim taking refuge in sleep, the absent aggressor, the smoke and the spilt drink, the inquisitive sympathetic bystanders. In the past she had been the undertaker in charge of disposing the body and dispatching the belongings but now she looked at the scene as if it was a photograph in the evening paper. She wasn't there. But when Félix and Perla left and Tomas disappeared into the sleeping alcove she was alone, once again, with the body. She sat on the sofa and studied Jordan. Her hair was less perfect than usual, loose brown strands strayed against the white of her neck, the blouse and skirt had become unanchored and twisted in sleep. She bent over and breathed in the delicate perfume. Yes, that was still there. The chaste ear rings still nestled in their lobes. No self-inflicted scratches on the cheek. No unbecoming smear of tears and mascara. The case wasn't mortal.

Yet she felt a kind of nostalgia for the Milo drama. The sleeping woman could have been herself years ago. She could have been the girl set adrift by his strange demands and pushed into a maze of mirrors by his abrupt outburst of anger and sudden changes of mood. Years ago there was this secret excitement as the pain and bewilderment undermined her. There was intoxication in the loss of control and a perverse pleasure in her deafness to the warning voices of self-preservation. There was distress now but it wasn't hers. It was an echo somewhere of a voice in the distance. She could shut her eyes and put her hands over her ears and it would go away.

The room was quiet and chilly, someone had turned off the stoves. She covered Jordan with another blanket and went to bed.

Tomas wasn't asleep. His body was warm but his hands were cold on her. His palms were dry and his touch was rough and demanding like a prisoner reaching for food. Ada searched for his eyes but they seemed to be turned inwards or probing for someone, not herself. He said nothing and his breathing was laboured and panicky. She tried to calm him with slow caresses and shushing sounds but this seemed to make him angry and he turned away from her and curved into a ball.

In the morning they woke to find Jordan gone and her blankets neatly folded on the sofa. She had left a note: *I guess I made a fool of myself. Sorry and thanks.*

Later in the day outside the police station in the Russian Compound Ada met the lawyer Margarian. He had been hired by the Ethiopians to get Eyob out of trouble. Margarian had a way of turning the tables, putting judges and policemen on trial for their scandalous ignorance of the practices of the mysterious Christians on their side of the ceasefire line. Whenever some nunnery or church institution was sued for non payment of municipal taxes or allowing a wall to crumble, Margarian was called in. He was particularly good at producing obscure Ottoman rulings allowing the Franciscans or the Latin Catholics to pay a reduced tax or to define a shop on church property as an educational charity. Although he was generally a calm and mild-mannered man he could for such purposes put on a performance of deeply-hurt pride and sorrowful anger that such a learned man as Judge Berman or such a dedicated public servant as Chief Inspector Siman Tov were so badly informed of the ancient, deeply-rooted rights and traditions of the ancient Christian orders with whom it was in the interest of the comparatively new Jewish authorities to be on the best of terms.

'Don't worry,' he said to Ada, 'I'll get him out. He was stopped by a patrol on the border by the railway line and, you know, they were not so gentlemanly in their treatment. This is good for us because they will be defensive and we will convince them he was lost or perhaps undertaking a religious quest. That is usually a good argument. They cannot doubt a religious quest. It makes them uneasy. The religious search is an invincible argument. Go home young lady. Leave the monk to Margarian.'

The next day Eyob was released and back in the monastery but Ada was not allowed to see him. She was told he would be spending some weeks in silent meditation.

JAFFA ROAD

TOMAS, CAUGHT UP in a frenzy of work, hardly took an interest in his book stall and spent the days attacking a large canvas as if he was a mountain climber and it was the implacable, unyielding rock face. As he worked he drank arak and chewed on carrots and cucumbers and olives. Ada, when she stayed there, left the ruin in the morning, sometimes while he was still asleep, his face, hair and arms stained with the colours of the day before. Often when she came back the house was empty and the canvas, covered by a large sheet, glimmered faintly in the near dark. Tomas liked to go walking after a day's work. He would set out by himself or with Julius and walk out of town as far as they could go along the treeless ridge towards the UN headquarters. At the DANGER BORDER sign they would turn back and end up in one of the run-down basement shops near the market where alcohol over the counter was cheap and illegal gambling went on in a back room.

One evening Ada came and saw that Tomas had left the canvas uncovered. She put all the lights on and stood in front of it doubly curious because he had said so little about it.

It was Jaffa Road, detailed and crowded, gay bright and sunny till it disappeared, ambushed by some kind of chaos. Patches of canvas were still bare, like broad grey fingerprints. But the street was all there with shops and a café, and billboards advertising films. One side of the canvas was unnaturally crowded as if the street had been invaded by trainloads of people from somewhere else. The café was full, impossibly full. People, often gesticulating wildly, were packed together with no space between them, tables were piled high with bottles and glasses and food. The clothes they wore were dated but elegant yet the crowded scene lost its cohesion as it spread across the canvas and melted into something Ada couldn't comprehend. A chaotic and brutal storm of thick brushstrokes in violent reds, smeared browns and creeping grey smudges spread everywhere but created nothing stable. It wasn't forest or heath or countryside. It wasn't desert or water. Nor was there any shape of a hill or a wall or a path to give the eye a direction. It wasn't even outside the city. Ada stared till her eyes watered trying to penetrate the thick undisciplined brushwork to discover some shapes beneath but she gave up and turned to the figures in the café. Julius was there, not in his usual beret but in a cork sun helmet and holding a tennis racket. There was also a red-faced priest in a soutane with a girl on his lap. And the waiter had Kronberg's high forehead and steel glasses. Milo, wearing plus-fours, dangled a fishing rod over the kerb. It took her some time to notice a boy in the street near one of the tables. He was on his knees on the pavement, drawing.

She lay down on the bed. She couldn't see the painting from where she was but closed her eyes and the street and the café appeared blurred and unsteady like an old newsreel, beyond the street there was nothing. She tried to hold onto it like a photograph in a frame but it broke into little dots of green and red light. She was left with a sense of betrayal. Why wasn't she there?

Tomas and Julius came back in high spirits. Julius had quarrelled with one of the drinkers, a grizzled olive seller from the market. He had cursed Julius in Kurdish Aramaic and Julius had thrown back some obscene rhymes picked up at school in England. The onlookers had made peace by getting Tomas to translate. The result got everyone laughing though Julius who needed quarrels as exercise would have liked it to go on.

No-one spoke about the painting though it hung above them like a banner. Tomas and Julius sat down to play sheshbesh. Ada watched them critically. They played too slowly, lacking the noise and the macho élan of the players she used to watch in the Arab cafés in Haifa. In this game you needed swooping hand movements and the rhythmic, click clack of counters picked up and slapped down and shouts of triumph and curses. Julius played erratically moving his pieces, then trying to take them back. Sheshbesh wasn't a game for European hands. Tomas was agonizingly slow. With his head in his hands and face in a grimace he looked like a chess player under torture.

He lost his patience.

'Enough! Before we send each other to sleep. Play like this in the drinks shop and you get your ears cut off.'

Julius was slumped in his chair. He had forgotten the game and was pointing at the painting.

'No-one there playing sheshbesh. Why are they so crushed together. Isn't that Père Félix with the girl? And what's Milo doing with a fishing rod?'

'You're there too,' said Ada.

'So what are we all celebrating?'

'Mardi Gras.'

'What are they doing here?'

'Are you sure it's here?'

'I'm not an idiot. Jaffa Road with the crooked bus stop. But the tables outside Café Vienna, you definitely made that up. The pavement's too narrow for tables.'

'Alright it's here and it's the end of the road for them so they're celebrating getting here. A holiday. They've been on the road for years. Some have forgotten when they started and where they wanted to get to. But they're glad they got somewhere, even if it's only here.'

'You're talking about a refugee camp,' said Ada.

'No, Jaffa Road and Zion Square,' said Tomas, unyielding. 'Outside it's much worse. It's something they don't want to know about because they've been there. I can't paint it.'

'That's you isn't it?' asked Ada pointing at the boy drawing on the pavement.

'Yes, you can't see what I'm drawing but it's a whale with a family in its belly eating supper. The boy doesn't know about bullshit. All that mess beyond Mardi Gras is bullshit. It's an excuse for not painting what's out there.'

'So leave it empty,' said Julius. 'That way the street party is stuck on the edge of blank space and people will fill in what they think. Why am I holding a tennis racket and waving under that ridiculous hat?'

'Julius, can't you see? You're waving at the crowds looking at the painting in the Louvre. You want them to notice you... Julius is here.'

Later Tomas told Ada that Kronberg was coming back.

'He settled his property case and, though you might not believe it, he's homesick. He's fed up with being observed like a stuffed owl. And it got to be dull. But he still means to go back and take up that job. It's a matter of honour.'

BETHLEHEM GALILEE

ADA HAD TO go to see Suzi. Since she had improved there were fewer phone conversations so she decided to take the long bus ride on the week end to the Walzer Sanatorium in the Galilean village of Bethlehem Galilee. It was strange that Perla should have chosen this little Templer village on the road to Nazareth which was abandoned in the war after the German evangelical farmers turned Nazi and the British deported them. But the Sanatorium had a good reputation and its director was Perla's army friend from the Monty days.

Ada knew Bethlehem Galilee as a sister village to the German colony in Jerusalem where the narrow lanes of sturdy, solemn houses and market gardens had been sucked into the city, but when she got off the bus she was still surprised to see how similar the houses were. They were more clearly farmhouses but their gentle proportions, arched windows and the earth colour of the stone gave them a seigneurial look. Surrounded by oaks and tall eucalyptus trees in the sharp winter sunlight they looked as if they had sat on ancestral lands for centuries. Ada had heard about the madness that made the pious farmers fall for Hitler right here in British Palestine and when she asked Suzi about it the answer was simple: 'He was the new Saviour so they abandoned Jesus and they didn't think the British had it in them to fight.'

She had found her mother on the porch of the sanatorium smoking and reading. Without make-up, sunburnt in a simple white blouse and skirt and with her black hair that was flecked with grey pulled back severely off her broad forehead, she seemed a neat *hausfrau*, belonging more to the evangelical past of Bethlehem Galilee than its present. But her kiss was earthy and immediate and she spoke fluently without the hesitations and silences of the past.

'So you've come to check up on me, sweetheart. I must be doing well because even Perla approves. I'm getting better at yoga. Gerri Walzer is an excellent master. You know he studied in London with some Indians. You should see him on the mat. A brown lizard. And I feel so clumsy and stiff. But the yoga helps me talk. Strange, the body is stuck and I'm still smoking, but the tongue breaks loose and when I finish a talk time with him it feels like I've run a marathon but I can see the end. Adamia, why are we making this trial?'

Ada looked at her mother, astonished by the question.

'The Nazi, why?'

She was serious. Her eyes were searching Ada's for an answer.

'It will bring up bad memories and it won't look fair. They should have killed him right there in Buenos Aires and made it look like an accident. That's not so hard in Argentina. Tell me, are they filming him in his cell? Did you see pictures? They need to be careful because somebody's going to try to do away with him, like poison, and then we'll get the blame. And maybe, you know, maybe he's sick with the memory of what he did. Maybe he has nightmares. How do we know? We can't know.'

Suzi was talking fast. Her face was flushed and her fingers were playing on absent piano keys.

'How do you think they recognised him? Didn't he grow a beard or something? Why can't we wait for them all to die? Why can't we let it be?'

'Shhh shhhh, Ima, shhhh.' Ada shushed her like an overwrought child.

'We've been looking for him for years. It's what police do all over the world, keep quiet and wait for a sign. We're no different and he's just another of many like him on the run. Don't let it upset you. Anyway I know less about it than you think. Just because I

112

work at the television means nothing. Nobody knows any details about him.'

Suzi took her hand and pressed it in hers.

'If they let people into the courtroom will you get me a place, somewhere close where I can see?'

Ada was at a loss. They had never spoken about the Big Shit, only about Ada's work at the centre. But Suzi wouldn't leave it be.

'We don't have judges in wigs and antique robes like London. We are disorderly and naked. Have you ever been in a courtroom here? It's like a market. The police uniforms are shabby and the noise…People sit there eating and cracking nuts so you can't hear the judges. How can we put him on trial in this way and broadcast it everywhere? They'll laugh at us and who'll believe it's fair? And he wasn't the worst of them.'

Suzi frowned. She looked as if she wanted to get hold of all the policemen and the judges and shake them by their ears till they agreed with her.

Ada decided to bring Suzi up to date on the opposition.

'You remember Milo, Ima? Well he's back and he doesn't think the trial is going to do much good either. So he's doing something crazy. He's plotting to upset it, create a diversion.'

Suzi didn't look surprised. She was used to stories about Milo's hypothetical extravaganzas.

'What's he going to do, lead a parade of dancing bears and naked girls past the Great Synagogue?'

'No, it's serious. It's about real things and making people wake up. So Milo is going to put Noah, you know the old man from the Bible, on a stage in his Ark, and perform a play to the crowds outside the trial. The Flood. That's going to be Milo's challenge to the show inside.'

Suzi looked interested.

'This is one of Polly's big ideas is it? I don't suppose anything will come of it. But why The Flood? He never gave a damn about Bible stories.'

'He quite likes this one. You see it's about the end of the world and that makes Milo happy.'

'The end?'

'Well, near enough. Near enough to tell people who ignore it that they're going under. Milo thinks the trial is going to create mass hysteria. It's a revenge fantasy controlled by politicians and can do no good. So he's going to take over the street with this protest, create a showdown, warn the people. And we'll probably get arrested. But at least we'll get noticed.'

'WE? What are you doing in this?'

'He asked me to build the Ark.'

'I thought you were doing the television studio.'

'That as well. You know, everybody's got two jobs.'

Suzi looked upset.

'I don't understand you, my love. You finished with him and here you are serving him again like you did in Paris, building him ships, getting arrested, losing your job because they won't keep you on when they find out. I don't know what hold he has over you now. You're not sleeping with him again, are you? Just because he was your first doesn't give him a season ticket. Aren't there any other men around?'

'There is someone but I can't tell you about him now.'

'Aha. So how come you have no colour, sweet? Let's look at you. What's the point of a man if he doesn't give you a flush? When you're all in black and pale like this you look like a nun before breakfast.'

She laughed and brushed an imaginary curl away from her forehead.

Ada saw cunning and aggression in Suzi's eye and was encouraged. She could imagine her looking in the mirror again, outlining her eyes with the thick dark pencil Ada coveted as a young girl. At home years ago she understood there was a price for having a glamorous, interesting mother: her absence not only from the daily procession of meals and the weekly floorwash but also from intimacy. Conversations on the balcony in the evening cool were rarely with her and the silent goodnights at bedtime came from a photograph taken in a Frankfurt studio. It was bordered with feathery kiss signs, crosses in green ink.

114

At lunch in the spartan dining room Ada understood that Suzi and Gerri Walzer were intimate. Although there were other patients and staff at the small glass-topped tables, he paid little attention to them. He was a handsome, spare, sunburnt man who didn't look ridiculous in shorts but could have been the commander of an intelligence unit operating behind Rommel's lines in the desert. His face was heavily lined but his light blue eyes under a shock of unruly grey hair were sharp and mischievous. He spoke about vegetarian ideals and the transportation of survivors from Europe to Palestine in the same breath, all the while slicing a cucumber and a bulbous radish into thin strips which he arranged in a starlike pattern on his plate. He cut up a salad for Suzi with the concentration and dedication of a watchmaker, not setting the bowl in front of her till he had built up a green and red hillock, irrigated with olive oil and lemon juice and flanked with glacier-like slices of white cheese. Ada half expected him to plant a toothpick on the summit and salute the flag but she responded to Suzi's pleasure at being looked after so solicitously and listened attentively to his words. He spoke with a slow ironic formality which she took to be his way of emphasizing his distance from the too-easy camaraderie around him.

'So, mademoiselle, where are the vegetarian restaurants in our neglected capital? Politicians who eat meat are unreliable especially in a precarious place like this. If Ben Gurion admires Gandhi as much as they say he does, he should stop his followers eating meat. It would be a good start. Mondays and Thursdays, no meat days.'

Ada looked for signs of amusement in his eyes but he seemed entirely serious and picked up a spoon to feed Suzi some of the salad mountain. She pouted and turned her head away at first but then took the spoonful with the beginnings of a blush, or so Ada thought. It was only the first bite, they continued eating in a normal way, but Suzi had for a moment revealed her dependence on this man who was watching her eat as if he would remember every move of her lips. Ada resisted the impulse to look away. Why should her mother's half-hesitant gesture embarrass her? If he was protecting

115

her, taking care of her that could only be for the good. Still the sight of Suzi, momentarily a child, being fed by a man put Ada on edge and afraid of what might happen if she found herself alone again.

'Suzi tells me you are engaged in preparations for the trial. Does this seem good to you? Does it make anyone happy? So we've shown we can follow them to their lairs. So what? Revenge, is that what it is? Aren't we taking Adenauer's money instead? Revenge is madness. After the war some of us wanted revenge nothing else, and we were right there among the Germans with British trucks and weapons. There were insane ideas like poisoning the drinking water in the whole of Munich. We were just boys and had seen terrible things. But the only thing that made sense was to go after somebody we knew was a criminal and alive like Mengele or Brunner. We didn't have enough intelligence and they got away. This one, I don't remember anyone mentioning him. Now nobody talks about anything else. Why do we have to know what he eats for breakfast and how many showers he takes? It's demeaning.'

He seemed to sink into himself for a minute and drop shutters over his face. Then he came back.

'You've been living in Paris and now you're with us? But why Jerusalem? Isn't it full of old people and cranks?'

'And ghosts like here. I live quite near where your Templers had their Jerusalem colony. Their cisterns and rainwater channels are still there and the pines they planted too. So there are ghosts. Yes, it's a strange place stuck onto the rest of the country like an empty trouser leg. It's more an afterthought than a city. But I like it.'

'You came back but you didn't really come back here,' said Walzer. 'You found yourself a refuge.'

'From her mother and Perla,' said Suzi.

'I've got a brother there,' said Walzer. 'We came here together from Leipzig and we were together in the British army and in our war but after all the wars and makeshift utopias he was attracted to the poverty and disciplines of the godly people. He took his few shirts, his discharge papers and a camera in his army knapsack and

116

got on the bus to Jerusalem. To try it out, he said. I went to his wedding of course and he was quite different by then. He used to be muscular and had a builder's grip but when we danced in the men's circle his arm round my shoulder was as soft as a ribbon and his hand and fingers were white, thin and delicate. He's popular there because he can write well in English and German and he helps them with correspondence and claims. Do you ever get to their part of town?'

'Never,' said Ada.

'I'll give you a letter for him. He used to be Erwin, now it's Eliyahu. If you meet you'll see he's not as strange as you might think and even if he is, he's worth taking seriously.'

After the meal Ada and Suzi walked along the perfectly straight single street of the village to the empty Volkshaus, the community centre of the Templers. The building retained a certain civic dignity despite its decline into disrepair. It was taller than the other buildings and built of finely dressed stone. At its front, the remains of a formal garden led up to a wide stairway. They sat on the stairs in the shade of one of the eucalyptus trees. All you could hear was the whine of some agricultural machine far away and the bassooning sounds of the cows in sheds behind the farmhouses. It couldn't have been more peaceful but to Ada this was a thin curtain stretched over waves of disorder and violence. What group of people could have been more peaceful than the Templers? They had come here to live like Jesus and forget the world. She imagined a decorous Easter gathering just where they were sitting with elderly, soberly dressed men and women singing hymns and listening to the Bible reading. But the hymns were challenged and drowned out by a Nazi chorus from the street where the swastika flag was raised by the young nationalist hotheads to remind their elders that they were Germans first and Christians afterwards. Months later, British army trucks would have lined up in this same street to load families, suitcases, toys, bits of belongings and drive away with them to some camp leaving the village empty, the animals disposed of somehow, the workshops swept and abandoned. Years later the street would fill up again with similar trucks bringing other people out of other camps. These people had no belongings and opened the doors of the empty Templer houses only to sit, strangers, on floors of dusty, echoing rooms and wait for someone to tell them why they had been put down there and what they should do.

'Why are you so quiet, Adamia?'

'A tiny place like this and it's full of ghosts.'

'You mean the Germans, the Templers? Why lose sleep over them? It was war wasn't it and they chose to fly the swastika flag right here in Palestine. Heil Hitler with the British army round the corner? It's absurd. It's easier to laugh at their stupidity than think about what they lost. Anyway they ended up in Australia and a lot of people here would give an arm and a leg to be shipped out to Sydney right now.'

Her mother was in no mood to respond to the melancholy of a deserted Templer village. She seemed light-hearted and brittle. Her freckled, sunburnt forehead and shoulders were signs of health but also of the absence of cosmetics. She must have stopped using her expensive foreign creams because Walzer disapproved. What else did he disapprove of? Pyjamas? Sugar? Chocolate? Ada found herself resentful of an imaginary spartan regime imposed on her luxury-loving mother, made to get up at the crack of dawn to stretch and tie her body in knots on a mat and then breakfast on grated carrots, wheat germ and camomile tea.

'How long do you think you'll stay here?'

'The quiet is wonderful and Walzer wants me to help him run the place. He thinks he can expand it and make it a centre for meditation and a stressless life. What do you think of Gerri? When Perla introduced me to him I was quite disappointed. She described his exploits in the war in such a way that I expected Trevor Howard or Robert Taylor and there he was quite small and reserved in shorts and sandals with a pipe in one hand which he never put in his mouth. Yet I never saw Perla listen so respectfully to anyone. Maybe because he began to stammer when he was describing the truck he drove to Toulouse.'

'What truck?'

'It was carrying people who had been sent to the DP camps after '45 and were desperate to get away. They wanted America, Canada, Australia and they were scared of being shipped back to Poland or worse. It seems there were debates and loud arguments about their journey. Only some wanted to come here. But they couldn't turn back as the whole thing was illegal and passing through check points was touch and go. Then one night they stopped at a monastery. It was a place where the monks had hidden children during Vichy. Some were still there as nobody had claimed them. Then at supper with the monks people from the lorry started to sing. They had picked up songs from the American soldiers and the radio and the favourite was 'Don't fence me in'. You know, Bing Crosby and the Andrews Sisters.

'Give me land lots of land and the starry skies above.'

Suzi sang and Ada joined in, *'Let me ride through the wide open country that I love*
'Don't fence me in.'

'Well Gerri described that refectory, bare and gloomy, a few pale robed monks at one table and long tables with bread and cheese and jugs of water and the travellers from the truck, loud and restless in their scraps of uniforms and ill-fitting clothes picked out of relief parcels.

'One kid, a boy of about ten, he said they called him Bublik, was their star solo. They stood him on his bench, put an American army cap on his head and had him perform.

'Then Gerri did an imitation of his song:

Ye vanna ry to deridtch wer de Vest commentzes
End geyz et demun antil iluzmei zentzes
Kent luk at howels and kent stend fentzes
Don fentz me yin

'It was very strange. I watched him stretch out two hands as if he was rolling a ball of air between them and bring into Perla's room a boy singing in a garbled language something that should have been a cowboy jingle but turned into a prisoner's dream. And when Gerri sang he couldn't complete the *Don't fence me in* line. He stumbled on it twice, seemed to lose his breath and was quite embarrassed. Perla covered up for him. She knew just the kind of truck he drove on that journey, a Bedford MWD. They had them in the desert with no armour against the Messerschmitts, and of course, she could still do basic repairs on the engine. Blindfold.

'So that's how I met him.'

On the bus back Ada found herself surrounded by soldiers shouting to each other across the rows of seats. *Don't fence me in*, she hummed to herself as the knapsack on her right banged down on her knee and the overladen racks above threatened to spill their loads of sweets, towels, fizzy drinks and water canteens on her head. *Don't fence me in.*

WUNDERTOPF

ULLI ARRIVED AND declared her intention of crossing over into the Old City for Christmas. She had heard it was possible for Christians to get through the Mandelbaum Gate for Holy Days and all she needed was a letter saying she was a regular churchgoer. Félix recognizing in her a kindred adventurous spirit said he could fix the letter and boasted he could even get one in Latin from the Papal emissary.

Rudi seemed ill at ease around his young wife. Her startling blonde hair turned heads in the street and her effervescent winning ways made everyone her friend. The nuns took to her as one of their own even though she resisted their invitations to join them for Mass. Mother Superior, who was born in Munich, would call her *unser Ullichen* and give her gaudy little picture books of Bavarian churches and shrines. Ulli herself, used to Californian impersonality and the unwritten law of keep your distance, was flattered by the interest she aroused and laughed at the stares and calls directed at her as she negotiated the narrow pavements of Jaffa Road. For Rudi this was upsetting. The young woman who had always been in his shadow and unwilling to talk about her past was now singing *Hoppe hoppe Reiter* with the nuns and getting lessons in street Arabic from Père Félix. Milo's admiration was no comfort either.

'That's some girl,' he said. 'She's like a balloon floating in the sunlight. How come she fell for a square guy like you?'

Rudi tried to talk Ulli out of going over the border for

Christmas. There had been incidents in the past, and the Jordanians were very prickly about people pretending to be churchgoers just to get into the Old City. There was the case of Joe Gould once a Jew, then a Buddhist and an Episcopalian who had sat for a few miserable weeks in a Hashemite jail accused of religious fakery. Rudi had heard these stories from Margarian who took a very dim view of people crossing borders between communities for trivial reasons such as tourism. But Ulli reminded Rudi that she was a Christian even though her father was an anarchist. She was Christian because her grandmother had whispered the Lord's Prayer to her and she remembered some of it: *Geheiligt werde dein Name.*

'You're just jealous,' she told Rudi. 'You're the big tripper, always on the way to somewhere and here's a line you can't cross. But I can. Don't worry I'll come back. Félix will take care of me.'

So Ulli went to see the American Consul in the company of Père Félix to get her letter of churchgoing and bona fide Christianity. The consul and Félix were old friends and the interview to establish Ulli's credentials was perfunctory.

She remembered the sign on a vast artificial-looking lawn in front of a rambling bungalow in Oakland:

FELLOWSHIP OF APOSTLES
COME AND WORSHIP
GOD IS YOUR FRIEND

It was Rudi who had explained what Apostles were. She thought they were pharmacists.

'Fellowship of apostles,' she told the consul who scribbled something on a pad and gave it to a secretary to type.

'If they ask you, say it's an Episcopalian outfit. That's the safest. Quiet and very American. And what do you plan to do over the line? But you're with Félix, I forget. He'll show you everything and stop you paying good dollars for fake oil lamps and Roman coins.'

A few nights before they went Julius invited everyone to a Mandelbaum Banquet of sharp white cheese and rough red wine.

Crossing over to the other side by a friend or a neighbour was something that needed to be marked and celebrated so he was going to put on a performance to make it doubly memorable. He had been writing a puppet play for his randy philosophers, Ibn Battuta and Abarbanel, and wanted to try a bit of it out as a curtain raiser. The whole work he would be sending to some editors of little magazines who, as usual, would not reply.

Julius had arranged the room to form a small arena with cushions and mattresses set around his kitchen table which would be the stage. He had borrowed a couple of desk lamps from Ada and she had covered them with red and blue cellophane and focused them so that the crude lines of the rickety wooden table were blurred into an indistinct cloudiness that could have been sky or sea or mountain peaks. On the table was nothing except for a dented *Wundertopf* of the kind in which German ladies like Die Tanten baked their round marble cakes with a hole in the middle which they called *kugelhupf*.

Guests of honour in the audience were the Sasson brothers, who entered the dimly lit room holding onto each other and staring shortsightedly into the darkness as if they were afraid of being ambushed by a bat. Ada greeted them as Julius was making last-minute preparations in the shower.

'Julius will be so glad you could come. All our friends here know where these wonderful puppets came from.'

Ezra looked displeased and refused a glass of wine but his brother Sami stared at the group one by one as if he was looking at stuffed animals in a museum cabinet.

'It is not easy to walk up here,' said Ezra. 'There is not any pavement and the hill is steep to climb.'

'But isn't the view great?' said Ada with false confidence.

'For tourists yes. For us, we have seen it.'

There was a sound of drumming from the shower. It was the overture, Julius slapping his large dustbin lid calling the audience to order.

He came into the light dressed in a glittering pied Bokharan silk robe with a tassled red fez on his head, lipstick smeared in dots on his forehead and his lips lined in red and black. In each hand he held a puppet covered with a large white handkerchief. Ibn Battuta to the left, Abarbanel to the right.

He bowed and the philosophical pair under their handkerchiefs bowed with him. The audience clapped gently.

The Philosophers' Quarrel over the Miraculous Wundertopf

he announced in a voice quite different from the mellow English drawl of his everyday speech. This was a clipped, metallic voice, part Laurence Olivier and part Mr Leech, his sarcastic English master at Manchester Grammar. It was a voice that took no quarter and abided no inattention. The Sasson brothers looked astonished.

Julius placed himself squarely behind the table, raised a handkerchief and hoisted up Ibn Battuta by his spinal stick. His voice changed again. It was now mellifluous and seductively close to song.

Noble audience, learned, generous and well-appointed guests of the Caliph's court, Ibn Battuta has journeyed here all the way from Samarkand, surviving earthquakes, storms, whales and ravening lions, to answer the summons of the great Caliph and demonstrate to you the mysteries, the secrets of the Wundertopf.

Julius turned away from the audience in a majestic, solemn dervish-like move and picked up by its stick from behind the table the other puppet. When he turned back to face them, this time abruptly, his nose and beard seemed to have grown pointed and his mouth stretched unnaturally across the gap in his beard.

He didn't raise this puppet above his head, instead he thrust him out aggressively towards the audience.

Lies lies lies,
Abarbanel says.
The journey is no journey

The wild animals are cats and mice and flies
The adventures hearsay
All figments of a brain heated by wine.
I, Abarbanel, a scholar and scribe
Unrewarded by great kings
But protected by Almighty God,
Delved into the secrets of the Wundertopf
Before Ibn Battuta was relieved of his foreskin
Before he dived into debauchery in the hammams of Basra

On cue Tomas took a tin flute out of his pocket and tootled a fragment from *Scheherazade*.

Ada got up from her cushion and placed on the table one of her dolls, Rusalka, a nubile blonde with long eyelashes and red-painted toes and fingernails. She was wearing nothing and she sat there curiously sedate, beside the *Wundertopf*, her pudgy little arms stretching out as if welcoming an aunt or an older sister.

Now Julius was holding both puppets so that they were staring at each other like wrestlers in a ring each trying to dominate his rival by look before the struggle began. He again moved in dervish-like steps. And they circled each other without losing eye contact. Then he stood over them, his beard like a thundercloud in their sky. He first growled and made threatening sounds and muffled curses but then his breathing grew soft and sighs replaced the growls. They were sighs of love and yearning, sighs of unrequited passion or of body separating from soul. He began to sing, not a tune but a melancholy chant:

It isn't fair to hold your lover captive—
come close and the wandering chariots draw away.
Turn my sickbed into a bed of pleasure—
and feed your lover honey and milk

Ibn Battuta swooped down towards Rusalka like a buzzard and landed on the table by her painted toes. Julius tenderly placed the puppets' hands in a supplicatory position so that he was prostrate before her.

> *Ophra washes her clothes*
> *in the stream*
> *of tears*
> *I've shed*

Julius with his free hand took a kazoo out of his Bokharan pocket and made the scornful braying sound of a hoarse hyena. Abarbanel raised one accusing arm and pointed at the suppliant

> *Stolen, stolen, stolen verses*
> *Picked up from a table in*
> *A rich man's library*
> *The Jew Halevi made them*
> *For wise and graceful lovers*
> *And for God*
> *Not for forgers and liers*
> *Not for seducers of virgins*
> *Or defilers of the Wundertopf*
> *Like this miserable scarecrow Ibn Battuta.*

Abarbanel hovered over his rival and inspected his still body from above. Slowly Julius lowered Abarbanel's lividly painted head until its nose was almost touching Ibn Battuta's turban. The tension in the room was noticeable as the space between the puppets slowly diminished. Julius breathed heavily and stamped his foot. At the cue Tomas put the flute to his lips and played the opening phrase of the muezzin's call to prayer. Ibn Battuta, raised up very slowly from the table, looked around him as if in bewilderment.

> *I have had a dream, a vision of Paradise*
> *I saw a pure maiden bathing in a fountain*
> *Floating in the water at her feet was the Wundertopf*

Encircled by rose petals and goldfish
But sealed with a band of silver thorns
As the maiden put out her hand to caress the Wundertopf…

Blasphemer, Liar, Plagiariser

Abarbanel's nose was now touching Ibn Battuta's. Julius's brow was damp and his eyes were red with effort and concentration.

Plagiariser
Your so-called dream is taken verbatim from Abd Rabbihi's
Conversations with the Divine Messenger
In your mouth it carries no conviction
Look at Rusalka
Does she show the slightest interest?
Your mention of the sealed Wundertopf
Brings no blush to her cheeks
Why?

Julius put down both puppets and crossed their arms gently over their supine bodies He stood over them and over Rusalka and the *Wundertopf*, folding his hands together in a clerical manner. He could have been a vicar burying a parishioner's favourite dog. He cleared his throat.

The Wundertopf is a work of great mystery. Our philosophers, now exhausted and temporarily laid to sleep, are engaged in a centuries-long quarrel over it, a quarrel which delves deep into the Koran and the Talmud and Augustine's City of God. *Like the Holy Grail, the Wundertopf has inspired the bravest men and the deepest thinkers to seek it out risking everything to answer its seductive question:*
What do I conceal?

Here Julius with a conjurer's flourish of both arms pointed dramatically at the *Wundertopf* and made as if to lift it over his head.

127

Should I open this humble copy, thereby desecrating it, you would see nothing. Emptiness. Dust. Crumbs. Perhaps you would notice an odour of cakes once baked. These are earthly signs, traps to mislead the unlearned seeker.

For the true Wundertopf encircles the origin of life, created when God made Eve and cut her, as the angels wept, from the sleeping body of Adam. When Adam woke he saw her and the Wundertopf in all its pristine beauty. But when they were driven from the Garden, when they wove a leafy cover for their bodies, the original Wundertopf was lost, replaced with base imitations. And we search for it all the years of our lives, in vain.

Julius's voice broke and he covered his eyes with his hands. His shoulders shook and he seemed to be struggling to control his sobs.

There was quiet for some minutes until Ada came forward and put a comforting arm around Julius's shoulders. Tomas piped some of Rondo alla Turca and the audience, relieved by the jaunty, familiar music began to clap.

It took a while for Julius to uncover his face but when he did his eyes were red but lively with excitement and pleasure. He picked up the philosophers and brought their noses together in a kiss while Ada took Rusalka under a protective arm. The *Wundertopf* remained, appropriately enough, untouched on the table.

Ezra and Sami Sasson sat stiffly in their chairs. Julius still resplendent in his Bokharan robe brought the puppets and laid them face up in Ezra's lap.

'Here they are, back with you in good condition. I hope they haven't shocked you.'

Ezra stared at the puppets as if seeing them for the first time.

'You see,' said Julius, 'they need to speak and sing. That is what they are made for.'

'Our father had a robe like yours,' said Sami, 'but he never wore it. He said it would make people think he was rich.'

'Rich?' said Ezra. 'He was a miser. He would not buy us new clothes, only hand-me-downs from charity. Did you have a *Wundertopf* in Manchester?'

Julius laughed. 'No, I first saw one when I came to Jerusalem.'

'Then we will give your philosophers back to you because they should continue their quarrels and searches,' said Ezra. 'Who knows, they may uncover the mystery. But you must be careful to whom you show this performance. Certain narrow-minded people could be angered and shocked.'

The brothers stood up and shook hands gravely. Then they made a dignified exit after Félix had forced the door open for them with a grunt and a mighty push of his shoulder.

RETURN

KRONBERG WAS BACK but didn't come to the Mandelbaum Banquet. No-one had seen him but Tomas, who said almost nothing.

'He's getting over the shock. He keeps the shutters down all day and complains that the light is destroying him. He lives on coffee and chocolate.'

One morning he turned up at the entrance of the Television Centre asking for Ada. She came down to the lobby to find him dressed incongruously in a grey suit with a red handkerchief in his breast pocket.

'Where can we talk?' he asked. 'This place smells like a police station.'

He said nothing more as Ada led the way to Jaffa Road and a small kiosk in a courtyard where the chain-smoking proprietor fried omelets and made glasses of muddy coffee for the local shopkeepers and office workers.

Kronberg looked at the scratched formica table with distaste and brushed away some imaginary crumbs before he sat down. He wiped his brow with a perfectly folded handkerchief. There was a hint of stubble on his usually smooth shaved cheek and the eyes behind the golden wire of his glasses were not calm.

They drank their coffee in silence and Ada watched him grimace at the unaccustomed bitterness. He's forgotten what it tastes like, she thought.

'How are the dolls?'

'Neglected but no crisis. You missed Julius's performance. Rusalka was in it.'

'What did she do?'

'She sat still and played the femme fatale, naked.'

He polished his glasses with the white handkerchief and squinted at the sun.

'No escape, is there,' he said.

'From what?'

'From this, from the light. It's so-called winter and it's relentless. It makes me want to hide behind closed shutters. I wouldn't have come out now but...'

He hesitated.

Ada who was used to the confident flow of his speech and the forward march of opinions punctuated by short pauses while he caught up with breathing, resisted an urge to encourage him to say what was on his mind.

They sat there for a while silently. Then he took a fountain pen out of his inner pocket and started tapping on the table.

Knaben liebt ich wohl auch
Doch lieber sind mir die Mädchen

He looked at her accusingly. 'You don't follow?'

'Something about boys and girls,' she said.

'Indeed,' he said ironically. 'Old man Goethe discovered Eros late in life. In Italy of course. "Boys and girls both will do, but I prefer girls," at least that's what he says.'

'So what do you think that's got to do with me?'

He was teasing her.

'Tomas,' she said.

'Excellent.'

He raised a hand and saluted her. 'Excellent, Fräulein Ada. Not a new story, as you probably know. And it's nobody's business even in this little rabbit warren. So I wouldn't be talking about it. But there's a problem. Tomas. Tomas has made it clear that he won't

131

come with me if I go back to Würzburg. I don't know if you understand, I made an excellent arrangement for him – a studio and a teaching job and a good sum of money. He'd be able to work and be independent. I know this sounds strange but he'd be freer and safer there than he is here. He took a long time healing here and the people around him didn't help. I know because I protected him. Würzburg will take him out of all this and put him into a studio in a wood that looks like nothing has changed in a hundred years. It's green and perfectly clean and ordered and that's good for him.'

They looked at each other almost nakedly, as if hiding nothing.

'I know Tomas has…has formed an attachment to you. He has been frank with me. We have no secrets and I'm not jealous.' He laughed, seemingly at himself. 'I am not possessive. Maybe years ago. Now my aim is to make Tomas safe. He can't be safe here. He might have moments, but he'll always be in danger.'

'You want me to tell him to go?'

Kronberg was arrested by the directness of her question. He blew into his glass of coffee dregs and didn't answer.

Ada didn't believe him. He wanted Tomas for himself, not Tomas's well being. Kronberg was not telling the truth and in her eyes now he looked mean and dangerous, a bully disguised as a reasonable man. In the past, the dangerous look in his steely grey eyes had been attractive. He had secrets that made him interesting. Now she was looking at a man playing a part badly. He was disguising his need for Tomas as unselfish. He was also underestimating her. She could see through him.

'You're wrong about Tomas,' she said. 'He's stronger than you think. He doesn't need a protector. Maybe once, but no longer. And the wound you talk about. He doesn't parade it or nurse it. He paints it. And, by the way, I love him. I couldn't let him go. I can't think he would be happier with you in that forest. He's got his ruin here and that's home.'

Kronberg banged on the table.

'His ruin. Exactly. An old shell of stones dangling over no man's land. Why do you think he's set up in there? Because he can see the mosques from his broken windows or paint pretty scenes of goats and olive trees? You know that's not Tomas. So why then? It's a dangerous place. Admit it. For him. Not because of guns and shooting and what they call border incidents. No, for him specifically. It's dangerous because he has set himself a trap, a burrow with unusable exits. It's not happening yet but he's going to bury himself in that ruin. To go on living he has to get out.'

'Then he can decide for himself whether he wants to or not.'

She looked closely at Kronberg. He seemed older, with more lines around his mouth and eyes and the suit was too tight for him. His cheeks looked oddly bronzed, not smoothly but in patches as if he had been visiting an inefficient tanning parlour in Würzburg. She was close to feeling pity for him, a learned, sharp-witted man stranded in a place he had no attachment to, among people he barely liked or tolerated. She had never before felt it was shameful that he was repairing refrigerators and radios and sticking toys together. He wasn't the only one. There was a well-known Marburg lexicographer who had a paper and magazine stall on Gaza Road and he was a kind of hero for those Berliners and Frankfurters who considered Palästina an opportunity for self-reinvention. But Kronberg carried around an air of dissatisfaction that allowed no positive view of the forced removal of people like him from Europe to the Levant. Like him? He was a homosexual in a small society of transferred Europeans who were simultaneously puritanical and tolerant. They cultivated a respectable façade with religious zeal but behind their heavy pianos and bookcases they stored their sins and their foibles, taking them out like stolen jewels only when the shutters were firmly down and the doors locked. Kronberg was part of this heavy-footed shuffle but didn't for a moment pretend to be at ease in it.

He got up abruptly and with a quiet *au revoir* he was off, his straight, grey-suited back incongruous among the packing cases and piled-up planks and metal sheeting in the commercial courtyard.

'Who's that, a consul?' said the kiosk owner.

'Not a consul,' said Ada. 'A refugee.'

133

Halt Merry Christmas

THERE WAS, EVEN in the early morning, lively confusion at the approaches to the Mandelbaum Gate when Ulli and Félix got ready for the Christmas crossing. Rudi, Julius and Milo came along, Rudi, still reluctant to let Ulli walk through a gate closed to him and the other two unusually excited by the 'miracle' of the passage which Milo compared to the annual liquefaction of San Gennaro's blood in Naples. 'It's a sacred flow, a kind of annual menstruation and it keeps Naples happy and fertile. Here it's more like opening a blocked water channel for a day. It's a pretence at irrigation... Nothing grows. But at least something's moving.' Julius was more optimistic. It reminded him of the miracle on the Red Sea with the Children of Jesus crossing over through a narrow defile while Hashemite and Israelite armies confronted each other from opposite shores. Miracle or not, something momentous was happening. The road towards the Gate might once have been a real paved road leading from one place to another in a real town but now it was a miserably pocky, wounded and orphaned track which kept getting lost in the earth of no man's land. At the start however, as it wound downhill from the grand white Russian church with its green domes to the stately Italian Hospital, it was still a road belonging to one part of the city. Above, over the hospital wall, a fair copy of the Signoria tower borrowed the skyline of Florence to give the scene an illusion of stability. Then chaos took over. The road dribbled down through a scattering of hollowed-out houses, turned into minor ziggurats by the crazy sculpting of shell fire. They had once been wealthy residences of pink stone set in generous gardens. Now a lone fig tree or a stunted palm poked up out of mounds of rubble and clumps of weeds. An odd green or blue shutter hung precariously from its window like a trapeze artist holding onto an invisible wire. Instead of balconies holes gaped. It was a stage setting for the aftermath of a disaster — but the crowd hurrying along towards the Mandelbaum Gate was colourful and noisy with the excitement of travel. Rudi pushed forward with Ulli and Félix but Milo and Julius took advantage of a crumbling garden wall and climbed up to watch the scene from a distance. It was a flowing mosaic in brown, black and white, Christian colours. A stream of monks, nuns, priests, Christian Arab families from Nazareth and Galilee, the women in black, men in formal suits and white keffiyehs, old men and women in wheel chairs and prams, some with nuns and nurses in attendance – all were picking their way ahead, as if along a narrow bridge to heaven. Ignoring the ruts and debris, they were intent on their goal, their gate of iron set in stone: Mandelbaum.

From their vantage point Julius and Milo picked out the patchwork of bewildering signs warning and greeting the travellers.

DANGER NO PASSAGE TO FRONTIER
DEFENCE DE PASSER TERRITOIRE ENNEMI
FRONTIER POST
WELCOME TO ISRAEL
HALT
MERRY CHRISTMAS

Ulli and Félix had long disappeared into the compound surrounding the Gate and all that could be seen inside the fences and the barbed wire were the black and white of police jeeps and UN trucks. Most of the travellers had been swallowed up into the various huts, tents, and doors of the crossing process.

Julius thought he saw a Jordanian soldier in a spiked helmet.

'A hallucination,' said Milo. 'They couldn't still be wearing stuff left behind by the Kaiser.'

But Julius definitely saw two familiar figures walking away from the compound towards their vantage point. It was Rudi and Lewis.

Lewis was angry, his normally white complexion was red and his eyes glowed with righteous scorn. His goatee was as sharp as a spearhead.

'The nincompoops on this side wouldn't let me cross. Those idiots. The damn British Consul had okayed my letter from the bloody Welsh church but the idiot on the desk said NO, I was a government employee and I was working on a buggering sensitive project. Would you damn well believe it? Sensitive my arse. How was it sensitive you nailhead, I asked him. It's not a damn secret that you've bagged the Hun. Pigmies and Eskimos know about it because you've been bragging on every radio station and every bloody newspaper in the world. THE JEWS GET THEIR MAN. And you're worried I'll spill your beans. My God, use your pitiful noddle. But he just sat there and nodded, the bastard.'

'You need first aid,' said Milo and pulled out his hip flask.

Lewis gulped down the restorative medicine and sat down on a boulder. His pride was hurt by the rejection. What next? They had brought him here to run things and now they were ordering him about, telling him where he could go and where he couldn't go.

'What makes them so bloody obstreperous?' He looked at Milo but Rudi answered.

'Look, you weren't desperate to get across. I know what that's like. You're not a pilgrim and you're not a refugee. You probably looked like John Bull having a fit...And it's Christmas. That must make them more edgy than usual.'

'Why?'

'It's like the world is having a birthday party and you're not invited. The big event is happening over the barbed wire with popes and kings and wise men and miracles and you're just the doorman checking tickets. Nobody will ever let you in. So at least you can keep some people out.'

The path to the Gate was almost deserted now. The big crush had come and gone and only a few stragglers hurried along like children late for school. The usual silence returned, disturbed only by honking cars from the other side as the travellers were ferried to their destinations. The compound itself looked orphaned and useless. *Danger Welcome Merry Christmas* proclaimed their gospel of contradictions to the wind.

Lewis, reluctant to let his defeat be known at the Television Centre, went home to sleep. Julius and Milo needed breakfast but Rudi was ill at ease. Although he was used to travelling alone and living away from Ulli for weeks at a time he felt strangely abandoned here in this limbo between where he was living and where Ulli had gone. She had been taken away from him like a girl in a Greek legend, spirited off into a dark kingdom, accompanied by a swarm of ghosts in monks' habits, keffiyehs and nuns' black robes. He wanted to bang on the iron Mandelbaum door and demand her return. 'Give me Ulli back,' he would say to the uncomprehending policeman. 'She doesn't belong there. She belongs here with me.' He would show him the photo he had in his wallet. 'See this. She may still be out there. Tell her Rudi wants her to come back. Look, this is her picture.'

He would wave the wallet in the face of the policeman to make him look. He would have to look, that's what policemen do, like the German inspector in the train from Vienna. That was a look Rudi hadn't forgotten. It passed before him brightly and unnaturally lit making him dizzy and he put his hand in his pocket to feel the wallet. The smooth, soft leather, source of dollar bills and home of social security numbers and driving licences comforted him and brought him back to the crumbling garden wall where he stood and the path he must take, up the hill to the noisy buses and broken pavements of Jaffa Road.

Once there he was at a loss what to do. He didn't want to go back to the convent where the nuns were madly busy with cooking and cleaning and spiritual preparations for their Christmas and where the number of guests had doubled. Even if Mother Superior gave him time, he could hardly explain to her his discomfort about Ulli being swept into the hidden Christian kingdom behind the Gate. As he walked away from the centre of the city he thought he heard bells through the noise of traffic. The farther he walked the stronger the jingling sound until he could make out: 'Hark the Herald Angels Sing' coming from the direction of the King David Hotel, or more exactly, the YMCA tower right opposite. As he approached the tower he saw that it was decorated with garlands of lights, switched on despite the day making it look like an exotic, expensive and giant fountain pen in a Fifth Avenue Christmas window. The carillon's mechanical, happy tinkle brought home to him the incongruity of this European-American wintry Christmas with its dark forests and log fires, imposed here on the treeless, stony, grey and brown landscape of the Valley of Jehoshaphat. It was an import, like the carillon, like the whole rambling YMCA building despite its Mameluke arches and domes and mosaics and Armenian tiles and inlaid damascene chairs. It was all a masquerade. So what was real? The muezzin? The Holy Sepulchre? The unattainable Temple Wall? The countless prayer rooms all around the city? He had feared the bewildering currents of religion would take hold of Ulli but now they were buffeting him making what would elsewhere have been an invitation for the curious tourist into a riddle, dangerous to probe and impossible to solve. How could his expertise in the easing of conflicts through language learning be of use in this labyrinth? Where would you start? How could you transform all the incompatible jarring dialects into harmonious sentences? He was walking aimlessly now but in the general direction of the rough, high concrete wall that cut off Jaffa Road just before the danger line. Soon he found himself in front of Notre-Dame, the huge white pile Ada had pointed out to him. Massive, heavy and episcopal, it mimicked Rome and Lourdes so that Catholic pilgrims would feel at home in Jerusalem. But war had emptied it out and turned it into a frontier bulwark. Now it straddled the border like a Titanic run aground, almost leaning against the Old City wall as if ready to breach it with its weight.

Ada had told him about the roof and its view over the divide, so he decided to go in. There was an old man, a porter probably, at a small door at the end of the courtyard, but he paid no attention to Rudi who walked into a cavernous, dark entry hall smelling of disinfectant and kerosene and stale air. Massive stairways led up in different directions and dark corridors branched out on either side. Some young people who could have been students walked out through one of the corridors. There is still some kind of hostel dormitory here, thought Rudi and started up the stairs. The first floor was quite different. There was much more light and the walls, coloured sky blue, bore naïve paintings of mounted crusader knights in armour parading across the scene with coats of arms and pennants and scrolls announcing their titles in heavy Gothic lettering:

RAYMOND DE POITIERS
BAUDOUIN DE BOULOGNE
GUY DE LUSIGNAN
GODEFROID DE BOUILLON

My God, they must have sweated like pigs in this climate, thought Rudi as he looked more closely at figures he knew mostly from Richard the Lionheart and Hollywood spectaculars. The painter had obviously enjoyed working on the heraldic devices much more than the knights' features which were pugilistic, pug-nosed and blunt-jawed. The heraldry though was gay and fanciful. The griffins and falcons were fierce and decorative. Fish had wings and eagles clawed onto shields. The lozenges, bars, circles and crescents on the armour and the banners looked like symbols in a game of cards. These knights were fitted out for a pageant not a battle. Rudi understood that was how the pilgrims pictured the crusades. Banners and plumes and Christian princes. No blood or torn limbs. No horses trampling over dead Saracens' spilled brains.

'Qu'est-ce que vous voulez, monsieur?'

139

His reverie was interrupted by a small nun with glasses carrying a bunch of keys. She was incongruously wearing slippers.

'Je cherche ma femme,' he said truthfully, in a way.

'Elle est ici?' she said incredulously.

'Elle a monté l'escalier par là,' he pointed up to the higher floor, 'et je l'ai perdue.'

She looked bewildered. 'Restez ici, monsieur, je vais chercher le gardien.'

Rudi took a chance and bounded up another steeper flight of stairs. He found himself in a spacious hall with tall windows blocked by sandbags. Bare beds were placed haphazardly around, some turned over on their sides. A few open packs of bandages were piled in a corner. It seemed to have been a hospital ward or a dormitory. The walls were pock-marked, sprayed with bullet holes and stained with black traces of fire. Irregular patches of faded colours suggested some decoration or painting in the past. Rudi went over to a window and tried to peer out through cracks in the pile of sandbags. He could just see a corner of stone which, like a stray piece in a jigsaw puzzle, defied attribution. If this was right on the danger line it was very frustrating. The emptiness irked him. He explored further and found a much smaller door which opened onto a narrow dark corridor and another steep stairway. Finally at the top, through a landing, he encountered a soldier. He was a heavy bald middle-aged man in an ill-fitting khaki shirt and a bright orange pullover. He was smoking and sitting on a hollowed-out armchair, on his knees was a gun.

'*Hey Atzor*,' he said in Hebrew.

'English?' said Rudi.

'What you do here? Is forbidden. Military.'

'I am a tourist.'

'Yes, from where you are?'

'America.'

'America.OK.Hereonlyarmy.Danger.Boomboom.' He grinned and aimed his gun at the ceiling. He had a mouth full of gold teeth. Rudi had seen such shining displays in the mouths of Russian officers in Nuremberg. A smile of flashing gold spread good humour and genial camaraderie around the staff at the trial. The Americans called them Goldheads.

They looked at each other silently for a while. Then the soldier said, 'You have cigarette Chesterfield?'

Rudi considered trying to bribe him with dollars but behind him he heard footsteps and the voice of the nun.

'Monsieur, c'est défendu. Ah mon Dieu. C'est une zone militaire. Venez toute de suite.'

He turned around and went downstairs with the nun clucking and muttering in front of him. Downstairs a man in a black suit was waiting for him. He looked at him suspiciously.

'Did you find your wife, sir?'

'No, she must have left the building by some other door.'

'Do you wish to enquire about the student hostel accomodation?'

'No.'

'There is nothing else here. Just nuns from St Joseph to attend to the chapel. It is an empty shell and on top there are soldiers encamped. But it must be kept up. Would you give a donation?'

Rudi, seeing an opening, took some dollars out of his wallet.

'I am told that there is a view over the line from here.'

The man took the money.

'The military section is forbidden but there is a very partial view from a window in the nuns' room. You bear no weapon?'

Rudi spread his hands in a gesture of surrender and appeal and the man turned abruptly.

'This way.' He seemed to have done this before.

They walked up some backstairs and through a series of dark passageways, past many padlocked doors and collections of broken chairs and torn straw floormats until they came to a door which had been recently painted blue. It bore the name St Denis in bold white letters.

The man took out a set of keys and unlocked the door.

'Up there' he said pointing to what seemed like a porthole set in the wall above a heavy cupboard. The room had a bed with a crucifix over it and a small table covered with an embroidered tablecloth. Apart from the porthole there were no windows or if there was one, it was blocked up behind the cupboard.

'How do I get up there?'

The man moved the table and set a chair on it. He made a sweeping, ironic gesture which covered the table, the chair and the look-out point.

Rudi levered himself up slowly, stood on the chair which seemed stable enough, and grunting, pulled himself onto the top of the cupboard. Dust got into his nose and mouth. He couldn't raise his head because of the ceiling and so he crawled up to the porthole putting his face into the cracked and grimy, half-open glass pane. What was he looking for?

He had asked Ada where the real Jerusalem was when she came to his hotel the first day. So here he was. This was it. But what was it? It was an absurdly small opening onto a patchwork of grey and yellow-grey stones, some dropping down into what might become a street if you could only adjust your angle of vision, which you couldn't. No feature of any wall or stretch of masonry was unambiguous. They were kept from joining into structures by a law of perspective that made them pieces of an illogical, eye-defying puzzle. Nothing in this patchwork showed what was mine as opposed to yours, what was there as opposed to here. It was all the same. So why were Ada and her friends drawn to places like this? Because through the keyhole they spied a forbidden scene? What scene? Naked parents? Ali Baba's treasure? The slaughter of the innocents? His mouth was dry and his neck was hurting from the strain of the unnatural angle but he felt reluctant to crawl back even though a cough below reminded him that the official was waiting. Then something made him stop concentrating on the stones. It was a sound, the clip clop of horses' hooves coming from below, from the hidden street (if there was a street). He felt a surge of excitement and happiness. There was someone down there riding a horse. He listened so intently that the clip clop seemed to come closer, teasing

142

him with the imminent appearance of the animal itself, up against his window like a jack-in-the-box. More dust invaded his nose and he sneezed. The clip clop was gone, if it had ever been there. Now he was ashamed. He had peeked at nakedness. The fact that it was only a naked wall made no difference. It was shameful and fruitless. It was shameful when he had peeked at his sisters in Vienna and had been caught and smacked. But that at least was worth it.

Rudi climbed down wearily, brushed off the dust and insect droppings and followed the silent gardien out of the building.

MIDNIGHT MASS

I'm dreaming of a white Christmas
Just like the ones I used to know

BING CROSBY WAS crooning across the hills of the Hashemite
Kingdom on Radio Ramallah but Milo could pick him up well
enough in his large room overlooking the Temple Mount. They
were sitting at different ends, each at a window, Jordan with her
research notebooks on the culture of faith-healing in Spanish
Harlem and Milo smoking and writing in a thick exercise book.
Hunched over his desk, enveloped in smoke, frowning, his thick
black hair and beard gleaming in the light of the lamp, he looked
like an Italian alchemist, a friend of Caravaggio, busy at work
calculating the elevation of base metal into gold. Jordan looked up
from her description of a case of *mal de ojo* treated by Asuncion Soto
in her tiny room in East Harlem and considered how strange this
all was. First that song. Who would willingly listen to it? Not
anyone she knew in New York. They would throw shoes at the
radio. And here? Irving Berlin's dime-store nostalgia was a balm
for Milo. It lulled him into good will and calmed his pessimism by
its cheap, outrageous self-assurance. Milo had proved its
invigorating effect when they were mouth to mouth, half-naked,
exhausted and sweating on the couch. May your days be merry and
bright, he had hummed, tearing at her again hungry and bearlike,
and all your Christmases be white, spooning into her more gently

144

but purposefully like a skilled rider heading for an Olympic jump. Milo's lovemaking, like the sound track of a French film, featured classical music. Schubert, lyrical, melancholy and flowing with clarity was the favourite. Jordan, coming from younger love affairs played out to Sinatra and Billie Holiday while the music burbled in the background like in hotel lobbies, was intrigued by the alliance of deep cello strokes and leaping violins with Milo's priestly dedication to the ceremony of sex. This was definitely more fun than years of piano practice under the best teachers. But she sometimes felt more like an audience than a participant as he led her through elaborate steps of rituals mastered only through discipline and concentration. And, truth to say, Schubert sometimes stole her spirit away from Milo even though her body stayed behind. Not that she didn't respond. She learned to submit to the sway of the music and, within its sweep, play her role as Milo's antagonist whose struggle could be tolerated, even encouraged, but who must always, in the end, surrender.

'Can God look like Kronberg, my dear?'

'Does he have to look like anything?'

'In the play he does.'

'Can't you leave him out? Just do a voice. Having him on stage will only cause trouble.'

'What d'you think makes the flood happen. A cloudburst? It's him. The God who lives here round the corner. He's an angry old man with a bad back and haemorrhoids and he's had enough of all this shit.'

'You get angry when you talk about him. But his anger also makes you happy. You want this flood to be a success. Why? What makes you go after this washout with such determination?'

Jordan's eyes met his. They were bloodshot and dark in their deep sockets. His face though, in the light of the lamp, was touched with an unnatural glow.

'I watched my father drown kittens on the porch above our grove and the orange trees. I was only a pisher and he was wearing shorts and a torn undershirt and I could see his brown skin and his muscles curving under the cloth. He was smoking and shouting to one of the workers in the grove while he held the kittens under the water with one hand. He was the Boss, the death-dealer. His legs in their boots were as smooth as polished wood. Then he went down into the grove and I was alone by the pail with the kittens. I looked down into the water and there they were floating face up peacefully. When I asked him why he couldn't let them live in the yard he said they'd be eaten by jackals or dogs. Drowning wasn't painful. It was quick.

'Drowning. That would be a great finale. A major drowning and goodbye everyone. No Noah. No Ark. A clean rush, a great wave and nothing. It would be an escape.'

'For us?'

'I said us, of course. Noah is a cop-out. It would be a surprise. Sudden. We couldn't prepare for it. But if we were lucky it would catch us fucking our heads off and high. It wouldn't be painful if it was quick.'

Jordan strained to see if he was serious.

'It gives you pleasure to imagine this doesn't it.'

'Sure. It makes living bearable, bearable to think it possible. Bearable to think of a great emptiness.'

'Isn't suicide more real, more just. Why everyone? Why not...?'

'Me alone?'

He took a long pull of his cigarette.

'If I took an overdose it would be insignificant. They would say Milo finally does it. Years of talk and finally he does it. The shits would say I told you so. So they'd be justified. Milo would go and nothing would change. There would be no emptiness just a clean ash tray.'

'So you're doing the play to infect people with your fantasy.'

'Yes maybe some, even some of the solid householders will get the thrill and will be able to imagine the drowning, the absolute taking of everything...If they could imagine that and forget the trial it would help them grow up. We'd get a prize for public education.'

'You wouldn't regret...?'

'What?'

'Us.'

'No. That's just the point. Where is regret? Where is a you, a me or kittens? Where? There's only emptiness.'

Milo was hunched over his desk like a beast over his kill. Instead of the victim's bloody gore there was a pile of papers and an open book and a fat fountain pen leaking ink.

It's his melodrama, thought Jordan. He's alone on the stage of his own making, mouthing murderous thoughts like some actor-devil, invoking the collapse of the stage and the whole theatre together with its audience into the destructive tide bashing against the doors. But there was no tide and the melodrama was just that, lurid and thin, a parody of a tragedy. She almost pitied him for the helplessness he worked so hard to conceal. Yet Jordan had never met a man as weatherbeaten as Milo. Her American boyfriends had been young and untried by the world. They knew what they knew from books and films and had the unsophisticated idealism or toughness absorbed from their favourite authors and actors. They had a thirst for the world but were still protected against it by money and anxious, watchful parents, too near even if they were at the other end of the continent. Compared to them Milo had no anchor, no ties to anything. He seemed to come from nowhere and the fact that he spoke Hebrew and lived in Jerusalem was just chance, an accident. He was like an orphan with the prickliness and wild temper learned from self-defence in dangerous surroundings.

And he had an orphan's contempt for a world in which fathers and mothers protected children and had breakfast together on weekends. He would rather see it go under or, until it disappeared, cast it aside for any momentary madness, a sudden woman, a wild treacherous friend, a long-lasting high, drink and sleep.

In their first months together he slept so much that Jordan thought he was sick and in decline. It was a total, overwhelming sleep, noiseless and short on breath but not deathlike. She watched him, brown and bearlike, in his down of black hair, fascinated by the energy his sleeping body gave off. She would have pressed

147

herself totally against his warmth like a lizard on hot stone but she held back, reluctant to expose herself in this way. Now she was in his lair, a prisoner of a kind, serving the commandant by learning the hidden rules of the compound but unwilling to be sucked under by the currents of his anger.

'Listen,' he said.

And I stood upon the sand of the sea and saw a beast rise up out of the sea having seven heads and ten horns and upon his horns ten crowns and upon his heads the name of blasphemy.

'That's John, it's what he saw in the waves from Patmos. He must have been high on some weed but he had the picture right. He had it in colour and in fire and full of detail. Noah is a child compared to him.'

Jordan, who grew up with colouring books which depicted a sturdy Ark with a happy greybeard Noah welcoming a procession of animal families onto the gangplank and no sign of drowned creatures except for a page with a watery space for her blue crayon to colour, found it hard to accept the justness of Milo's wish for the annihilating deluge. In her heart she knew it was as fake as Irving Berlin's whitewash of Christmas. It wasn't venal but it had a strong whiff of kitsch, the kind of damnation kitsch that sustained Milo's sense of difference from the rest of the world. She couldn't easily laugh at it because of her love for him but she was wary of it, knowing that it could be turned against her one day when she would become a real victim not of the flood but of Milo's cruel hand drowning her in the pail with the kittens.

It was already dark and totally quiet. As there were no curtains, the large, handsome windows gave onto a landscape in darkness which remained itself even though hidden to the eye. There were hillsides, terraces, cypresses and olive trees as ghostly presences that the eye might strain to detach from the all-surrounding night. The stillness encouraged you to picture what you couldn't see so that you could be reassured. The world you knew was still out there.

148

Milo had quietened down, his pen scratched in a regular rhythm of writing. Jordan had learned to cope with this deep surrounding silence by listening for meager sounds here and there. It could be a dog or jackal, wind, a faint whistle, the drone of a small plane. These she picked up like a bird pecking crumbs.

Then in a moment the loud rattling of stones on the gravel path and the noise of voices changed everything.

Tomas gave a shout and pushed open the door, followed by Ada who was carrying a package wrapped in tissue paper.

She gave the room a quick look over to check there was no crisis.

'I've brought the model,' she said and put the package on a table.

They were flushed with the cold of the night and in good spirits. Compact and wrapped in coats and scarves they looked like a pair of wooden Russian dolls about to unpack themselves.

Milo stared at the wrapped Ark for a while before opening it up like a birthday present. He was quiet. They all looked at it.

'Turn off the light,' said Tomas.

When the room was dark Tomas pressed a small switch and the Ark began to glow.It had no resemblance to a ship. It was a rectangular, flat platform, a dock, made like a city square with marked pedestrian crossings and a traffic policeman's stand. Commanding the square was a detailed replica of Zion Cinema complete with posters for *Gone with the Wind*, rails to tame the queues and ticket booths protected by iron grills.

There was complete silence. Ada spoke.

'The Ark is a place everybody knows, Zion Square. It's right next to where you want to perform the play. Five minutes walk up the street and there's Eichmann. So the Flood is happening right in the middle of the city and the survivors are going to walk into the square and into the cinema just like they do every Saturday night dressed in their best white shirts and blouses. And those who laughed at Noah and think he's nuts they're in the streets and houses all around the square. But they can't get there. They see the waters rising from their balconies and there's no way, the square's afloat and the water is going to cover everything.'

149

'And the animals?' asked Jordan.

'They're in the cinema. Giraffes at the back. Elephants and other bulky ones on the sides and all the others, first come first served.'

Milo bent over the model as if it was a baby in a cradle. He seemed at a loss for words.

'What do you think?' said Ada.

'You're a witch. Only the devil could have put this brilliant idea into your head. When did you sell him your soul?'

He went down on hands and knees and kissed her shoes, a separate kiss for each.

Ada's usual reserve gave way to exuberant activity. She fished in her bag and pulled out the animals one by one and Noah, Mrs Noah and all the families. Like a girl in her birthday best fussing over her doll house, she placed each figure carefully on the model, mentioning their names and keeping the families separate, even contriving to push a couple of giraffes inside Zion Cinema so that their long necks and bulb-eyed wistful faces stuck out above a fire escape like banners.

'There you are,' she said. 'The world can begin again.'

Tomas switched off his little stage light and the room was dark. Jordan didn't put the lights back on and all four melted into the stillness and the black. No-one spoke. A solemn bell, deep and monotonous, rang from the direction of the Dormition Abbey and Mount Zion. The insistent, resounding blang blang made the room seem doubly locked into itself as waves of sound lapped against its walls.

We are detached from the town. We are floating down the valley into the desert, thought Jordan and was angry with herself for surrendering like this to the mystique of the place. All it is is a bell over the valley. It's a church getting on with its business for Christmas. She switched the light on.

Tomas and Ada were lying on the sofa at the other end of the room face to face. Milo was at his desk his chin propped up by one hand and his writing book open. She went over to him and cradled his head to her.

150

'Jingle bells,' she said.

Looking down on his bearded face cupped in her hands and seemingly detached from his body she felt an unfamiliar power. The man she loved was her toy. His head, lit by the desk lamp, was a ball for her to caress or fling away. The eyes were closed, the brow smooth and the lips slightly parted. He was submitting to her and she could enfold him with no challenge. It was as if he had surrendered life to her and become her victim like the women in Ada's drawings.

He opened his eyes.

'What are you looking at me like that for? Did I catch something?'

Jordan laughed. 'I had a Judith moment. You were the big marshal honcho and I was the Hebrew girl with the knife.'

Milo sat up. 'And it was my head you were going to chop?'

He fingered his neck dramatically.

'They didn't teach you that stuff in Bible class did they?'

'No way, I was in Rome and I saw the Caravaggio. It's a thriller. She's got Holofernes by the hair and she's slicing through his neck, bone, muscle and everything. It's hard work. She's concentrating and a bit shocked but firm on the sword. The look on his face, Milo, is incredible. He's horrified and he can't believe what's happening to him. But it is happening and the blood is spurting out thick and strong. And he's not dead yet, he's more horrified than dead.'

'Poor bastard. Why didn't she just chop off his dick after what he did to her.'

'He didn't.'

'He did.'

'Never. When did you read it? She didn't even get into bed with him. She was a respectable widow and she was clever. She matched him drink for drink till he passed out. He was too blasted to lay a hand on her. Holofernes, that's who he was.'

Milo got up and took her by the hand to a book case.

'Ok let's get the evidence. Did she or didn't she.'

He pulled out a Bible.

'It's not in there' she said. 'You've got to get the Apocrypha.'

'Fuck the Apocrypha. I'll ask Ada. She went to a good school.'

He went over to where Ada and Tomas were lying with their eyes closed, apparently oblivious to what was going on around them.

He kneeled down and put his mouth to Ada's ear.

'Ada'le, Ada'le, come out of it, it's Christmas. The kids are tracking up to the abbey. You remember, Ada'le?'

His voice was gentle, more of a coo than a whisper.

She looked up at him. 'I wasn't asleep, just exhausted. What was that you were arguing about?'

'Holofernes. Did he screw her?'

Ada sat up. She glanced at Jordan who was standing by Milo's writing table looking embarrassed.

'What's this? A Bible quiz?'

'We have to know whether she chopped him after he screwed her or not.'

'Why is it so important?'

'Because in this struggle the death blow and the sex blow are in the balance.'

'She didn't,' said Ada. 'She got him pissed and she didn't. Definitely no.'

Milo seemed crestfallen.

'Do people still go up to the Dormition on Christmas eve?' said Jordan trying to get away from sex and death.

'We can go if you like,' said Ada. 'It used to give us a thrill years ago.'

Milo was quiet.

He stayed quiet while they made arrangements to take the steep walk up Mount Zion and the abbey. Tomas too was strangely quiet. He had never been to the Dormition mass. He had stored Polish masses in his memory and laughed at his fellow students' excitement over the midnight climb to the massive, ugly church on the border line. But they all put their coats on and stepped out into the cold night. There was a bell somewhere far away, not at the abbey and the only sound as they walked was the crunch of footsteps on the ground. After the sharp descent into the valley they began the climb up the trail. Soon they were part of a line of walkers making their way quite noisily and with a lot of laughter and shouts back and forth. Halfway up a crowd was gathering around two men holding placards.

NO TO ROME
DANGER FALSE GOSPEL
PAPISM=IDOLATRY

The men said nothing and looked impassively at people who asked about the placards. They were well-dressed in winter coats and broad hats. Neither was bearded and they looked foreign.

Milo said 'They're Christians but they're against the mass. They've been here before.'

'So why do they do it?' said Jordan.

'They say the mass is Catholic propaganda and they don't want young Jews to fall for it. But they keep quiet. They're not missionaries.'

He saluted them gravely as he walked past.

The abbey seemed more cavernous than ever and the responses of the prayer echoed hollowly as they rose and fell. The monk at the entrance pushed them nervously along one side of the outer circle into the curious crowd. They looked like children to Ada, too lightly dressed for the cold night's outing, their hair wild and windblown, noses red and cheeks flushed. There were T-shirts everywhere. Fidel Castro, Ho Chi Minh, Marylin Monroe and Sigmund Freud were carried in procession like revolutionary banners into the sanctum of orthodoxy. There was a peculiar lack of attention and gravity in the crowd. They seemed to be communicating with each other by glance, whisper, gesture or touch all the time and ignoring the mass they had come to see. Perhaps they were watching out of the corner of an eye or listening to it as background music while more significant thoughts and sounds occupied them. They were good-humoured and happy to be together, though they could have been anywhere, at a football match or a parade. For Ada as well the mass

153

receded into the background. She watched Milo, whose fingers were stroking Jordan's neck under the whisps of her gathered hair. She could only see the back of his head but she knew by its pose that he was looking at nothing, at emptiness. Next to her Tomas was looking down at his shoes, concentrating hard as if plotting an escape shaft deep under the polished stones of the church floor. Only Jordan's attention was a riddle. The back of her graceful neck under Milo's caress absorbed his tribute but Ada couldn't guess what her eyes revealed, perhaps only the acquiescence of a woman to a man's loving touch. The organ boomed and the monks' chanting swelled and filled the great space, perfumed now and smoky with incense. Ada was hungry and the ridiculousness of their situation struck her with blunt force. There was no mystery or secret anymore for them in the music and ritual of the mass. They had all been in it before. Tomas knew more than he would reveal. Milo had been in combat with it, attracted and repulsed by it here and wherever he had lived. They had all lived outside the tight cocoon of their one religion. And Jordan, she came from a place where religions had no secrets or mystery at all but were on public offer in attractive packs with sell-by dates and consumer guides.

Jordan turned round. They looked at each other. Jordan raised an eyebrow and grimaced. I've had enough, it seemed to say. Ada beckoned to her and they slowly pushed their way out of the crowd.

The trail outside was deserted. A torn anti-Papist slogan on the ground was the only sign of the protesters. Perhaps there had been a scuffle and the monks had forced them to leave. As they made their way down Milo was walking beside Ada.

'Not so fast,' he said, 'take in the stars. No reason to hurry.'

She felt his presence beside her keeping pace with her like a hunter shadowing his prey. If I had a coat of fur it would bristle, she thought, pulling her jacket tight around her.

'What d'you think?' he said.

'What?'

'The mass and the children. Wasn't it very different …'

'When we used to come? We were thirsty for something. These

154

kids came for a party with music and fancy dress. They're younger and tougher.'

'Thirsty?'

'Yes, we thought there was a secret hidden from us, some shame and scandal kept away from the children by parents and dull teachers. So we came up the path to find out.'

'Did we?'

'O mi Dios quando sera

'You remember that?'

'You scrawled it over my painting.'

'I could have scrawled it over your belly, you slept so deeply. And then turned you over and scrawled the rest on your tiny buttocks.'

'Why didn't you?'

'There wasn't enough room there but seriously, I was afraid.'

'Afraid? Of what?'

'I don't know. Maybe John's passion was too genuine for me. It must have made me ashamed. His lust for God scared me. I couldn't write it on you.'

They walked along silently.

'What was that about the general and Judith? Why did you want to know what happened between them?'

'It was Jordan. Something odd happened in the room after we looked at the Ark. She's got a thing about Judith and the man. It's like the story was about us, her and me, and we got into an argument about what happened…'

He sounded more troubled than amused.

'She didn't try to get you drunk, did she?'

'No, Ada, don't play dumb. She stood behind me and took my head in her hands and bang there I was, the general ripe for the knife. That's what she told me.'

Ada laughed.

'This worries you? Everybody's got a murder or two in them. You know that, even well-brought-up girls. Anyway, maybe she's getting even with you.'

155

'How?'

'Maybe you're rough with her.' Ada was searching for diplomatic language.

'When you're with her, I mean, rough like a soldier fighting hand to hand.'

Milo was quiet.

'Was I rough with you?'

'I knew nothing else.'

'But you said it in those drawings.'

'I said it about women you brought in like peaches from the market. I was embarrassed by them even though I wouldn't show it and I thought I saw them cut open and damaged. I looked at them hurt. But it was really me. And that's what I drew.'

Even as she spoke, Ada heard the echo of conversations with Milo years ago. She had, at first, tried to make him see her as she was. But his rage for conquest wouldn't abide it. It was as if his very life, certainly his writing and thinking, depended on taking prisoners, women tribes of women, fallen into the hands of the imperial army of one. And Ada? She was the keeper of the gate. How had she come to this? She now felt a shame stronger than she had felt then. It explained her obsessive return to those drawings as a kind of self-punishment and, if other people saw them, a public confession of her ignoble weakness and surrender.

Now Milo's cruelty seemed almost comic to her. The obtuseness and vanity that underlay his charm stood out, in her eyes, like red blobs on a clown's white cheeks. The imperial army was growing older and its plumes and uniforms were getting shabby. As for the emperor himself, he was losing his grip if he felt threatened by a Judith from Berkeley with perfect teeth and worried parents.

Milo stopped and stared at her. In the dark she felt rather than saw the intensity of his gaze.

'Show me how I'm hurting her and I'll kill myself.'

'No-one can show you Milo. You have to know it yourself or you'll never be able to stop.'

Milo's threats to commit suicide weren't new to her. They were

156

part of his Byronic pose and were supported by a good deal of learning in the literature of suicide. In the past they weren't even connected to some crisis or disappointment but were marshalled to lead an argument about the emptiness of life. He had never actually tried to do it as far as she knew. But the aura of possibility and even common sense he granted the act hung about him like a cloak and gave him the distinguishing marks of a gladiator about to enter the arena of death.

Milo took her hand roughly but Tomas and Jordan had caught up with them and he let go.

They walked on till they got to the Turkish bandstand. Jordan noticed a light in Julius's window and they followed her up the path to his door. From outside they heard a mooing sound and an irregular plucking of banjo strings. They knocked and walked in.

Drink to me only with thine eyes
And I will pledge with mine

Julius was kneeling next to one of his three folding chairs singing with his hand outstretched in supplication. On the bed Kronberg was holding a small banjo and plucking strings in a haphazard fashion. He looked up flushed and embarrassed but Julius held his suitor's pose by the chair. His face was ruddy and his large head seemed suspended over the scene by a string from above. He could have been a puppet, a large mannikin with dangling limbs and a body stuffed with straw.

Milo knew him well enough not to disturb the performance and cause a tantrum so he beckoned to the others and they sat down quietly on some pillows by the wall. They were now part of the audience and Julius could go on.

He stared at the chair, creeping closer and closer on his knees humming to himself. Then he looked around the room, taking them all in, one by one as spectators of his experiment.

157

It breathes.
It distinctly breathes.

He moved around the chair on his knees inspecting it gingerly.

Curious, curious.
In general it breathes.

He gasped and raised his hands towards the audience.

Maybe it will lash out at me like the Great Cat of Madagascar.

He placed his palms on his thighs.

That would be intolerable.

Julius paused and seemed to pull himself physically out of his act by spreading his arms wide at first and then waving them from side to side like windscreen wipers. He stood up.

'Just an impromptu rehearsal,' he said. 'Trying out something I've been writing about love and furniture. Kronberg doesn't think chairs can be dramatic. So I've been trying to convince him he's wrong.'

'*Ladies and gentlemen, meet Gertrude.*'

He pointed at the chair with a ringmaster's flourish.

Kronberg looked around the room, got up and walked over to the chair. He was wearing a suit which seemed out of place and a little too tight. Gravely he stretched out a hand:

'*Delighted to meet you Madam. Such a fine performer...*
And what brings you to our remote province?'

Julius clapped.

'Kronberg, you have seen reason. I won't be scared anymore of your Prussian positivism.'

He turned to the newcomers.

'*Welcome Rosencrantz. Welcome Guildenstern, the delicate Ophelia*

158

and her younger sister Gudrun. Welcome good friends to our far province. This night we will hear a play recently performed in Vienna and Stockholm. It concerns the murder of Duke Gonzago by poison and his betrayal by the chair he loved most in the world.'

Julius turned to Kronberg.

'It begins.'

Kronberg stood by the chair looking around as if for help. The paleness of his closely shaven face and the blue glint in his eyes behind their glasses hinted at tension without surrendering to it. He seemed to be struggling to retain his composure.

'It begins.'

Julius repeated his stage direction and made a sweeping histrionic gesture which included Kronberg, the chair and the rest of the room.

Kronberg stood frozen for a while. Then he looked at Tomas and his stiffness gave way to resolve. He knelt down and laid his head on the seat of the chair. He sighed and closed his eyes but when he opened them again his look was still directed firmly at Tomas. Then he addressed the chair.

'Dear, I loved you like no-one ever loved a chair. I attended to your every need. I stroked you to health when you were broken. When no-one understood you I learned your language and spoke for you. You were mine and I was yours. But Oh, Oh what a falling-off was there.'

Kronberg closed his eyes again and held his pose. His head rested on the seat of the chair. No-one spoke.

Julius helped Kronberg get up and hugged him.

'Well spoken and with true accent.'

'Kronberg, who would have thought it,' said Milo? 'A Prussian and so familiar with Hamlet?'

'I acted in Hamlet at school. I was Polonius but I knew most of it by heart in German and in English.'

'You must have been a very convincing Polonius,' said Milo.

'I wanted to play Horatio but our teacher thought I was best suited for an old man. I wonder why.'

He grinned at his self-mockery and turned to Tomas. As he

approached him he stooped, furrowed his brow and folded his hands over an imagined pot belly.

> *The friends thou hast and their adoption tried*
> *Grapple them to thy soul with hoops of steel*
> *But do not dull thy palm with entertainment*
> *Of each new-hatched, unfledged comrade.*

'He talks sense the old pedant. Doesn't he? Drybones knows a thing or two about friendship.'

Tomas said nothing.

'Tomas didn't study Hamlet at school. He was too busy hiding,' said Ada.

'You think I don't know. We read it together here one very hot summer. You remember, Tomas? The Ghost, he made you sit up. "Confined to fast in fires." You said you could feel the burning walls on your skin. That's what you said, I remember.'

'Enough nostalgia,' said Milo. 'We came here because we heard music. Let's have Radio Ramallah. It's party time.'

He went over to the radio and twiddled with the dial until the Andrews Sisters came up clear and bright: *Don't sit under the apple tree with anyone else but me.*

Three chirpy, clean American voices rolled happiness across the room like gaily coloured balls for three healthy American girls to bounce on in front of a world of admirers.

Milo led Ada into a kind of polka. Julius and Jordan jigged awkwardly between the table and the bed. Kronberg turned to Tomas, bowed from the waist and put a hand out in invitation. Tomas got up and Kronberg steered him alongside Milo and Ada.

They hardly moved and they looked quite incongruous; Kronberg stiff and grey in his suit, like an elderly bachelor at a hotel tea dance and Tomas slight and pale in a paint-flecked sweater with holes at the elbows. Next to Kronberg he looked shorter and frailer than he was. Ada watched his face for any sign but it was impassive and empty. His eye seemed to rest on a button of Kronberg's shirt.

160

Then abruptly the Andrews sisters fell silent and a slow, dark and sinuous Ellington glide took over. Time for romance said the soft Ramallah voice. Milo enveloped Ada in a bear hug, pressing his body against her but Kronberg, seemingly bewildered or embarrassed by the change in the music and the mood, just stood there holding Tomas in a tenuous embrace. Ada looked at them over Milo's shoulder. They seemed to have lost the will to move and stood as if some inner clockwork had stopped and needed rewinding. She wanted to intervene in some way, call out or turn Tomas around to face her but the mad thought struck her that, if she did, Tomas would disintegrate, just collapse into fragments on the floor. Except for the music the room was completely still. Julius had stopped trying to make Jordan laugh with grotesque dance movements and now her head rested on his shoulder. Her eyes were closed and he semed to be making a great effort to sway to and fro smoothly and not disturb his graceful burden. Ada had the strange feeling that she was the only person awake in a room of dreamers. Milo was so close that she couldn't see his face but she imagined his eyes were shut because he seemed to be humming, from somewhere deep inside, a variation on Ellington's luscious, complex chords. Where are we, she thought? What compass and pencil on a map can find us out? What watchful eye can picture who we are?

Nowhere else had she felt the urge to find a hidden logic in the apparently accidental collision of lives, splitting from one trajectory to another, meeting and spinning apart again. The secret had something to do with this terrain, she was sure. It was how she saw the little group as balancing together on an edge over a chasm with no rope, no net, no promise of a safe landing. Tied to nothing stable, only each other, they existed in giddy suspension over an emptiness they refused to fear. How long before they fell?

The spell was broken by a cry of pain from Jordan. She had slipped off her shoes and Julius had trodden on her bare foot. She fell back onto the bed and Milo knelt by her feet and sucked her wounded toes with murmurs of compassion. Julius stood in a corner like a dunce cursing his clumsiness and punishing his shoes by kicking hard against the wall. Kronberg and Tomas, no longer touching, stood opposite each other as if struck dumb in the midst of a conversation. Then Tomas turned away and called to Ada. 'We should go, it's getting cold in here.'

The kerosene heater hadn't been refilled and the chill had crept relentlessly into the room. No-one had noticed. But now Ada realized how cold it had become and how the acrid smell of the neglected heater had filled the air. Tomas already had his coat on, Milo was still kneeling by Jordan's wounded toes, Julius, head bowed, was tenderly moving the chair he called Gertrude. Only Kronberg was still frozen in the middle of the room, pale, tall in the grey suit too tight for him. He held his glasses in one hand and was blinking myopically at the bare bulb above his head.

ULLI

RUDI WAS RUNNING up steps and along corridors in a bombed building with a Russian officer looking desperately for a lost passport when he woke up to find Ulli unpacking her bag. It was late afternoon and Félix had brought her from the Mandelbaum Gate and delivered her into the safe hands of Mother Superior Schwester Clara. She was tactful and didn't pepper Ulli with questions but helped her quietly into the room where Rudi was asleep.

The convent was tranquil after the exertions and bustle of the Christmas days. The courtyard hadn't beeen swept and a smell of cooking hung lazily in the air. The only noise was that of the crows croaking in the tall, wrinkled pine trees of the German Colony.

Rudi rubbed the sleep out of his eyes and they looked at each other as if they had been apart for months and not five days. This was a new situation for them. Instead of Rudi returning from far away with his story of a trip full of meetings and language laboratories, Ulli was now the traveller returned from the far country, fifteen minutes walk down Bethlehem Road past the King David. When he got up to embrace her, Rudi noticed a strange perfume in her breath.

'What did they give you to eat, liebchen?'

'Nothing today except one of these.'

She fished out of her bag a long thin bread shaped like a flattened oval hoop. It was covered with roasted sesame seeds.

'And this.'

She pulled out a small twist of what looked like newspaper torn out of a telephone book. When she opened it out Rudi saw that it was a fragment of a telephone book. Along the columns of names in Arabic lay a tiny mound of green dust. A strange but not unpleasant herbal smell emerged.

'*Zaatar*,' said Ulli. 'Look,' she broke off a piece of the hoop wetted it with her tongue and dipped it in the green mound. Then she offered it to Rudi.

Suspicious at first, he took it and observed the piece of bread as if it were a live crab or an unusual mushroom.

'It's good,' she said. 'Go on try it. It should be dipped in olive oil not saliva.'

Rudi took a bite. The bread's surprisingly sweet taste was tempered by the sesame seeds. The green stuff was salty and tart. Its greenness was in the taste also.

'Félix says it's hyssop. It's what they gave Jesus on the cross. On a wet rag to make him more thirsty.'

She broke off a large piece, rubbed a finger in the zaatar and sucked away with relish. 'I can't get enough of it.'

'Do you know someone called Margarian, an Armenian?'

'Yes, he's a lawyer, the agent for Julius's landlord.'

'I've got a vase for him and some pastries. They're from his sister over there. Félix knows them.'

There was something different about her, something new to Rudi. She had always been girlish in his eyes, slight and fragile with an open, trusting face. Now there was something else in the set of her mouth and chin, some pleasure in what she had achieved. She was flushed and excited with it, her blue eyes were bright with energy and brio, her blonde hair was tied in twin pigtails and over her multi-coloured jumper she was wearing a weighty string of beads made of strange stones and blue glass. He assumed she had bought them in the Old City.

She sat down on the bed next to him and rested her head on his shoulder.

'I'm such a fool, Rudi. I went through the Gate like a stray cat. It was there so I went through but I didn't know why it was there. So I was on the other side and I didn't know of what. It was the other side of the same thing. The bit of wall that you see here, so you see it from the other side and the road with the stones and the holes you see that too. It's the same. Yes, I know you told me about the war and the way everything was split apart but you can't imagine what it's really like. It's not like an apple cut in half, normal and clean. This isn't. It's crazy, rough and a mess. So I stood on a pile of sandbags and looked back over where I just came from and there I was, me here, and myself there, two people and we were meeting at the barbed wire. I got giddy, Rudi, like a crazy mirror was put in front of me, the kind you see in a fair.'

Ulli lay back on the bed. She was exhausted despite her excitement and flow of talk.

Her eyes were closing as she mumbled something about the Holy Sepulchre and repeated the words '...black, black, all black.'

Soon she was asleep.

Rudi watched her quiet breathing and was puzzled. How had they got here, the two of them, to this narrow convent bed in Jerusalem under a banner declaring *Amor Vincit Omnia*? He was only meant to be here a few weeks to help train the translators. Then he was to go. There was a new project in the works: a language-learning Olympics in Japan or Singapore, an ambitious idea bridging cultures and continents, sure to arouse the interest of the press. Just up his street. So what had derailed him and what had made Ulli come? She had never before dreamt of such a thing. Oakland was home where she felt secure. The streets of San Francisco were world enough for her while Rudi's reports and photographs from the frontiers of language learning left her uncurious. She had over the years asked him about Perla and Suzi and about Vienna and their parents. But as he was reluctant to talk she didn't persist and made do with adding a few words of greeting to an annual Thanksgiving dinner photograph. But a visit of the Bleis, relatives who had managed to get away from Vienna to Argentina had changed all that.

One California summer, Gisl and Sigi Blei had come oddly dressed in heavy coats and woollen sweaters. They were carrying battered old suitcases bound with string and patched with scuffed bits of leather. They were not only bewildered by the weather. They were giddy in the world. Their life in Buenos Aires had been a series of catastrophes and miraculous changes in fortune which they retold with fits of laughter: money was lost, stolen and recovered; menial work at home, glueing together parts of fake leather handbags, gave way to their own importer's office in the back room of a restaurant. Rooms, flats and houses followed each other across the stage at a dizzying pace. Sigi became Sergio, Gisl – Graciella. As they described it, Buenos Aires seemed more like the backdrop for a comedy of errors than a capital city. Sigi's favourite expression was *ken eine horre*, a magic Yiddish formula to ward off the evil eye used like an air raid warning, to alert everyone for incoming trouble whenever something good happened ('so we got a licence for importing corsets and they sold like hot cakes – *ken eine horre*'). It seemed to have worked, in general, for them. They had stayed afloat through many storms and though they had no children they didn't look forlorn or beaten down.

They had discovered Rudi, through Perla, for a reason. They had left Vienna at the very end and were the last people in the family to see Ossias Maiberg and Bertha. On the last day of their stay, after dinner, Sigi took Rudi aside and they went into the study. He was a burly man with broad, dough-kneading hands that could have been a baker's and large flat ears. He put his arms round Rudi's shoulders and they closed the door.

Rudi was uncomfortable. He guessed what Sigi wanted to talk about. That was why he had closed the door on Ulli and Gisl. It had to be something difficult. The big hands on his shoulders steered him right into the furthest corner of his study to a chair under a framed photograph of the Nuremberg courtroom, all grey and black except for Rudi's head which was encircled by a white halo. Rudi knew Vienna was coming up. Vienna was what he avoided in his letters to his sisters. They might try to bring it up, but he was able

166

to skirt over it with news of his international seminars and his ideas for a universal spelling agreement. As for Nuremberg, he never mentioned that directly. Instead he wrote about his lecture tours, the nice audiences and the pleasant hotels he stayed in. Now he was being pinned down by the big man in a brown baggy suit who was standing over him breathing more heavily than usual and wiping his brow with a handkerchief.

Rudi would have liked to take charge of the conversation but the right words and usual gambits failed him. He had to wait for Sigi.

'Your father,' said Blei, 'he was a distinguished man and clever too. He was in a tough situation, as you know. Your mother was losing her sight. She needed treatment but...Anyway you know all this so why am I telling you again? What you don't know and I only found out by chance, is that your father could have got away quite easily. He might even have been here with you, a free man in his last years enjoying the California sunshine. You see the Aryan who took over the law office, Grebner, also a Rechtsanwalt, was a Nazi, one of the insiders in Vienna and he knew one of the top men in the Central Office, Stahlecker. That bastard disappeared you know. They even think he got to South America. So Grebner fixed it for your father to see this Nazi in their headquarters, the Hotel Metropole. He thought it would help. He wasn't such a bad guy, Grebner.

'Your father told me he dressed in his black suit and shirt with the stiff collar and he went in his hat and walking stick to that hotel. He didn't tell Bertha where he was going. She would have been out of her mind with worry. So he is brought in by Grebner, past all the uniforms, and the secretaries running around with files and papers and outside the main office there is a delegation of Austrian Jews waiting, well-known people like Loewenherz and Kritzler. But Grebner takes him straight in. Inside he is face to face with the Nazi who decides everything. Where the Jews can go, where they can live, what papers they need, how they pay their money, if they can have a radio in jail, everything. He was god in Vienna. Your father is out of breath. He isn't so healthy any more. He is also dizzy from nerves and from the steps. He asks to sit down. The little god behind the desk is surprised. He considers the request. Then he makes a sign and points to a chair. It's a joke and he's laughing to himself, a quiet laugh like a smile on one side of the face. So what does your father do? He doesn't think too much. He doesn't know what gets into him. Maybe to refuse would be worse than to accept. He goes and sits in the chair, not before he says thankyou. There is silence. It's like a game of chess. The opening moves are made and now it gets deep and dangerous. Remember, your father is a serious man, not a gambler, not a joker. When did you hear him tell a joke? But he is left alone. Rudi is gone. Perla and Suzi just left. He is alone with a wife going blind. And now he is in the chair opposite the little god. He has to speak or this game will not end well. It's his move. He isn't going to beg for his life. There's no gun pointed at him. Ask for a visa to Spain? That's absurd. Asking for anything is absurd. Loewenherz and Kritzler outside, that's their job to ask for something big. He's just Rechtsanwalt Maiberg and he can't ask. So he opens his mouth and he's back in school, in the gymnasium, a keen scholar with a good memory. Let's see if I remember it. I learned it by heart at school also.

Wer reitet so spät durch Nacht und Wind?
Es ist der Vater mit seinem Kind;
Er hat den Knaben wohl in dem Arm,
Er fasst ihn sicher, er hält ihn warm.

'He stops. Who's standing there? It isn't his distinguished teacher at the Obergymnasium. It's the Nazi and why should the Nazi listen to this?

'"Go on," says the little god. "Finish it."

'But he can't. For the life of him he can't. His throat is dry and his head is full of empty noise. He also feels burning and pressure on his bladder. To pee himself here would be the worst shaming hell.

'So he gets up, with some difficulty, pressing his thighs together on account of the bladder and asks permission to go.

'The Nazi is more amused than annoyed. He signals to Grebner to stay and shoos your father out. They are both laughing.

'He told me this just before we left. He was alone, Bertha was in bed and he didn't say so but I knew he wanted me to remember it, every detail. And I didn't ask him why he hadn't used the meeting to get something out of the Nazi for himself like a hospital for Bertha. What would have been the point?

'So when we left he gave me this photo of him and Bertha. I copied it. You can have it if you don't have it already.'

Rudi handled the small yellowing photograph gingerly like a butterfly. Two people dressed in black looked into the camera's fish eye. One stood stiffly with a nicely trimmed white beard and a firm, sharp stare. The other was bent in her loose black dress. Her face was soft and round, her eyes dulled with glaucoma. They were looking out for Rudi, looking everywhere. Now they had found him after he had abandoned them on the railway line out of Vienna. There was a quick pang under his ribs and then nothing. He had cut himself away from them well before he had let their photograph fly out of his hand. The man who summoned up Goethe's ballad out of his schooldays as he sat in the chair opposite the Nazi was certainly a brave, perhaps a foolish old man and he had been Rudi's father for some years. But to be honest he had never felt the pain of his loss. He had left them behind like his child's bed and stamp collection. That was all. It was shameful, he knew, that he cared more now for hungry children in a Brazilian slum than he did for these two ghosts in black. Yet he could bear it, this shame. It was the price he paid for living in the present and working, like Sisyphus, to push a reluctant world up the steep mountain. That work had to be done. If he and people like him didn't concentrate all their energy and push, life would become ever more unbearable not just for the usual victims – the poor, the hungry the dispossessed – but for people like himself who thought that, after all they had lived through, they were safe now.

When the Bleis had gone Rudi began to feel the photograph had designs on him. He was determined to tear it up and throw away the pieces or burn them. But he kept forgetting to do so, and then he didn't. He had it in his wallet when he went walking by the beach but he didn't pull it out and throw it into the foam where the waves hit the sand. Once he had it ready between his fingers when he was driving and rolled down the window to throw it out but it stuck to the sweat on his hand. Instead of persevering he put it back into his wallet between the business cards and the dollar bills. Intending to keep quiet about the photo, he nevertheless told the story to Ulli.

'You threw it out of the train window, why?'

'I was getting free of a burden.'

'What?'

'Maybe that's not it. I was scared that passport control would suspect me of not being who I said I was.'

'Why would the photo make trouble for you?'

'Well, they don't look Aryan.'

'So, you had a photo of a couple of old Jews. So what?'

'It was the only thing on me connected to the past. Even my clothes were new. It was irrational but I felt they were weighing me down.'

'Those two old faces?'

'There was some embarrassment in it too. I had nothing of theirs except that, no letter, no keepsake, no embroidered handkerchief. So it was a reminder of something I didn't want to remember. I was cocky and I imagined I could be born a second time, all my own work. No parents. No baggage.'

Rudi could see Ulli had little sympathy for what he had done. She took the photograph under her protection, had it enlarged and framed. She then put it under the reading lamp on her side of their bed. Whenever Rudi reached over to draw her small warm body to him they were there, Ossias and Bertha, looking upon the nakedness of their prodigal son and asking him why he wasn't making a son of his own.

O For A Muse Of Fire

THE OLD ICE factory was coming back from the dead. It was infiltrating the brand new, unfinished Television Centre, emptying the offices, spreading fine dust onto the desks and the heavy grey drawers of files, stripping naked the notice boards and filling Lewis Meredith's heart with melancholy. Someone high-up had got cold feet and decided there would after all be no experimental television station, not yet, not even a trial run. Television was too much of a gamble, a monster with a million eyes and a hungry stomach. The high-up was struck by the thought that it could become uncontrollable. Too many faces and voices, too many opinions and therefore dangerous. As for weather reports and chatter, who needed them? Weather was mostly predictable and there was enough chatter on the radio and the buses to fill the country twice over. The centre, it was decided, would be a base to help the foreign press and to document the trial but nothing else. No news, no sports, no Mickey Mouse. Just a film of the courtroom, an eye on whatever went on inside. How many people did you need for this? The building was once again quiet. Office partitions divided up vacant squares like empty egg boxes and the remaining staff flitted about like spirits in the underworld.

Shpitz had been kept. Why, no-one really knew. Rumors went round that the important man in London wanted to keep him away from his daughter; but that seemed far-fetched. More likely he had been to see the high-ups and had convinced them that an old hand like his was still needed in case of sudden change. If they changed their minds again late in the day, under pressure from the big guns of the news corporations in America and Europe, it would be burdensome to start all over. But with Lewis still in place it could be done quite smoothly and quickly. The sharp white face and the perfectly symmetrical goatee must have worked some kind of magic. And as a goy with a resonant bass voice he was so different, so unusual that he had to be handled with circumspection.

Ada was also still there. Perla had talked to a deputy minister who had been with her in the Egyptian desert and, as a result, she was kept on with a cut salary and a vaguely defined technical brief. This meant she had plenty of time to work on the Ark, which was beginning to resemble Zion Square in considerable detail but in miniature. She spent much of the day working with Tomas in a windowless gym-like space deep in the bowels of the building which, apparently, was to become a communications bunker for the government in case a new war broke out and Jerusalem was cut off again just like in the old one.

Tomas was excited. Caverns and tunnels were, for him, protected places and here the stark white walls, so white they gave birth to flapping sheets and flying banners if you looked at them too long, encouraged his inventions. He started by painting Zion Square in more and more detail. He traced the cracks in the paving stones, the erratic lines of the pavement, and the letters on manhole covers. He made the pedestrian crossings bold, even lurid in their stained whiteness like markings on the flanks of a large animal. He had the railings, street lamps, electricity poles and traffic lights entangle with each other sometimes high, sometimes low, like structures and wires in a circus tent. He painted the façade of Zion Cinema in the colours of a carnival weathered and battered by time. Exhausted pinks, ashamed reds, defeated yellows all looked beaten down by winds and blasted by strong sunlight. Yet the square didn't look ready to be released from the land. Nothing suggested its coming detachment from its solid surroundings, the streets, alleys and rubble-strewn empty lots of downtown. Tomas thought of indicating the catastrophe with a crack breaking the ground at the edge of the set where the square met Ben Yehuda.

'No' said Ada, 'no cracks and no hints. Here's a downtown crossing and a cinema. Nothing could be more normal and familiar. You'd have to be crazy to imagine it sailing away. That's why they laughed at the old man.'

She had become possessive of Milo's Ark, building it like Noah himself with the cackle of a crowd's laughter and ridicule in her mind. She pictured herself standing there on a Saturday night as the moviegoers crowded into the square. They were mostly young, the men in white shirts and slathered with aftershave, the girls in blouses and floral skirts. Occasionally an older couple came along, he in a suit, she in a tailored outfit, a handbag over her wrist. Everybody was talking, friends calling to each other loudly across the square. It was a summer evening. The air was cool now but the day's heat still radiated from the stone of the buildings and the concrete pavements. An ice cream stand was besieged by part of the crowd and others milled around the narrow, barred windows of the cinema's box office and made a wrestling match out of buying a ticket. At one edge of the crowd she stood, alone. She held a placard:

EVERYTHING MUST DROWN

But she said nothing. Milo's contempt for the citizens rang in her ears. They were a base herd seduced by demagogues, unable to think, unable to see where they were being led, ignorant of the truth. But his diatribe clashed with the fellow feeling she had for the moviegoers. They were her neighbours. They waited for the bus to Haifa with her. They fed stray cats with her by the garbage cans. They were busy, ordinary people eating peanuts and ice cream. Why should they fear a tidal wave sweeping away their half of a town, here on the edge of a desert?

She held her placard stoically. Hardly anyone in the crowd looked at her. Some pointed at the placard and laughed, then hurried past to join the queues.

'Why are you so quiet, my love?' said Tomas. He came over to her in a corner of the room where she had taken refuge.

'You look upset.'

'I'm taking this too seriously. I know it's only a stage for Milo's anger and his fantasy of doom but what's it saying? Everybody drowns, OK. Except for a few, what few? It's a shameful story. Building a lifeboat for yourself and leaving the rest to go under. It's shabby. Didn't Noah have any sympathy? Couldn't he build a bigger boat, an armada, a navy? Couldn't he have saved more, many more?'

'Nobody listened to what he said. Anyway, you can only save a few. There's never enough time. Never enough room. It's like there's a cellar or a hollow space behind a wall. How many will get in there? There's only so much air to breathe.'

'So why save any if the whole world is set to go under? He could have said it to Supremo who gave him the orders: *If you're so fed up and want to put an end to it, do it. Get rid of it all. Who needs it, if you don't?*'

'But he was given a chance. He was on the spot. You have to be superhuman to give up a chance to live.'

'He wasn't even man enough to argue and bargain for his cousins, his sisters-in-law, his brothers, nephews and nieces. This story is depressing. We're all alive thanks to a coward with no imagination.'

Tomas seemed reluctant to go on with this and busied himself with the set. Ada was sorry. She had touched the wound. She watched him working in a corner of the square concentrating on the detail of a painted manhole cover. Crouching on the platform he looked like a fox guarding its kill, ears pricked up to detect any threat. She felt how immense a distance separated Perla's sunlit balcony high over the sea, from the dark places where Tomas had lurked.

She went over to where he crouched and touched the nape of his neck.

He was painting words in what looked like Polish on the mancover: *Krakowie Miasto.*

'What's that?'

'Krakow City.'

'Why there?'

'There, here, it makes no difference…It's all the same when everything's under water.'

He wrote some more Polish letters in a circle on the manhole cover. Concentrating, his lips forming the words as he painted.

'There's more?' she said.

He read it out: '*Rzeki niech klaskaja rekoma*, Floods will clap their hands. It's a psalm.'

'And you know it by heart like a good choir boy in the village church?'

'No, not from over there, from here. I found a Polish Bible in the hostel and I got to read some when I first came. It was new to me and weird but it was Polish, something I understood. I even learned bits by heart by repeating them when I was out walking. It was like a drumbeat.'

Tomas stood up looked at the painted Zion Cinema and began to speak in a pleasant musical voice: '*Spiewajcie Panu piesn nowa, bo dziwne rzeczy uczynil: dopomogla mu prawica jego, i ramie swietobliwosci jego.* So I had to learn Hebrew, I know, but Conversation: Stage One, was so idiotic and here was my own language talking to Pan, this big Polish God, in grand words about singing new songs and mighty arms and the voice of waters and marvellous things. I walked a lot with that in my head, alone.'

'Say it again,' she said.

When he repeated the verse his face gained colour and she heard the unfamiliar tongue and tooth work of the Polish shedding its strangeness as he spoke. He sounded like a young man speaking or singing in front of an audience in a hall or in a field by a river. His message filled him with hope for the people. 'The Floods aren't going to suck you into the belly of the deep. The Floods clap their hands in friendship. Hear the word of Pan the Polish Lord.'

'You didn't hear that in a church?' she said.

'No.'

'So how come it sounds so happy?'

'It sounds happy because you've come out of the worst and you're still alive. You can shout loud and you won't be ashamed. You're not betraying anybody. You're just happy.'

He clapped his hands and the echo was hard and dry like smooth planks of wood falling on ice.

They both went back to the set, moving over it methodically, crouching before doors, shop windows, bus stops, and standing on crates to reach areas still unfinished. They hovered over the structure like a pair of bats first swooping low and then withdrawing to survey it from a distance. Although the Ark of Zion Square was a different place for each of them – for her the outcome of a shabby deal with a bully, for him a gift to be seized greedily – they were partners in the work of picturing it, as an everyday, scuffed and shabby patch of city chosen to survive an apocalypse that would leave it afloat, alone in a drowned world.

Shpitz walked in while they were in the back room with the paint cans and bits of board. He knew the Ark was being built under the empty studios and had visited to check its progress from time to time. He didn't understand why Milo wanted to create a scandal outside the court where the Nazi was being tried nor did he comprehend his contempt for the ordinary citizen. But he was tickled by the incongruity of a piece of Christian mediaeval street theatre put before a motley crowd at the top of Ben Yehuda Street in full view of the bearded zealots in their Munkacz quarter across the road. Although Milo was patronizing towards him, considering his presence in the town as evidence of a failing career in England, Lewis Meredith was eager to help. How could he resist the lure of a makeshift stage on wheels pushed into a noisy, ribald crowd with amateur actors dressed up as God and other characters out of Genesis. It excited him and filled him with nostalgia for his student days at a drama school in London.

He climbed onto the set, stood in front of Zion Cinema and became Laurence Olivier:

O for a muse of fire, that would ascend
The brightest heaven of invention
A kingdom for a stage, princes to act...

Ada and Tomas came out of the back room. Meredith smiled at them.

'Sorry, I couldn't help it. It always gets me, the smell of it, the paint, the varnish, the stage perfume. I look at it and I see it in the middle of a crowd, hundreds of faces pushing close. I can inhale the actors' excitement, just thinking about it makes my pulse gallop.'

He was flushed and his hand movements were large and unnatural, influenced slyly by the empty stage he was treading on.

'It's a virgin stage,' said Ada. 'No-one has performed on it till now. You'll bring us luck.'

She liked Shpitz and felt sorry for him. How had he come to be stranded on this aborted project in a strange city where his theatrical manners went unnoticed and his intelligence and quick ability to adapt to his new environment were taken for granted? He hovered on the edge of the tables of talkers and arguers in Taamon Café raking through his goatee with his fingers and looking for an opening to put in a word or two in his growing vocabulary of Hebrew. The talkers tolerated him but didn't listen much and he sat there a fixed smile on his face with a glass of Medicinal and a cigarette waiting for someone to really talk to in English about the disasters and excitements of metropolitan theatrical life. He was a goy and not a journalist or a UN worker so he was exotic but his uncanny, growing knowledge of Rabbinical quirkiness, such as opposing definitions of kosher and laws governing menstruation and sex, moved him close to the line separating goy from Jew. No-one knew where he got his fragments of information from and for some it was an embarrassment to be corrected by this goy on rules for the disposal of foreskins.

Evenings he was often alone in Fink's, not eating but staying on the Medicinal and writing in a small notebook which he would put away if he got talking to someone. Ada had asked him once if he was taking notes on the habits of the natives. Not at all, he said and after some time and a few more glasses he told her he was jotting down bits of his mother's Welsh-inflected talk when they lived in a mining village during the war and that he couldn't bring up her voice in a quiet place or at his desk but needed noise and bustle, a wobbly table and the glass of brandy. Since the Television Centre had emptied out he could be seen most days walking the lonely road on the ridge up to the checkpoint before the UN headquarters on the Hill of Evil Counsel. He would walk it again and again in all weathers, invariably bareheaded a cigarette in his mouth and perhaps talking or singing to himself.

'How are you going to get this up and out?' asked Shpitz.

'They didn't show you the big equipment lift in the back when they took you round the building?' said Ada. 'It's actually left over from the ice factory but it was brought up to date and looks quite safe. Anyway we can take the set up in sections.'

Then she took a risk.

'Come to the rehearsals. It will be chaotic but it'll be interesting.'

She hadn't asked Milo who would be suspicious of anybody with some real experience in theatre production but she felt responsible for Shpitz and wanted to alleviate his loneliness and enforced idleness by bringing him into the certain chaos of the Flood. Shpitz said nothing but raised an eyebrow in a sign that he had got the message, looked at his watch and left them.

'What's he doing here?' asked Tomas. 'Why's he staying? What's he running away from? A woman?'

'Maybe, but he's also staying here because he wants to disappear. Look at the way he hovers on the edge of the chatter in the café. He's learning how to get lost, among us.'

'I can think of better places.'

'Can you? Our town? It's so aimless and empty that you get lost in it for want of anything better to do. I can see what Shpitz is doing. I did it myself. He's looking for shelter. Disappearing into the shadows.'

Tomas laughed and cupped her face in his hands.

'Disappear? What's the matter? Look we're still here and you came because you chose to. Really, you chose it. To get lost? I was dropped off by the immigration machine, an old bus from Haifa port. Nobody asked me if I preferred Paris or Buenos Aires. From their point of view I was a shipwreck and here I'd be salvaged and repaired. Look at me. Am I a success? Did they put me together right?'

He set his face close against hers, and bent down so that their foreheads touched.

She asked herself why she felt they were twin children lost in a wood afraid of the dark and the broken light through the trees? Who would find them and lead them out to the warm welcoming house they had never known? Behind them Zion Square waited to be lifted out of the cavern and begin its journey up Ben Yehuda to the place of judgement.

Nazdi Eikamenn

Eyob knocked on Ada's door in the Ethiopian mansion. He was with a smaller and even thinner and very silent monk who had been assigned to stay near him since he had completed his period of isolation. He looked gaunt and stood there with head and shoulders bent as if he was ashamed of his height or was bearing a heavy burden of contrition.

They stood at the door saying nothing and the smaller monk seemed to be inching closer to Eyob as if to take shelter in his shade.

'Madame, God bless you.'

Eyob's voice was unchanged, thin and reedy like a desert nomad's pipe.

'Madame, this I must return to you.' He was holding a bundle of drawing paper, presenting it to her gingerly as if it was glass and could break and smash into pieces.

Ada took the papers. They were sketches and watercolours he had worked on with her.

'You should keep them Eyob. They are yours. But why are we standing here by the door. Come in. I will make some tea.'

The little monk stirred uneasily at Eyob's side but Eyob entered the room with a large step that was almost a leap. He looked around, seemingly pleased to be there. There was silence while Ada made the tea. Then the only noise was that of the two monks gulping the hot drink. The little one's gulp was full of breath, Eyob's was more like a struggle in the plumbing.

Ada jumped into the breach.

'So Eyob, you have spent some time alone, without company. Was that very difficult for you?'

'I was not alone. I was with the Father.'

He did not sound very convinced. He might have spoken for the benefit of the little monk. He put his palms together, concentrating. Then after some false starts and clenching of both fists, he said: 'What is this Nazdi Eikamenn?'

'What?'

'Nazdi Eikamenn. Nazdi Eikamenn. In the Muskubiye Police prison there were fighting and one man shouted to the policeman: "You Nazdi Eikamenn." They were drunk. But the police was very mad and beat them and they were put in a special cell after that. Is this a curse, Nazdi Eikamenn? Is it from the Book of Moses?'

Then Ada understood.

'No Eyob it is nothing to do with the Book of Moses. It's a name. You heard it wrong. It's the Nazi Eichmann.'

He looked at her, puzzled.

'Yes, Nazdi Eikamenn. Who is that? The name of who?'

She was at a loss. This was a door that shouldn't be opened. Would you take a child to the charnel house? Would you push the door against the piled-up skulls and bones and hold up a torch to light the scene? Or would you find a lollipop and change the subject?

'He was in the big world war. A German.'

Eyob nodded.

'Yes, Mussolini, a bad man. He did bomb our country.'

'Nazi Eichmann was even worse. He tried to kill everybody.'

'Everybody? Even American people? One man, kill everybody?'

Eyob stared at her. The white pools of his eyes grew larger and larger and he seemed to be weighing the absurdity of what she had said.

He furrowed his brow in thought searching for some clue that would explain the vision Ada's words had uncovered for him.

'You mean Atom? This is the way to kill everybody in the big war?'

The thought seemed to have cleared his way to understanding. He seemed relieved. Atom was a sufficient weight against 'one man' and 'kill everybody'.

Ada looked at the little monk, who was probably asleep. His eyes were closed but he was sitting stiffly in his chair his hands neatly spread on his knees.

She couldn't go on with this. The door of the charnel house was open and it had a name on it: ATOM. Wasn't that sufficient? Who would she betray if she didn't give it that other name, unfamiliar to Eyob and unpronounceable as well. What good would that do?

But Eyob was excited by his advance in knowledge and wanted to press on.

'Nazdi Eikamenn has ATOM? Where? He had it in the war. In a bomber aeroplane? Like the Americans for Hiroshima? Yes?'

Eyob's eyes were bright with achieved understanding. Knowledge at this moment was more important to him than anything else. Ada was struck by his happiness. This was not Mussolini's bombs on Addis Ababa. That was destruction. This was a name.

'But Nazdi Eikamenn bombed the ATOM where?'

Ada had enough.

'I'll tell you later Eyob. Now show me your drawings. Show me what you've done.'

He was reluctant to give up his quest but gave in when she spread out his papers on her work table and they looked at them together. Ada was surprised: there was something direct and honest about the crude sketches that were mostly in black crayon. There were repeated attempts to draw a monk's black habit draped over a bed or arranged on the tailor's dummy she had lent him. In some the gown was a featureless flat splodge on the white sheet. But in others the gown became alive. It imitated a body, asleep or floating on water. It had arms and shoulders and its length indicated feet but there was no head, no neck. When she looked and held her gaze the black gowns seemed to be trying to slide over the sheet, away from the bed, off the paper and out. There was one finished drawing of the gown on the tailor's dummy. It was more finely done than the others, more exact in structuring the lapels, arms, skirts, pockets against the dummy's torso. In place of the absent head Eyob had drawn a large, bold outline of an eye. It looked like a cross-section of a fish with a black ball in its mouth. It was the eye of Horus the Egyptian god. Eyob looked at her eager for her praise.

'What is that Eyob?' she asked pointing to the eye.

'It is the eye of Pharaoh. It can see the whole world. It is never closed.'

'So why did you put it on the dummy?'

'You are angry?'

'Why should I be angry with something you drew? Why Pharoah's eye? Where did you find it?'

'When I was alone. There were some books in the room. They were holy books and prayers for singing and for saying. The masters want me to sing loud a long time to make me holy. So I sing and sing but I also looked at all the books. Many pages are torn and falling out. So in one book I saw this. It is drawn with a pencil on the last page under the word AMEN. First it looks like a little child has drawn it, an animal, a creeping animal. I look at it every day. But one day I see it looks at me like an eye, a big eye like of a horse. Then I tear it out, the page with the AMEN and the eye. And when I finished staying alone in the room I find the lawyer, the Armenian, Mr Margarian. He comes to the masters for his business and the courts. I find him in the street and I say to him what is this? Mr Margarian knows many books and languages. You know him?'

Ada nodded.

'He looks at the page and he says: "You mustn't tear the holy book." But I say it fell out. Then he looks and he says, "It is an Egyptian god, the eye of this god. And it is from Pharoah. And this eye is always open and sees the whole world." The masters shall not see this drawing because it is the eye of a strange god and Pharoah.'

'So why did you draw this eye on the dummy?'

'You are angry?'

'No, but why did you put it there in the place of the head?'

'He is always there to look at me.'

'Who, Eyob?'

'You are angry because Pharoah threw the children of Jacob into the river?'

'I tell you I'm not angry. Why do you want him to look at you?'

'Because Pharoah's god is magic and it will find my way to run from this place.'

Eyob was whispering and keeping an eye on his sleeping companion.

Ada folded the drawing with the eye and handed it to him.

'Keep it Eyob, hide it. It is a good drawing. It should be near you.'

They went towards the window where they had often sat listening to the birds and the street sounds. A radio nearby was broadcasting the evening news at full volume. Eichmann this and Eichmann that. How far must she go not to hear this?

Eyob listened attentively.

'Eikamenn,' he said and looked at her expectantly.

'Like Pharaoh,' she said. 'Throwing children into the rivers everywhere. Many children. He is here, in this country.'

Eyob stared at her.

'He is in prison here. The police watch him all day and all night and the judges will judge him.'

'Pharaoh,' said Eyob. 'His heart was hard and he was drowned in the sea.'

'Yes,' she said. 'But the children of Israel crossed over onto the dry land.'

Eyob took her hand. Maybe he was comforting her.

FINK'S

'YOU KNOW, DON'T you, that Ham emasculated his father. We've talked about it, how he cut off Noah's schmock when he was drunk.'

Milo and Félix were sitting in Fink's drinking Armagnac as Félix seemed to have made some profitable transaction in the Old City which he wasn't talking about. The small bar was quite empty for a change. Just a few of the regulars were there like Ziggy who worked for Peltransport and could get whole crates of contraband car radios through the customs, if you paid him well. But the place was always welcoming; the low, erratic lighting over the little tables promised discretion. Marlene Dietrich, Danny Kaye, Kirk Douglas and Simone Signoret, photographs signed and hanging askew on scruffy walls, looked down on you with professional good will. Like you, they had been here and enjoyed the warmth and hospitality. Unlike you it had cost them nothing so the signed photograph was the least they could do. Above the bar and above the many coloured ranks of liqueurs and brandies, framed front pages of *The New York Times*, *The Daily Telegraph* and *The Palestine Post* announced victories and disasters in bold print and indicated why the place was foreign yet familiar, like an embassy of a friendly world power which offered asylum to thirsty exiles.

'Remind me where you get that diseased notion from?' said Félix. 'You just want to see trouble. It's a happy ending we're talking about. The waters go down. They start all over again. Then the rainbow, the sacrifice of thanks. It's all good. God is happy. Man is happy. The book says the old man planted the vine, that's certainly good, and got drunk on the first bottle. Understandable after all that abstinence. Then he has a nap. Ah now I see what you're getting at. The old man's fly is open and Ham takes a look. *Verboten*!! Also understandable. I didn't ever see my father's. Though I'm sure I knew it was there. But how do you get from sightseeing to castration?'

'Rabbis.'

'Rabbis what?'

'Rabbis with enquiring minds filling in bits left out by Genesis. Like Ham and Papa's penis. I wish I could put it in the play. So what happened over there at Christmas? What did you see? How did Ulli get on?'

'She hit it off with the Franciscans in the hospice. They want her to come back at Easter. She liked the confusion and all the babble of the pilgrims. She was rubbing shoulders with Arab bishops, Armenian priests and old ladies in black from Cyprus but she was unsure whether her grandmother was a Catholic or a Protestant. It seemed to matter to her.'

'Ulli and Rudi, that's an odd pair. Hard to imagine the dreamboy translator and the German waif meeting in the ruins of Nuremberg. Did she ask him for chewing gum? I never got to meet him when he saw Ada in Paris, I was kept away.'

'She must have been afraid you'd rub him up the wrong way. Were you and Ada still a couple then or what?'

'It's hard to say what we were. It was like she was somebody I grew up with, kind of incestuous. First a younger sister and then an older one. She began by depending on me in ways I wasn't used to. It was a burden. I wasn't all that much older and we were in the army, but it was as if she had joined a church and I was the Father Confessor – me! I was used to keeping women at arm's length or just close enough for what I needed and Ada almost made me ashamed of that. There was a lot of innocence in her. Telling me her secrets, making me swear I wouldn't give them away and looking for ways of getting secrets out of me. I suppose her trust flattered me. And as for my secrets I had none worth hiding. I was doing my sophisticated bastard act. Being the cynic suited me and I had enough money to make me different from the rest. She was just beginning to find out about music and Braque and Hemingway and was painting as well so it was exciting and infectious being with her. But it got harder for me to put on an act with her.'

'What about the beast?'

'Strange and chained up at first but not for long. In many ways she was a little girl or even a boy. So it was borderline criminal and that was exciting. Then she cottoned on to this and started playing little girl, tears and fear of being found out and sudden shame in bed which had to be overcome roughly. It was quite a game, even for me. And her Aunt Perla came into it as if she was spying on us. But games like that don't last. Well maybe they do, in old, dark places like Paris or London, but not under this sun. Not under this relentless searchlight. Then there was an abortion and she became an elder sister. I felt she knew more than me, not books and stuff like that but about pain and mourning and regret, real things. Instead of sympathy this made me cruel to her. And she reacted as if she expected it. So we dragged on and got to Paris a kind of a wreck but held together by bits of string and glue. And we still are.'

Félix was not surprised. He suspected that the ties that bound Milo and Ada were a hidden knot that kept the group around them from slipping away in different directions. They were like Adam and Eve in the memory of later generations; a famous or notorious couple, apart but together, the subject of stories and fabrications. It gave the little cluster of friends who lived on the edge of no man's land a shared legend with a plot that connected the army to a love story and a journey far away and included a return to the hill with the ruined Turkish bandstand.

From an outsider's point of view Félix could conclude that this was an intimate, erotic and unpolitical version of the Hebrew national myth. He knew it too in his way; the maiden's journey into the desert following love. Jeremiah had revealed it to him: *Je me souviens de ton amour quand tu étais jeune, quand tu me suivais au*

187

désert. In Bordeaux at the seminary the prophet's words had seduced him, in technicolour. He had imagined them lovingly as a desert romance with Gerard Philipe in a burnous, weapon in hand, gliding through the waste on a camel while behind him on a white donkey came Ava Gardner and a trusty brown servant, half-naked and on foot. In the hills above them an envious sheikh with a ferocious band of followers prepared an ambush. It was Jeremiah who turned Félix's cold bed into a perfumed tent for Gerard and Ava and breathed the hot breath of desire and adventure over the young seminarist's enforced chastity.

'So where is Jordan in all this? She is the real thing, after all?' There was a distinct note of disbelief in Félix's question.

Milo took some time.

'Yes but so was Ada and so were others. You don't mean it, *mon Père*, when you say "the real thing". You're making fun of the way cheap songs colour our love affairs. I admit I am a bit like that. Believing it's the real thing is like believing in God. It's absurd but you shut out all the contradictory evidence. You bury your head in a woman's breast and you declare it real. It's the real thing and you are its prophet. What's real then? Not the skin you brush with your lips. Certainly not the spread of flesh and bone and veins and muck that hides under the skin. That's revealed only in sickness and it's not the real thing for you. No, you are well out of that. Real is the excitement that travels like an express train between your body and your mind and links the two like they are never linked by any other means. Why do you think the old mystics used to call high ecstasy a "transport", *mon Père*? It's when your body and your mind have escaped together, taken a one-way ticket to a destination that's not in the timetable.'

'So where is Jordan in your travel schedule?'

Milo ran his fingers through his shiny, thick black hair and bent his head over his glass as if looking for his fortune in the honey-coloured brandy. He was half-listening to scratchy songs from *Countess Maritza* on the gramophone.

'She took a big gamble coming here and I'm responsible. I hate

188

that word. It reeks of lawyers and signatures. But it was a storm that flung us together in Berkeley and made havoc of her well-arranged life in the States. I know it sounds absurd but I didn't play such a large part in that big disturbance. I was more of a spectator. That's what I felt anyway. Jordan was the lightning and the thunder. She broke off her engagement, quarrelled with parents and old friends, threw up the chance of a job and joined me. I was honest with her. As much as I can be. I didn't put on an act or go down on my knees. And she was honest too. She told me she knew now what it meant to be carrying the wound and I was its cause. I had cut it into her. I had torn her flesh and imprisoned her soul. Félix, *mon Père*, I hadn't heard this kind of thing before. Or, if I had, I put it down to hysteria or lying. But Jordan was like Joan of Arc at the fire. She was commanding and I couldn't not love her.'

Milo looked at Félix with disturbance in his eyes as if asking for absolution.

Is this Milo, he thought, or the third glass of Armagnac speaking? Could Milo have been unmanned by the Maid of Berkeley's resolve to burn as a martyr? Was he afraid of the fire he had caused, perhaps negligently? And now? She had followed her love into the unknown, but where was he taking her? Félix felt some of Milo's perplexity but especially, though he hadn't spoken to her much, Jordan's danger. She had come after her man into the wildernesss and she might lose him in a sandstorm or be left in a tent to wait the long hours for his return. Félix himself took a distant view of grand passions, preferring minor ones which were manageable like head colds and didn't progress through your throat and lungs to become pneumonia.

'If it's the real thing,' he said, 'you are on your own, my friend. No-one can confirm it or deny it for you. I'm no expert but I know this. It's not a currency. You can't buy and sell in it. It's yours alone. Only you know the value of it. That is you and she and even then her value may be different from yours.'

Félix felt odd to be speaking seriously and without irony. He and Milo were most at ease in noncommittal banter which revealed their learning and wordliness but touched on little that was vital to their lives. Talk was a sport like fencing, with masks and thick protective layers over your breast. But Milo had manoeuvred him onto the confessor's bench and seemed to want Félix to cleanse him of any doubts and send him on his way to happiness. Ridiculous, thought Félix and kept silent for a while. Brubeck had replaced Maritza on the record player and some noisy journalists had come in from the radio newsrooms nearby. Félix took advantage of the distraction to deflect the conversation into a description of the homosexual culture of the Old City.

'How come you haven't asked me about sins of the flesh across the line? Surely it still interests you. Sodomy, as you might know, is a favourite entertainment and medicine for boredom. A kind of exercise. It makes it possible for God's workers to stay comparatively sane despite the easy way to depression and madness. It embraces all the sects and religions. Like the black market, it's unseen but it props up commerce and social exchange. Don't quote me on this. I'm still persona grata on the other side and you'd be amazed how easily resentment crosses the border.'

Milo was hardly listening. His head was low over his glass and his face was in shadow. Félix observed him from the side. He looked like a wrestler contemplating a chess board. The stocky trunk and powerful shoulders and hairy arms and hands were anchors to a dark head that was seemingly preoccupied with thought. In profile his nose, lips and jaw struck Félix as uncommonly Afro-Semitic; they could be a gladiator's in a reverie or a muscular slave's awaiting a command from his Roman lady.

Then Milo looked up.

'This Armagnac takes me far away. I'd better go before tears start dripping into my glass.'

Both walking a little unsteadily they pushed their way out of the now-crowded bar into the windy darkness of the empty street.

ARARAT

JULIUS WAS NO friend of the Bible. He had a brief struggle with some barely understood Hebrew passages in Manchester at the age of thirteen but once past that he rarely looked back and now he considered Moses, Joshua and Elijah to be strange giants pursuing stories he could remember mostly in idiosyncratic versions edited by himself. He was, briefly, curious about the Patriarchs and the intrigues and dangers of their family lives. He called them 'The Uncles' and considered 'The Aunts' to be more interesting especially the two who were interchangeable at night in Uncle Jacob's bed. Julius would have liked to compose his own Bible like his idol William Blake but unlike the great Englishman he found no Angels willing to guide his hand and the presences that floated through the windows of his house were more likely to be Sufi spirits or essences from the *Book of Zohar* with names that sounded magical to him, like Shemhazai and Ishtahar.

Milo's obsession with the Flood didn't draw him in at first, mainly because he didn't share his friend's anger and idée fixe of the approaching catastrophe. Here they were, living on the invisible line between DANGER BORDER and STOP GO NO FURTHER and who was worrying? Painters were painting, professors were typing footnotes, poets were chasing words onto pages and most of them had jobs of one kind or another. Nearby lived the chicken lady with her coop and noisy rooster and in the shack next to her a family of pious Persians whose patriarch sat on his chair outside on mild

191

afternoons and chanted psalms facing the Temple Mount. He would often cover his eyes with his hands as if the sight of the holy place was dazzling them. He was old but his chair was there every sunny afternoon. So what was there to fear? Weighing all this up while struggling to force his boots on to his outsize, painful feet Julius realized with a shock that he was thinking the thoughts of Noah's doomed and foolish contemporaries.

'A big tidal wave to drown everything? You mean all these houses and bus stops? Ridiculous. Leave us alone, old man.'

'All hell break loose across the ceasefire line? Swarms of locusts descending on everything? No water in the pipes? Bread only for the rich? Now? Here? It couldn't happen. Nah.'

But it could. So maybe Noah was not an old bore but someone who saw it coming – even though it couldn't come. He couldn't be an old dullard because he was witness to a disaster. To think of him as boring because he survived was perverse. Was the Ancient Mariner boring? Robinson Crusoe? When he imagined Noah after Ararat, poking around an empty, washed-out, sodden landscape, wondering how he could begin to make it liveable again, Julius found in himself a well of sympathy for the old navigator. Look at what he had seen, swimmers fighting each other in the waves, holding children up to him to take on board, naked bodies, bloated and disfigured, pushed aside like algae by the prow of his vessel. Then, in the Ark, his despair, thinking that the journey would reach no end but the old would die and the young after them. Yes, he had a promise. But outside there was nothing, nothing but water. Who could have enough faith to imagine all this becoming a world. Again?

This was a man Julius could talk to, so he went to the National Library and began to look for Noah in the General Reading Room. When he found him in the pages of Louis Ginzberg's *Legends of the Jews* with his whole perplexing history before and after the Flood, he found events and details and colour and scandal added to the Biblical account which looked grey in comparison. Here was a believable mariner tossed by storms and thrown onto an empty land.

He was ashamed that he had not given the old man his due and he had overlooked the most important turn in the story. Noah wasn't a prophet of doom. He wasn't saved, he was a survivor.

If you look into the eyes of a survivor you see, compressed into them, everything that cannot be said. And you, yourself? You are struck silent but also thirsty to know the worst. Julius felt shame at having slighted, even mocked this Ancient Mariner. He resolved to make amends.

Burdened by this, Julius went to carry it to Jordan rather than to Milo. He could confide in her without fear of Milo's aggressiveness against anyone poaching on his territory. Noah was Milo's. No Tresspassers. But Jordan had become his good friend and confidante. He treated her with a Chinese formality and politeness which, though eccentric, didn't create distance between them. Rather it was a ceremony he elaborated to warn onlookers that this pair was outside the commonplace and casual goings-on between men and women in their world. When he spoke to her his face went through a gamut of histrionic expressions. There was a mask with furrows in its brow and delicate pouts of the lips showing concern and sympathy and a mask, round and polished, beaming a moonlike glow of veneration. These masks, usually set at an angle on his neck, were puzzling because they seemed to have a life and a rhythm separate from the conversation, communicating things that words failed to convey. So Julius could not be casual with her and Jordan was initially upset by this. She was an American woman after all. But she gradually learned to interpret the masks and understand their tangential relation to the talking which, over time, became easier. In the end she could accept her friend's formal care and reverence without coyness or embarrassment. Julius's courtly friendship was another facet of the little tribe's way of life here on the edge of no man's land and she felt sometimes like Margaret Mead in Samoa pondering the meaning of a girl giving a boy a pair of coloured feathers. But, unlike the great anthropologist, Jordan had no obligation to be objective because the tribe she was studying included herself.

Julius waylaid her between the oranges and the soda bottles in the local grocery shop on Hebron Road. She had meant to go back home and dive into her notebooks but Julius, after some hesitation and unfinished sentences, took hold of her shopping bag and led her to the old Karaite graveyard on the steep slope below the path that led to Mount Zion. They approached it down a rough path and through formidable clumps of thorns and weeds. The graves were flat, spotted by age and bird droppings, and covered with Hebrew inscriptions like pages of a large, stained prayer book. Julius led the way to a recess in the hillside that could have been the mouth of a collapsed cave. They sat down on stones pushed together to form a bench. She offered him an orange and they sat silently as she peeled the fruit methodically and split it releasing the innocent, fresh citrus perfume.

He turned to her and his face was troubled. His eyes were bloodshot and moist and his nose quivered like a sensitive instrument picking up signals from below the earth's crust.

'What's the matter, Julius,' she said and touched his hand.

He shivered visibly.

'Are you cold?'

'How can we avoid it?'

'What, Julius what are you talking about?'

'The female waters swelled up from below and the masculine waters streamed down from above. The waters copulated in an orgy of destruction.'

'Who?'

'The waters. Nature decreating.'

He took a crumpled notebook out of his pocket.

'It's here in Ginzberg. The detail of a calamity. It's like they imagined it in minute fragments, every bit of suffering is described, every inch of chaos, like Bosch painting Hell. I wrote it down.'

She took the notebook and saw page after page filled with Julius's spidery handwriting. The only signs she could make out clearly were exclamation marks. There were lots of them.

'Ginzberg is a collection of fantasies, Julius. It's how people a thousand years ago imagined God being angry and having a fit. A thousand years ago. What's it got to do with us?'

'Everything, because we are only pretending things are normal. Don't you know we are living on the Syrian African Rift. It's a fault line in the earth. It makes everything above it unsafe and we ignore it.'

'But Julius, a fault line means earthquakes and what can we do about earthquakes?'

Jordan was trying to calm him with common sense but she understood the disquiet of her friend and indeed shared it in some way. It wasn't thoughts of calamity, of floods and earthquakes that haunted her but a nagging unease about the thinness and fragility of the lives she had encountered here. They came from elsewhere and were tied to nothing. They could be swept away suddenly or go under slowly and who would notice? As for her, the newcomer, one morning, waking up, she might find everything gone. No Milo, no ruins turned into houses, no stunted olive trees, no rusting shells of burnt war machines, no crumbling Turkish bandstand, no beaten paths of friendship between the scattered houses on the edge of the valley. Just a bare hillside with its warning signs oddly intact and the clumps of thorns and barbed wire and in the distance the flat pink table top of the hills of Edom, unreachable, indifferent. Her disquiet was, at heart, her sense of the unpredictability of Milo. Would he suddenly turn against her and insult her like he had done before? Would he get bored with her, with his work, with Noah? Would he abandon her, leaving a note to say he'd taken a boat to Greece and she should leave the key with Julius?

She shivered and cupped her face in her hands.

Julius put an arm around her shoulders to warm her with the heat of his body.

'I'm sorry, Jordan,' he said, 'you're cold, I shouldn't have. I shouldn't be telling you my bad thoughts. But the old man got into my head and I couldn't keep it to myself. He knew something important after the flood. It could all be repeated because children would continue to be born. It was inevitable. He got dead drunk

195

because he had a horror of rolling over his wife and making her pregnant. He wanted to stop all that, stop creation and forget. STOP.'

Jordan knew Julius well enough to understand how he turned his reading into drama and dialogue. There was no point in reminding him where these legends and phantasies came from. Noah's continuing premonition of disaster was now Julius's. It was Julius who drank himself to sleep so he wouldn't touch a woman's flank and fall into the trap of procreation. It was Noah's sodden, deserted world that Julius was seeing when he walked out of his door and looked over the valley. But such dramas wouldn't stay with him for long with such intensity. They wouldn't disappear entirely but would inhabit the background of his imagination's plot together with older scenes and stage furniture. Thinking this of the man whose arm was warm over her shoulder made her smile and dispersed her angst. Her friend was a vaudeville company of one and he could perform tragedies and comedies and philosophical puppetry and biblical epics. He needed no fellow actors but travelled alone with a typewriter, some dolls and a chair or two. He had almost no audience but that could never stop him. Nothing could stop him except the mighty jaws of the Syrian African Rift opening up to swallow them all.

Jordan laughed out loud.

Julius looked at her startled.

She couldn't stop and spilled the bag of oranges on her lap. They rolled into the thorns between the Karaite graves and Julius bounded after them clumsily. When he picked one up he turned and threw it to her so it became a game of catch as she threw them back and he had to jump for them. Soon they were both flushed and sweating. Julius turned and kissed her on her damp brow. Then they clambered back up the path she holding his hand, he holding the bag of oranges.

Milo wasn't alone when they got back. The familiar, sweet weedy smell filled the room and he was lying on the sofa deep in a pile of cushions, apparently asleep while Amalya, one of his students in the Satan and Eros seminar was typing at his desk. She was besotted with him and would have spent her days and nights in the house cooking, rolling joints, cleaning up, dusting books and typing his papers just to get a glance of recognition. But Milo, while treating her with politeness, was oddly impersonal as if she was an umbrella or a potted plant. Sitting at the machine, her soft shoulders and neck curving over it, she seemed like a neat beast of burden under the yoke she was born to bear.

Jordan found this unnatural and sometimes even suspected it was a charade set up to hide what was really going on. But Amalya was so fleet and nunlike in her dedication to work and took up so little room in the house that any suspicion seemed unnecessarily prurient.

Julius dropped the bag of oranges and cursed. Milo sat up and sank back again onto the cushions. He looked at them through half-closed eyes and said nothing. When he did speak his voice was flat.

'I'm tired of it all. It's hopeless. I thought I could fix it with the city. They have no idea but they won't let us do it. I took the British Council man to the mayor's office. So they told him the Mandate was over and he should mind his own business. Then they said I should go to the Ministry for Education if we wanted to do a play about the Flood. The idiot there said we could possibly get permission to do a play in infant schools as long as it was done in mime with a narrator reading passages from the Bible. They are pieces of shit, all of them in their miserable offices with their miserable kettles and dirty cups of coffee. I've had it.'

He seemed exhausted by his outburst and sank back. Jordan couldn't find his eyes so she spoke at the furniture.

'Why ask them? You don't need permission. You're going to do guerrilla theatre for the beginning of the trial. You set it up in the night and surprise them in the morning with the Flood on the street. Then it'll be gone before they know what happened. Whoever sees it will remember it. They wait on line all night to see Eichmann and who turns up? Noah and the weather forecast. In the end they'll arrest you. So what?'

She was surprised at her own eloquence. Her encounter with Julius in the Karaite graveyard had fired her up. She understood now how the Flood might disturb the crowd lining up for the trial. They might get it: God's promise was unreliable. It could happen again thousands of years later. It did.

But Milo didn't answer. He seemed to have drifted away and lost interest. Amalya who had interrupted her typing was now busy again, frowning at her Hermes.

Jordan went over to the sofa and sat down. Milo turned his head towards her. His eyes were bloodshot and unfocused. His skin and eyebrows seemed to reinforce each other's darkness but the usual power in the set of jaw and mouth was not there. Instead there was a looseness and lack of tension which could have been the joint or, the thought shook Jordan with a jolt, post-coital indolence. She looked again at Amalya. Wasn't her application to the typewriter overdone? Were those fingers, now hitting the keys so smartly, just drumming softly on Milo's skin? There were no signs on the girl. She was as neat and silky as ever. Jordan could almost see the symmetrical perfection of her nails as they moved over the machine. Milo closed his eyes. His anger at the idiots in power could be camouflage. Nearly caught with Amalya, he lets go at the government, the perfect decoy. She had observed this in her father who said horrible things about the mayor, the governor and the president when he was losing an argument with her mother in the kitchen.

'Drat you. Drat you, you pair of muddy clods. Bleeders.'

Julius was fighting with his boots again, trying to pull them off without tying his whole body into a rheumatic knot. When he got them off he sighed and walked over to the sofa in his socks. He kneeled down by Milo and whispered loud in his ear.

'Listen Milo.' He put his hand gently on Milo's forehead. 'Listen. I know everything about the old sailor. I know the worst. You can't just give up, leave him snoring drunk in his dirty smock and waste your anger on the mayor. The old man is going to bleed. His son's got a knife and is after his balls. It's urgent. You can't sleep all that away, Milo. And what about us? We're living on the Syrian African Rift. We're on the arse crack of the earth and nobody wants to look. Nobody wants to listen.'

He picked himself up clumsily and walked over to Amalya.

'Type it dear,' he said. 'Type it in capitals. Underline it.'

DANGER THE SYRIAN AFRICAN RIFT
LOOK WHERE YOU TREAD

Amalya stopped typing.

Milo heaved himself off the cushions and sat looking around, taking in the room methodically, slowly. His glance was neutral and cold, meeting the books, the big windows, Jordan, the bottles of wine on the table, Julius, the typewriter, Amalya as if they were all equally lifeless. They were all tied to him as property, friends, lovers, slaves. He felt a chill he was not used to. It was the chill of responsibility. He was responsible for all this and the oranges on the floor. They surrounded him, made demands, assumed his presence at all times. If he made to escape there would be carnage. The bottles would smash into sharp and evil splinters, the women would turn into harpies screaming for his blood, the books would starve for want of reading, the friend would write his name into an anathema. And where would he be? He couldn't see where. He only saw the room around him frozen in obedience to his brain's command. If he blinked it would begin to live again. If he held his stare it would stay frozen.

He got up and without speaking crossed the room to the toilet. He needed a piss more than anything.

He took his time in the freezing toilet to calm the turmoil in his head. The pee charged out reassuringly making a defiant, manly splash. This is Milo's, it said, no sad, ashamed tinkle but a mighty flood. The smell too was fruity and rotten, a ripe, animal, marshy smell. His head was clearing. He looked out of the little window at the cypress in the garden. It was quite still, a brush-shaped, compact and beautiful thing. Nothing protruded to disturb its grace. No branches or stray growths; just the strong but delicate green brush tapering up at the sky. He felt proud and then humbled. It wasn't his tree. He hadn't planted it even though he, in a way, owned it. If someone felled it or it was consumed by lightning it would be the end of the world. Worse even, the UN might come and draw a line around it giving it to the Hashemites. Never. A wave of patriotism filled his chest. He would defend this tree with his life against all its enemies. *No pasaran*. Milo buttoned his fly with new confidence and, jabbing at the reluctant door with his knee, went back into the room.

Things there were the same as when he had left except for Amalya. The typewriter was abandoned. The girl was gone. Milo found it hard to break the silence. Jordan and Julius were sitting on the sofa. Julius was bent over holding his head in his hands. For a moment Milo thought he was weeping but he was mooing, a kind of chanting breath which came more from his stomach and the earth than from his lungs and throat. Jordan was patting his back the way a mother might comfort a baby with colic.

'Where's Amalya?' he asked.

Jordan continued the patting.

'She left, just like that without saying anything. Took some papers and left.'

Milo went over to the desk. There was a piece of paper in the typewriter with a few words printed in capitals and underlined
DANGER SYRIAN AFRICAN RIFT
LOOK WHERE YOU TREAD
He took it off the machine.

'What's this?'

'Julius wanted her to type it but she left, so I did it.'

'And what's it for?'

She was still patting Julius on the back though the mooing had stopped.

'A warning. Danger. He caught it from you and he takes it seriously.'

'I infected him with something?'

'He listens and it invades him. First he watched you bring on the Flood then he put himself into it, really into it. It's alive for him. You'd be surprised how much.'

'The Syrian African Rift?'

'That's right here. You can't deny it.'

Milo couldn't pin down her tone of voice. Was she accusing him of leading Julius to the brink and then abandoning him? Was she speaking from outside or from within Julius's fears and obsessions? Did Jordan look down at her feet and see the geological fault line?

Milo was up against a blank wall.

She wasn't looking at him but was concentrating on Julius and making soft shushing sounds to calm him.

Milo was perplexed. He knew well the difference between his idea of an impending disaster and the way Julius saw such things. He wanted to wake people up but also to draw attention to himself. A *succès de scandale* wouldn't hurt his reputation even if it made him enemies at the university. Setting off a colourful riot outside the Nazi's trial would get headlines even if it changed nothing. Julius's despair was none of his doing and he had to defend himself against it because it was primitive, absolute and infantile. Who but a child could be afraid to walk on the Syrian African Rift? Who in his right mind could heed such a warning? It was mad.

Julius had raised his head from between his knees and was staring at the large windows and the mist and fast-moving clouds over the valley. When he spoke he spoke slowly, licking his lips to ease the dryness and stopping frequently to swallow.

'I'm sorry, I panicked like at night when I'm proofing at the Post. There's an e missing in some word. One bloody e. And I stare on and on. But I can't find what's wrong. It looks right then wrong, then right. I try to hide the sheet. Panic. I've got to lie face down on the floor to get rid of it. And I don't give a penny in hell for the Post. I don't care if it's full of missing e's. But the panic gets hold and chokes me.'

When he swallowed his Adam's apple behind his beard moved up and down like a yo-yo.

He stood up and walked over to the typewriter. He looked around puzzled.

'Where's the warning?'

'Here.'

Milo had it in his hand.

Julius inspected it mouthing the words silently.

LOOK WHERE YOU TREAD

He looked at Milo and Jordan. His voice was calm, even resigned.

'So I'm mad when I'm working at the paper and chasing letters. But this isn't madness Milo. It's science and geology. It's like being a water diviner. Something in your hand twitches and you know what's underneath – water. I know what we're walking on. It may be just a geological name but it's the writing on the wall.'

Syrian African Rift

He pointed at his feet in their threadbare socks.

'Stay on guard you flat corporals, stay on watch! Report any rumbling below stairs. Dismiss.'

He went over to Milo and hugged him.

'I should be angry that you treat me like a child. Not just with you but with myself for leading you on. You know I've tried to break with it, go and put myself into the ward and feast on pills. You were there, you've come with me. But I can't. I'm afraid. So I'm your baggage and if you lose me or if you leave me behind I'm on the dung heap.'

He kneeled where Jordan was sitting on the sofa, took her hand and placed his forehead on her palm. Then he left.

Alone in the room, they were going to quarrel but instead they lay side by side on the sofa and didn't speak but watched the scudding clouds and listened to the clatter of bits of corrugated iron whipped by the wind on a patched roof nearby.

YMCA

PERLA AND SUZI were staying at the YMCA. They had arrived for a short visit ostensibly to attend a reunion of British army veterans at the Menorah Officers Club in town but really to inspect Ulli, with whom they had only spoken on the phone since she had joined Rudi. The visit started dramatically enough with a short curiously quiet snowfall that quickly covered the city in a thin white dust like talcum powder and spread a pale sheet over the hills and the soft ridges approaching the desert. There was almost no traffic as the very thought of snow paralysed the town's meagre transport service and no owner of a car would think of moving an inch till God called off his winter manoeuvres.

From the window of their spartan room Perla looked out towards the Old City wall and Mount Zion. She had come here with friends in the British days before '48 and remembered the soldiers in their ridiculous baggy shorts at the Jaffa Gate. The British army in Haifa looked smart and polished. It was something to do with the blue of the sea and the white ships in the bustling port. Haifa looked like an imperial link, a port of call on the way to India and Australia. But Jerusalem was a backward way-station. Here the British soldiers looked bedraggled, overburdened and underfed. Their knees were ungainly and too white and their headgear – whether it was berets, caps, hats, peaked or unpeaked – never seemed to fit the skull they sat on. Perla felt a comradely, sisterly affection for these younger versions of the soldiers she had served with in Egypt. But the danger, dirt and glamour of the desert war were absent here and the men at the Jaffa Gate and on patrol in the restive city were strange, unpredictable and vaguely threatening, even to her.

Suzi wouldn't even look at the view.

'Nothing I haven't seen before. It's tiresome. Look how long it took for the bus to get here. I thought we wouldn't make it up those last hills. The engine seemed to be suffering from asthma. I know why I don't come here much. Whenever I do I feel sick. Give me one of your headache pills.'

Perla always travelled with a well-stocked medical bag, marked with a red Star of David, taking care to keep all the pills and salves and plasters up to date. As a head nurse she had standards. They were to meet Rudi and Ulli in the lobby and go for a meal in the YMCA café. This was one of the few places in Jerusalem where you could eat bacon and ham or pork chops and was therefore frequented by rebellious Jews as well as by foreigners and local Christians. The food was dull and sweet, a copy of what was served in minor college cafeterias in pre-war America. But the clientele was uncritical and those who knew even appreciated the Y's oddness as a patch of small-town America disguised as a Moorish palace across the road from the King David.

The lobby, quiet and eerily imposing, was like the entrance hall of an ambitious undertaker's parlour. There was not much light and the blue Armenian tiles on the walls glimmered like distant stars while the inlaid damascene tables and chairs were formal and stiff, and seemed to be waiting for a long delayed visit of Lebanese business men. They were mostly unoccupied. A few young Arab men, students, talked quietly in one corner. From the basement areas a faint smell of cooking and of swimming-pool chlorine crept in as if to mark the place as unashamedly collegiate and ordinary, the opposite of the grand hotel across the road.

'These Damascus chairs are the real thing but they are impossible to sit on,' complained Perla as she pulled up a humble kitchen chair she had found behind the reception desk. 'They were made by people who prefered to squat on their haunches or recline on divans. Me, they give me a backache after five minutes.'

Perla was in a somewhat warlike mood. She had argued with the bus driver coming up about turning down the volume on his radio. She had appealed to the other passengers dramatically, standing up to rally support. They didn't react but read their papers and munched their sandwiches. The soldiers on the bus were mostly asleep anyway so Perla had to accept defeat and was therefore ready to continue her war in a different arena.

'Ulli shouldn't have crossed over for Christmas. It'll make trouble for Rudi. People who cross over are always watched. So he's living in a convent with a German wife and she jumps across the line at the first opportunity. Doesn't it look odd?'

'She's a Christian tourist, that's all,' said Suzi. 'What's odd about that? It was Christmas, wasn't it?'

'Fine, but what if she was given something to bring back, something innocent-looking like a pot of jam or a rosary? It could arouse suspicion. They could be dangerous. And how would that look for Rudi?'

Suzi closed her eyes. Perla's fantasies of foul play were out of a B picture. She felt her sister had prepared a villain's role for Rudi's German wife and meeting her wouldn't change the script.

They waited in silence watching the patch of grey daylight through the glass doors. No-one came or went. It was as if the entire association of young Christian men was fast asleep and would stay asleep till Easter when the carillon would play again and awaken the sleepers with news of the risen Saviour.

The big doors creaked and Rudi and Ulli came in. There was a moment's hesitation while they took in the dark and empty lobby then they noticed them, waved and came over.

Perla became the official welcomer: 'You look lovely – just like your photographs, Ulli. It's a good thing you had someone take them. I'm sure Bubi wouldn't have taken the trouble. So we know who you are and here you are. And you've already been in the Old

205

City. Here such a short time and you've already crossed where we can't. Does it still smell of sewage?'

Ulli nodded, smiled and seemed to want Rudi to do the talking.

'Félix took care of her so she was fine.'

He pulled a thick envelope out of his briefcase.

'Look I have something to show you, reactions to my project for a Spelling Olympics. I thought no-one was interested but they're going to try it out in Singapore. Next year. Teams will come from many countries and we're beginning to work out rules and procedure. There will be spelling matches and games in fourteen languages. Spelling relay races and marathons. Can you imagine it? A jubilee of language sports and internationalism. And maybe I can get an event going in Esperanto.'

Perla fingered the envelope as if it was a wet fish.

'To me this sounds like the Tower of Babel. So many languages in one pot. That's a queer stew and how can you stop them quarrelling?'

'That's just the point. Interlingualism is an exercise in tolerance. Different language groups learn to sympathise with each others' spelling challenges and attempt spelling in each others' languages. It's a *paix des braves*.'

Ulli had pulled out of her bag a miniature camel train made of olive wood. Five camels chained to each other were led by a donkey. She tried to set them up on the table but they kept falling over.

'It's for you,' she said, looking forlornly at the pile of beasts of burden on the table.

'Perhaps the table isn't smooth enough,' said Suzi.

'They used to make them out of thicker cuts of olive wood,' said Perla, 'and with real embroidered miniature saddles.'

They all looked at the fallen camels.

'Let's go to lunch,' said Rudi. 'I have a better idea than this café. Ada will meet us at the Berlin ladies. I think you've been there Perla.'

It was too windy and cold to walk so they took a taxi to the little dining room behind Jason's Tomb.

There were few guests this early and Frau Hermine greeted them warmly, smiling broadly across her flat face and smoothing her apron with vigorous strokes.

'Ah Herr Rudi und Frau Ulli, *schön schön.*'

Without much ado Perla established her past connection with the establishment and soon they were all seated at a table where Ada and Tomas were waiting. Tomas had dressed for the occasion, wearing a black sweater with fewer holes and no paint stains. Both slight pale figures in black, he and Ada looked like waifs on display at a modest charity dinner in the grey, neon-lit room with its rickety glass-topped tables and windows overlooking Jason's Tomb. Suzi knew about Tomas and had indeed praised her daughter for 'getting out of the Milo jail' finally but this was their first meeting.

Perla launched into the probe.

'So Tomas do you sell any of your paintings? Ada tells us they are unusual and historical too. You're not painting Biblical maidens, are you? Or *schmaltz* like that?'

Ada answered for him. Out of habit she respected Perla's opinions and needed to encounter them however angry they made her.

'Tomas has done a painting of Bathsheba in her tub but you'll see it's nothing like historical kitsch.'

'So what is it about and why Bathsheba?' asked Perla.

Tomas seemed to be struggling with a gag against speech but after an effort that wrinkled his brow, he said; 'It's a painting of a memory, I think.'

'A memory of Bathsheba?'

'No, my mother.'

There was a silence as Perla called off the advance, sensing that she was getting into dangerous territory.

'I saw it,' said Rudi. 'A woman in a tub on a roof. It's an odd place to put a tub.'

'Did you lose your mother a long time ago?' asked Ulli.

'In Poland.'

'But if I remember right,' said Rudi, 'you put her on the roof of

207

a house like those old Arab houses near the ceasefire line. That wasn't Poland.'

'I put her there because I imagine her in this place.'

'You mean it's a kind of escape for her.'

Tomas struggled more.

'No. No escape. I put her here because she joined me in not escaping.'

'But you did get away. You came here,' said Perla. 'So you're painting her from a distance.'

'No distance. She's on the roof of my house in a looted bathtub.'

'Whoever looted bathtubs?' said Rudi.

'Soldiers and civilians,' said Ada, 'in the war when the city split. Houses were emptied of everything, in minutes.'

'Who would take furniture and soup spoons out of an abandoned house? I mean the owners might come back.'

'If they do Tomas would get out,' said Ada.

'You're living in an abandoned house?' said Ulli. 'Somebody will come back and say it's mine, and then you'll leave?' She looked startled.

'Nobody's coming back,' said Perla. 'There was a war and the city was divided up. People left. Houses stayed. New people came in. That's the story. Worse happened to our houses over there. They were flattened.'

'I didn't realize,' said Ulli. 'I was on the other side and I looked over here from there and I didn't understand that people left their houses behind. I thought that the line divided one side from the other and people had to stay where they were. They couldn't cross but they didn't leave everything on the other side.'

'I have a key,' said Tomas. 'It must have belonged to whoever lived in my ruin. I found it on the path as if somebody had lost it. The door was forced open anyway.'

'Why do you call it a ruin?' said Rudi. 'It looks good and sturdy. Patched up but all together.'

'I couldn't call it a house because it isn't mine. It was somebody's house and it was empty and falling apart. When I pushed open the door for the first time the smell of shit was so strong it could have kept the walls from collapsing. Inside it looked like a rhino had run wild. But the piles of rubbish and plaster didn't hide the windows. The windows were like eyes in a skull looking inwards at the ruin. I didn't look any more. I left and wasn't going to come back. But I did. It was somewhere to live.'

'That does leave some hope,' said Rudi. 'Because people on both sides lost so much. They all lost. So it's mutual. Now if they could agree on ways of compensating each other it would be a move towards reconciliation and who knows, even getting rid of that stupid dividing line. They were once neighbours after all.'

'It's not a game of Monopoly,' said Perla. 'There's no going back and making nice. And neighbours make the worst enemies. They listen to conversations and look through windows. They know too much about each other.'

When the food came Ulli didn't eat. She sat looking at her plate.

'What's the matter Ulli?' said Rudi.

She didn't answer for a while.

'In the bombing walls of whole houses were torn away and sometimes you could see a bath just hanging on. It was easy to see because the tub was white and the rubble around it was black and grey. It was like a white boat stranded on rocks. I noticed the tubs because we didn't have one.'

'You can't compare wars,' said Perla.

Rudi came to Ulli's rescue.

'But you can compare tubs. They are bits of a household left behind when the people who used to wash in them have gone. It doesn't matter what country or what war.'

'We had a tub,' said Tomas. 'It was like a monument, it was the whitest thing in the house.'

'It does matter,' said Perla. 'There are victims who lose everything and there are people who make wars and lose everything. That's the difference. Some deserve to lose the lot. Save your sympathy.'

'And what are we?' asked Ada.

'Surely you know, we are sucessful victims and some of us are looters and Tomas here can record our shame in his painting of Uriah's beautiful wife. There's a looter for you, David our musical king. He stole the bathtub and the woman in it.'

'He just took her?' said Rudi making a scooping movement with his hand.

'Worse. He sent her man to the war, to the front line where he got the bullet. Then he had her for himself.'

There was silence for a while as they dealt with their food and tried to digest the treacherous lust of the Psalmist.

Suzi had enough of stolen bathtubs.

'I thought the Ark was your big surprise for the opening of the trial. The Flood and Noah and the Nazi. What ever happened to all that? Forgotten?'

'Not forgotten' said Ada. 'We've built it. Tomas and I have got the Ark almost finished in the cellar of the Television Centre. We've been working on it for weeks. Milo's coming to see it today. We can all go.'

Ulli looked worried.

'What's the Ark got to do with the trial and the Nazi?'

'The Ark is in a play about trouble and disaster.'

'Disaster?'

'Yes, like the Flood. Big trouble, a big wave, everything here could be swept away.'

'Swept away? By what? This place looks so normal.'

'A town with a dead zone in the middle is normal? Danger Border Stop signs at the street corner, that's normal?'

'No, but people learn to live with worse. I saw it after the war, disaster. We were crawling in it. Streets and houses piled high like mountains. No food no water almost no light just choking dust.'

'You think that couldn't happen here?'

'What kind of comparison are you making, Ada?' said Perla, red-faced. 'In front of Ulli too. Look how pale she is. It's unthinkable and shameful. You know what Nuremberg was. Hitler's showpiece. Those boots and flags and standards. They were trampling on

210

civilization. They brought destruction on the world and on themselves. How can we even think such a catastrophe will hit us? Milo's idea is crazy. Why is he warning us? Why on earth link the Nazi's trial with the end of the world? Who does he think he is, Jeremiah?'

Ada didn't find it easy to defend or explain Milo's idea. But Perla's anger made her understand better the need for the Ark on Ben Yehuda Street. Perla's self-righteousness spreading everywhere was the trap. Perhaps the Big Shit's trial wasn't a polite setting for a flood warning. People would be thinking of what had happened twenty years ago. It was overwhelming them already and would do more and more. Then they were victims and now they would be judging their executioner. So why not leave them to it? But she couldn't explain to Perla that to leave them to it and to the display and counting of their many wounds was trouble. The man in a torn grey suit who ran through the centre of town every day with a toy shovel in his hand shouting LOBKA LOBKA had been driven mad by that. There were many like him all over the country. Now there would be more, stirred up by the trial to scream wildly in the middle of a concert or in the theatre, at a play or during prayers in a synagogue. Noah's medicine for that madness was repentance and ark-building. Occupational therapy. It was a strange kind of therapy because it replaced self-pity by self-examination and worry but it was about the future. It was constructive and it showed you how to build something to float on and stay dry.

But if she talked like this to Perla she would have a fit and put her hands over her ears because nothing, nothing in the world should be allowed to question their innocence. Now she had gone on to interrogating Ulli about the destruction of Nuremberg. Ada heard this confusedly through the screen of her own thoughts and the growing noise in the dining room, crowded now with regulars coming in from the cold with heavy coats and red hands and faces.

One question she heard Perla repeat: 'But did they understand they had brought it all on themselves? Did the people understand?'

Ulli looked at Rudi for help but it was Tomas who intervened.

'When you're there who can understand? Hunger, you understand. You are blind and cold. Understanding is buried under the ruins. You've got anger instead and self-pity, bags full of anger but nothing...'

Tomas stopped in mid-sentence and stared at the door. He had seen Kronberg at the entrance, wrapped in a fancy tweed coat with a felt hat, talking to Frau Gertrude. Standing at the door, Kronberg surveyed the room looking for an empty chair. For a moment he hadn't seen Ada and Tomas and their party and he seemed vulnerable, an outsider at the edge of a crowd uncertain how to interpret the hum of words, perhaps wounded by the lack of interest in him, perhaps planning an intervention to break into the ring. But Tomas had noticed him and when their eyes met he waved and motioned to Kronberg to join them. There was a moment's hesitation, then he manoeuvred nimbly between tables and chairs and stood next to them with his head slightly bent like a distinguished doctor listening to a patient's symptoms.

When he sat down Ada noticed small cuts from shaving on his cheek dusted over with some perfumed talcum powder. His complexion was ruddy and polished and gave an impression of health and well-being though the cold blue eyes behind the glasses seemed to be searching for something concealed behind what they saw. Despite the formality of his manner and presence he was soon whipping the conversation along, talking with a thirst perhaps created by an unaccustomed period of silence.

Ada guessed why he was so eloquent. It was the aftermath of an upheaval in his life. He had come to see her in the Ethiopian mansion a few days before and, hesitant at first but glad to see she was alone, told his story in great detail like a witness before a judge. 'I am telling you this' he said 'because I can't tell Tomas now or anyone else and, ever since you came to me with a legless doll, I know you care for broken lives. It began when my apartment became a prison cell with bookshelves. It was always cold and no amount of newspapers and cotton wool could stop the draughts curling in and blowing cold around my neck and ears even in bed.

Broken dolls and ailing electric kettles weren't enough to fend off winter boredom and both of my Plato students had been called up for reserve training. Even my customary walk through the centre of town, you know, the triangle, King George, Ben Yehuda, Jaffa, turned into a convict's exercise in the prison courtyard. The streets were never lively. My fellow convicts walked by, their coats pulled up as far as their noses, their eyes looking down at the mean pavements. Eventually the curfew bell rings and the line of walkers gradually dwindles as each is swallowed up by the cells assigned to them where they eat identical evening meals of bread, white cheese and olives. It was not always like this.

'In the past the triangle had been the liveliest walk in the city for me. It was the way to the cinema, to one or two good cafés, to the shop where you could buy *Le Monde* or Schimmelpenick cigarillos, to an upstairs haven which smelled of new books and glue and had good connections with publishers in Frankfurt and Paris. I found reassurance in the Euclidean logic of this urban geometry. What had changed? Nothing but my growing dissatisfaction, loneliness and the darkening of my imagination.

'I needed to get free of the triangle and find an open space with light enough and air to blow away the mists in my brain. Then I discovered the sea. My friend Hava, the waitress in Atara, told me about her trip to the seaside at Ashkelon. She described it as just a village, small square houses and Nissen huts built on the bluff overlooking the sea. It was empty of bathers at this time of year. "There are Roman ruins, you would like it," she said. So I packed a book and pyjamas, endured the slow bus ride and arrived in the small forlorn town which was to me new and attached like a trailer to a crumbling Arab town which was old and partly in ruins.

'I had been given the name of a lady who rented rooms for bathers. And I quickly installed myself in a bare monkish room with an army-style bed and a card table with a small vase of artificial roses. The woman spoke only Roumanian but we communicated in gestures and wrote down prices on a slip of paper. For some reason she wouldn't shake hands with me but nodded

213

her head vigorously and folded the paper with the numbers into the pocket of her apron.

'It was afternoon by the time I had slept off the fatigue of the bus ride. I bought a roll stuffed with bland white cheese and a bottle of soda in a tiny grocery and made my way towards the sea – which meant following the light. Although I couldn't see the sea from my street there was a definite brightening of the sky in one direction. I made my way towards it hardly noticing the shops and the life in the street. It was pleasantly warm and windless and I encountered no cars, just a bus stop with a cluster of people waiting stoically.

'As I walked, the collection of sporadic houses and huts gave way to a scruffy open space with some empty flower beds, a bench and a few fragile, newly planted trees tied like prisoners to wooden stakes. Then an abrupt drop revealed the sea, strangely quiet, grey-blue, licking the edges of a long nondescript empty expanse of sand. It was a shock, like a reunion with a parent absent for years. It was at the same time familiar and sudden, a surprise. I breathed in the salty air. I was excited and I stumbled down a steep path and found myself on rough sand and grit which made walking harder. So I took off my shoes and socks, tied them to my belt and as the warm sand embraced my feet I was hit by the powerful, unfamiliar iodine sea smell, so strong it made me giddy and I had to sit down. I stretched out on the sand like a crab, spreadeagled. I closed my eyes and let the sun roll over my face. Then, flat on the ground, I began to hear the quiet splash and lap of the waves but in the splash and lap there was something else. Sometimes faint and sometimes louder, weaving into the sea splash, I heard what sounded like the high-pitched call of trumpets and the throbbing of violins. I put it down to the hypnotic effect of the waves falling on the sand but when the sounds persisted I sat up and looked around.

'Though weak, the sun had made me lightheaded and the strip of sand with the line of bluffs behind it jiggled up and down like a ghostly earth tremor. Slowly and with difficulty I got myself standing and began to walk in what I thought was the direction of the sound. There seemed to be nothing on the beach. I stumbled against broken columns which I would have looked at closely if I wasn't in search of the sound. But it played with me mischievously depending on the breeze. Sometimes it was there then it was gone. Yet it seemed to be getting louder as I walked away from the waves towards the yellow-white cliff. Soon, as I got further from the sea, there was no other sound. Just music or its echo. I stopped to get my bearings. I was surprised to find myself breathing quite heavily and there was an intermittent ringing in my ears. I needed water but I had none and I decided to retrace my steps to the path up to the town. Then there was a distinct roll of drums, big tympani whose loud, defiant pulsing seemed to address me directly from nearby. Then quiet. Looking at the cliff side again I noticed a water bucket standing upright in the sand. The beach was so empty and featureless that the pail signalled to me like a lighthouse. Approaching it I noticed a line of stones leading towards the cliff. After a few steps it veered to the right and I was in front of a small oddly-shaped structure built in a hollow hugging the cliff. It was made of planks and bits of building material and some kind of sheeting. It could have been a shower stand or a primitive changing room. No music was coming out of it. I moved right up to it and knocked on one of the planks. I called out but there was no answer so I pushed aside some sheeting and stepped inside. A man was lying on a torn mattress. He could have been asleep but his eyes were wide open staring at the light filtering in through the material on the roof. Next to the mattress stood an orange crate holding a battered gramophone. A cup and a plate were set on a stone next to a jerrycan.

'"Ho," I said.

'The man hardly moved but raised an arm in greeting.

'I came nearer and saw a thin brown-skinned face, wrinkled, unshaven under a crown of greying wiry hair.

'The man made some strange high-pitched sounds like the yelping of a dog and his fingers hovered over his mouth moving to and fro in a gesture of denial. He shook his head and seemed to be saying no. No. No to speech.

215

'"Do you hear me?"

'The man nodded and took a piece of cardboard out from under his mattress. He held it out. On it the word YIDDISH was written in large letters.

'I shook my head.

'The man sat up and pulled the jerrycan over to the bed. He held out the cup and made drinking gestures.

'I would have refused in any normal situation. Who knows where the extended cup had been? But this was desert hospitality. Refusal was out of the question and I was thirsty.

'I took the cup making sure to nod and drank the tepid water gratefully. It tasted of rust and stale tea.

'I sat on the floor pointed to the gramophone and then at my ear making conducting gestures with both hands like my hero Otto Klemperer.

'The man reached out and shook my hand. Then he picked up the gramophone and showed me an electric cable that led to a light fixture in what remained of a shower cabinet at the back. He smiled a wide clown's smile as if to congratulate himself and the whole world on his luck. I smiled back a genuine smile. I was happy that the man had got himself this connection, a simple enough click of a switch in any room in a house up on top. But here on the beach, a miracle.

'The man signalled me to pay attention like a magician preparing his audience for his coup. He pulled out another piece of cardboard from under his mattress and held it in front of my face like a mirror.

'MAHLER

'My pulse raced. That was the music that had been lurking in the sound of the waves. That was the call. I heard it now in distant recollection more clearly than when I had heard it by the sea. The harsh call of trumpets, the skeletal plucking of harps, the swooning and groaning of the strings, the plangent bird-song of the woodwinds; it was the music of my young manhood, my loneliness, my exile, my love. It was the music that never left me.

'I turned to the man and took both his hands in a gesture of brotherhood. The man lifted up some sacking by the bed and pulled out a record. He held it like a thin and delicate piece of porcelain and opened the gramophone lid. He made a move with his hands over his eyes and pointed at me. At first I didn't understand. He did it again and it was obvious. He wanted me to close my eyes.

'So I sat there, eyes closed, conscious of a trickle of sweat on my forehead. But I didn't move. The man made impatient, cajoling sounds. The gramophone hissed and then stopped and hissed again. I heard the man get up and do something perhaps to the cable but I didn't open my eyes. The hissing started again. Then the doom-laden staccato fanfare exploded accompanied by the chorus of quaking strings leading into the tenor's cry for wine.

'Schön winkt der Wein im gold'nen Pokale

'I fought with my racing heartbeat and shortness of breath. The cry hit me a hammer's blow to the nose. It released tears. But the man had told me to close my eyes so only some of the salt stream got through and slid down my face. The music hurtled on. The high tenor flew into the orchestra's sound like a hawk into a violent storm. He battled the currents, climbed and fell and fell again. The falling was a drunkard's swoon as he sought oblivion in sleep. And the sound became gentler as the voice, looking for rest, found darkness.

'Dunkel ist das Leben ist der Tod.

'I stretched out on the sand. I couldn't sit any more. I listened to the rest of the record half-asleep and dreaming, till the contralto's slow, repeated, retreating farewell, *Ewig Ewig* came to me from close by as mother's gentle call at my bedside: wake up, wake up, wake up.

'Then silence till the hissing of the gramophone returned and I opened my eyes to see the man sitting on his haunches quite close to me staring. He was ageless. Old but with the smooth cheeks of a young man. He ran his fingers from his eyes to his jaw and dabbed at his face with a tragic grimace. Tears.

'Yes, I nodded.

217

'I picked up the record cover. On it was a gaudy, tinted picture of Red Army cavalry riding through a forest under a banner bearing a Russian slogan.

'I laughed and waved it in the man's direction. He made some squeaking noises and shrugged his shoulders in the shtetl gesture of "What can you expect in a dump like this?"

'Then he picked up the Mahler placard and kissed it with a rich smacking sound.

'I was at a loss. How could I reward this man for his music. Would he be offended if I offered him money? How much? Who was he and why was he stretched out in this hovel with a record of *Das Lied von der Erde* and a gramophone?

'I cleared my throat and signalled a speech by pointing at my mouth. I was going to try in minimal Yiddish, even though, to me, it's a clownish jargon. My father used to mock the Polish Yiddish pronunciation of the Hebrew word for soul, so I remembered that.

'"*Neshume*," I said. "*A groisse neshume*."

'The Yiddish word is almost German, slanted over. Now what?

'Dead but alive. In Paradise. Paradise, there was Hebrew for that.

'"Gan Eyden" I said pointing at the holes in the roof. "Ewig" I added, appropriately. Proper German at last.

'The man smiled and moved his lips carefully as if enunciating a word. I couldn't make it out. He burrowed under the mattress and pulled out a small book. It was a German book of black and white reproductions of paintings. Quickly he put his finger on one. Angels singing over the Christ child. He pointed at one of the angels, a perfect oval face with an open mouth. Then he pointed at the record and crossed his hands over his chest.

'"Angel" I said.

'He signalled me to carry on.

'"Engel?"

'He shook his head and pointed at his mouth.

'Carefully he moved lips and tongue and jaw in an attempt to produce the word.

218

'I followed as best I could.

'M A O K

'He half-nodded, looked disappointed and then dismissed the whole thing with a wave of his hand.

'I reached for my wallet. I took out a few banknotes and offered them. The man took them without hesitation and with no word of thanks. Then he stretched out on the mattress and closed his eyes. I could go.

'Later on I found out that the Yiddish for angel is Malokh. That's what he was trying to mouth.'

'I returned to Jerusalem immediately. I didn't ask anyone about him and what he was doing on the beach. I had it in me – all of it, the sea, the music and the man. I was afraid to talk about it, because I might waste it in babble. But I arranged it all in my mind, I worked over it again and again like an actor learning a part. This has never happened to me. This need to say something exactly with total truthfulness. I talk a lot but it's mostly chatter, nothing really. What happened at the beach is not something to chatter about. No, I had to tell someone and not casually. I needed someone to pay attention, alone. If I tried to tell this to Tomas it could only be misunderstood. It would open up old wounds and I would spoil it by trying to make him pity me. I would falsify what happened to me because I want him to love me for it. So I came to you because something about you forbids pathos and sentimentality. There is some Antigone in you, Ada. Don't dismiss it. Don't look away. I picture you before all this, pale and quiet, wearing black, alone at your table at Frau Hermine's…You were born to listen and be trusted.'

That's what he said, thought Ada and her confusion was still with her days later. The man chattering at the table had made her into his chaste witness.

'What do I do with your story?'

'Treat it as my confession. Absolve me.'

'Of what?'

219

'Despair. Don't look so startled. I didn't think anything good could ever happen to me. I was set on being a prisoner. For life. I was wrong and I'm telling you this to unburden myself so I can escape from my jail.'

'You witnessed a miracle. You saw the angel and heard him sing. But what are you going to do? You're still Kronberg. If you'd seen Jesus would you change your name like Paul and rush to tell the world? Probably not. Show me your hands.'

His palms were soft, pink and slippery with sweat.

'No stigmata. No blood. Mahler's wounds were made of music. Still you had a vision. No-one will deny you that – if you tell them. But you probably won't. It'll stay your secret if you want it so. And it may not change your life all that much. Kronberg will be Kronberg. But if Mahler on the beach at Ashkelon is a sign, it could be telling you – don't go back to Germany. That's a start.'

She felt strange assuming oracular wisdom like this in front of learned, suffering Kronberg. He might regret coming to her. But he received it quietly and naturally, leaving her room a little more heavily than when he had come.

'*Gut geschmeckt? Zur Nachspeise Torte mit Sahne.*'

Both Hermine and Gertrude were standing by their table like large cherubs at the altar. They had brought everyone an extra portion of chocolate cake with fresh cream, *Torte mit Sahne*, as they felt there was some kind of celebration going on. The cake was dry and nondescript but the *Sahne* was the Tantes' rarely offered holy grail, a sacred libation, sweet, white and velvety poured on each slice. It never left the kitchen without ceremony.

Kronberg stood up and embraced Frau Gertrude.

He was on the verge of tears.

'Thank you, thank you, today is my birthday…'

Some diners in the room looked up and clapped. One tried to sing but it didn't catch on.

Tomas whispered to Ada, 'It isn't. What's got into him?'

'Gustav Mahler,' she said.

Ada's Journal

Who's going to be God? Kronberg? Milo's surprise choice. He refuses at first. 'I'm an atheist from the cradle. I wasn't circumcised. My father was an atheist and my mother was a gymnast and a vegetarian. Every drop of my blood is progressive and I can't speak those mediaeval idiocies.'

Why did he come to rehearsals at all? He wants to be friends. He's tempted by acting though he pretends to look down on it. It's a way of getting free of the Kronberg burden. So he's offered God.

Reheasals in the cellar of the TV building are aimless, even chaotic. It's cold. Milo's friends and some students are here (Ayala) but not all the time. It's hard to get parts set and actors committed. Some come just to look. No-one talks about the Big Shit and the trial. Some are perplexed by the set, surprised even shocked that Zion Square has become the Ark. To go and stand in front of the Zion Cinema box office and declare the end of the world is ridiculous. So they keep their distance. They avoid stepping up on it. Tomas notices this and takes it personally. They can't bear it happening here, he says. They can't imagine this ground melting under their feet. Tomas understands Milo's idea better than most. But he doesn't talk. Apocalypse is real to him, even normal. He also won't say a word about the Big Shit. But the Ark makes sense to him. He has studied escape.

He was so exacting about the detail in the set because that is what highlights the danger. The more normal and everyday it looks the more shocking. It's like a doll's house made large, a getaway toy for escaping children.

In the old plays Noah claps the Ark together on stage or they wheel it on after some banging and thumping behind a curtain. Here it is in view from the start. That serves Milo's purpose. We see it but we can't imagine what will happen. It's a kind of shelter like the ramshackle war shelters dotted around the city. Nobody notices them and they are full of garbage and shit. This shelter is only too visible. Therefore it's even easier to ignore.

Ulli isn't succumbing to the Milo mystique. On the contrary she seems to mistrust and dislike him. Her pure blonde opposes his brooding dark. He can't stand a woman's indifference or rejection so it makes him even more aggressive. When he tries to catch her eye she shuts him out. She just doesn't notice, unlike me. I am always aware of Milo's eyes even when he's behind me. The back of my neck picks up his look like a rear mirror.

She starts a row with him. She is thinking about the trial. She told him he was scraping at an old wound for no reason but his own vanity. 'So much pain and shame is going to come out of this' she says. 'So many people will be made to remember and you want to tell them it's not the worst? You want to tell them there's worse to come? Here outside Zion Cinema where they go to see Grace Kelly in a Cadillac?'

Milo treats most objections with deafness. He's thought it through and people are reluctant to argue with him. With Ulli he takes the trouble to defend himself.

'You know what happens when sheep all run in one direction? It ends badly. They fall off the cliff. Where are the outsiders? Where? Have you heard any, seen any? We are the only ones. It's our job. Somebody has to be outside the trial. Because when everybody's in there and all together the madness takes hold, they lose their minds. Somebody has to stay outside to remind them.'

When Kronberg first saw the set he was speechless. All he could do was point and stutter: 'Here here. It's here? This?'

I suspect Kronberg has particular associations with Zion Square. Like everybody, he's there on Saturday nights and if there are pick-up spots in town this is it. Sufficiently crowded to be anonymous, this is where he touches a young man and they go off to the darkness of the park. Now he's going to tell the people they are to be destroyed for their lusts. God will have a guilty conscience.

Milo answers Kronberg's objections.

'You fit the God description. You are tall and you've got a high forehead. All you have to believe in is God's anger. When you tap your own you'll find the voice for God. He's full of rage and so are you.'

'But a man with glasses acting God. It's going to drive the audience crazy. Jews can't swallow a human God. They'll riot and throw stones.'

Yet Kronberg has agreed to look at the part and he got Milo's OK to change some of the speeches. He started so hostile but now he wants God to sound more like himself. He's flattered secretly and relishes the hypocrisy. He's no Tartuffe but his double life will make his God-playing more interesting. He also likes the prospect of giving Félix orders.

Félix, the happy Noah. He's one of the few who are not troubled by the Ark on Zion Square. He strokes the painted walls lovingly. He says the setting is right for a mediaeval play. In Rouen they had a cathedral and a market. For us, he says, Zion Cinema is just that: Notre-Dame de Sion. He doesn't really believe the play will get out of the cellar and this makes it easier for him to act excited. He'll do anything that makes Milo happy. He would even be an animal, a large one.

Noah is right for him. He looks cheerful and he'll get the crowd to like him. He swigs from a bottle. He is ruddy and healthy. He's going to take the *nebbich* out of the old guy and make him manly and attractive and dangerous to the womenfolk, like a country preacher. So he's playing against the script. He's supposed to be a henpecked fart. But Félix is always trying to charm some woman, all women. Who specially this time? Ulli? Jordan? Ayala? A devout maiden in the crowd? He is Jean Gabin at the wheel, a grizzled steersman full of knowledge and sap.

Much depends on who is finally going to be Mrs Noah. Given the right woman with Félix their scrapping and fighting could become sexy, a wrestle before tumbling into bed. But remember. No sex once inside the Ark. 100 days and nights of abstinence. SS Chastity.

Julius has shaved off his beard to play Shem. He was waiting for the opportunity he said. The hairs were getting in the way of his thoughts. He and Mr Margarian have an argument about geography. Margarian came to the cellar to see if he could help with the police and legal objections.

He suggests Milo request police permission for an interfaith religious display. 'That sounds healthy and quiet. Like Madame Tussaud's. They will ask you why there outside the trial and you will say it is a display of the victory of good over evil as written in the Bible. Could they object to that?'

But Margarian has devious intentions. He wants Armenia in. He's got an Armenian verse for Noah to speak when he steps on to Ararat, preferably in Armenian but if not in English or Hebrew.

'Ararat is the cradle of civilization,' he says, 'but who knows this apart from us Armenians? This is the second Creation, a better, drier world will begin on Armenian Ararat.'

This annoyed Julius, who is responsible for the script. Julius is touchy about borders and frontiers. He knows that any change on the demarcation line, like moving a fence or adding a light bulb, can cause trouble.

'Ararat isn't Armenia,' he says.

'So what is it?' asks Margarian. He is flushing under his olive cheeks.

'It's in Turkey.'

Julius must know that this will enrage Margarian but he seems not to care.

'The people in the Ark are everybody. Everybody left alive. They've no passports from any country. There aren't any countries.

Everything's washed away and they are just people. There's no name for that flood either. It's just endless water and they land on something called EARTH, mud and rock and slime. Not Babylon. Not Arcadia. Not Nubia. It's not on a map. It's just earth. Drawing lines and calling it Armenia is an act of rape.'

'Rape. Who was raped?' shouts Margarian. 'Thousands of Armenian women, wives and daughters, young and old. The crime will never be forgotten. And in your trial here you must remember it.'

He is a tidy little man but in his anger he inflates like a balloon, his ears grow red and his shirt slides out of his trousers. He feels the Jews have run off with the Armenians' victim medal and taken all the credit for themselves.

Félix puts an arm round his shoulders and gives him a brotherly caress.

'We do not forget, Monsieur Margarian. I shall write a letter to the Armenian Patriarch in the Old City to express our solidarity. From the Ark to Armenia. They will publish it in their newsletter. I will mention the duty of remembrance and the spirit of Ararat.'

Margarian quietens down and Félix looks pleased. He likes to be thought of as a peacemaker, a kind of doctor in the desert equipped with precious salves and ointments for the nomads. Jordan told me how he intervened in a quarrel when Milo threatened her with a bread knife. Félix walks in and deflates their anger by treating it as melodrama overdone. Jordan imitates him: *O mes enfants what is this grand guignol? Hostilities? Here? By the line of ceasefire? Lay down your anger for a friend.*

Jordan has been playing Mrs Noah and, taking the cue from Félix, she is much younger and more attractive than the old baggage in the original. She prefers drinking and smoking to worrying about the Flood. Jordan does some vamping out of Gina Lollobrigida and it becomes her. Félix tries to bully her as Noah should but is more tempted by her lipstick than angered by her lack of respect for God and himself. When he grabs her by the arm she fakes surprise and turns it into an attempted embrace. Then she pulls away. Come and get me. She has power over this older man who knows time is running out but is still a prisoner of his blood.

Milo tries to direct this love quarrel scene urging them to stick to the text but they mostly ignore his comments and instructions and the others crowd round as the rehearsal catches fire. The scene gets better the more it deviates from the text. Milo's face is a mask. He knows it's more interesting the way they do it but it bothers him. Or does it? Strange for me to see him impassive as Jordan and Félix act their battle of the sexes without reference to him. His thoughts, once so obvious to me when he seemed in control of his seduction games, are now a blank. I've lost the code. I can't imagine him wounded. Once his jealousy would have given itself away to me as part fake and part true. I could have calculated the ratio. But now I can't figure out his pose. He seems hypnotized or is his mind elsewhere? Could he be bored?

Eyob appears out of nowhere. His tall black figure looks oddly appropriate near the painted façade of Zion Square as if he has just wandered down from Ethiopia Street round the corner to buy some batteries for his torch and stumbled on a street performance. He was told about our rehearsals by Julius and is attracted by the biblical subject. He stands for a while close to the wall, separate from the others. Against the stark white he looks like a charred tree trunk. He watches the confusing starts and stops of the rehearsal for a while. Then he comes over to me. 'Why is there anger between them?' 'She is Mrs Noah and she doesn't want to get into the Ark. She doesn't believe what Noah is telling her.' 'She is foolish,' he says. 'There is great water coming from God.' He looks around perhaps wondering how the flood is going to arrive. Can others enter this exhibition, he asks. He is excited. Here is Ham, I think, the father of the African peoples come to us out of Ethiopia Street. Then I realize how impossible this is. 'Others can,' I say. 'But there are only a few in it. Just Noah and his family.' 'No animals?' 'Yes, animals too.' He is silent, calculating. 'So where is Ham?' I have to be careful. 'They are looking for the right person.' He holds back for a bit. 'I

226

am him.' A long finger points at his face. 'Eyob you will never get permission. How will you come to rehearsals? They won't let you go.' He presses my hand as if to say trust me and slips out.

A discussion about Ham and Eyob.

Milo thinks it is a good idea. Black skin is an unusual sight here and Eyob will make people look.

Jordan: Look at what, a zoo? It'll be racist. They'll think of Ham as the African who gets the father's curse and spreads it through all the black peoples like a disease.

Ulli: Why was he cursed?

Félix: According to the Bible he saw his father's nakedness.

Ulli: So what? Didn't they all go around almost naked? Just cache sex?

Milo: The Rabbis think he raped him while he was dead drunk. Or maybe castrated him.

Rudi: Does our audience have to know all this? It's not actually in the play. It doesn't happen on stage.

Kronberg: They know it anyway. They are folktales like Grimm. They are whispered from one generation to the next.

Jordan: So by casting Eyob we fortify their primitive racism. Black Ham is a sex offender. We know that because he's black. A *shvartzer*. What else could he be, a chess champion?

Félix: No chess for Ham. He is the only one who doesn't observe the sex moratorium in the Ark.

Ulli: And his wife?

Félix: It's not obvious he did it with his wife. Could have been sheep, goats.

Rudi: We have to distance ourselves from this ancient racism. Noah can make it clear at the end that Ham was never found guilty of any sex crimes. He should embrace Ham and show him respect as the father of all Africa.

Milo: So let's have a white Ham and no-one will lose sleep about his being a bugger.

I am torn between boredom and watchfulness. I am not a

227

performer but the Ark is my work and Tomas's. Every bit of damage to the set hurts me. Mind the boards I want to shout as Félix and Jordan wrestle on the floor of Zion Square. Tomas spends much of the time drawing. He has a sketch of Jordan which brings out her character's wily voluptuousness. She is a market woman and Carmen. Nobody's girl. Playing a part brings out a side of her that I missed. The civilized intellectual beauty, carefully put together, is gone. In its place there's a feline creature searching, but not for food. For what? A territory of her own. Freedom from the law of the man-god? Ownership of her feminine treasure? When she appeals to the audience against the rule of men, the clarity of Jordan Loew mingles with an agitator's raw energy. She's a sexy Rosa Luxemburg and she sweats too. What does Milo see when he watches this? It's aimed at him isn't it?

When she refuses to step onto the Ark she's telling Milo you don't own me. I go my own way.

Eyob turns up at the end of a particularly disordered session. The parade of animals was a queer stumble. Julius was never in step and couldn't hold his lion's mask The giraffe's cardboard neck kept collapsing. The musicians were bored and didn't get to play their sections through. Eyob walked in. He wasn't wearing his monk's habit but an ill-fitting white shirt and khaki trousers.

'I can be Ham?' he says to me.

'How come you aren't wearing your monk's clothes Eyob? What has happened?'

'I have freedom, for some weeks I have freedom.'

'How is this possible? The monastery just let you go?'

'I speak to the Master. I told him I am sad for my mother and sisters. And I dream of Satan beating my head with the big bell of the church. It is true. I also told him I dream of Eikamenn throwing the children into the sea. So he asked me if I wish to go away from the Church and I say no but I beg him to make me free for some time. To do what he says. To be Ham I say in an exhibition. The Master does not know what is this exhibition. I say it is showing Noe and the Flood for people to know the work of God in the street when the evil man is judged. The Master is an old man and kind. He knows my trouble and he forgives me. I love him.'

Eyob didn't explain exactly on what terms he was freed from the monastery. He will stay with Julius and Milo will decide if he goes on board. Can Ham's villainy be hidden from Eyob? If he finds out will he want to play the part?

Shpitz has taken to coaching God on the side. He comes to all the rehearsals and watches hungrily but is quiet. He's careful not to undermine Milo. Yet he takes on little jobs and Milo pretends not to notice. Kronberg is one of them. Kronberg's Jehovah has become a Prussian martinet. God has to wear a golden crown, a beard and a purple robe yet he still sounds more like a prison warder than the king of the universe. The prisoners have rebelled and he is out to punish them. Shpitz tries to get some humanity into him. 'Maybe you're disappointed,' he says. 'You're hurt because these kittens have fouled the carpet and you're going to have to drown them. You are God but you're a father goddamit. You recognize yourself in them. Remember you had high hopes of them. Think like a Christian, Kronberg. Give the Almighty fucker some humanity for Chrissake.'

Shpitz picks at his goatee and mouths Kronberg's text along with him. He makes him speak it first blindfolded and then with sweets in his mouth. Then he has him whistle 'Tipperary' before each section.

Strangely Kronberg doesn't protest. He must like being a puppet to Shpitz's master. God is learning how to be human. I see in him what Tomas must have responded to. There's a pliant core somewhere inside the confident, opinionated exterior. He loses his rigidity when Shpitz, waving his hands and staring at him with burning eyes, takes charge of him. He wants to be played with, made to say this and that, speak with his mouth full, give his words one meaning then repeat them another way and then a third way, till they become nonsense. Then his habitual wall of confidence begins to crumble. He's learning not to be Kronberg.

Tomas watches this carefully but he doesn't try to draw Kronberg. When I ask him why he says he's drawn him too often in the past. Where are those drawings? I ask. Kronberg has them. Tomas's silence has been uncanny in the babble of the cellar. The music starts and stops. Noah and wife's loud quarrel, the interruptions and laughter from the watchers, all this cacophony envelopes him as he sits alone and draws. He doesn't even watch consistently as he concentrates on his pad but takes a swift look now and again to make sure the scene is still there. He could be alone in a forest drawing the outlines of a deer half hidden by trees and undergrowth. Never has he seemed further away than in this crowded place. When I come close to him he half turns to me but says little. I see him working at his pad head down while Kronberg, a more broken, contrite God than before, is listing his grievances against mankind. I look over his shoulder and he has drawn nothing. Instead he has written some Polish words in bold calligraphic strokes and decorated them with disembodied wings. 'What's that?' I say.

'*Zalowal Pan*, God repents he made man on earth just like a Catholic sinner. Punish yourself by drowning your mistakes in the river, like unwanted babies. Then forget everything and start again.'

'Why Polish?'

'That's how I heard it. The farmer read the Flood story aloud to his family. Sometimes I heard it from below. It sounded real to me, the threat of rain and flooding. Nothing strange about that. If the flood came they would leave me behind. They would all push away in a boat with the cow and the dog and I would be in the pit under the planks and straw waiting for the water. First mud and slime and sodden earth then more and more water and I couldn't swim.'

Eyob starts Ham disastrously. He is teamed with Ayala as Mrs Ham. A beautiful pair. They remind me of the lanky jazz players and their girlfriends in the Rue de la Huchette. Eyob is carried away by his role, laughing all the time, eager to hold Ayala's hand or any part of her he can get to. He has to plead with Mr and Mrs Noah to stop quarrelling and come on the Ark. But he steals Ayala's lines

230

and misses his cues because he is too interested in what's going on around him. He doubles up over Julius's lugubrious, unstable lion's head and when he laughs his warm bounding peals set the audience going and this delights him. But he has found out something...He comes to me.

'Is God angry with Ham?'

'Why do you ask?'

'Julius says Ham is trouble.'

'Well, his father is angry with him.'

'Why? Noe is a righteous man.'

'Yes but he's angry because Ham didn't respect him.'

Eyob sits down with his head in his hands. When he looks up his eyes are red.

'I promised the Master that the exhibition will show the good work of God but I am showing disrespect for my father? How is this good? What will the people say? They will say a brother from Debre Ganet in Ethiopia Street is bad to Noe his father. The church will get shame from me.'

'It isn't you who is bad Eyob, it's Ham. Ham from the Book. And anyway Ham isn't bad, he made a mistake. Everybody makes mistakes.'

'What did he do?'

'He stole his father's blanket when he was sleeping.'

'Ham was cold?'

'He was selfish. Eyob, this happens after the end of the play when the Flood is gone. No-one will see it happening.'

'Is there also anger for his brothers?'

'No.'

'Only Ham?'

'Yes.'

'Is it because I am black?'

Jordan was right. The colour thing is a trap. Eyob isn't a child and I can't fend him off with lies.

'You are black Eyob but Noah wasn't angry with Ham because of his colour. Colour isn't even written in the Book.'

'Was Noe white?'

'Nobody knows what anybody's colour was. Adam and Eve, Cain and Abel. They could be red or yellow we just don't know because it isn't written.'

Eyob is dissatisfied with my answers. He misses two rehearsals then he's back a different Ham. He shouts at Noah instead of pleading with him to stop fighting with his wife. He paws Ayala and she has to push him off. He comes out with words in Amharic and he's not laughing. When Milo tries to speak to him he listens but keeps his head down and drums with his fingers on his knee.

It comes to a fight. Today he tugs at Félix's shirt and says, 'You curse me.' Félix tries to free himself but Eyob hangs on. They land on the floor and Félix shouts 'What's this about a curse, have I cursed you?' 'Afterwards,' says Eyob, 'after the water goes away. You curse me. Afterwards.' Félix doesn't try to free himself or get up. He seems defeated by the savage story. Jordan intervenes. She takes Eyob by the hand and coaxes him up off Félix's stomach.

They go off into a corner, meanwhile the musicians doodle until 'It Aint Necessarily So' gets someone singing, 'Now he made his home in/That fish's abdomen.'

The rehearsal continues. Ham is subdued, almost whispering. It's hard to hear him.

I ask Jordan what she said?

'I explained to him about racism in the Bible.'

'You what?'

'You have to be open about it. I said didn't Moses marry a black woman? And didn't his sister Miriam say ugly things about her? And didn't God punish her with a disease? God punished her for that. Then I took a chance and I said, Do you know why Noah was angry with Ham? Not because he was black or because he stole his blanket. He was angry because when he took away his blanket he showed…I got a bit stuck there but I had to keep going, because he uncovered his father's secret underhair.

'That's what I said. Eyob looked startled and maybe he blushed.

232

Do black people blush? Anyway he kept his eyes down looking at his shoes. He said nothing.'

The incident has affected the rehearsals. The actors are bored and burdened with a labour that has gone flat. Even Félix has lost conviction. Mr Noah is tired of crying wolf. He'd rather forget about the whole Flood thing and go back home.

We disperse without a peptalk from Milo. These are now empty rituals as the actors don't feel he has a grip on what's happening. They do what they want and it works sometimes. But the ship is rudderless. It could easily fall apart and sink.

From the door I look back. The Ark lurks miserably in the chilly and dark cavity of the cellar. Zion Square never looked more forlorn. Zion Square? It's a shabby scarecrow made out of bits of wood and cloth and cardboard. All life has deserted it. The trial hasn't begun and the Ark is already foundering. And us? We'll lose interest and abandon it, leave it locked away and forgotten. Years later they'll find it covered in dust, unstuck, all shrunken with dryness and wonder what purpose this contraption was meant to serve. Why would anyone want to build a replica of the cinema and the square underground? A pagan cult? Voodoo? Monopoly for mice?

I lock the doors and we make for a warm place, any warm place. The early evening is bleak and empty. There's not enough light in the street. The rehearsal may have been a failure but it creates a bond between its survivors. We share disappointment like a blanket and huddle together in the street unsure of a direction but reluctant to separate.

We wander aimlessly until we realize that Rudi seems to know where he's going. He picks up speed as we walk through the market as if to say don't linger. Don't be tempted by the mounds of oranges and tomatoes. He is our captain warning us not to listen to the siren calls of the fruit sellers on each side as we walk off the afternoon's depression. The cold evening and the bright naked lamps over the stalls disguise the street's drabness and make it seem like a fairground in a small town among forests and lakes. Where's the firemen's band tootling marches and polkas? We leave the market and it gets darker as we walk through narrow lanes and courtyards where children are called in from play and smells of the evening meal drift out of half-open doors. Rudi it seems is taking us to the Convent where Schwester Clara has shown some curiosity about the Flood and urged him to bring Noah and the family to taste her tea and cakes. Rudi produces a key and pushes open the high heavy gates of Soeurs de Sion with a flourish, to announce his belonging there. There's no-one in the courtyard. From inside comes a sound of girls' voices singing. We follow Rudi through a couple of doors and along a dark corridor into a dimly lit room with chairs and benches around the walls and a heavy table in the middle with a vase full of anemones on a copper tray.

We sit there like patients in a waiting room while he goes in search of Schwester Clara. Félix is unusually subdued. Perhaps the move from the noisy cellar to this Catholic stillness and the monastic aroma of flowers and floor wash has opened up a wound. In this place he could be considered a renegade or a clown. Gulping from a bottle and fighting with his wife? What sort of behaviour is that from someone who is at least partly a churchman? Shame on you Père Félix. Shpitz is whispering with Jordan. She is writing something in her notebook. Milo has withdrawn into himself. He didn't speak on the way and now he has become a meditating Buddha in a rickety chair, all torso and head. His eyes look nowhere. Not a muscle moves in his face. In the dim light his skin glows like embers. Only Tomas moves around the room inspecting garish pictures of popes and saints. Why do I think of him as an orphan? We all are but he fits it best. His slightness as if he needs food, the signs of neglect about whatever he wears, sweaters with holes, jeans with no belt, accidental shirts and shoes, the paleness of his skin and, above all, his talent for loneliness. When he is asleep against me I can still feel bereft. It isn't him. Not Tomas but a double whom he has cunningly left behind. He is somewhere else. I know where. A clear white space, brightly lit but not by the sun and Tomas is in it alone. He comes over to show me a leaflet about a pilgrimage to

Compostella. I take hold of his extended hand. The skin is gnarled and creased. It is a real hand, moist and warm. I kiss it and he looks startled.

Jordan is laughing at something Shpitz is saying. After the wiles and mischief of Mrs Noah she is again her composed self, but not entirely. She laughs without any reserve. Her head and shoulders fall back, her mouth is wide open and her cheeks are red. Her shoulders under her blouse are gracefully curved and strong. Shpitz looks around pleased. His boyish grin sets his beard at a slant to the rest of his face, a cartoon grimace on a comic demon. Milo seems to notice but doesn't speak. The afternoon's defeat has driven him inwards. I know this silence and the gloom inside it.

It's what drives a woman to question herself, search for her offence against him. Let her find it and she must beg forgiveness for the wrong she has or has not committed. Nothing can be more fearful to her than the wound of the silent lord. But this woman here is laughing with Shpitz, uncaring of Milo's silence. A few hours ago she was playing the hussy with Félix by the Ark on Zion Square. Shpitz is laughing too, embracing his knees and repeating what sounds like a punch line 'She was the headmaster's wife dammit and she needed my shaving brush.'

Rudi comes back with Schwester Clara and a tea trolley. She doesn't waste time. Once the food is passed around she sets her perfectly arranged habit around her small stout body and looks us over from behind her glasses.

'I have heard about your Noah and the Flood. It is so unusual and even shocking to put it here on the street opposite the trial of the evil man. In public! We have plays, holy stories, in our school for the girls but always private, inside, behind our big walls. So no-one from outside will know. There is much anger here in the city. It waits to jump like the dead cat and the rotten tomatoes thrown over our wall. Your Noah is a Christian play and it will make a noise. The evil man is also a Christian. So it is not good for us. Somebody is always watching to set us on fire.'

We are all looking at Milo. Buddha doesn't move or show that he has heard. Félix red-faced and breathing through his nose takes over. He and Schwester Clara know each other well. He has found refuge in the convent in the past when he was in some crisis or had run out of money. He is her problematic younger brother. Félix stands silent for a while and I imagine him wrapping his cassock around himself to help him concentrate on his sermon. 'You are right Schwester Clara there is danger in it. But it's for us not for you. We are putting our necks on the block by making the end of the world worth attention to people who know about it only from a book which they read year in year out but forget in their daily lives. They will ridicule us for reminding them. How can God wear shoes? How can Noah be so impotent? How can a mighty wave swallow up the world beginning with Ben Yehuda Street and Zion Square? And why show it outside the trial? Why distract attention from the big crime inside when the victims are still here, in the line outside? They want to see this man face his crimes. They don't want to see the world given up for lost again. What have they done to deserve that? For God's sake what?'

Félix is redder than ever and the veins in his neck are standing out like electric wires. He has hit a climax in the argument by turning it against himself. He has put Noah in front of people who don't deserve to be drowned.

Schwester Clara intervenes. She raises a hand and points to one of the paintings on the wall. 'Did you forget, Félix? The world was saved, twice, by a righteous man. Once Noah and then Christ. If you could only show that to your audience there would be no place for resentment. And perhaps they would learn to follow the best example and forgive. Forgive the sins of the evil man.'

Milo emerges out of Buddha. He raises his head and looks at Schwester Clara with an open-mouthed stare as if she was a Gorgon with snakes in her hair. 'Forgive? That's a diversion. We have something more urgent to do. Schwester Clara, we are plotting a look at the end of the world. True, as Félix says, no-one wants to hear about that. And they can laugh at it because it seems comical. But really it's like an air raid drill. It isn't happening yet but you go through the motions and accustom your feet to act quickly and the mind to face collapsing walls and staircases. The church is a great builder, Schwester Clara. That's admirable. Your convent has thick walls and deep foundations. But the security they offer you is false, a trap. If you trust them they'll betray you. Suspicion of thick walls is what can save you. Not forgiveness.'

Schwester Clara's eyes grow large behind her glasses and her white forehead seems to gleam and vibrate but she says nothing and Milo goes on. He is rallying his armies after the defeat in the cellar.

'You want the people to forgive. I want to make them uncertain and suspicious of their own innocence. You will forgive the hooligans who throw dead cats over your walls. I value doubt over forgiveness and out there in the street outside the trial we need to make the case for doubt. Because the people are being told they are triumphant when they aren't. We are the other voice. We say the opposite of what everyone hears on the radio. So don't be afraid of anger against Christians. It will all be directed against us. We'll get the dead cats, not you. And there are no thick walls to protect us only a wood and paper Ark on a platform as we pretend to wait for the great wave that's going to wash everything away. And then comes Ararat and the story starts all over again.'

Milo isn't talking to Schwester Clara or to anyone. He's talking to himself. Not the general any more but a martyr to his mission of waking up people who don't think they are asleep.

Julius has been slumped in his chair, drowsing, his Humpty Dumpty head always ready to fall off its perch on his shoulders. The mention of Ararat pulls him up. He looks round the room and seems to count us.

'Where is Ham?'

Rudi looks worried. 'I think he followed me when I went to look for Schwester Clara. After that…'

Schwester Clara sweeps out of the room followed by Rudi. We sit there embarrassed. Eyob could be up to anything among the nuns and the schoolgirls. He is Ham after all. A few minutes later Rudi is back with Eyob, who is looking sheepish.

'I found Eyob in the kitchen, his mouth full of whatever the nuns were cooking. They had put a bib round his neck and were enjoying the spectacle. They don't see a really hungry man very often.'

Eyob pats his belly gently. We stare at him the way Jordan said people would at the play. We know him. I know him well but we all stare at him. He is Eyob, lithe and long-limbed, his face glowing and heavenly from the nuns' care.

Schwester Clara comes in and claps her hands.

'Our guests must leave. It is the evening hour. Although we disapprove, the Sisters will pray for you in your dangerous venture. And we will offer you refuge if the crowd in the street wants to break your bones.'

We troop out of the quiet courtyard through the thick wall and out into the unprotected city.

SANVY SANSANVY SAMANGALOFF

THE SCRAP OF purple ribbon felt like silk in Jordan's hand. She had found it between pages of Milo's copy of *The Anatomy of Melancholy* which she had taken off the shelf by mistake in her search for *A Thousand and One Nights*. Two Burtons side by side. Melancholy, suiting her mood, caught her eye and she opened it. *Melancholy baby.* Sinatra's drowsy voice called her as she peered at the small print.

Come to me my melancholy baby. Cuddle up and don't be blue.

He sounded so innocent, such a polite young short-haired suitor offering his sweetheart the cuddle cure. So no more melancholy, baby. Lucky girl. But her melancholy it wouldn't cure and Milo was not a cuddler. He pursued her with more complicated moves, the bite of the dragon and reverse chin lock. Such wrestling fended off his dark moods for a while but left hers intact. Not that melancholy was new to her but here it had been spreading its tent, enveloping her with feelings of emptiness and isolation. Attempts to keep in touch with her research were sporadic and increasingly the materials she had gathered in notebooks and diaries seemed like a half-forgotten language which had once exercised some power over her imagination. Where was Spanish Harlem? Where was she now?

Living here on the ridge over the deep valley in winter with its mists, its gusts of wind and sand over the stunted trees and caves seemed more and more incongruous. No domestic rituals could make the strange overpowering house a normal place to live in. Cooking in the tiny kitchen produced familiar smells and smoke and heat yet something uncanny hung over the most natural activity as if making soup was projected in silhouette against a huge white wall and watched by disembodied eyes. When she washed the floor she was amazed by the deep pink colour and the monumental breadth of the flagstones under the rugs and books and papers. They didn't belong in a living room with ashtrays and a gramophone. They were, she imagined, captives, deported survivors of some great hall of a monastery or a fortress now crumbled away into rubble. She had, nevertheless, adapted to the ways of the house even though the eccentric water heater in the shower made the groaning and wheezing noises of a sick camel and switching on the light started a war between fizzing and quivering fronts of electricity. She was often alone there and even when wrapped in warm blankets and lulled by the comforting ebb and flow of music she could in a moment feel unsafe as if a hole was opening up in the floor and the house was beginning to sink away with her, or worse without her, leaving her stranded on the couch next to a pile of rubble, alone.

Milo's temperamental behaviour became more predictable. In America it was his unsettling, extravagant strangeness that had set him apart from the young graduates and eligible men who were her friends. It drew her to him. She seized on it hungrily to steer herself away from the sedate comfort and honeyed good will of her family. Becoming his she could stop being the good daughter, accomplished, clever, marriageable, neat in all things and experiment with the evil arts by apprenticing herself to a sorcerer. It was a kind of servitude that offered her the thrill of breaking bounds, mental and physical, and let her taste the pleasures of offence. But it exacted a price. She stopped thinking for herself. She caught herself saying what he would say and anticipating his reaction to whatever she said or did. His approval was so necessary to her that she could sink into a torpor, a state of near-paralysis for fear of his disapproval. No-one could see this. Jordan struck everyone as more attractive than ever and happy in his company. Any disquiet she labelled cowardice and locked it away. So she followed him to the end of the world, to the house by the ruined Turkish bandstand.

The end of the world got smaller. In one direction you could go no further. Danger Border. In the other there was the town regarded with suspicion and disdain by Milo and his companions. This cul-de-sac was his element, narrow and circumscribed for all his worldliness. Here his angry melancholy was familiar, still threatening but also comical. Like all obsessions it had ovious weaknesses and could be dismissed as an affectation. But his companions tolerated him as the Professor of Darkness. His adoring students were under his spell and suspected nothing. To Jordan he was a wounded sorcerer, wounded by a love which hampered him by lasting too long, built him up and undid him, fed him and made him impatient. He was impatient with her but also with people he cared little for like the tribes who would line up one day to get into the trial. To express his impatience he would throw the Flood at them as if in some perverse way he could justify his anger and authenticate his misanthropy by wielding an age-old threat of universal destruction.

Even with the play in rehearsal Milo and Jordan never talked about the trial. But it was everywhere. As it came closer she heard words on the radio she had never heard before. They were alien forbidding sounds, the vocabulary of a system not revealed to her and place names on a map she had never consulted; *Umschlagplatz*, *Einsatzgruppen*, *Obersturmbannführer*, *Endlösung*, *Sobibor*, *Plaszow*, *Sonderkommando*. At first they were just ugly twisted sounds, then they turned into places and scenes brought into being, it was said, by the man whose small sharp face, mean brow and thin lips turned up in the same photographs day by day in all the newspapers.

She had put down the Post and, to chase the photograph out of her mind, had gone to look for a tale about cunning young wives and miserly husbands in *A Thousand and One Nights*. Instead she found *The Anatomy of Melancholy* and the ribbon. When she looked at it more closely she made out a row of Hebrew letters in ink faint and smudged but legible.

241

SANVY SANSANVY SAMANGALOFF

They made no sense. When Milo came home Jordan asked him about it.

'Look what I found in your book.'

She held the piece of ribbon in the palm of her hand. Something about it said: *Handle me carefully.* He was smoking one of Ada's Gitanes and pouring glasses of wine. He squinted in the direction of the ribbon. There wasn't much light in the room. Then he reached for it and laughed.

'What made you pick up Melancholy?'

'I guess I thought it was a self-help book. So what's the ribbon?'

'I lent the book to a student and she must have put it in there, a bookmark.'

Jordan left it at that but a while later she came back to the ribbon.

'What are those odd letters on the ribbon, a name, some kind of riddle?'

His head was in the cushions enveloped in smoke. 'No it's a spell.'

'A what?'

'Magic. It came up in a class. One of them wrote a paper about desire ungratified and occult ways of heating up desire. Burton is a great source. He's full of the maladies of love. You watch them spread through the bile and liver and kidneys. Then they eat up the brain and poison the imagination. It's sometimes repulsive, sometimes, but then there's a passage like this.' He turned some pages and began to read:

Love universally taken, is defined to be a desire, as a word of more ample signification: and though Leon Hebreus, the most copious writer of this subject, in his third dialogue makes no difference, yet in his first he distinguisheth them again, and defines love by desire. Love is a voluntary affection, and desire to enjoy that which is good. Desire wisheth, love enjoys; the end of the one is the beginning of the other; that which we love is present; that which we desire is absent.

242

'That's it. There it is, "that which we love is present; that which we desire is absent. The end of one is the beginning of the other."'

'The end of what?' she said.

'Desire.'

'Does he mean love begins when desire is over?'

'Probably but he also says that what you desire isn't here with you. She's absent.'

'And doesn't she become present?'

'Yes, but then it isn't desire any more.'

'So it's love. It's present and you have it but it sounds like second best, silver, not gold.'

'What you have is not what you want.'

'So where does magic come in?'

'To provoke and focus desire.'

'And the letters on the ribbon?'

'Listen. Here's another bit. He's good on the madness.'

But this love of ours is immoderate, inordinate, and not to be comprehended in any bounds. It will not contain itself within the union of marriage, or apply to one object, but is a wandering, extravagant, a domineering, a boundless, an irrefragable, a destructive passion…

He blew out some more smoke.

'She could have found a spell in some book and was trying it out.'

'In the spirit of research? So how did it get to you?'

'She left it in the book.'

'Who was she?'

'Ayala, maybe or one of the others, Zina.'

He seemed to be enjoying this. His eyes were half-closed and his head was comfortably propped against the cushions. This was the seat of a destructive, extravagant, irrefragable passion? Not likely. It was the head of an idol sated after being fed incense and the daily sacrifice. She knew.

243

He had been with Ayala or Zina or Tilly or Nadine.

She knew but she didn't care. His complacency made him ridiculous, like a cuckold, not one robbed of sex but one cheated with a grant of sexual favours. Ayala, Zina and the lot weren't deceiving him with someone else. They were deceiving him with Milo. They were collaborating in his self-deception by selling him the drug. Their soft skin and fragrant hair, their shining maidenly legs all fresh from the shower and prepared for the seigneurial embrace spun the web of the illusion he had become addicted to. Lucifer, the weakening rebel angel, had to have Ayala and Zina and their sisters to decorate his doom and people the fading, falling star which he pictured for them in his lectures.

Milo's eyes were closed and his face looked peaceful in spite of its deep furrows and the shadows under the eyes. He was at rest. Jordan stroked the ribbon and wondered what Ayala or Zina or Nadine had hoped to make happen with the spell. It could have been a light-hearted gesture, a parody of a black art. But why not a more serious gamble? Why not a desperate attempt by one of the maidens to win for herself the hidden heart of their Lord. Why not an attempt by magic to get hold of that heart, its blood, its slippery pumping muscles, its enveloping arteries to capture its secret and make the Master her prisoner for ever. Or perhaps kill him?

Jordan was surprised at her wheeling thoughts. She was not oblivious to the parallels between the maidens and herself. She had pretended to herself that her encounter with Milo was one of equals, a mutual fascination. He had listened to her with what she found to be interest and admiration. He knew nothing about Spanish Harlem and seemed to rely on her for information that was important to him. She could see even now his eyes fixed on her as she spoke, excited, about a healing prayer with its rhythms and shouts and smells in a small hot room in a tenement. They were thirsty eyes. He had told her she knew about secret things that made him feel blinkered and ignorant. Flattery, maybe but it encouraged her to open herself out to him. She was nourishing him as much as he was feeding her with his reckless rejection of a stable life. But as

244

their relationship deepened she found herself playing the part of his companion in distress or the nurse of his wound. His black moods and the anger, directed at himself as much as at others, when he would tear at himself in disgust, physically and verbally, drew out of her an almost maternal tenderness which he both tolerated and resented. She could see herself serving him like this for life, warming his trembling body, calming his rage, praising his daring and helping him live with the deceit he accused himself of practising.

Milo asleep, propped up against the cushions, didn't look as if he needed such dedication now. Simple services more frequent and in quantity would do. Deceit perhaps had ceased to disturb him and the ease with which he practised his spell had dulled in him the feelings of betrayal and anger which made people curious and then attracted them. She carefully arranged a blanket over him. Was she deluding herself that he needed her and that the dead end where they lived was, after all, a station on some unmapped way? Not a terminus?

She took the slip of ribbon and went to look for Julius. He would know about spells and magic letters. She had seen a roughly drawn amulet hanging on a wall over his two angry puppets. Julius said it was a peace-making amulet and would in the long run bring about at least an armistice between the warring dolls.

There was no light in the house but the door finally opened when she heaved at it with the full strength of her hip and shoulder. She stumbled into the dark room and called out for Julius. No-one answered and she felt her way along a wall till she found a switch. The light was dim and the room seemed empty and quite cold. At one end stood Julius's desk with its old typewriter and little mounds of paper and open exercise books. On the floor there were more mounds of paper, books, some oranges and sweaters, trousers, socks and slippers. But along the opposite wall there was a mattress with someone lying on it wrapped in a blanket and turned to the wall. Jordan called out. There was no answer. She drew nearer and saw Eyob's head thrusting out of the blanket. His eyes were closed but his breathing was agitated. She thought of leaving Julius a note but there was nowhere clear enough of clutter for him to find it. So she sat on the bed and waited.

The feuding philosopher puppets looked down on her from their wall with bulging eyes and beefy flat noses. They bore a distinct family resemblance. Like brothers, she thought, who could never agree about anything. The amulet was framed and hung on the wall. She squinted at it in the poor light and made out a crudely drawn figure half-animal, half-human with a bird's head and a woman's breasts. Lines of undecipherable Hebrew writing were arranged in loops and circles around the figure and in the centre, more boldly, three words stood out. These she could make out. SANVY SANSANVY SAMANGALOFF exactly those drawn on the ribbon in her pocket. She turned them over on her tongue and repeated them again and again. They beat a syncopated jazzy rhythm like 'Yessir that's my baby' or 'Five foot two eyes of blue kuchi kuchi kuchi chu.' The familiar beat undid the distance between her and the strange scrawls. They weren't necessarily threatening even if she had no idea what their power was. Julius had told her they were amicable charms and she was inclined to trust him in such matters. SANVY SANSANVY SANVY SANSANVY set her fingers drumming on one of Julius's bedside books when Eyob's head popped up. He looked at her with startled eyes.

'I am sorry. I am sleeping. I am very sorry. Julius is not here? It is cold and I go to lie down. Excuse me Mrs Noe.'

He motioned to her but she couldn't make out what he meant. He fidgeted in the bed then he motioned more graphically, grimaced and pointed in the direction of the shower while making circular movements with one hand. Then she understood he was asking her to turn round while he got out of bed and made for the toilet. She did and heard some scuffling and a door bang and then silence. It had got colder and she was looking for matches when Eyob came out. His brow was wet and he smelled of aftershave.

He stood by the desk silently watching her rummage in the kitchen.

'I make it warm,' he said and bent down to light the kerosene heater.

'I'll make some tea for us while we wait for Julius,' she said and took the box of matches from him.

As he handed her the matches he caught her hand and said 'Mrs Noe, you are my mother.'

Jordan turned quickly back into the kitchen.

'Yes, Eyob. In the play I am your mother.'

'You do not want to go in the Ark? You quarrel with Noe? He is not a good man?'

She tried to concentrate on the kettle and the tea pot.

'Noah is a good man, Eyob but Mrs Noah is…' she looked for the right word. 'Mrs Noah is a bit wild.'

'Wild? Wild like animals? But Mrs Noe is my mother.'

'Yes but she is free. She is not Noah's slave. She must do what she wants.'

She poured the boiling water into the tea pot. They were both silent for a while warming their hands on the hot mugs.

'Woman is free?' he said.

'Yes, just like a man. They are both free.'

'I am not free,' he said. 'I am staying in. I am only wearing black clothes. The master forbids me.'

'You are serving God,' she said and was ashamed at her stupid words. Her fake piety had nothing to do with Eyob's troubles.

'Noe is my father and he curses me because I look under his blanket. Is this why I am staying locked all of my life? I am young and I have strength. I can run far, even so far as Ethiopia. You can help me go to America?'

Eyob reached out over the table and took her hands.

'See how strong I am.'

His long fingers pressed hard against her wrists and moved up her forearm. He was holding her now by both arms and mumbling words she did not understand. His face was working in grimaces she couldn't read. She tried to free herself but his grip resisted.

'You must not hurt your mother Eyob. It is forbidden.'

247

'Ham is black and this is why Noe curses him. Which father curses his child? This is not forbidden?'

He was still holding her by both arms. She twisted her body and knocked over a mug spilling the hot tea over the table and her clothes.

Eyob released his grip.

Jordan wiped the table and her jeans with a dirty dish cloth while Eyob stared at the ground. Neither of them spoke.

'Take this,' he said, and drew a large handkerchief out of his pocket. It was a white square in her hand, embroidered with a red thread of letters in a strange alphabet.

'It is from my mother,' he said.

'*Geta yebarkih* God bless you.'

She gave it back to him.

'Show it to Noe,' he said. 'So he will not curse me. You can take it to him. He will listen.'

I will not pity him thought Jordan. I will not treat him as a child. I will not fall into that trap.

She reached into her jeans pocket and pulled out the purple ribbon.

'Look Eyob,' she said.

She gave it to him and he looked at it casually.

'This is for the hair of a girl, no?'

'There are words on it. Look Eyob.'

He looked more closely.

'What is that?'

'Hebrew' she said. 'SANVY SANSANVY SAMANGALOFF.'

'Say the words. Say them.' She repeated them,

'SANVY SANSANVY SAMANGALOFF
SANVY SANSANVY SAMANGALOFF'

and he followed her

'SANVY SANSANVY SAMANGALOFF
SANVY SANSANVY SAMANGALOFF'

And again

'SANVY SANSANVY SAMANGALOFF

SANSANSANVY SAMANGASNSANOFF'

Faster and faster they jumbled the words till they were shouting, stamping feet and banging on the table. The second mug toppled over and a pool of tea trickled onto the floor.

When Julius came in he saw them both on their knees, laughing and wiping the floor with his two dishcloths.

Jordan stood up and gave him a kiss.

'We got carried away by a spell and had an accident.'

'What spell?'

'*Sanvy sansanvy samangaloff*, the one on your amulet.'

He made a mock grave face and pressed his hands together in priestly fashion.

'You mustn't take those words in vain. They have to be used for their cause otherwise they lose their power.'

Julius warmed his hands by the stove and sat down with them at the table.

'Seriously,' he said, 'these are three angels SANVY stands on the right SANSANVY on the left and SAMANGALOFF in the middle and they are the only ones who can stop the demon Lilith murdering newborn babies. She sees them and runs away from the cradles.'

Eyob was agitated.

'Nazdi Eikamenn killed babies. Was he stopped?'

Julius looked at him, perplexed.

'Who?'

'Babies,' said Eyob. 'Many babies and children. Now he is caught by police and there will be judges. Nazdi Eikamenn. He is here.'

He pointed to a page of the Post spread under boxes of cereals by the sink. Peeping out between the cornflakes and the puffed wheat was the blurred grey photograph of the face with the narrow lips.

'Why did the angels not stop him?'

Jordan got up and tore the page to pieces.

'Why do we have to see this every day. How can people stand it? Day after day.'

'The papers have to keep showing that we actually caught him,' said Julius. 'But people want to see. They are trying to get press passes to peek at him in jail. They want to know what he eats and if he has any books? They want to know if he sleeps in pyjamas.'

'Why did they not stop him?' said Eyob.

'Angels are not there all the time,' said Julius. 'Most of the time they are nowhere and we can't find them to help. They are like air, we can call them but we can't see them.'

Eyob sighed and went back to his mattress. He pulled the blanket over his head and turned to the wall.

'Are you going to work tonight?' said Jordan

'Yes, the midnight shift.'

'Don't go, call them, I want to stay over.'

Julius looked startled.

'Has Milo gone off somewhere?'

'No, he's in the house.'

'Did something happen?'

'Nothing that hasn't happened before.'

Julius looked troubled and stared at his boots. He was silent for a long time. When he spoke he was firm and politic, Julius the character witness.

'He appeared out of the dark the first night I was here. I was sitting in this shell, right over there by the sink, with some candles and a leaking roof and he comes along, arranges for electricity, gets some cover for the roof and gives me Rochester's poems and a mattress. I ate with him every day after that. When I went over to his house there was always a woman there. Sometimes even the same one. He paid attention to them each in the same way, like cats. After a while I didn't much notice and he gave up trying to fix me up with some woman or other. I took too long taking off my boots, that's what he said. You have to be quick and certain like a fencer, like Rochester, he said.'

Julius looked at Jordan with his head tilted to one side and a trace of a blush on his brow. It was a shy look but also a frank one. She understood he was trying to be honest about his friend and at the same time asking for understanding. If he didn't much notice those cats in the background, neither should Jordan.

'You don't need to excuse him,' she said. 'I've had the list from Ada. She's kept count.'

What could she tell Julius? Milo weakened by Ayala, Zina, Nadine and company and locked into a bed of self-delusion was not a description he would recognize. It would be, in his eyes, a lie, a hateful caricature. Their friendship was Julius's anchor. Because of it he could endure the storms and earthquakes his mind surrendered to without doing harm to himself. She had seen him in Milo's study curled up in a corner on the floor with a blanket thrown around him crooning curses against himself and his enemies and God and someone called Uncle Bildad, sometimes even sitting in a pool of pee. Milo brought him drink and underwear and cleaned the pee and put an arm across his shoulders and said nothing but sat by his desk and smoked. He knew Julius would come out of it eventually. The important thing was his presence, near but not too near and silent. *His* presence, never hers. He did not let her into it.

'Let me stay here tonight. I'll be gone tomorrow.'

'I haven't got enough towels.'

'We'll share.'

She opened the fridge. There were two eggs in it, a dish of olives, something that might have been a radish and a cube of white cheese.

'Are you hungry?' she said.

He looked at her, startled as if the material reality of her staying had just hit him.

'Did you have a quarrel?'

'No, I left him sleeping.'

'Did you leave a note?'

'No. I thought I'd just look at your amulet and find out how it can help me.'

'Help you?'

'With this.'

She took the purple ribbon out of her pocket.

Julius fingered it like a leaf of thin gold.

251

'Somebody wrote the angels' names, the angels who guard against Lilith. Who gave it to you?'

'I found it in a book of Milo's, a book a student borrowed. Maybe Ayala or Zina. Maybe Nadine.'

Julius looked worried and put the ribbon down as if it had turned electric and burned his fingers.

'Why would a student want to put this spell in the book? What was the book?'

'*The Anatomy of Melancholy*. In Milo's seminar, he said, they were doing work on desire and magic.'

Julius put a finger to his forehead and stared at the names as if they were dangerous bacteria.

'They got it wrong, whoever wrote the names. They went up the wrong path. Lilith is a killer, a baby killer because she hates Eve's children. It's the subversive creation story, the anti-Genesis. She is Adam's first woman and they quarrel because she wouldn't lie under him. So she left. Lilith had to be on top, always.' Julius's forehead was reddening by the second.

So I'm Lilith, thought Jordan. The foreign woman. They want to spook me away and why not try those names?

'How would the amulets be used against Lilith?'

'By hanging them over the bed where the woman with the child slept. Amulets and garlic and coins. I'll get it down.'

As Julius went into the other room Jordan worked out the plot against her. They (or was it she) hid the spell among the books to spy on the bed where she slept with Milo. The big bookshelf was opposite with the bed in full view. SANVY SANSANVY SAMANGALOFF were put there to spoil her embraces and hinder her blood. She could imagine them giggling as she guided Milo's head down on her belly. They were deriding her lovemaking, calling her a selfish suburban bitch, waiting for her to press down over her lover so they could curse her by the name of Lilith, the man-rider, the succubus.

The amulet itself, written on cheap paper, looked puny and ill-formed in Julius's hand. The writing from close up was spotty and irregular and the drawing of the bird with breasts had no force. It was a poor man's amulet if it wasn't a fake, scratched out in the Bokharan market for tourists. Only the names SANVY SANSANVY SAMANGALOFF stood up boldly, perhaps the forger out of fear had called in a true scribe to write them.

The door rattled and Milo walked in.

'I was looking for you. You disappeared.'

He had not bothered to put a coat on and was looking dishevelled. The bags under his eyes were dark and deep and his beard was unbrushed.

He touched the amulet on the kitchen table.

'Where's the witch?'

'Here,' said Jordan. 'I am the witch.'

'Then you're in the right place, m'amie. This house is full of spooks. Julius feeds them.'

Jordan felt him looking at her and turned away so their eyes would not meet.

'Tell me, chuck, it's about the ribbon isn't it. You figured it out, Lilith and the three stooges. Don't say you're pestered by this voodoo talk. It's a sickness. You catch it from an overdose of monotheism. Students fall for it.'

He made a lunge for the amulet but Julius pressed it to his chest as if protecting his baby. He lit a cigarette and sat down.

'Satan and Eros is a big hit, you know. I get better students and they're motivated. They talk about it, so people think I'm some kind of shaman. The Faculty of Black Arts. That's shit. But I do hit on subversive ideas that were ignored or censored and repressed. Students are drawn in, some too much.'

'Especially the women,' said Jordan.

'There are no men,' said Milo.

She imagined him in the classroom, half posing, half transported, speaking in a careful vibrato. He is Don Giovanni contemptuous of Hell. He is Lucifer, preaching rebellion to the angels. Excited among the girls, Amalya, Zina and Nadine feel their hearts beat faster and a creeping dampness moisten their limbs.

253

What stops them all from rushing out of the university gates onto the street to assault and tear at any symbol of authority, a policeman, a soldier, a bus stop?

'It's not a sickness,' said Julius. 'It's an attempt to build a bridge over darkness. People are terrified. You can't laugh at that. Babies die.'

Milo was silent. Looking at him Jordan saw an older man leaning on the table. The rebel angel had been marked by deepening lines across the brow and under the eyes, the rich black of the hair was robbed of its gloss by Julius's naked kitchen light and the neck and shoulders were burdened and bent over. He seemed to be putting all his energy into drawing the tobacco into his lungs and keeping the tip of his cigarette bright and flaming red.

He got up and as he walked out he said, 'Come let's go.'

She didn't follow him.

For a while she and Julius sat opposite each other at the kitchen table with the amulet between them. Not looking at her he whispered something as he traced the outlines of the bird with a finger.

'What's that, Julius?'

He moved his finger round and round the bird, humming.

'She's been in a quarrel. I've got to pacify her. It isn't just decoration, you know. At night when the searchlight from the border patrol hits the window the bird lights up. After the night shift she's the first thing I see when I open the door and switch on the light. When you're by yourself you bring all kinds of things in to live with you. They're company. You rely on them. You speak to them and they answer, sometimes.'

He touched her hand.

'You don't think I'm mad.'

She took his hand in hers and put it to her cheek. It was a rough wrinkled hand, dry and warm.

'Never,' she said. 'You're as sane as anybody this side of the border. You're so sane that the cats line up like skittles outside your door to get their cheese and milk. You're the most reliable man for miles and I love you.'

The blush on him was ferocious. It surrounded his eyes and

254

tinged the tips of his ears. She noticed his eyelashes were long and feathery in contrast with the severe dark curve of his eyebrows.

Julius looked at her, worried.

'If you want to stay here tonight I'll go over to Tomas's.'

'No, stay here, stay with me. I'll be one of the things that come in for a while and you speak to them and they answer, sometimes. I can do that better than puppets or chairs.'

She had made him smile. Something in what she had said had chased away embarrassment and fear. She had placed herself in the society of his constant neutered companions and put aside for the while her difference and strangeness as a real woman.

'Come,' she said and led him onto the main room. 'You put the amulet back in place. I'll go and get some food and make supper.'

Before he could answer she had stepped out and made her way to Milo's house.

She had acted on impulse not knowing what she would say if she found him at home. But the house was empty and she put food for supper in a bag with a bottle of wine and some candles. They would have a banquet.

When she got back he was sweeping the kitchen floor wearing a fresh shirt.

'The house is empty,' she said. 'Milo's not there.'

'Do we need a tablecloth?' he said, 'because I got one from the Post for a New Year's present. I've never used it.'

He pulled it out from under some pots and a frying pan. It was a white nylon sheet bearing bright blue silhouettes of Ben Gurion and Theodor Herzl crowned by garlands of olive leaves.

'It's another amulet,' said Jordan. 'Old men watching over us while we eat.'

She set about cooking an omelette while Julius searched in corners and drawers for plates and glasses. He knocked over a pot and quickly Eyob appeared.

'You are cooking,' he said.

'Come and eat, Eyob,' said Jordan. She had forgotten about the sleeper on the mattress by the window.

They sat at the table awkwardly without talking till Eyob noticed the figures on the tablecloth.

'Who is this?' he said pointing.

'Idols,' said Julius.

'They are forbidden in the Book.'

'Yes, but people want idols. So they print pictures of them.'

'And you eat on that?'

'It's all we've got and we don't look at them.'

'He's joking,' said Jordan. 'It's not idols, Eyob. They are leaders of the people.'

Eyob had lost interest and was eating with passion. Julius opened the bottle of wine.

They drank and ate mostly in silence. Eyob seemed intimidated by the company and kept his head mostly down over his plate until, sated, he looked up then gestured around the table in a wide embrace.

'Mother Noe, you have two sons here. You have Shem and Ham. So where is Noe?'

'I know where he is. Noe drunk too much wine and so he sleeps.'

He laughed.

'He sleeps and makes whistles in his nose like Julius.'

Eyob's laughter embarrassed Jordan. The mention of Julius snoring was oddly uncomfortable. It was like a family secret brought up impolitely at the table by a rebellious child. We make a strange trio, she thought. Two runaways and their host in a house with talking chairs and quarrelling dolls. Two runaways, but she was different. She resented Eyob's claim on Julius's hospitality because it robbed hers of its novelty. Now she was just another candidate for a place to sleep in the big room. She had come to Julius on impulse, with the ribbon and the spell and her anger but also with a half-admitted desire, to face him unmasked. Was Julius's shyness and eccentricity a way of painting over a wound, camouflage for a shame he was afraid to admit? She thought of persuading him to be open to her, by speaking frankly about herself. He trusted her and he

256

might let her get beyond his maze-like defences. To what? The elaborate masquerade he lived in was fascinating but also frustrating. It couldn't be all there was. What would happen if he was moved to abandon it in her company? Was it dangerous? Could he set down the shadow puppets and phantoms and come out alive from behind the white sheet? Could she touch a nerve and wake up a different Julius? And how could any of this happen with Eyob around?

Eyob's laughter at the thought of Noah and Julius snoring had died down and he was sitting at the table fidgeting, ill at ease in the silence.

Jordan wished him gone, back to the monastery to check his mail, down the hill to Hebron Road to sit at a bus stop, up the hill to St Andrew's to get a cup of tea from the Scottish minister. But in reality there was nowhere for him to go. Julius was staring at his plate as if he was aiming to burn a hole through the fine cracks in the china. In the dark outside some cats were wailing.

'Bildad is on the prowl,' he said.

I will lose him, thought Jordan. I will lose him if he makes a run for the neighbourhood spirits. I must turn them away.

'Dessert,' she said. 'Milo gets homemade Tiramisu from one of his colleagues' wives.' She didn't mention he bartered a few joints for it.

'There's a full moon,' said Julius. 'After dessert we'll go for a walk; you've never been to Government House where the Brits put their High Commissioners.'

'I am always tired,' said Eyob. 'I will go to sleep.'

In her hurry to bring the food from Milo's house Jordan hadn't noticed how bright the night was. The sky was a velvet cloth punctured by sparks and the moon's clock face hung from invisible wires over the desert. They walked side by side.

Hearing the clump clump of his boots on the gravel, Jordan abandoned herself to their rhythm without paying much attention to the route they were taking. There was no wind and, surprisingly, it wasn't cold. Eventually, after some climbing, they were walking along the ridge towards Government House, the Hill of Evil Counsel.

The hollow, empty palace lay along its hill like a grey crocodile beached on rock.

'The guards know me,' said Julius. 'They're only supposed to let UN cars in but if you're just a walker and they know you, it's OK.'

The barrier in front of them gleamed white across the narrow approach road. In the cabin by the roadside a man was sitting and smoking.

Julius went over by himself and after a brief conversation the barrier was pushed aside.

'I bring them a pack of American cigarettes when I've got some. They're OK.'

Soon they were in what remained of a formal garden with sunken flower beds and graceful terracing. At its centre there was a fountain and a dry ornamental pool. There was no debris. It was almost surgically clean, as if a posse of gardeners were employed just to keep it tidy and ready for the return of an imperial governor or Roman ProConsul to control the unruly city nestling on the lower ridge opposite.

Julius led the way into a small stone structure which might have been a sheltered belvedere. It smelled pleasantly enough of dried grass and herbs. They sat down on a ledge and Julius took a paper bag out of a pocket. It was full of roasted watermelon seeds. Jordan had never mastered the local art of splitting the kernels between her front teeth to tease out their salty heart. Instead she got a tongue tipped with gritty sawdust. 'You're American, you'll never get it right,' she was told. But she took a handful and watched Julius pop seed after seed into his mouth, catch them, tongue them into position and split them with a click. The salty heart was eaten and the debris made its way out of his mouth and into his pocket with no sign of effort or litter. It was a way of pacing the hours and taming worry. Like the worry beads of Arab shopkeepers, it befriended time. You forgot the clock and measured the minutes with teeth and lips and tongue. You could go on for ever or till you had enough.

She said, 'How do you do it?'

'I watch the delivery boys at the paper. I can teach you.'

He took her face gently in one large hand and with the other he placed a watermelon seed carefully in between her teeth. It was like a dentist's probe but tender and delicate.

His large face moved close to hers in the half light and his eyes focused intently on her mouth.

'Cut down on it, as if it was a small chocolate bean.'

Was he making fun of her? No, he sounded serious, concerned for her to get it right.

She pictured a small chocolate bean but when she sliced down with her teeth the seed collapsed into gritty dust again. She had no handkerchief and spitting it away with Julius so close was an embarrassment.

He tore off a piece of the bag and gently wiped her tongue and lips with it.

The touch was so intimate it unbalanced her.

She took his hand and placed it on her throat.

'Who's playing doctor?'

With no hesitation he kissed her throat and with a quick pressure of his arms on her shoulders he laid her down opposite him on the ledge. Side by side, face to face and still, they were stretched now like a monument on a tomb. But after his quick movement he seemed lost and remained stock still. She drew him closer till their foreheads touched and her breasts felt his warmth. When she kissed him he responded with a kiss and a sigh.

'Where's the pain, doctor?' she said.

She led him at first slowly and with hesitation along the paths of her body, unwinding a thread to guide him. He moved as if he was blind or uncertain who she was. She was his guide but he resisted, seemingly not knowing whether to trust or fear her. She led him along a path that made him stop for breath at every step.

259

The irregular rhythms of his breathing she heard as a plea for help and answered with patient moves of her body. Blotted against each other as they were, the dark was total. Then for a second his head over hers was lit up by a flash. It was a torch. One of the guards on patrol had walked by outside. In that moment she caught his eyes staring, unnaturally white and a grimace of pain and tension over his mouth and jaw. She enveloped him in her arms, breasts and limbs as much as she could to comfort him and wrap him in a warm cocoon but he began to tremble uncontrollably. Then with a shout 'BEULAH BEWARE BEULAH!' he broke away from their embrace.

He sat on the ledge huddled over with his arms sheltering his head as if to ward off blows. Then with a quick lunge he pulled off one of his boots and threw it out of their shelter. 'BAGGAGE,' he shouted into the dark. He kept his eyes fixed on the darkness outside. Jordan moved away along the ledge. Where had she wanted to lead him? Did she know what she was doing? She was ashamed of her light-headed presumption that she could release him from his demons. Instead she had lost him. The moment of their intimacy had not prevailed against the currents that pulled him further and further away. She had misunderstood the masquerade. It was not camouflage but part of his running battle with chaos and she blamed herself for not taking this seriously. She reached out and touched his shoulder. It was bent under his burden but he got up, looked at her blankly and shuffled out to find his boot.

A wind had risen and they walked home fast in the cold. Jordan folded her arms around herself to preserve some warmth. As they approached the Turkish bandstand some cats were wailing and a light went on in one of the windows nearby.

When they reached Julius's door he took her hand.

'I'll give you the spell and you'll go back,' he said and darted into the room. He came back with the ribbon. She took it and turned to walk back to Milo's house.

He was in bed asleep with *The Anatomy of Melancholy* open beside him.

Jordan put the ribbon with its spell under her pillow. In the morning Lilith would wake him up with her demand. They would wrestle and she would smother him while Sanvy Sansanvy and Samangaloff, envious, impotent and breathless, choked beneath their weight.

Blood Frogs Lice

Something akin to Julius's phantom quake was approaching the city and it wasn't coming from the earth. The mighty tectonic plates under the Syrian African Rift seemed not to be moving. Those great blocks were perhaps not snug and quiet down there but apparently still in place in their fiery home. Above them, in the city, people walked on solid earth, now drying into dust after the winter rains. Over by the ceasefire line the ground also seemed firm enough. The balustrades of the ruined Turkish bandstand had not shed any more masonry and the cracks in the walls of Julius's house had not spread or shifted as far as he could tell. So the Syrian African Rift was biding its time. But an earth-shaking movement was indeed happening, calculated not by the sensitive dials and digits of the Richter scale but by the calendar, the diary and longer days and shorter nights.

Passover was approaching like a big ship making waves, steaming into port closely followed by its younger but more popular sister, Easter. Crowds would soon flood the city. The great festivals would clash, each in its space separated by borders and walls and barbed wire yet sending to each other rumbles of disturbance and upheaval. Some of the crowds would pour into one half of the city, rich in its relics and monuments. Some into the other half, into its bareness, disorder and neglect. On the one side old Cypriot women in black prepared for the miraculous fire of Resurrection to emerge from the Holy Sepulchre through the usual fight between the

262

Armenians and Greeks. Meanwhile, in the market they bartered cans of olive oil for sustenance while Franciscan monks swept the dust of the alleys and streets with the hems of their cassocks. On the other side families prepared for the Paschal sacrifice marked by a week's abstention from bread. In the cause of breadless purity normally sedate and empty streets became alive with tension and business. Expanses of neglected concrete were cleaned and whitewashed. Metals on door knobs, doctors' plates and banisters were polished. Walkways were weeded. Flowers planted in boxes. Books shaken and slapped. Soot was expelled from ovens and chimneys. New curtains were hung over glass so freshly pure that the world looked paradisal. Entire kichens were dismantled, sink by stove, and put together again stripped of a year's worth of detritus and droppings. Balconies, usually empty and neat, filled up with banished chairs, tables, mats, cribs, carpets, mattresses, washed and unwashed laundry while, inside, the work of cleaning went on through empty rooms. Shops greeted the coming event with a great show of newness in everything. Pyramids of cups and plates in dull white, pale yellow and prissy blue, sat in windows alongside cutlery snug in fake wooden boxes like chess sets. Imitation crystal decanters presided over arrays of wine glasses parading above each other in neat ranks. Tablecloths waited in piles to be spread out in their Terylene finery and suffer the spilt wine and heavy stains of family meals. In food shops sections of shelves disappeared under white sheets like shrouds. These were the forbidden foods, contaminated by their association with bread and sent into quarantine for the duration of the festival. People in need of them would have to stockpile and enjoy their guilty pleasures at home, behind closed shutters and in the dark.

Yet the clash of the great festivals was not the deepest cause of turbulence. The Christian fire of Easter and the smoke of long extinct Hebrew sacrifices could live together, side by side, here because they were separated. They were like unfriendly farmers bound to an ancient quarrel yet ploughing fields that touched each other. Close but distant. The approaching tremors had another darker origin, heard on the Voice of Israel Radio in the Hebrew, English, Hungarian, Yiddish, French and Arabic news bulletins, heralded in the large black print of newspaper headlines. At their epicentre was the grey blob of a face that looked like a bacterial specimen enlarged under glass.

Only X more days till the trial. He had a book. He was reading. The Bible. Not the Bible. He had lawyers. They were bad men, good men. They were interested in the finer points of law. They were secretly Nazi sympathisers. They were scrupulous, unscrupulous. They were Germans. He was apathetic. Nervous. Hungry. Watched. Examined by doctors. Never in the dark. Washed. Fed. Was drugged. In Buenos Aires. Injected. Argentina objected. Was bundled up. Spoke. Was silent. He was on the way to be tried and would get to the hall at the top of Ben Yehuda Street after Passover.

But first *our* tables were to be set for the Seder and the reciting of the Exodus story. The wine was to be poured. The family was to sit down to the festival meal. The words were to be spoken, by *us*, over the flat squares of fresh, crisp, virgin Matza.

THIS IS THE BREAD OF AFFLICTION.

Rudi wanted back to Oakland. Nuremberg and Passover were hunting him in dreams and making him sweat at night. The courtroom came as a clear, frozen image; a palimpsest over another more fluid image of the Passover meal with American soldiers in the base. The courtroom was silent. The accused sat in rows. The guards stood stiffly. The judges sat impassively. It was like a wax museum. Madame Tussaud's, cold and bloodless and he was observing it from high up, a bird in the rafters.

The Passover meal with the soldiers was full of noise. Ranks of uniformed men and women sat at long tables covered with white cloths. They were singing and chanting. It was a dream of sound rather than sight and he was in the middle of it, hearing noise. Words and phrases resounded in no particular sequence or order. They clashed and were repeated. They began with a tune and went on to split into competing tunes. But sometimes the entire hall

would ring and echo with a loud chant. Rudi at first couldn't make
out the words. He guessed what they must have been. They were
from the Passover Haggadah recitation, words he had heard as a
boy at home. But in his dream he wasn't sure he heard them. Not
clearly. He woke up with them on his lips.

'What?' said Ulli.

Rudi was silent.

'What did you shout?'

'I shouted?'

'Yes, out loud.'

'I never talk in my sleep.'

'You did. It sounded like: *Now do do*. It didn't sound happy.'

'I dreamed of Nuremberg.'

'The trial?'

'No, the Seder. The Seder with the Americans. It was their
singing. I must have mouthed the words and they woke me. Was it
a tune?'

'No, a croak. *Now do do. Die you do*, or something.'

Rudi knew it. He had woken up with that word, the chant that
rang through the hall in Nuremberg like a football cheer. It was the
word he remembered most clearly from his father's measured
recitation because it was more mellifluous, easier on the ear than
other Hebrew words. It had soft consonants and cooing vowels with
a harmonious and flattering sound.

DA YE NU.

It would have been enough.

His father read it in German as well for emphasis: '*Es hätte uns
genügt.*'

What would have been enough? It didn't trouble him as a boy.
IT would have been enough. OK. *Dayenu* and all that. It was one
of the many lists in the evening's chanting. Something to do with
adding up all the good things that happened to us, any one of which
would have been enough. It joined the other lists. The plagues:
blood, frogs, lice. Miracles, questions. Chants: Who knows one, Who
knows two? It was a counting game with a delicious meal attached.

But Nuremberg was his first Seder without his father and the war just over. Lurking behind the noise of hundreds of young men and women in uniform singing and stamping their feet was his father's thin voice quavering over the white table cloth and the crystal decanter. *Es hätte uns genügt.*

And the soldiers yelling *Dayenu!*

He remembered looking at the English in the Army-issue booklet.

It would have been sufficient.

It would have been sufficient.

It would have been sufficient.

Here again was the list of happy escapes and lucky breaks endured by the Children of Israel on their long journey from Egypt to the Promised Land. And they were too much. One lucky break would have been enough. Thank you dear God but you really overdid it. It was grotesque, this devious list of thankyous for too many good things which wouldn't cease but kept pouring out like the flush of coins from an overheated gambling machine. Rudi felt much older than the soldiers around him even though he was younger than many of them. He alone knew what the words covered up. The people were happy with those things that *would have been enough* because they were alive. But it was a fraud. The lucky breaks were fantasies repeated by his father out of respect for the old words and by the soldiers at Nuremberg to cheer themselves up in the teeth of all the evidence. The singing was there to drown the truth and he, Rudi, knew the truth. It wasn't happy and he didn't want to join in the singing. But wasn't he one of them? Wasn't Rudi one of the lucky beneficiaries of unnecessary miracles? Hadn't he been saved?

The chant in his dream grew shrill with repetition. Red-faced soldiers near him were singing. The tables rattled as feet stamped to the rhythm of the word. It banged on his skull. They banged on the tables. The entire hall was filled with one word, the word on his lips as he woke up. It was a warning. He had to leave, go back to Oakland before Passover, before the trial. If he stayed he would lose his way. He would be forced to enlist. World Peace through Language Learning, Spelling Olympics, International Syntax Games, Verbal Table Tennis – all would recede into the distance and sink under the burden of repeated, determinedly happy *dayenus*. *Dayenu* would recruit him and dress him up in a white robe. His name would be added to the list of miracle recipients. He would rejoice at Pharaoh's sinking chariot and stagger under the weight of looted Egyptian treasure. He would be funneled into the long wandering through the desert and told to shout *dayenu* by every well and miraculous trickle of water. Yet *dayenu* was the word he, even he Rudi May, Nuremberg translator, couldn't control. What did it really mean? *Es hätte uns genügt?* It challenged him like a call to mortal combat and he had no ready answer, only panic and the urge to flee. *Dayenu* was the war cry of the horsemen galloping in pursuit. It was the name of his captor who claimed he was his brother. *Dayenu* would be tattooed on his arm as a token of identity and belonging.

'We are going back,' he said to Ada.

'Why, why now when the trial is on the way. Don't you want to see how the young translators cope? You're not jealous, are you? And what about Noah and the Flood? Don't you want to see what happens?'

'I've got to get back to my project. There are funds to raise and I have to be there to deal with the Babel Foundation. They don't need me here. Milo's play will be a catastrophe and he'll enjoy the riot and the scandal. I see the whole thing is leading me astray. From Oakland I can see the ocean and know where I can go and what I can do. Here I'm pushed into corners. I feel hunted, locked in. And Perla.'

Ada looked at his handsome troubled face. Bubi again. Bubi the charmer, worn and creased but still uneasy, the quick mover and escape artist. Once he had fled for his life with the Swiss dancer. Now he felt the breath of pursuit again on his neck. Who was after him?

'It's that time of year, it's the Seder isn't it?'

He probably dreaded sitting down to the Passover meal with

Perla and Suzi and their stories of Vienna and all the family history and being quizzed about what he remembered and why he had forgotten.

'It doesn't have to be at Perla's,' she said. 'We can have it here. Père Félix wants us to lay the table at the Soeurs de Sion. That's even unusual enough to get Milo interested and Schwester Clara has developed a soft spot for the Noah people. She's afraid about what will happen when the trial starts and wants to offer a refuge.'

'You mean a Seder with nuns?'

'Well, Schwester Clara and one or two other seniors. They've got a nice room where they entertain visiting bishops and they'll set it up perfectly for us. Félix has been going into the details. We can cook our own meal so it won't cost them anything. Rudi, this is something you know about. Is Seder in a nunnery so unlike Peacemaking through Language Learning? It's right there, an ancient conflict and old enemies reading a book together. Stay. Oakland can wait.'

Ada hoped she hadn't sounded flippant but Rudi seemed to be considering her point.

He brushed the tip of his fine nose with a finger and his clear blue eyes met hers frankly.

'The Seder business doesn't give me a thrill you know. It was Ulli who made me go back home and I've been having bad dreams about Nuremberg and Passover there. But what you say does make sense. If we had it at the convent it could be a kind of experiment, an original way of getting out of Egypt so it includes everybody. The Catholic sisters bring Jesus and Milo brings Satan and Père Félix brings Don Juan. It would be an Exodus open to all comers.'

There was more than a trace of enthusiasm in his voice and he seemed to have dismissed the threat of Perla's inquisition. He had changed again quickly from Bubi the escapist to Rudi May the reformer, the liberal explorer in search of the passage to a better world.

'I'll talk it over with Ulli.'

*

268

Meanwhile Milo had been interrogated by the police.

He was contacted by someone called Raban who said he had been his student in the Satanic Rebellion seminar and was now in the police. Could they have a talk one day at the police headquarters in the Russian Compound? Milo was expecting it and was tickled he would be seeing a policeman who had studied the plot to overthrow God with him. When he walked through the Turkish courtyard by the lock-up where drunks and thieves were kept for the night he passed a cluster of women with food and blankets waiting for visiting time. Sitting on a stool near them was a man with a typewriter ready to write petitions for a price. He gave the typist some money and told him to do the petitions for free. The man said nothing and pocketed the cash. The women stared. He should have given money to each of them. Useless gesture. He hurried on to find Raban who was sitting in a cubicle with a shabby desk, a phone, and a photograph of Simone Signoret on the wall. She was the girl in *Casque d'Or*. Her moody, hopeless eyes stared out at her sisters, the women by the prison entrance.

Raban was friendly. He shook hands and gestured at the peeling paint and small window.

'Why this is hell nor am I out of it.' You see I haven't forgotten, professor. You made me feel damnation. Like hell is here in this room, not in some cellar with fire and torture.'

Milo was flattered and intrigued that one of his few male students had become a policeman with a lively sense of what a desperate soul endured. Then Raban started, 'You're setting up a performance outside the court on the day the trial begins?'

'Yes.'

'We understand it is about the Flood.'

'You are well informed,' said Milo, 'the Flood, the Ark, the end of the world. The few survivors.'

'Do you really mean to set this old story on a stage in the street with the Nazi inside and the whole world watching?'

'That's exactly why. The world is watching for the Nazi but they'll have us to watch as well.'

269

'Who is us?'

'Just people…'

'So who wrote it?'

'Probably a monk in England ages ago. But we changed things. We added and cut quite a lot.'

'God is in it isn't he?'

'Certainly, God is the star.'

'You expect an audience in Jerusalem to stand quietly by while you put God on a stage in a Christian play?'

'They don't have to be quiet. They can yell. It's the street after all. And the story isn't Christian, it's our story.'

'So why are you doing this?'

Raban's tone had become less friendly.

'The Nazi is our obsession, you can see that. You see the papers. Nothing else except us and him. Us and him. It's driving us crazy and we can help balance things with this play. It's also about a disaster but it's not about us – not specifically, that is. It's about everybody, Jews, Arabs, Christians, Mongols, Eskimos, Japs. The Flood happens to everybody.'

'So why is that important now to us?'

'We're in the same boat. Or more exactly we're in the same water, or we would be if the world went under again.'

'But that's absurd. Why should the world go under and why should you be warning people about this in the street outside the trial?'

'Noah wasn't a Jew.'

'What's that got to do with it?'

'Whatever bad things happened to us in the past doesn't mean we are insured against the next disaster. We're not. We're in the front line and we should know it.'

'Maybe, but right now we are dealing with the Nazi and his crimes. That's the real disaster. It happened. There are people here it happened to. So what's the point of bringing up this old wives' tale? Where are the bodies of the millions who drowned? Where are the children and the pregnant women? Where are the piles of

270

boots and gold teeth? Your flood is trivial, who cares about it? They'll laugh at your bits of painted wood and cardboard. Zion Square on wheels! We know you've got it there in your cellar. It's a joke and it's disrespectful. We can't have nonsense like this causing a disturbance in the street outside the trial. But if you do it we'll arrest you. Call it off professor. Take your friends and your doll's house and show them off to the faculty on Students Day. Is the Devil in it?'

Milo felt Simone Signoret's mournful gaze directed at him. He looked back. She was resigned to her fate. It was her beauty had laid the trap and the guillotine waited for her doomed lover. Milo felt tears of anger welling up for her and Serge Reggiani. He saw the prison steps and felt the hands pushing Serge to execution. Raban was waiting for him to speak.

'I have nothing but contempt for the police.'

The brutal gendarmes were dragging Serge to his death and no-one dared protest.

'Nothing you do will stop us.'

He stared over Raban's head at Simone. She would accept his defiance as a tribute. It couldn't save Serge but all was not lost as long as there was some resistance.

Paris, Jerusalem, Berlin, Madrid, Budapest; it didn't matter as long as there was some resistance.

Raban got up.

'Think it over professor. These are serious times. Leave child's play to children. I mean it in a friendly way.'

Milo left the office without shaking hands. The women at the gate were gone but the man with the typewriter was still there.

Milo went over to him. He pushed a handful of coins at him. 'Write,' he said.

'To Inspector Raban,
    We are worried about the future. We have it on
reliable information that there is to be a mighty flood
which will drown everything, men, women, children,

271

synagogues, police stations, kindergartens and schools. As you know the trial of the Nazi will soon take place in this city. This will also create a mighty wave, of emotion, anger, shame, pity and disgust enough to threaten the sanity of this nation. Though neither the great flood nor the trial can be prevented, we urge preparation. For the water, strong high places, bunkers, sandbags, flood walls, shelters, civil defence guards. All these are of no use but should be prepared. It will prevent rioting as hope is a great pacifier. For the trial, hours of tranquil music on the radio would ease the tension. Also we recommend the unrestricted import of choice foods and luxury goods from Europe and free showings of comic films – for example Danny Kaye, Bob Hope or Charlie Chaplin.

In past disasters a remnant of our nation was always saved. A few will be spared this time. If you wish to be one of them, allow us to perform the Flood and we will find a berth for you on the Ark, though you should bring no luggage.

Noah, Shem, Ham, Japheth, and wives.

The typist tapped out the letter laboriously showing no interest. He clearly wrote about disasters all the time, though probably few petitions contained such a brazen offer of a bribe.

'Where do I put it?' asked Milo.

The man pointed to a battered tin box by the gate. Milo went up to it, folded the page neatly but didn't drop it in.

This Night Is Different

THE RECEPTION ROOM at the Soeurs de Sion had an unusual, airy look. The sunlight flowing gently through the windows tossed little puffs of dust from beam to beam. The nuns had polished all the heavy mahogany chairs and burnished the copper and pewter bowls and vases till they shone with an unearthly light. Flowers in white and yellow with lilies for Mary were everywhere and bushels of fragrant herbs from the garden spilled over shelves and nooks. The large windows, newly washed, watched over the central table like martial angels. After some sharp words with other senior nuns, Schwester Clara had removed a large, gaudily coloured Passion from the wall and put in its place a smaller reproduction of the Last Supper by a minor Italian painter. She liked the touch of the sleeping apostle with his head on the table next to Christ. It gave the scene a warm, domestic look and didn't children fall asleep at the Seder table? Three popes in a row looked down sternly from the opposite wall. To remove them would have fomented rebellion among the sisters. The church needed to overlook the proceedings, however uncatholic they were.

In fact they would be less so than might have been thought as Félix had taken on the task of master of ceremonies. Milo wasn't even asked for obvious reasons so Ada had turned to Père Félix.

'You know more about the history and the language than most of us and you've got a foot in both camps.'

Félix was flattered and, though estranged from the official

273

church, he was glad to take on this ceremony as a primitive Christian, borderline Jewish though uncircumcised and closer to Galilean Jesus than the three moon-faced popes on the wall.

A sense of occasion had affected the appearance of most of the participants and, as the evening light settled on the room, the travellers on the Ark and their friends gathered in an unusually formal manner. Kronberg had put on a grey suit with a waistcoat and a tie with a pearl pin, Shpitz was wearing a high-collared Indian shirt with a polka-dotted scarf at its neck, Eyob had borrowed a long white robe from Ada's treasure chest. She wore black as usual but had put on make-up and her lips were startlingly red against the paleness of her face. Tomas had made no concessions and had come in jeans and a stained pullover. Escorted by Milo and Julius, Jordan looked like a fairy queen. Her hair was loosened and flowed over her shoulders. At her brow she had placed a chaplet of spring flowers. Félix had brought her a *djellaba* from the Old City and the long striped Bedouin dress made her moves into a kind of sailing. Julius had put on a sea captain's hat he had found somewhere. Rudi had persuaded Ulli to wear the Japanese robe he had brought from Kyoto and she had bundled her hair tightly round her head so she looked more like a doll than ever. Milo was determinedly scruffy, unshaven in black leather with signs of a hangover in his bloodshot eyes.

At the last minute Perla and Suzi arrived, Ada had invited them though she knew it would put Rudi on edge. At first Perla had sounded hostile. 'How can you do it with them? They stole it from us and baptized it. Those nuns might be nice, as you say, but they are the enemy when it comes to the Seder. For them the wine is the blood of Jesus. You'll have trouble swallowing that.'

Yet they came bringing Walzer who had jumped at the chance of reliving his adventure in the French monastery with the refugees and Bublik.

At first there was some tension in the room as they all stood awkwardly around the table which was set with the nuns' best dishes and glasses and a large copper tray serving as the ceremonial

Seder platter. Félix had made sure all the symbolic morsels were in order and had the matza piled up in the middle like a lighthouse in a sea of white.

He was in high spirits but also solemn. He felt at home here in this convent room leading the motley crew of Noah's Ark out of Egypt and across the Red Sea on dry land. He would read out the blessings of the wine and the celebration of the divine choice of the Jews in his French-accented Hebrew with peculiar identification. *You have chosen us from among the nations.* Yes, he thought, *Seigneur Béni,* us you have chosen. Ethiopian monk, Soeurs de Sion, runaway seminarist, Lucifer, unbelieving Jews. *From among the nations.* From among the United Nations Truce Supervision Organisations. You have sanctified us – German orphan, American princess, Welshman impresario, improver of hostile languages, Mandelbaum poet – blessed us, waifs and strays, blasphemers and Ark builders. You have exalted us to speak of the journey out of Egypt in many tongues. Amen.

'Why is this night different?' Félix asked in Hebrew and in English.

Eyob answered, 'It is the fall of the Egyptian children asleep in their bed, each one asleep and dead. This is the night.'

There was a long silence in the room.

'Only the first born,' said Perla. 'And it was Pharaoh who brought it upon them. Didn't he order all the children of the Jews thrown into the river?'

'Only the boys,' said Ada.

'On all other nights we eat all kinds of herbs. This night bitter herbs,' read Félix.

They all munched lettuce and parsley solemnly except for Milo who sat still and stiff, hands by his side, eyes closed.

'The Children of Israel might have been swallowed up by the sea or lost in the desert,' said Perla. 'Maybe it was miracles that saved them but certainly they had a great leader, a genius like Monty at El Alamein. He saved us alright.'

Félix dipped his finger in the wine cup and waved it at everyone so that they would follow suit. Then he read out the list of plagues letting one drop of wine fall on his plate for each.

'Blood.'

'Blood,' they said.

The sisters watched Schwester Clara. After some hesitation she dipped a fingernail delicately in the wine.

'Blood,' she said in a whisper.

'Blood,' they whispered after her.

Félix went on.

'Lice.'

'Frogs.'

'Darkness.'

Rudi interrupted with a sharp clink of his knife on a wine glass.

'Does this grim recital make anyone happy? What's the point of counting these disasters? Say you're a doctor in a hospital ward, would you read out a list of all the deaths that day: Cancer, Tuberculosis, Anemia, Typhus, Dysentry? It's shameful and inhuman. If they happened, they shouldn't be broadcast like this... We should pass over them in mournful silence. Just thinking about all that suffering is enough.'

Félix raised his voice and dropped the last drop for the last plague: 'The Slaying of the First Born.'

'Look at this,' said Rudi. He opened his Haggadah at a poorly executed drawing of a woman raising her hands in lamentation. He held it up. 'Whoever drew this was no Leonardo but he saw a woman wailing. He knew her sorrow. Who is she? The Unknown Mother? The cowherd's wife? Give her a name.'

'She is the Wife of Potiphar,' said Eyob 'and she did lust for Joseph but he ran away. She was punished.'

Kronberg cleared his throat: 'It happened in Würzburg too. The bombs got everybody. They didn't discriminate.'

Schwester Clara wiped the wine off her finger delicately with her napkin. 'I have read that the drops of wine falling on the plate stand for tears. They are tears of sorrow at the suffering of ordinary people whoever and wherever they are. The Lord wept when he saw the glorious Temple before its destruction. This list of suffering tells us how weak we all are, our bodies are weak, our towers and palaces are not safe. We depend on the mercy of God, like the Children of Israel at the Red Sea.'

Schwester Clara blushed, as if taken aback by her own speech.

Julius examined his Haggadah closely. Ada had picked them out of a pile in a shop full of decrepit German classics in Gothic print and other abandoned books of the recently dead. His was printed in Trieste and had a drawing of a family at the Seder table on the first page. A stern-looking father wearing what looked like a tasselled fez, a mother, two daughters and a son. Above them on the wall hung two portraits, presumably of ancestors. The father was gesturing in the son's direction and the boy stared back at him as if astounded. He must have asked the boy a difficult question, thought Julius. Did the Children of Israel leave Egypt on foot or on camels and donkeys? When darkness struck the whole of Egypt how did the Children of Israel see where they were going? Julius had a vague memory of such questions fired at him by an uncle and of his own terror at being unable to answer.

'Darkness,' he said. 'It was darkness so thick that you couldn't see your own fingers. It's when the sun dies and all light sinks. I can imagine that happening to us here,' he said.

'It could have been an eclipse,' said Shpitz. 'That sort of thing is always taken as a sign of doom. It's in Lear: *These late eclipses in the sun and moon portend no good to us*. But old man Gloucester was wrong. The evil is not in the sky. It's his own son, the bastard. The evil is in us.' He stroked his beard.

The light was declining though the room still held traces of the afternoon's glow. Shadows were spreading and dulling the gleam on the copper bowls and polished glass. The popes on the wall were already in shadow. They all sat and eyed the pools of wine on their plates where the plagues had dribbled down.

Félix felt melancholy in the air and searched for some relief. He found four sons on a page.

277

'There were four sons,' he read. 'One wise son. One wicked son. A simple son and the one who doesn't know how to ask.'

It might have been the beginning of a fairy tale of adventure with a forest, giants and a princess in a bed of gold at the end. But it wasn't. He read on, 'The wicked son says: *What is all this to you?*'

Milo opened his eyes. 'He is the only one with brains,' he said. 'He's got the guts to say what's all this nonsense about? Why are you doing this? None of it happened; plagues, seas opening up, food falling out of the sky. Pie in the eye. It's so absurd, it's comical and still you sit there and dribble plagues off your fingers. Wake up!'

He raised his glass. 'Here, I drink to the wicked son, Baruch Spinoza. Baruch Spinoza, I invite you to the Seder.'

'Isn't it customary to invite Elijah the prophet?' asked Kronberg.

'What's the point of that?' said Milo. 'He's part of the fraud.'

'But what would Spinoza do at this table?' said Jordan.

'He would engage Schwester Clara in a discussion of divine revelation,' said Kronberg. 'He would prefer arguing politely with her in Latin. With us he would lose his temper.'

'Who is this Spinoza?' said Schwester Clara. 'Is he one of the Rabbis?'

'He was a philosopher and a lens grinder and he thought the Bible was an unreliable work of the imagination,' said Kronberg.

'And our Lord and his gospel?'

'Moses and Abraham and all of them. Imagined, by dreamers, storytellers. He was a man of reason.'

Schwester Clara laid a delicate hand on her breast. The sisters looked at her for a sign.

She was in deep water but had to speak to save the Lawgiver and the patriarchs and the prophets, not to speak of Jesus, from this man of reason with the curious name.

'Reason,' she said, 'cannot bring comfort to the poor and the suffering. It does not offer hope. This man Spinoza, did he repent? Did he die saved or in sin?'

'He died in Holland,' said Félix, who saw the Seder heading in a dangerous direction. 'He had no religion.'

278

There was an uncomfortable silence.

Rudi picked up one of the Haggadahs. It had a German translation printed in heavy Gothic letters. He opened it and stared at the words his father had chanted forty years before over the white tablecloth and its crystal and silver and burning candles.

'Es hätte uns genügt.'

'Es hätte uns genügt,' he read. It wasn't him reading, it was the thin voice of his father. The hand holding the Haggadah was the old man's hand with lines of blue veins beneath the pale skin. It was trembling and with it the page trembled too. He could barely make out the German print but the words crowded forward and pushed onto his tongue. *Hätte Er uns aus Aegypten geführt und die Aegypter nicht gerichtet. Es hätte uns genügt.*

Who was speaking? What could Rudi May, the experienced courtroom translator, make of this? Nothing.

It was still untranslatable, *dayenu*, this cry of extra thanks for the abundance of gifts from which he had fled in anger years back after Nuremberg. It was still a riddle but his anger was mostly gone and here in the darkening convent room with Jesus at his supper on the wall and the popes watching, the words humbled him. His father was blind but so was everyone around him. He was blind but happy to be alive with the white tablecloth in front of him and his wife, son and daughters arranged around it. The old man was happy for the familiarity of the scene, for the feel in his palm of the silver spoons and the clink of the decanter on the wine glass. Rudi understood. The gift of life alone was enough and more than enough. It wasn't miracles, one after another; it was putting on his dark suit and white shirt with its stiff collar. It was sitting at the heavy desk in his study eye to eye with Beethoven's heroic bust. It was the sealed and framed lawyer's diploma on the wall and the cane with its ivory handle. It was the silver letter opener and the newspaper every morning. *Es hätte uns genügt.* These were the gifts and they were over-gifts in their persistence day by day, week by week, year in year out as if they could have no end. Until.

Until.

Dayenu, said Rudi, under his breath hoping no-one would take up the tune.

Jordan began to sing in a soft falsetto and looked around for support but no-one joined her and her voice wavered and stumbled as she struggled to fit the words to the tune. The repeated chorus should have been sung triumphantly by all, just like at home with her parents, aunts and uncles, brothers and cousins trying to outdo each other. Here she carried on alone, her voice persisting up the mounting ladder of divine gifts as if she was being tested in front of her class. The nuns looked on with approval. It was the kind of maidenly voice they recognised even though the words were strange. When Jordan finished the last *dayenu* they hummed a soft amen.

'That was happy, a song of thanks, I understand,' said Schwester Clara. 'Like *Gratias agimus tibi*.'

'But much longer,' said Shpitz. 'Why does the list go on and on?'

'A roll-call,' said Walzer. 'It's a roll-call after the battle to see who's still alive. If we're alive, we're happy. *Dayenu*.'

'And if we aren't,' said Rudi.

Then Suzi spoke. She had been silent all the while hardly seeming to pay attention only whispering now and then into Walzer's ear.

'Papa was not a believer. He did all this, year by year, the way it should be done but he was not a believer.'

'So why did he do it?' said Shpitz.

'They all do it,' said Milo 'because they are scared to stop. To stop would be heroic. Spinoza threw the book into the canal. He stopped.'

'But he wasn't a father,' said Perla. 'He didn't have to pretend for the children at his table.'

'What pretending?' said Félix. 'Look at us, look at the *mélange* at this table. Are we pretending?'

'Maybe playacting,' said Shpitz.

'No,' said Félix. 'We are composing. We are making it up out of words we overheard, out of songs somebody once sang. We are collaborators like Rogers and Astaire, like Django and Grappelli.'

We argue because we are together too much in Milo's Ark and we get on each other's nerves. But we are now guests of the Soeurs de Sion and we must go on.'

Félix stood up and motioned the others to do so.

'Open the door, Tomas,' he said. Tomas looked puzzled but went over to the heavy door.

'Open it wide.'

'Elijah, Prophet, come!' Félix sang it out like a trumpet call.

He had watched this ghostly invitation at Seder nights before and it tickled his sense of drama.

Then again, softer in a kind of plainsong and raising his hands in a priestly gesture of welcome:

'Veni Veni Helias Propheta.'

The door gaped open revealing a corridor in deep shadow.

All was silent. It was almost dark. From the trees in the garden a loud, quarrelsome cawing swooped into the room.

Eyob spoke. 'The birds, they gave Elia food. They brought him bread and he was not hungry. They were black. They were black like Ham.'

Milo broke the silence.

'I'm hungry. Isn't everybody hungry?'

The meal consisted of a grand and rich vegetable and fruit risotto with aubergines, leeks, courgettes, prunes, pumpkin, artichoke hearts, beans and rice deeply-flavoured with saffron, coriander, cumin, and all the local spices Ada could find. She and Félix had agreed that a copious, aromatic vegetarian dish would be a good riposte to the ancient, bloody Paschal sacrifices.

'No *agnus dei* tonight,' said Félix. 'Just treasures of the good earth.'

As the company ate Jordan was lost in a mist of sadness. She felt bereft, abandoned at a table of strangers. Singing the *dayenu* list of miracles alone had made it clear. There were tears in it which she had choked back with difficulty. SOS she had sung and no-one had responded. No voice was thrown out like a rope to save her. The absence of her parents made her feel like a little girl lost in a house with dark corridors leading to locked rooms with heavy wooden doors. From the wall the popes stared at her coldly. Their faces betrayed no humanity only vacancy as if they were beyond any ordinary feeling. She suppressed an urge to throw her plate at them. As for Milo he was almost asleep with his head lolling on Ada's shoulder. The table was mostly quiet. Only Shpitz was talking to no-one in particular describing the taste of deep-fried artichokes in a restaurant in Rome's Ghetto. They told me Nero was fond of them. *Carciofi alla giudia*. Unbelievably crisp all around and soft inside, soft as a baby's buttock…He made sensuous sucking sounds with his lips. Then he too fell silent.

I have to bring it to an end thought Félix. But this was something he had not prepared. He imagined it would just end of itself when the food was over but it was clear to him now that there had to be some closing sign like the whistle at the end of a match or the curtain falling on the stage. Meanwhile something strange had happened to the group around the table. Each one seemed to be enclosed in a transparent bubble. They sat closely by each other but the space between them seemed impenetrable. Only the sisters were united, looking at him with a gaze that seemed expectant or reproachful. Had he been a believer in witchcraft he might have suspected a spell fallen on them to freeze them all in their places until a redeemer broke it with a trumpet call or a loud challenge. But it was up to him to make the move and he had no trumpet or healing magic. The table, once so decorous, was now a mess with the debris of their supper. The white cloth was stained with daubs of red where the wine had spilled. The words in the book in front of him seemed strange and irrelevant now the meal was over and the ceremony emptied of whatever promise it held. Félix would have to invent an ending. So he stood up and began to sing:

J'attendrai
Le jour et la nuit
J'attendrai toujours ton retour

*

He hadn't planned it but it struck him that this could be Jesus returning or why not Elijah? The people were waiting and the door was still open for them both. He stood at the head of the table, florid with the food and the wine, his big frame and puffy handsome Gabin face and crop of greying hair making for a commanding presence as he swayed to the simple flow of the tune. The company stared at him in some surprise as he sang on. It was Tino Rossi's soft, high tenor guiding him now as it had filled him with longing years ago for a girl in Orleans. But now – *J'attendrai car l'oiseau qui s'enfuit vient chercher l'oubli dans son nid* now it was a different longing. Round the table they were all waiting, most obviously for the Seder to end. But the lively memory of how the melody had haunted the lovesick boy filled his voice now with a strange new resonance and authority. Here they were, travellers on the Ark and they were waiting on the empty expanse of water with the foul mess of the world packed in the hold. How long could they wait? It was up to him to give the sign. It had come to him unexpectedly, the bird, Tino Rossi's bird. He had sent it over the water. Would it return? He sang the words as the melody requested, with a sigh but not without hope:

En battant tristement dans mon coeur si lourd
Et pourtant j'attendrai son retour.

One of the sisters sighed audibly. She too might have grown up with the song, perhaps fallen in love to it as he had done. Félix was still standing, hoping the company would get up when Schwester Clara spotted the allegory.

'Your bird, Félix, will return with the olive branch. The white dove will bring us all hope. Certainly.'

She looked down at Milo and smiled. He was apparently asleep with his head resting on the table just like the apostle in the painting of the Last Supper. She was thinking of Milo when she gave the signal for the end.

'We have worked hard and we have come to the end. Some of us are already asleep. It is a good sleep in a safe place. When we all wake up in the end finally Elijah will come and announce the Redeemer.'

The company shuffled chairs and stood up. Milo, awake, looked around and scratched his beard.

'I dreamt,' he announced, 'I dreamt I was in a restaurant in Paris with Simone Signoret. She fed me with her own hand. Truffles.'

Noah's Flood

The trial was almost upon them. The People's Hall recently built on Ben Yehuda had become a courtroom theatre. Where once a British officers' club had stood and girls, careless of gossip, had attended the noisy and drunken dances, now there was a gloomy pale grey building set on its hilltop like a lazy tortoise squatting inside a cage of wire fences, rusty railings and police barrriers. NO GO signs were scattered everywhere on walls and barriers like badly sown patches on old clothes. Soldiers and policemen patrolled the streets and empty lots around the building, poking suspiciously at garbage cans, charity collection boxes and piles of rubbish while the painters and carpenters putting finishing touches to the interior were checked time and again.

Soon enough the area became empty even during the busiest times of day. People avoided walking by as if some contamination lodged inside the blank walls. But at night a few homeless beggars lay curled up in their rags near enough to catch the eyes of the patrolling soldiers as if they were hungry for some attention, even a curse and a kick, though sometimes they were given food and a hot drink.

The nearest inhabited area to the People's Hall were the narrow low stone dwellings of the Munkaczer Hasidim. They were right opposite the big building and predated it by a good half-century from Turkish times, but they turned their back to the street and huddled under low red-tiled roofs around cobblestoned inner

285

courtyards with their synagogue and ritual bath and school. During the day you heard sounds of men at prayer or children chanting their lessons. At night there was nothing, complete silence. No radio, no loud conversations, nothing but the whirr of the street lamp and the yowling of cats and corrugated iron sheeting rattling in the wind.

Walzer's brother lived there and some days after the Seder, persuaded by Ada to test the reaction to the Flood of its nearest audience, he went to visit him. He walked along a path between dustbins, rusting children's bicycles, broken furniture and plastic toys and knocked at a door which was partly open but protected by a curtain. From inside he heard the sound of children shouting in a game or a quarrel. A thin, graceful man, bearded and with large dark eyes behind thick glasses wearing what looked like a silk dressing gown came to the door.

'Erwin,' said Walzer, embracing his brother. 'Eliyahu, you haven't been answering my letters.'

'Busy, busy.'

'What with?'

'Come I'll show you.'

He led him through the kitchen into a room, clearly the dining room, with a large heavy table covered in books. Books were everywhere, some arranged neatly in shelves behind glass. Others piled on chairs and window sills even balanced precariously on earthenware jars and wooden orange boxes.

'Suri,' Eliyahu shouted, 'Suri bring a glass of water.'

A ginger-haired girl with a long ponytail peeped in and came back with a tray and glasses of water.

'This is my work on the Red Heifer,' said Eliyahu making a sweeping gesture at the books and papers scattered around.

'It's probably not familiar to you but we know the Red Heifer has disappeared. It hasn't been seen since the destruction of the Temple. But that doesn't mean to say it has gone, gone for good. Should the Temple be rebuilt we'll need this cow because only the ashes of the red heifer can purify the priests. Without that they couldn't do their work. So many of these books are about attempts

286

over the centuries to breed it or find a red heifer somewhere. Books from Poland, Germany, Baghdad, Bombay even Meshed. Of course some scholars think it's an allegorical beast, an emblem of purity, an idea more than an animal. But I think it's real. An animal so important for the Temple work has to be. It was the priestly antibiotic. It expelled impurity and it was bred right here in this country. So I think we can reconstruct the conditions needed to breed this animal again. I am in touch with a farmer in the village of Binyamina who is willing to try. He sends me photographs of his calves year by year and they get redder and redder but not quite, not red enough yet.'

Walzer looked at his brother. There was no trace of obsession or fanaticism in his voice. His gestures were calm and his eyes behind their lenses shone with happiness and intelligence.

'I must excuse my wife. She is visiting her sister with some of our children.'

'Do you think about our future here, brother? Do you think about the possibility of miraculous change, of something great and amazing ever happening here again?'

'Well, not really but it's odd you should ask because something very unusual is about to happen right here, and soon, the trial.'

'What trial?'

'The Nazi. The big trial. It's beginning in a few days right opposite your house.'

Eliyahu made a clicking sound with his tongue.

'So that's what those policemen and barriers are all about. A trial. A Nazi. Well...'

'You mean you didn't know it was Eichmann who was captured and brought here for trial?'

'Perhaps I heard something about it but I try to keep my mind clear of inessential matters. The details in the scholarly arguments about the cow and especially the definitions of its redness are a great challenge to a man's concentration. I have to focus on what's important. This trial will be held according to Hebrew law or secular law? If it's secular law then it can have no lasting significance.'

287

'Eliyahu there's something else apart from the trial. On the day it opens something strange will take place in the street outside your Munkaczer dwellings.'

'Strange?'

'There's going to be a play in the street.'

'A play? Aren't plays supposed to be performed in theatres?'

'Yes, usually, but this is going to be in the street just outside here.'

'So why should we care?'

'Well, it's a play about Noah and the Flood.'

Eliyahu looked startled.

'Since when is that a play? It's a chapter in the Book, not a play.'

'It's a very old play written hundreds of years ago.'

'In Hebrew?'

'English, but it will be performed in a number of languages.'

Eliyahu looked astonished.

'What do the English have to do with Noah?'

'Everybody, the whole world, the Chinese even the English are interested in the story of the Flood and the Ark.'

'So, say some mad people want to do this here, in the street, why are you telling me about it?'

'I want you to keep the Munkaczer people from rioting.'

'Why should they riot? We are peaceful people.'

'Well, God is in it.'

'In the play?'

Walzer summoned up all his courage. 'Yes and acted by a man.'

'By a man? A Jew?'

'Yes.'

Eliyahu sat down on the only chair in the room not carrying a pile of books. 'Is this perhaps a play organized by missionaries?'

'Not at all. It's simply a repetition of the Bible story: the Ark, the Flood, the new beginning.'

'And why are they doing this?'

'They want to teach the people.'

'Teach what?'

'That we are all living on shaky ground, that we could all go

288

under in spite of our army and our flags and that the trial and capturing the Nazi doesn't make a difference to how vulnerable we all are.'

'We don't need a play to teach us that. Every dawn for us is a new miracle of creation. For us the world could end any minute and we would be prepared. If I may speak frankly, brother, this sounds like child's play. A man acting the Creator speaking English here in the street. It sounds like the work of lunatics not children.'

Walzer was heartened by his brother's lack of anger and, if pressed, would have agreed with him about the craziness of Milo's project but he had promised Ada so he went on.

'If the play creates a disturbance and the actors are attacked could they perhaps find refuge in the Munkaczer dwellings?'

Eliyahu was silent for a while. 'You say they are Jews?'

'Mostly.'

'And they are not working for any missionaries?'

'None whatsoever.'

'Well, I could give you the key to our old bakehouse where years ago we used to bake bread. It's doubly off-limits now because of Passover. It's underground and probably a mess and full of soot. How many are there in this play?'

'Not many. Noah and his family and the animals.'

'Animals?'

Walzer laughed. 'Not real animals. Masks, just a few actors with masks.'

Eliyahu looked relieved. He took Walzer's hand. 'You remember when we were ferrying the illegals from the camps to the coast and we were breaking all the rules of the British army, all the orders. You were fearless and the best actor. The way you talked us round the roadblocks and the inspections. None of us was as light-fingered as you. Your voice alone unlocked all the gates. Now you're here ferrying your lunatic actors with their masks into Munkacz and I'm giving you the key to the bakehouse. It will get me into trouble, even though they all respect me here. They respect me for my research. They know that the red heifer could be the beginning of an immense change in our condition. Come to think of it, I see some connection between your mad actors and my search, the connection of opposites. They are saying things will go wrong for us, we will go under, and I am saying things will change for the good when the red heifer is born.

'Tell me, Gerri are you content with your Hindu philosophy and your bending and stretching of your bones and joints. Does it give you hope?'

Walzer groped in his pockets for his pipe but it wasn't there. 'Hope. It's not something that occupies me. When we were in the Brigade I hoped we would live to see the end of Hitler but since then, hope doesn't signal to me. It's just part and parcel of living and working. When I meditate and teach others it's the present I belong to and live in. My discipline is to be open completely to mind and body in the present.'

Eliyahu looked at his shoes. 'The present is an illusion. It's a screen beguiling us with false images. It takes a lot of discipline to resist this fakery. That's what I learned here, the discipline of that resistance. But come, brother, I will show you where the bakehouse is. It's not so easy to find.'

Walzer followed his brother along a path behind the houses which led past a cistern to a dome-shaped hillock overgrown with weeds and strewn with garbage and broken furniture. Hidden by thorns and creepers and built into the hillock was a rusty iron door. NO said half of a painted message on the door the rest of which was unintelligible.

'I won't open it now,' said Eliyahu, 'but I know it works. We stored some wood for our stoves there. It was used as a shelter also. How are you going to show the waters drowning the world? Can you do that on a stage, in the street, without rain?'

'The actors are just acquaintances and I know little about it. But there's no realism. No water. It's a flood made by words the way a reader might imagine it.'

'So why not just read it aloud in the street?'

'It wouldn't attract attention and they want to compete with the trial. They want to make people look away from the Nazi and imagine everyone in the world drowned except one family and some animals in a ship.'

Eliyahu looked troubled. 'It sounds so savage the way you describe it.'

'I won't deny it. It's a savage spectacle. Imagine if we had to count the dead or lay out the bodies of the drowned from one end of the earth to another. Like the camps it doesn't bear thinking about and perhaps we shouldn't.'

Eliyahu's voice thinned to a whisper. 'But if your actors wish to set this in front of the people in the street they had better be ready for some roughness. It won't be an audience of scholars. Why do you think Noah was chosen to live? Even the Rabbis considered his times to be lawless and uncivilized. Noah, he wasn't a particularly good man or outstanding. He was just less stupid than most. People around him existed on the level of animals.'

'It's our story on a primitive level, Eliyahu. Something always survives. Somebody gets away somehow and carries on, remarries, has a new family. People forget how they got away. They just found themselves not dead. Noah was lucky he was a bit of a carpenter and he had instructions. The actors have an Ark too but I am told it's built to look like Zion Square on wheels.'

Eliyahu looked so startled that Walzer didn't elaborate. They walked together to the low wall that marked the limit of the compound. Ahead of them the People's Hall was being fed furniture and equipment by a line of trucks watched over by police.

'I should go back to my work,' said Eliyahu averting his eyes from the scene. 'Remember, return the key when it's all over.'

They shook hands and parted.

STREET THEATRE

THE TRIAL HAD begun but the Flood project was in limbo. Milo had lost hope of confronting the police and soldiers outside the trial. He was chainsmoking, fighting with Jordan, cancelling lectures and coming home irregularly stinking of brandy. Rehearsals such as they were went on without him so the play developed in directions he had not foreseen. Félix moved it closer to the Biblical story and removed some of Milo's doctrinaire pessimism. Without Milo and with no performance date the actors were freer to improvise and there were bursts of laughter as Noah and his wife clowned their quarrel or the sons mimed the Ark-building in slapstick. But above them, the old ice factory was totally deserted as a foreign television crew had arrived to take over all the filming with its own equipment. Only the massive police presence outside the People's Hall and the slowly moving queue trailing into the courtroom indicated something was happening. A short distance away, downtown, the thin daily bustle went on unchanged, apparently unaffected by the big event though it did fill the papers while hourly accounts dominated the radio. But the trial's opening stages dealing with the bureaucracy of expulsion and pillaging of Jewish property weren't in themselves dramatic or sensational enough and the newsboys weren't shouting 'Dead and Wounded Strewn About, Dead and Wounded All Over' as they did whenever there was an incident along the borders. 'Vienna Jews Expropriated' wasn't going to sell papers.

Yet there were new people in town, mostly foreign journalists. In the cafés and in Fink's Bar they stood out in the kind of linen suits and dark glasses not often seen there. Rudi who knew one or two from his Nuremberg days tried to interest them in a strange and dramatic event that might occur soon in the street near the trial. But as he wouldn't go into any detail they paid little attention. He had also been attending the sessions observing the young translators at their work.

'They're enthusiastic and professional. They don't let the hours of dreary stuff slow them down,' he told Ulli. 'Of course they have it much easier than I had. My polyglot table was opposite two rows of murderers. You could practically smell the blood on them and our young men only have one mouldy guy shut in a glass box. So no smell. The Big Shit, Ada calls him. But he's more of a dry turd.'

Jordan, homesick and bored, had taken refuge in her thesis and was spending days in Café Atara trying to revive the ideas in her notebooks. The warm, cosmopolitan atmosphere of the place with its smell of cinnamon and coffee and its motherly waitresses in sensible padded white shoes helped her forget what was happening between herself and Milo.

Margarian walked in and tapped her gently on her shoulder.

'The young lady is alone. Père Félix told me there is trouble with Noah and the Ark. The professor is hiding. The players do what they like. Professor Milo knows the police will not allow his performing to take place. So he is moody and gets drunk and sleeps. I know. But all is not over. The saving of the world from Ararat and Armenia can take place. It can be shown so people can see. The question is which people and where it can be shown...'

Jordan looked at him. She said nothing.

He spread his hands like a magician over a box of tricks covered by a cloak.

'It will be by the bandstand of the Turks. The place is quiet. The people who live there are few but they will bring others, also the professor's students will come and the place is in view of the Holy

293

City, the Sepulchre and the Temple. It is like Ararat. It is an Ark sitting on the top of the valley over the old world.'

Margarian was flushed but measured his words with legal eloquence. He had argued cases like this in the District Courts, cases involving the strange behaviour of religious sects and quarrels over precedents and processions. He knew a thing or two about sacred processions from the days when the city was still in one piece. He was a fixer and a resolver of seeming impossibilities.

'Call the people together,' he had said to Félix. 'Spread the word.'

Call them to come and Milo will repent.

To Jordan he said, 'Come at night on Thursday, there is a full moon.'

Ada and Tomas, Kronberg, Rudi and the rest had been summoned by Margarian. Ada had deposited her pile of costumes in Julius's house, God's starry robe and golden crown, Noah's smock, Mrs Noah's rolling pin, the family's ragged brown tunics, a stuffed raven and a clockwork dove. Piled on Julius's floor they were a motley heap, a paupers' carnival.

Milo was still sulking. Perhaps in the garden of Government House, perhaps in one of the caves in the valley but Julius was hunting for him and was sure he could get him back.

Meanwhile Margarian had arranged for the Ark to be lifted out of the ice factory cellar by a truck owned by a fellow Armenian, Ohanassian, the owner of Ohanassian Removals in Jaffa who had been won over for the sake of Ararat and a small sum donated by Rudi.

Félix had borrowed a long electric cord and a lamp from his friend the caretaker of the Dominican Seminary telling him it was to help him light an archaeological dig under a house in the Hinnom Valley. It was in a flank of the valley that Julius found Milo. He was filthy and pale and stretched out in a trench some way below his garden inside a tangle of barbed wire. He had crawled through it and was bleeding over his eyes and smelling of piss.

'Milo, look at yourself! Filthy. Look where you are. You're

294

bleeding, man. You are in danger. How on earth did you get into this trench? You are almost over the bloody line.'

Julius was muscular and strong above his crooked legs and he pulled Milo by his arms out of thorns and over stones like a killed animal away from the trench, over a crumbling terrace and into his garden. Milo tried to resist but he was weak and seemed unaware of where he was.

'It's me, Julius. Milo look at me, you can't abandon the ship. It's going to happen. The Ark. They are bringing it up here.'

He ran into the house and brought a wet towel to wipe the blood off Milo's forehead. His hands moved tenderly over the scratches and bruises and Milo began to mumble, 'Cut my head off Judith, bitch. Get him drunk and cut my head off. No-one knows.'

'Milo, listen. The Ark is coming here. They are setting it up right here on the bandstand.'

Milo waved a hand feebly. 'No passing. Dead end. Quiet on the front.'

Julius propped Milo up into a sitting position and stared at him, his beak up against his friend's nose, like one of his puppets. His deep eyebrows brushed Milo's forehead.

'The Ark Milo. It is here. They've brought it from the factory. We'll do it!'

A spark of awareness lit up Milo's eyes.

'Not here. The street by the trial. It has to be in the street in their faces. Fuck the police. They have to see it. Outside the Big Shit.'

'They'll see it here. We'll trick them. We'll put it on our hill. We've passed the word around and they'll come.'

Milo looked crumpled.

'Our hill is nowhere. It's a dead hill. You walk up the slope and there's nothing.'

'Not nothing,' said Julius. 'We make it a landmark. We put the Ark right on the Syrian African Rift and we send our warning. I know about sending warnings to people who don't open my letters. They come to understand they are missing something. They get an echo. It comes to them from under the earth like my boots hear the rumblings of the Syrian African Rift. That is real, under us, waiting. I know it. You know it and the Ark will be in place on top of it. Here.'

Julius pointed into the gathering darkness towards the bandstand. Then he dragged Milo into the house and started cleaning him up.

As it grew dark the planks, cloth curtains, packing crates, cardboard screens and boards of the Ark on Zion Square were being put together on the bandstand by Félix, Rudi, Tomas, Kronberg, Ada and the women from Milo's seminar. Shpitz was conducting the work like an engineer on a building site, giving brief orders, 'Gently, gently' – putting his shoulder to a plank, smoothing and attaching pieces of cloth with professional care and a stapler.

To the Persian family living opposite it looked like their eccentric neighbours were stacking up a bonfire to celebrate some holiday, birthday or wedding. At first the structure looked random and shapeless. Gusts of wind almost blew it over but Shpitz proved himself a wizard at propping up the sides of Zion Square and the ship's poop with makeshift girders from Ohanassian's lorry. The Armenian had been infected by Margarian's enthusiasm and knew how to tie and strap together the different parts of the set so that as it grew darker the bulk of the Ark and the façade of Zion Square loomed against the grey pink of the sunset. From a distance it seemed a jagged shell of a house damaged in war and badly repaired, but from closer the shape of the square with its cinema and shop fronts made some sense. It was a broken city scene empty of life, open only to the wind. But when Félix connected his lamp with its long cord to Julius's house the square seemed ready for something, anything to happen. Tomas clambered over it catlike to test its stability and inspect his painting, his film posters and shop windows. They were hardly visible but he patted his Polish manhole cover like an old friend. *Krakowie Miasto*, his secret mark from a lost city.

People began to drift by and collect near the bandstand. First the Persians with their grandfather and the armchair on which he sat to look down on the Temple Mount, then other neighbours from the houses by the valley lured by the bustle. Schwester Clara arrived with a train of Sisters and their Arab gardener. A United Nations jeep from Government House drove by to have a look and aimed its headlights on the Ark so that Tomas's colours grew vivid, especially his big hoardings for *Gone with the Wind* and *The Flood: Coming Soon* in large Hebrew letters over the cinema. From below on the Hebron Road the hill with its bandstand seemed crowned with a halo. The Sasson brothers, persuaded by Julius, arrived in a taxi – something they had last done for an aunt's funeral. They held hands like children on a school outing and perched on an upturned oil drum. A police patrol car drove up the hill and an officer rolled down a window and asked what was going on.

'A dramatic performance, students from the university,' said Shpitz in his English-accented Hebrew.

The policeman seemed uninterested and drove off but a reasonable crowd had gathered. Soon there were some more United Nations personnel, Africans and Scandinavians. Perla had brought Suzi and Walzer on the bus even though she remained scornful of Milo's 'absurd catastrophe' which had enslaved Ada once again.

In Julius's house Noah and his family looked at each other shamefully. Dressed in the rags and patches of their costumes they felt naked. Kronberg stood stiffly in robe and crown staring grimly at Julius's shower curtain. Eyob had not arrived. Only Félix began to show some ease swigging from his brandy flask, whispering encouraging words to the others and pleased to have Ada smear rouge on his cheeks and rub thick eyeliner on him with her fingers.

Jordan sat quietly on Julius's bed. Although she had Mrs Noah's burlap dress and crimson headscarf in her lap she had not put them on. She suspected Milo was lurking in or near the house somewhere. Tomas came in and called for her. He took her by the hand through the dark, skirting the crowd to Milo's house and into the garden by the entry to the cistern.

'Down there' he said. 'Go.' He gave her a torch.

'Down there that's where he is.'

Jordan walked carefully down the rough steps. At first she could make out nothing but then the beam of her torch picked out a bundle rolled up on the floor against the wall. It was him.

'Switch it off,' he said. 'Switch it off.'

She approached him gingerly and tried to touch him but he pushed her hand away.

'I'm finished,' he said. 'I'm done for. I screwed up.'

Jordan stood distant above him like a doctor inspecting the symptoms of a hypochondriac.

'You aren't finished,' she said. 'You are scared. You're afraid of your own phantasy turning up outside your door alive. It's not in your head any more. It's not about you and everything you hate in this town and want to fight. It's not about your end of the world, *your* scandal, *your* flood. It's a birth, a living thing, a big bundle made of boards and junk by us and it's squatting in front of the people here outside your house.'

'People,' he sneered. 'Stray dogs, garbage cats from nowhere. If it can't happen in the crowd waiting for the Nazi and they turn their heads away it can't happen at all. Outside my house is nowhere. It's a dead end.'

There was a clatter on the stairs and a black figure in a white robe stood in front of them.

'I have brought the friends from Debre Ganet. They will see Ham and Noe saved from the flood. They are given permission by the fathers because Ham is the father of the African and we are his children. But then I must go back and no more showing of Ham.' He looked both enthusiastic and crestfallen.

'When are we beginning?'

Jordan turned away from Milo and said, 'Now right away,' and ran up the stairs followed by Eyob.

In the absence of Milo, Julius had taken over. He had sent the student band with trumpets, clarinet and a drum to one side of the bandstand. They began to play *O Mary don't you weep don't you mourn.*

298

The crowd clapped along though few knew the song except someone who shouted 'Pharaoh's army got drowned' again and again.

'Go,' Julius said to Kronberg. 'Go and be God.'

Kronberg couldn't move. He stood stiff as a flagpole by Julius's door. Tomas took him gently by the hand and steered him into the dark through the people and up onto the front of the scene. He left him there blinking into the headlights of the UN jeep listening to the music and laughter. He opened his arms wide. I am Otto Klemperer he thought and to his surprise the words came: *I am God who made heaven and earth.*

He said it in English then in Hebrew and there was no laughter, just the yowl of a jackal and a subdued drum roll from the band.

He said it again: *I am God who made heaven and earth, I made man and woman his companion.*

He had rehearsed the speech with Shpitz so often without bringing life to it that, embarrassed by Shpitz's disappointment, he told him about Mahler and the old man on the beach. Shpitz had seized Kronberg's confession to coax him into a show of sympathy which was not natural to him. Shpitz stroked his hand and said 'You created them, daddy. They are your children, the bastards. You really want to save them. You are a god person, a father, a disappointed lover. Kronberg, you could cry. Cry over lost love.'

As Kronberg started to describe the sins commited by his creatures, a wetness in his eyes surprised him and a secret tear came as he thought of Tomas and warned of the destruction he was about to visit on every living thing.

I repent I ever made man
And all this universe so full of sin—

He said it in both languages gesturing first widely at the audience then over their heads at the dark Valley of Hinnom, at the border waste land, its blocked wells and ruined terraces. Then he turned and faced the cinema, pointing at *Gone with the Wind* and *The Flood: Coming Soon.*

This evil world so full of people
Seeking sinful pleasures
Must drown

There was some laughter and boos but Kronberg's pain visible in the strain on his face and the wet glistening in his eyes was not an easy target. Schwester Clara touched her cross and felt, in a pang, the sorrow of the Creator who was now dependent on Noah and Jesus to save him from unthinkable failure.

This world so fair I will destroy
A flood I'll make to cover all
Man and beast, children, the old and frail
No-one, nothing will be left on earth
No Jaffa Road, no King George Street
Hebron Road, Bethlehem Road gone
All gone.

Zion Square and the cinema shook in a gust of wind as Kronberg spread both hands wide, took a Star of David pennant like a conjurer from under a sleeve, tore it violently into pieces as the crowd jeered and protested, then scattered the shreds at his feet,

All except one.

He held a blue and white fragment up like evidence in a court of law.

Everything will go
Except one man who will live
Noah my servant true
Noah Noah
Faithful old man

There was some commotion at Julius's door and Félix emerged red-faced and moderately drunk in a brown smock like a friar with an umbrella in one hand. He pushed his way roughly through the laughing, cheering crowd, shouting:

I come, my Lord I come!

Clambering heavily onto the set he bowed deeply to Kronberg, then unfurled his umbrella to waves of laughter:

I hear you call my Lord
I hear you call the waters
From above and below
To drown all living things
Jaffa Road too and King George Street
The bus station and the policemen
It fills me with fear
What shall I do?
Where will we go?
Kronberg took Félix by the hand and led him slowly round
Zion Square.
An Ark you'll build right in Zion Square
Your wife and sons will come on board
And animals also two by two
When everything on earth is drowned and lost
This city swallowed beneath the tide
You will remain.
Félix turned to the crowd round the bandstand
These people here, fathers, mothers, children can they not live?
Do they not suffer?
'Yes, yes, yes!' People in the crowd were shouting now. 'Enough!
Enough!' and waving hands and fists.
'*No-one,*' said Kronberg over loud boos. Someone threw a
watermelon rind. Apple cores rained on Kronberg.
He stood his ground. He seemed taller and stiffer and more
Prussian as he raised his voice:
You will all drown.
Your children
Your parents
Your money
Washed away.
'No! No! No!'
There was a surge below as some tried to climb onto the
bandstand. Félix pushed them down then the UN jeep's headlights
were switched off.

301

The drummer mistaking this for a cue began to roll thunder claps and Félix sensing a crisis called out:

My sons Shem Ham Japheth come
We must set to this work.

Eyob, Rudi, and one of Milo's male students pushed their way from Julius's house. They were each carrying a hammer and leading their wives by the hand.

When the jeep's headlights illuminated the scene again, Kronberg had disappeared.

There was some ribald whistling as the women presented themselves but when Noah's sons began to hammer to the persistent, driving beat of the drum while the wives tore at their hair and made shrill keening noises, the spectacle began to work.

Where is my wife? asked Noah waving his umbrella.

The drum beat thunder and the jeep driver, joining in, switched headlights on and off for lightning and storm.

Wife come!
Wife, you obstinate woman
Hurry. The waters are gathering
You will drown!

Jordan in her burlap dress with a crimson headscarf tightly bound ran out, a plastic shopping bag in one hand, the other waving a rolling pin.

She stood among the people on a step below the bandstand and yelled at Noah:

Crazy old man!
Have you been hearing voices again?
So call the police,
I've got better things to do than
Climb onto your clumsy tub.

Jordan turned to the audience

You women here – haven't you had enough
Of orders by drunken, useless husbands
Told to go here and there

Because of stupid rumours?
Speak out women
We're not following you old man
We have better things to do.

There was cheering, whistling and *Yalla Yalla Sharmuta* from the crowd.

From above the sons and daughters joined in the noise:
Mother come!
Mother the waters
Look the waters
At your feet.

Ham jumped off the stage. Looming over Jordan, shouting wildly in Amharic he manhandled her, half-carrying half-dragging her, tearing her dress and ripping off her headscarf. Jordan fought back scratching him and drawing blood but he forced her onto the stage where she stood bare-shouldered, trembling, hair loose and falling over her face pale as chalk. She was in shock and the sight was so disturbing everyone was silent.

From the direction of Julius's house a growling sound broke the silence and a brown bear appeared making its way in a rolling gait towards the bandstand. Once there it climbed on all fours onto the set, put paws on Jordan's arms and made as if to lick her hurt shoulders. Then he lay on his back at her feet and waggled paws and legs. Back upright he stood behind her and hugged her whispering, 'That Eyob is out of his mind.'

It was Julius in a bear suit Ada had found in the trunk of an old clothes shop. He was the only animal they could rely on in the rush to perform.

The band played 'Singing in the Rain' and Julius jigged slowly round Noah and the family then round Zion Square as the crowd laughed, clapped and threw orange and banana peel. Then he joined the family huddled together under Noah's umbrella putting a comforting paw around Jordan's waist.

The drum rolled and the trumpet burst into a shofar cry again and again, warning of danger and calling for repentance. Ada saw

Milo. He was standing at the edge of the audience next to Margarian who was whispering in his ear.

Félix, feeling the warmth of the bodies pressed against him under his umbrella, surrendered to an almost forgotten priestly calling:

Salve Regina mater misericordiae
Ad te clamamus.

He sang on the spur of the moment, quietly to himself feeling for an instant the brotherhood of his seminary days. No-one in the audience heard or would have understood. Schwester Clara did and clutched her handkerchief to her breast but immediately Félix, now in full throat, sang *Avinu Malkeinu*, Our Father Our King, the familiar Yom Kippur hymn calling for God's mercy.

The people joined in full-voiced and lustily. It was known to them all and could be sung again and again as in the synagogue. It enveloped the floodbound family under the umbrella with hope. Milo had objected violently to using the chant. There had to be fear and doubt, not hope. But Félix instead of arguing with him had resolved to sing it out repeatedly to get the Ark through the flood. The spectators cooperated admirably singing each chorus louder than the last, building up a sailing rhythm over high, rolling waters. Ada watched Milo closely. In his dark face she saw both disgust and fascination. 'Yom Kippur,' she thought. 'Of all things… Milo's got himself a Yom Kippur. He wants anger and panic and rebellion but he's got an audience captured by the story. The Flood is rising on Zion Square. The trial is going on up the road. So the world is going under. So what. Perhaps there were moments when the crowd felt their ground might also be unsafe. But Our Father Our King would take care of that.' Milo's attempt to cause upheaval, doubt and unease had become a journey of faith just as it had been in Chester and York 600 years before.

Noah pulled a black bundle out of a pocket. It was a raven puppet made out of curtain material and cotton wool stuffing. He held it up:

Cunning Raven

Far-flying bird
Go spy the waters
Look for land
Bring us a sign…

He threw the bird backstage over the cinema hoardings, then the family all except Noah hudddled together to sleep.

Félix alone paced the square scanning the sky and the horizon, counting time aloud on his fingers. Twenty, thirty. He spied Milo helping Margarian climb on a wall to get a better view.

Forty days and forty nights have passed
The raven is away
Perhaps he found food
Dear Lord
Let me try how the waters lie
Have they lesssened or will we starve to death?

He slipped off his rope belt and bending over the edge of the set threw it onto the feet of the front row of the crowd then drew it back slowly and inspected it;

My God the water is sinking
The earth is near
We'll send the dove
Come wife
Give me your sweet dove
She's a faithful bird
She'll bring us
A true sign

Jordan rummaged in her bag and took out a clockwork tin dove from Sasson's box of toys.

Noah spoke to it as he wound it up and made it rattle its wings.

Lu lee lu sweet bird we trust
Fly to seek a sign
Bring us the promise we wait for

He threw it over to Shpitz by the far side of the stage and Shpitz stuck a sprig of olive branch in its beak and gave it to the nearest child to give to Noah.

The girl ran up to the stage and Noah knelt down to take the
dove. He held it up
An olive branch
Dear Lord a sign
There is a world once more
Wake up children
The earth is found.
He took Jordan and with his hand over his eyes searched the
crowd up and down, right and left:
Where in this world are we?
Then pointing directly at Margarian:
Wife look there are the hills of Armenie
Ararat a sacred mountain chosen by the Lord
There we will land and begin our life again
Ararat will be our home
Margarian took out his handkerchief, wiped his eyes and
blew a kiss in the direction of the bandstand. Then Kronberg
came out of Tomas's ruin. He was walking unsteadily as if he had
been drinking Tomas's arak but it made him feel happy and
ready to forgive Tomas, the Germans and anybody else for
wrongs done to him. He was waving a rainbow-striped flag as
the band played 'Somewhere over the Rainbow.' And the family
began to sing:
Somewhere over the Rainbow
Way up high
There's a land that I heard of
Once in a lullaby
They were all on their knees before Kronberg when Milo could
stand it no longer. He ran up to the bandstand and jumped onto the
set between the kneeling family and Kronberg.
'Stop!
'Don't.
'There is no safe land. No safe land, never.'
Ham stood up, shouting 'It is promised!' He wrestled Milo to
the floor and held him down. 'Nazdi Eikamenn he killed the

children. He is taken by the police. And he will die. Noe saved the children. It is true. We will live. Ham will be the father of Africa. Noe, father,' he turned to Félix. 'Tell professor it is true. Tell professor I do not shame you. I am a good son. Tell the people Ham is a good son. I will not make you naked.'

Félix was lost. Eyob was writing his own play and there was no help not from God or Milo who was face down on the floor.

Jordan made her move.

She took Eyob gently by the hand and away from Milo who was helped up by Félix.

Then she led Ham back to the rest of the family and began to address the audience in her own words. Quietly but with authority. She spoke the English slowly like a school mistress, in defence of Milo's catastrophe.

'Why were we saved? Do you know? We are just like everybody else, like you millions who were drowned. Hundreds tried to climb on the Ark but we pushed them off.

'We had no food for them.

'We are no better than those who drowned. So why did we play you this story?

'We play it because we and you and all here are all escaped from drowning and we don't know it.

'We could drown again. It would happen quickly, Jaffa Road, Zion Square, Hebron Road. All gone. The city all gone. The Nazi in his box, his judges too would drown together with us, tonight or tomorrow. But we wouldn't be prepared. Nothing can prepare us. Not the police. Not the army. Not the newspapers or the radio.

'It would all go down like this.'

And she started pulling down the flimsy structures of the set. The cinema and shops of Zion Square shuddered. Bits of carton and cloth crumpled, sagged and split. Holes appeared in thin walls. The square was collapsing. Jordan out of pity and contempt for Milo was carrying out his plan of destruction and havoc.

With increasingly quick and agile movements she danced over the set warding off Eyob's attempts to stop her. Using her rolling pin she battered and lunged at whatever lay in her way as Félix and the rest looked on. Milo sat on the floor with his head in his hands. Infected by the confusion, people started climbing onto the bandstand to join in the work of destruction. The cinema hoardings fell, the shopfronts caved in, the square was now a heap of painted junk. Margarian ran up to the bandstand and shouted to Félix. 'Give the blessing Noah. Begin the world old man. Before it is too late.' Félix clambered over the ruins and took hold of Jordan. She was breathless and flushed, bewildered by what she had begun. He rocked her in his arms like a child and led her to the front as close to the people as possible. There was too much confusion for speech so Félix kissed her, a long lingering kiss full on the lips. There was quiet. He kissed her again and brought her to kneel on the ground and lie down as he lay beside her and put a hand on her breast... Most of the people had gone but those who were left pressed forward to look at the couple. The UN jeep's headlights were turned off. Only Félix's weak lamp threw some light at the derelict scene where Noah and his wife, exhausted, sought comfort in each other after God had finished with them.

Kronberg and the family had not stirred but Milo crawled over to where Félix and Jordan were lying and tried to move Félix's hand from her breast. Félix resisted and embraced Jordan more tightly. Eyob broke away from the huddled family and stood over Félix.

'Father Noe you embrace Madame in front of the people. This is not permitted. It is shameful for the family.'

Then he bent down and tugged at Félix's robe tearing at it to reveal a patch of white underpants. Then realizing what he had done he covered his face with his hands.

'No, Father, I do not shame you. You will not curse me. Ham is a good son for Madame to save her from showing sin.'

Félix, ignoring Eyob, heaved himself up slowly and helping Jordan to stand they made their way through the remaining bystanders to Julius's house. The family followed them quickly, heads down.

Only the moon lit up the bandstand now and its burden of ruins.

The slogan COMING SOON could be made out as a few spoilers picked their way through the debris hoping to find something worth taking away.

Ada watched Milo sitting on the bandstand cross-legged and staring into the distance. Julius still in his bear suit had an arm round his friend's shoulder and was singing his Sufi chant

LI LLAHI RABBI L ALAMIN.

The Sasson brothers approached the bandstand warily. Unlike most of the audience they had not left. They stood just beneath Julius and Milo, and Ezra spread his hands, palms upward in the Moslem attitude of prayer.

'Our neighbour Dajani would sing this,' he said. 'In the old times. It is a hope for God's peace after this destruction.' He pointed at the ruins.

'The dove we bought it in Bratislava. It is only one. Very precious. But the lady will keep it for another performance. Will you make another one for the people? Many of them did not understand. Next time perhaps they will.'

Julius went on singing quietly. Milo seemed unaware of where he was. Kronberg had not left the bandstand. He was still wearing his crown and holding the rainbow flag drooping by his side. He looked so forlorn that Tomas clambered up and embraced him. Gently he removed the crown and slipped God's robe off Kronberg's shoulders.

'God is discharged,' he said.

He took him by a hand and led him back to Tomas's house.

Ada kneeled down in front of Milo and tried to find his eyes in vain. They were pools of darkness, looking into nothing. She had never seen him so empty, so depleted. Soon they would all go. Jordan, Rudi, Ulli. Eyob back to his monastery. There would be remnants of their ruin on the ruined bandstand for a while till the wind scattered them among the debris of the desolate valley that split the city.

Shpitz was standing on one of the collapsed hoardings, eyes downcast and one hand plucking at his beard.

'All spirits,' Ada heard him say, 'melted into air, into thin air. This insubstantial pageant faded. But good fun while it lasted.'

He picked up Noah's dove, hidden among the debris, and wound it up. Its wings rattled. In the distance they heard police sirens.

Shpitz handed the dove to Ada.

'Here keep it with your dolls till next time.'

After The Deluge

Milo had disappeared. He had knocked on Ada's door in the Ethiopian mansion and stood there in the dark. 'I'm not coming in,' he said. 'Take this.' He gave her an envelope and a key. 'Take these and give the letter to her when you find out where she is.' He looked pale and spoke quietly as if he was afraid of being overheard. He was gone before Ada had time to say anything. She watched him walk quickly along the dreary corridor, a slight black shadowlike figure. Then he disappeared.

No-one knew where. He had cancelled all his classes. Some said he had quarrelled with the Dean and resigned. Julius knew nothing or said he didn't. Félix and Jordan were not in town. Ada guessed they might have taken a bus to Tiberias where Félix had friends at the Scottish Hospice. Rudi and Ulli had paid a hurried farewell visit to her at Tomas's house.

Rudi looked troubled and spoke hesitantly, 'I should have gone back earlier. The Babel Foundation was losing patience with me and some of the high-ups were getting sceptical about the whole peace-through-language-learning project. I guess I was bowled over by the way Milo's idea faced up to the trial and the Nazi. I saw all that bad stuff close up not so long ago and I thought this was a brave thing to do here with the Flood in the street and the Nazi in his glass cage. But I should have stuck with the young translators. At least that was a realistic job, something I could start and finish.'

He kissed her. 'I'll miss you my Mädchen. You'll have to say goodbye for me to my sisters. Tell Perla I'll write more often, even if my ideas give her goose pimples.'

Ulli was quiet and seemed to be holding back tears. She gave Ada a tiny olivewood camel she had brought from the Old City. It was wrapped in the torn page of a Jordanian phonebook and smelled of zaatar.

In the grey shoebox building at the top of Ben Yehuda the trial became sensational as witnesses, survivors from the camps, gave their accounts of what they had been through. They were emotional. One fainted as he spoke but the audience was totally quiet. People seen unwrapping sweets or chewing gum were quickly ushered out. In the street, the line was an endless coil, slow, grey like the building and strangely subdued. People waited patiently, didn't speak or buy the newspapers or packets of nuts thrust at them by passing vendors. A man dressed in concentration-camp pyjamas, who was carrying a placard condemning the Reparations Agreement with Germany as blood money, was roughly bundled off by the police. Eliyahu, from his window in the Munkacz Dwellings, looked out occasionally to see if any Ark and its passengers would appear. He had tidied up the hiding place prepared for the actors should the crowd turn against them but all was quiet. He assumed the eccentric plan had been given up and went on with his research on the Red Heifer with even greater concentration. Salvation was built up of such small things. The Flood was indeed a warning but nothing could be done about it now, while the heifer could be delivered at any moment and fall on the earth under its mother cow as a perfect sign of the great change that was to come.

Kronberg, Tomas and Ada met regularly for lunch at the Dodas where the absence of *die schöne frau Ulli* was duly noted. Kronberg was frailer now and Tomas paid more attention to his weakness, arranging his chair at the table and gently tucking in the napkin at his collar. His hands trembled and he had difficulty in using his knife. Yet he seemed oddly proud of his appearance as God and hinted at it to Frau Hermine. She laughed 'Herr Kronberg, the Almighty. A fancy dress show for the students?' but then she gave him a double portion of her famous whipped cream with his dessert.

312

GOD IS DEAD

HE RESUMED HIS habit of walking through the 'triangle' of streets at the centre of Jerusalem, Ben Yehuda, Jaffa and King George. But he only walked at night, even after midnight, fighting off his fear of lying awake for hours closing his eyes only to see his mother standing on the steps of their Würzburg house dressed in her best black coat and hat waving a white flag of surrender at a line of marchers singing 'O Tannenbaum'. He was often alone on Zion Square or in the company of drunks huddled together in a doorway. One night, exhausted and dizzy, he stood still under the portico of the cinema and shivered at the thought of it pitching and rolling on a surge of water rushing down Ben Yehuda Street. There was no traffic and the only sound he heard was a weak buzzing from the tall fluorescent street lamps. *I am in the city of the dead*, he said to himself. *They are all drowned, wrapped in their blankets and sheets, tied up in pyjamas and nightshirts, listening to their clocks ticking, switching off the midnight news. They are under the water mass but tomorrow they won't know it had covered them. They'll wait on line for the bus and they'll look as if they never drowned.*

Kronberg crouched down unsteadily and touched the fresh tar of the road. It was newly paved and still soft. It seemed to shine a welcome in the dark and its acrid pungent smell filled him with longing. Slowly and with difficulty he forced his body to curl over and placed his forehead on the tar. God is great, he said. He couldn't pull himself up. His arms wouldn't bear him, his knees were locked

313

in pain and his legs were numb. He called to the drunks for help but they didn't answer. *Get to the waste pile where you belong* he said to himself and crawled slowly to the garbage bin at the crossroads. It was full and smelled of pee and rotten fruit but it gave him a steady surface to lean his back on and stretch his aching limbs. *I have crawled ashore,* he thought, *onto Ararat.* He looked for a rainbow and found the blinking blue and red neon sign of Hadaya Shoes. COMFORT COMFORT it said in Hebrew and English. *Comfort ye my people,* hummed Kronberg. *Comfort them with the best shoes Italy can make.* He twiddled his toes to see if they were still numb and began to pull himself up with the support of the bin behind him. Sticky and wet slime trickled down his neck. Finally he was standing. Across the square from the cinema's hoarding a head stared at him. It was huge, a reddish-pink melon framed by a dense beard and a wave of greying hair. Set on broad, robed shoulders it glared straight down at Kronberg from a bright blue sky which announced *The Ten Commandments. Moses, my servant* said Kronberg as he stretched himself up to face Charlton Heston. *Are you angry with me?* He looked hard and long but the back of his neck ached and he had to lower his head. Moses was angry with him and with them all because Zion Square was littered with sin and the Flood hadn't washed it away. A wave of guilt made him shiver as he thought of his brief encounters with men in the square. His throat was dry and he turned to walk back along Jaffa Road but he felt the stare of Moses burning the night behind him as he passed the shuttered shops and the forlorn bus stops. Walking faster, he tried to look backwards over his shoulder and tripped. His forehead hit the ground with a dull thwack. There was blood and he felt dizzy but he had cushioned the fall with his hands and nothing seemed broken so he was able to pull himself along, half-walking, half-crawling, holding on to shutters, railings and lamp-posts until he got home. When he missed lunch at the Dodas next day Tomas went looking for him and found him asleep fully clothed on his bloodstained bed. There was a nasty gash on his forehead and when Tomas started cleaning it up with a towel and hot water Kronberg opened his eyes.

314

'I saw Moses and I ran,' he said.

'Where?' said Tomas.

'On Zion Square, over the cinema. It was the poster but I have bad dreams and see strange things. Tomas, Charlton Heston was looking down at me, with angry eyes, that fool actor made me feel guilty and I had to run. I saw my mother.'

'In the square?'

'No here, in bed. I closed my eyes and there she was on the doorstep in her best coat waving a white flag. *Mütterchen.*'

His eyes watered and his lips quivered. Tomas felt Kronberg's weakness almost as a betrayal. What would become of them if he gave in?

'She had no choice,' said Tomas, 'your mother. You have. You repair broken things we can't throw away. You repaired me. You won't admit it but you are stronger than any of us. Your discontent props us up. You could leave but look where you are. You're here talking. We need that. We need you to talk away and never stop. You don't have a white flag to wave, not for yourself. Not for us.'

Tomas kissed Kronberg on his lips. They were dry. He brought him some water and sat by his bed as his friend fell asleep holding his hand. But Kronberg's health was failing and Tomas decided to move him to his ruin where they could keep an eye on him. They arranged Kronberg's bed behind a large canvas of Tomas's and close to the grand double window which gave onto the valley. Kronberg was unusually passive during the move asking only for some books and his mother's pearl-inlaid opera glasses. He slept fitfully and they heard him talking in his sleep, in a soft musical voice sometimes drawing out the German words as if telling a story to a child, sometimes a kind of singing.

'He's telling bedtime stories to a child he never had,' said Ada. 'He's singing it to sleep.' Curled up against Tomas in the warmth of their bed she felt the sting of a dead child. Being a mother had never occurred to her. It was as if she had killed the thought before it dared appear. Now Kronberg's lulling sounds from behind the canvas

315

struck her with the pain of something lost and incommunicable to the sleeping man beside her. She stepped over to where Kronberg lay. His eyes were open but he was not looking at her. He was humming and breathing with some effort.

Selig blaue Blätter.

She made out the words but not the sense. She brought a damp towel and wiped Kronberg's forehead. His eyes remained fixed on some spot far away but his hands drummed on the sheet then reached out to grasp at nothing. He looked at her.

'Badly broken. Can't be repaired. No legs.'

He tried to lever himself up but failed and sank back. He made as if to take her hand and his thin white fingers brushed her forearm.

'Sing Mädchen Sing.'

Ada was at a loss. He was agitated and she needed to quieten him. Sing!

We'll meet again
Don't know where
Don't know when

Perla used to sing it when she showered her and rubbed her down with a nurse's rough grip.

But I know we'll meet again
Some sunny day

She stroked Kronberg's face gently.

'You have a cigarette?'

Ada was surprised. He rarely smoked now.

'A Gitane, your cigarette.'

She brought him one and put it between his lips without lighting it. He screwed up his face and made as if to puff. Broken. Useless. The cigarette fell from his lips but he took Ada's hand firmly and looked at her with the trace of a smile.

'You brought me here to make me give up my secrets. But I can't. I promised I would never give them up. I promised my mother but she was dead and looked the other way. Now it's you spying on me. I gave you everything.'

316

He let her hand go and closed his eyes. He muttered on in German till he fell asleep.

Sitting by his side Ada felt the disaster of his loneliness. He was shipwrecked on a desolate shore tied to a suitcase of possessions he had little use for. Now his weakness was loosening those few everyday ties that made for a kind of normality even though he scorned it. His café, his newspaper, his lunchtable, his workshop and library were becoming unattainable. Who would come looking for him to repair a toaster or help prepare for a Latin exam? Who would maintain his correspondence with the Commission in Würzburg? He was dependent on Tomas and herself in their ruin as he sank into a blur of memories and resentment. Betrayed by his body and weakened in mind he could only blame those who cared for him. Yes we are spying on him, she thought. We hear his secrets at night and wash the sweat off his body. He resents us for knowing too much and not bringing his old self back.

But one morning weeks later Kronberg was gone. He had left the sheets and blankets neatly folded and on them his mother's opera glasses with a note

DON'T LOOK FOR ME DON'T COME AFTER ME

When they got to his flat they found it locked but a neighbour said he had seen him leave in a taxi with a suitcase. Tomas had a key and once inside they found the flat as he had left it neat but smelling of dead flowers. A vase was full of rotting carnations. In the work room a few electric kettles, a toaster and a bulky gramophone were set on a table with notes stuck to them indicating whom they belonged to and a price. His books stretched up to the ceiling on their precarious boards untouched. On the small kitchen table they found an envelope addressed to Herr Paul Kronberg. It. was empty but the sender was Matthias Claudius Heim Würzburg. He's gone back, to an old-age home said Tomas. He's talked about doing it, but I didn't take it seriously. I never thought he could handle it.

Tomas looked around the airless flat. It was Kronberg's desert island where he had waited years for a passing ship to rescue him. But Tomas couldn't imagine him ever contented. He'll be washed and fed by the daughters of the men who took his parents. What will he think?

Will he say anything? He'll talk a lot no doubt. Too much. He'll have discussions about the gospels with the visiting priest and they'll give him the heavy food his mother cooked. He would die in the place where he left his youth.

Tomas thought of Kronberg rebuilding the city backwards from his bed as it was before Hitler, before the deportations, the smashed windows, before the bombs. He'd will it to be clean, orderly, pious. He'd leave the drunks and the bullies out. Then he would die hearing the nurses murmuring in the familiar Bavarian dialect and he'd have swept Tomas and Ada and everyone in Jerusalem out of his mind. He would be *judenrein*.

They sat bereft at the kitchen table. The querulous presence of their German friend was like an echo in the emptiness. God had fled to the Catholic home leaving his friends, his audience, his books and broken dolls and toasters to their fate. The city he had never made his home was as broken as ever. A hundred Kronbergs wouldn't be able to glue it together. Yet now it was broken in a place closer to them. He had insinuated himself into their lives so thoroughly that they felt abandoned as if the floor they walked on had collapsed. While they nursed him in their ruin they had for a while each recovered a lost father. It appealed to them both to think of him warm in bed with a thermos flask while they were away. Coming home to him made the house feel more stable, less likely to slide down into the valley and no man's land.

Tomas had placed his big canvas of the Jaffa Road café at the head of the bed so that Kronberg in the painting, the tall waiter looming over the tables, looked down on Kronberg lying beneath as if he was about to serve him a glass of cognac to get him up.

'What will we do with the books?' said Ada.

When they got back home the empty bed and the painting of the crowded café in Jaffa Road with its motley collection of people in transit and its painted slashes of foreboding and chaos in the distance made what had happened clearer to them. It wasn't just the desertion of another one of their number. It was a reminder of the precariousness of their life on this ledge over the chasm and the ease with which it could all fall to pieces. The café would become empty as people left never to return and the wind would blow more and more dust and sand from the desert through the streets of the depleted and divided city.

JORDAN

SHE JOINED THE long queue outside the trial. She had come back from the Scottish Hospice with Félix and taken the key of Milo's house from Julius, who wouldn't look her in the eye. The house was full of debris from the Flood, robes, scarves, boxes of paint, a drum but nothing of Milo's was visible except for some papers and a typewriter on his desk. In her hand she had Milo's letter Ada had sent to Tiberias.

'You were wrong to put any trust in me. Right to despise me. Nothing I begin finishes except my life, except my life. You never belonged here. You are too sane. You are well rid of me.'

She should have thrown it into the lake at Tiberias. But she put it on his typewriter and began to collect her few things.

In the middle of rummaging in her suitcase she came across a torn page of a newspaper with a picture of Eichmann. It struck her that she couldn't leave without going to the courtroom. That would be granting Milo a victory he did not deserve.

She advanced slowly as the queue shuffled forward. Heads were down. There was little talk. There was a thorough police search. She had a packet of chewing gum and was told she couldn't chew inside. It had been called a show trial but there was no show. Voices were subdued. A witness spoke more loudly and heads turned to look at her. She was a pale thin woman with her hair in a severe bun who spoke in measured tones, answering the lawyer repeating some of the phrases again and again with some emphasis. Despite this

Jordan could not make out clearly enough what she said. The judges sat stiffly, like a row of dolls in a fairground shooting gallery. It took her a while to look sideways at the Nazi in his glass box. But she soon looked away. There was nothing to see. Nothing was sitting there wearing glasses, hardly moving a head or a hand. Nothing had a neck, a face, a nose, a mouth. Nothing. Perhaps a smirk. Jordan looked with relief at the people next to her in the full hall. A large bald man with a thick moustache was breathing heavily and wiping sweat off his brow with strips of toilet paper he took out of a bag. A group of soldiers sat impassively, all straight-backed as if they had been warned not to slouch. A young woman dabbed at her eyes with a handkerchief. The man next to her put his arm round her shoulders protectively. Jordan was overcome by the ordinariness of it.

The newspaper headlines were wrong. It had nothing to do with the tragedy and disaster which was its *raison d'être*. It was stripped of drama like a film, unedited, naked and pale, without sound, colour or music. It flowed in front of her eyes and made no demands on her. She could be there or not. It made no difference. It was a procedure so it proceeded. She was no witness to the bloody open wound which lay at its heart. That was hidden under the foundations of the building, clues were under the piles of paper on the lawyers' tables. It couldn't be displayed. It was infectious. It was taboo. It couldn't be healed. She couldn't visualize it. She refused to try.

As Jordan stood up to go she felt she was being stared at. How could she leave? How could she be bored? Where better did she have to go? She wondered if people sat the whole day, unable to move. There must be some there who had seen the wound, even touched and smelled it.

They would stay.

But on her way out she heard someone at the door say, 'Quite enough. Let's go and have something to eat.' Jordan was surprised at the shame and anger that welled up in her. That woman in the smart coat was herself escaping by proclaiming herself healthy, hungry, uncontaminated by the festering wound, safeguarded by an American passport, free.

Later that day they all sat on Kronberg's bed under the painting. Jordan, Julius, Tomas and Ada. They were drinking some of Milo's abandoned Rémy Martin before Jordan's cab came.

Julius took a clockwork clown doll out of a pocket and wound it up. 'The clown's farewell,' he said as the doll swayed and bowed in jerking movements. 'He's saying goodbye by pretending to fall. This is how you'll remember us, almost falling. But he doesn't. He's my best balanced friend.

'You probably think we're foolish or mad, the way we live here.'

'No,' said Jordan. 'You are just separate like the hermits who lived in the caves right under here waiting for revelation. When I came I didn't understand that. Milo made it seem like I was invited to a party going on behind the backs of all the ordinary people. Something underground and different. I knew nothing of the kind of place he was taking me to. I didn't know about No Man's Land and Stop Border outside the door. I've always lived in the middle, comfortably. Never at the end. It took me time to understand and I could have understood earlier.'

'And left?' said Ada.

'No, but I could have been quicker to understand Milo's anger.' Julius pushed over his clown. 'Nothing stays balanced for long. It's the Syrian African Rift. It sends tremors everywhere.'

He reached over clumsily for Jordan's hand and kissed her wrist.

She got up and they watched her walk over to the old Turkish bandstand. There were still scraps of the Ark and Zion Square strewn over it. She turned towards them, a lone slim figure set against the twilight. She raised her arms and stood on one leg, gravely, swaying a little.

'I'm balanced!' she shouted. 'Balanced!'

Then she fell.

ACKNOWLEDGEMENTS

The author gratefully acknowledges the following use of copyright material: *Mr Charles's Chair: A Play* from *William the Wonder-Kid: Plays, Puppet Plays and Theater Writings* by Dennis Silk, The Sheep Meadow Press, 1996, Riverdale-on-Hudson NY10471; *To Those Born Later* from *Poems 1913-1956* by Bertolt Brecht, ed by John Willett and Ralph Manheim, Eyre Methuen 1976, London; *Poems from the Diwan* by Yehuda Halevi, translated by Gabriel Levin, Anvil Press, 2002, London.